The "SOCIALIST TRANSFORMATION" OF MEMORY

Through discourse analysis and a historical comparison of "Pernicious-Vestiges" narratives in the news text of *People's Daily*, this book is devoted to revealing primary metaphors of "Pernicious-Vestiges" and political functions in China.

"Pernicious-Vestiges" (Yí Dú 遗毒) is one of the most frequently used words in contemporary Chinese historical narration, as well as a constantly changing rhetorical direction in New China's media discourse, whose function is to remold memory. Over the past 76 years, the "Pernicious-Vestiges" narrative continuously constructed by *People's Daily*, the official newspaper of the Central Committee of the Chinese Communist Party, have reflected the views of China's political elite and represented the ruling party's evaluation and reevaluation of historical events. The findings of this book challenge the myth that memory is naturally superior to forgetting, reflect on the ethics of memory in "Pernicious-Vestiges" narratives and the erasure of their own justice, and suggest that the critical space compressed by "Pernicious-Vestiges" narratives should be returned to restore the order of memory and historical reflection.

This book will be an excellent read for students and scholars of Chinese studies, media studies, and those who are interested in political communication and collective memory in general.

Yusi Liu is Associate Professor at the College of Media and International Culture of Zhejiang University, China. Her research interests include comparative political communication and collective memory.

Ye Ma is a PhD candidate at the College of Media and International Culture of Zhejiang University, China. Her research interests include media and social thought, media memory, political communication, and intellectual studies.

China Perspectives

The *China Perspectives* series focuses on translating and publishing works by leading Chinese scholars, writing about both global topics and China-related themes. It covers Humanities & Social Sciences, Education, Media and Psychology, as well as many interdisciplinary themes.

This is the first time any of these books have been published in English for international readers. The series aims to put forward a Chinese perspective, give insights into cutting-edge academic thinking in China, and inspire researchers globally.

To submit proposals, please contact the Taylor & Francis Publisher for the China Publishing Programme, Lian Sun (Lian.Sun@informa.com)

Titles in media communication currently include:

Documentaries and China's National Image
Chen Yi

Rural-Urban Migration in China
The Impact of New Media
Zheng Xin

Social Mentality and Public Opinion in China
Fanbin Zeng

The Global Film Market Transformation in the Post-Pandemic Era
Production, Distribution and Consumption
Edited by Qiao Li, David Wilson, Yanqiu Guan

Cultural Representation and Cultural Studies
Zhou Xian

The "Socialist Transformation" of Memory
Reversing Chinese History through "Pernicious-Vestiges" Media Discourse
Yusi Liu and Ye Ma

For more information, please visit www.routledge.com/China-Perspectives/book-series/CPH

The "Socialist Transformation" of Memory

Reversing Chinese History through "Pernicious-Vestiges" Media Discourse

Yusi Liu and Ye Ma

LONDON AND NEW YORK

First published 2023
by Routledge
4 Park Square, Milton Park, Abingdon, Oxon OX14 4RN

and by Routledge
605 Third Avenue, New York, NY 10158

Routledge is an imprint of the Taylor & Francis Group, an informa business

© 2023 Yusi Liu and Ye Ma

The right of Yusi Liu and Ye Ma to be identified as authors of this work has been asserted in accordance with sections 77 and 78 of the Copyright, Designs and Patents Act 1988.

All rights reserved. No part of this book may be reprinted or reproduced or utilised in any form or by any electronic, mechanical, or other means, now known or hereafter invented, including photocopying and recording, or in any information storage or retrieval system, without permission in writing from the publishers.

Trademark notice: Product or corporate names may be trademarks or registered trademarks, and are used only for identification and explanation without intent to infringe.

British Library Cataloguing-in-Publication Data
A catalogue record for this book is available from the British Library

Library of Congress Cataloging-in-Publication Data
Names: Liu, Yusi, 1986– author. | Ma, Ye, 1989– author.
Title: The "socialist transformation" of memory : reversing Chinese history through "pernicious-vestiges" media discourse / Yusi Liu and Ye Ma.
Description: New York : Routledge, 2023. | Series: China perspectives | Includes bibliographical references and index.
Identifiers: LCCN 2023001325 (print) | LCCN 2023001326 (ebook) | ISBN 9781032530123 (hardback) | ISBN 9781032530130 (paperback) | ISBN 9781003409724 (ebook)
Subjects: LCSH: Ren min ri bao. | Collective memory—China. | Discourse analysis.
Classification: LCC DS721 .L67774 2023 (print) | LCC DS721 (ebook) | DDC 951.001/41—dc23/eng/20230214
LC record available at https://lccn.loc.gov/2023001325
LC ebook record available at https://lccn.loc.gov/2023001326

ISBN: 978-1-032-53012-3 (hbk)
ISBN: 978-1-032-53013-0 (pbk)
ISBN: 978-1-003-40972-4 (ebk)

DOI: 10.4324/9781003409724

Typeset in Times New Roman
by Apex CoVantage, LLC

Contents

List of figures		*vi*
List of tables		*vii*
1	Introduction: "Pernicious-Vestiges" narrative as legitimation profiles	1
2	Sheltering and domestication: strategies, historicity, and memory politics in "Pernicious-Vestiges" discourse	25
3	Body and politics: moral responsibility and authority construction of "Pernicious-Vestiges" metaphors	56
4	Developing from nothing: the evolution of feudal "Pernicious-Vestiges" discourse	88
5	From prosperity to decline: historical aberration and mnemonic silence	122
6	Paradigm interruption and re-narration: historical reversal as a source of "Pernicious-Vestiges"	156
7	Conclusion: the construction of China's political memory by "Pernicious-Vestiges" media discourse	200
Index		218

Figures

1.1	Overall time distribution of "Pernicious-Vestiges" discourse in *People's Daily* (1946–2022)	4
1.2	Classification time distribution of "Pernicious-Vestiges" discourse in *People's Daily* (1946–2022)	5
3.1	Narrative distribution of "Pernicious-Vestiges" discourse before the founding of the People's Republic of China	58

Tables

1.1 Source, duration, and main manifestations of "Pernicious-Vestiges" discourse objects in *People's Daily*   6
2.1 Number and proportion of enrollment subjects of colleges and universities in China in 1953   35

1 Introduction

"Pernicious-Vestiges" narrative as legitimation profiles

History is written by winners and forgotten by winners.
Aleida Assmann, Jan Assmann

Construct a "Pernicious-Vestiges" narrative: Taking *People's Daily* as a case

On Youth Day in 1978, the people of China had just emerged from the shadow of the Cultural Revolution and the Gang of Four, and the Third Plenary Session of the Eleventh Central Committee, which marked a new journey of reform and opening up, had yet to be unveiled. *People's Daily*, the official newspaper of the Communist Party of China (CPC), published an article entitled "Science and democracy" in its 2A. In this article, the newspaper's special commentator wrote:

> When the Gang of Four was rampant, whoever advocated science and democracy was the "bourgeoisie"; The fascist thugs who openly advocated ignorance and autocracy became the "proletariat". This reversal of right and wrong should be reversed again . . . We have to estimate the negative factors left over from China's long-term feudal society and semi-feudal and semi-colonial society, such as the Pernicious-Vestiges of bureaucratic autocracy, lack of democratic habits and backward economy and culture. Only through long-term efforts can the people directly manage all affairs of the country widely. The people of China, who have a glorious revolutionary tradition, have been tempered by the Great Proletarian Cultural Revolution. After smashing the autocracies of the Gang of Four, they are fully capable of fully exercising their right to be masters of their own country, and in the process of exercising this right, they constantly improve the level of managing state affairs. As you can remember, in 1966, those teenagers with a passion for combating and preventing revisionism flocked to the streets. Because of their inexperience, they were often deceived and chose the wrong target for rebellion. However, in 1976, the people were united as one, pointing the finger at the evil Gang of Four. This unusual decade has tempered the great people of Mao Zedong Thought's hometown. The

DOI: 10.4324/9781003409724-1

people's awareness of caring for state affairs and their ability to distinguish right from wrong have been greatly improved.

("Kēxué hé mínzhǔ 科学和民主 [Science and democracy]", *People's Daily*, 2A, May 4, 1978, by special commentator of this newspaper)

The vocabulary of "Pernicious-Vestiges" and its associated discourse construction is a very common discourse phenomenon and political phenomenon in contemporary public discourse in China. This vocabulary refers to the past, which is viewed by people in different ways under a specific trend, and is a part of memory and its construction. The term "reverse and re-reverse" in the article "Science and democracy" just reflects the key phenomenon of "historical reversal" in contemporary China (Dirlik, 1996) and gives a public discourse level to the phenomenon that one after another modern political movement in China, including the Cultural Revolution, come and go. This article was not the prelude to the practice of "Pernicious-Vestiges" discourse in *People's Daily*. In fact, as a metaphorical vocabulary and narrative tradition, "Pernicious-Vestiges" has been used familiarly since *People's Daily* was founded in 1946, and it has been in use ever since and given new vitality.

The word "Pernicious-Vestiges" (Yí Dú 遗毒) comes from Tàipíng Guǎngjì 太平广记 at the earliest, which refers to leaving something toxic behind. In modern Chinese, the word has three meanings: (1) It means leaving something toxic; (2) Metaphor refers to harmful thoughts and ethos left over from the past; (3) Harm and poison people. In addition to the original meaning in Chinese, this vocabulary is also influenced by the phrase "unassimilated remains" Háiwèi kèfú de yíwù 还未克服的遗物 put forward by Marx (The Works Compilation Bureau of Marx, Engels, Lenin and Stalin of the CPC Central Committee, 1972, p. 108; Jia & Teng, 1980). Wrapped with the meaning of such words, "Pernicious-Vestiges" has become one of the most frequently used words in the historical evaluation system commonly used in contemporary China, and it is also a rhetoric direction that continues to appear in the propaganda discourse of New China and constantly changes. It can be linked to any possible issue such as political cleanliness, utopian perfectionism, health, and politics. It continues the ancient tradition of the Chinese saying that we often need to sublate the past "ideas" and "ethos", and it also inherits the hostility of Marxism and its Chinese philosophy to the "bourgeois society". It inherits the successful experience of the Communist Party of China in shaping the "enemy of the people" through "labeling" during the Yan'an ideological reform movement during the Anti-Japanese War (Fairbank, 1986, p. 307). Its function is to "transform" our "memory".

However, the unexamined question so far is: Why does "memory" need to be "reformed"? How to "reform"? "Reform" for whom? In short, by reinterpreting the past, the state will be able to manage people's collective identity and at the same time deal with the historical burden accompanying development. History will not pass, but will only be re-expressed (Olick, 1998). These past practices or historical works often contain a set of logic and methodology for constructing history and selecting historical paradigms according to historical events under specific historical conditions (Dirlik, 1996) and become an integral part of "politics of history" or "memory politics" (Molden, 2016). At the end of the last century, some researchers in the field of memory research called for broadening the focus on the concept of "collective memory" to a series of commemorative practices and examining a broader social memory, that is, "historical sociology of mnemonic practice" (Olick & Robbins, 1998). Under the path of sociological empirical analysis, the rewriting of the past is no longer just the result of social construction but is regarded as a way for different groups to express their self-interest directly (Schwartz, 1991; Olick & Levy, 1997). This path advocates understanding the whole process in which various symbolic elements and issues settle in a relatively stable dynamic historical system with the passage of time through "legitimation profiles". Similar to linguists' perspectives that discourse is regarded as "the source of evidence" (Lakoff & Johnson, 1980, p. 3), a "legitimation profile" mainly focuses on the official discourse's declaration of the legitimacy of a specific historical event, the culture related to the topic, the discourse style, the construction of the past image, and the image of the enemy, etc., and changes in the constituent elements and forms of the "legitimation profile" in historical fragments. Although these changes are scattered and gradual, they can still help people understand the dominant trend of a specific era as a whole.

In the past 76 years, the "Pernicious-Vestiges" narratives has been continuously constructed by *People's Daily*. This newspaper was first published in 1946 as an official newspaper of the Central Bureau of the Communist Party of China in Shanxi, Hebei, Shandong, and Henan. Since 1949, it has become the official newspaper managed by the Propaganda Department of the CPC Central Committee. As a political agency that can directly set up a specific representation of the past, *People's Daily* performs many functions in the country, such as propaganda, organization, mobilization, and management (Bishop, 1989), and undertakes the historical practice with news narration as the carrier of fact construction and party ideology as the standpoint. This book defines ideology as "the general science of ideas" (Scruton, 2007, pp. 317–318), which not only contains the commitment to improve the social and political state, but also covers the critical construction differentiated by class concepts, thus forming an action-oriented belief system, a set of interrelations that guide or motivate rectification actions in some way (Heywood, 2014, p. 53). Then, the "Pernicious-Vestiges" narrative in *People's Daily* also has a series of meaningful historical manifestations, reflecting the views of China's political elites and representing the ruling party's evaluation and reevaluation of social reality and historical events (Wu, 1994). All kinds of "Pernicious-Vestiges" narratives produced by *People's Daily* because its spontaneous publication can be regarded as a "legitimation profiles", which is used by researchers to investigate the objects and ideologies advocated and opposed by mainstream discourse and reveal the historical meaning of the social changes behind it.

This book defines the object of analysis as "the current domestic political discourse events in China" constructed by the word "Pernicious-Vestiges" to facilitate the discussion of the shaping effect of the discourse strategy of "Pernicious-Vestiges"

4 *Introduction*

on the history of contemporary China. Among them, the standard of "present" excludes news texts that recount historical events, such as "From October 1976 to January 1977, Comrade Chen Jinhua made great efforts to expose and eliminate the Pernicious-Vestiges and influence of the Gang of Four and try to restore the normal order of the cultural and educational system" in "Chén Jǐnhuá tóngzhì shēngpíng 陈锦华同志生平 [Life of Comrade Chen Jinhua]" in *People's Daily*, 4A, July 9, 2016. "Domestic politics" excludes international news, translations, and comments to the scope of discussion. For example, in the article "Sīdàlín lùn sūlián tǔdì zhèngcè de jǐgè wèntí 斯大林《论苏联土地政策的几个问题》[Stalin's on several issues of Soviet land policy]", 5A of *People's Daily*, March 20, 1950 (by и Kuvnov), it is stated, "Comrade Stalin expounded the class struggle outside collective farms to overcome the individualism of some backward collective farmers inside collective farms". Finally, *People's Daily*, which is included in the analysis of this book, contains 838 articles on discourse construction of "Pernicious-Vestiges". The distribution of these articles from 1946 to 2022 is shown in Figure 1.1.

As a "legitimation profile", "Pernicious-Vestiges" discourse practice is a concrete breakthrough point to answer the questions raised previously. It is not difficult to find that the increase in the number of each kind of "Pernicious-Vestiges" discourse practice is often accompanied by a major external crisis or internal change in the society and its ideology. Therefore, in the same vein as the reversal of historical evaluation, the discourse construction of "Pernicious-Vestiges" also reflects the ideology of contemporary China and how various interest groups are "evaluated" and "reevaluated" to some extent. In order to intuitively outline which historical events, social groups, or ideologies are defined as the sources of "Pernicious-Vestiges" and in which time periods these "Pernicious-Vestiges" are reflected and explained, we have roughly described the use of the word "Pernicious-Vestiges" in

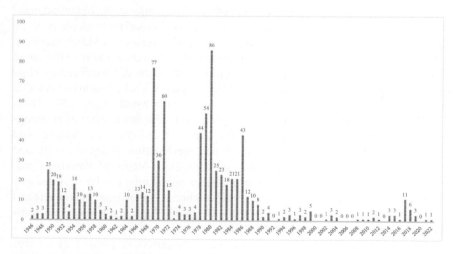

Figure 1.1 Overall time distribution of "Pernicious-Vestiges" discourse in *People's Daily* (1946–2022)

Figure 1.2 Classification time distribution of "Pernicious-Vestiges" discourse in *People's Daily* (1946–2022)

People's Daily since it was founded in 1946. From 1946 to 2022, any specific type of "Pernicious-Vestiges" appeared in *People's Daily* in each independent month was marked in one specific shape, which constituted a scatter plot that reflected the intermittence or even "self-denial" of different types of "Pernicious-Vestiges" discourse in the past 76 years, as shown in Figure 1.2.

It can be seen that the historical reversal in the form of "Pernicious-Vestiges" discourse presents quite different patterns, including from scratch (feudalism), from prosperity to decline (the old society, the Kuomintang reactionaries, capitalism, imperialism, and the "Pernicious-Vestiges" narrative as a whole), and re-narrating ("revisionism", Gang of Four, extreme "Left" ideological trend, Cultural Revolution), etc. This shows that the discourse representation of historical aberration is pluralistic. Although the history of modern China has always been entangled with the revolutionary paradigm and the modern paradigm, the two reversals of "Pernicious-Vestiges" from scratch and from prosperity to decline can coexist in the revolutionary paradigm and the modern paradigm. The existence of these discourse strategies can also help us to have a clearer understanding of the revolutionary paradigm and the modernization paradigm.

Different from the paradigm of conceptual history research or sociology of news production, this book does not intend to focus on "terms with the past" (Adorno, 1959/1986), nor does it intend to pry into the institutional logic of *People's Daily*'s

6 Introduction

construction of "Pernicious-Vestiges" discourse, but it takes it as a case of "legitimation profile" in the historical narrative of New China, focusing on "Pernicious-Vestiges". In order to provide an overview of the specific manifestations of the "Pernicious-Vestiges" texts in *People's Daily* at the beginning of this book, we also sorted out the 12 main "Pernicious-Vestiges" that appeared in these 838 texts from 1946 to 2022, as well as the objects, duration, and main manifestations of these "Pernicious-Vestiges". The results are shown in Table 1.1.

Table 1.1 Source, duration, and main manifestations of "Pernicious-Vestiges" discourse objects in *People's Daily*

Source of "Pernicious-Vestiges"	Duration	Main manifestations
1. feudalism	1946–present	Factional disputes, oppression of women, tradition, imperial examination system, violation of science, refusal to work, formalism, education of scholar-officials, conservative ideas, bureaucracy, contempt for folk art, valuing agriculture over commerce, commercial window display, separation from the old traditions of the masses, religion, the four old, exploiting class, conformism, Confucianism and Mencius' way, bloodline theory, paternalism, lack of legal concept, private concept and privilege, ignorance of the people, usurpation of the party, and theft of the country, cliques, denial of social division of labor, the idea of "unification", valuing officials and the people, valuing long-term development, giving up people's words, being headstrong, being loyal to friends, Gang of Four, specialization, unhealthy practices, administrative interference in academics, discrimination against intellectuals, poverty, backward culture, going through the back door, and corrupt social atmosphere, blind exclusion, closed-door, absolutism, ignorance and superstition, abuse of power, confusion between feudalism and socialism, literary prison, cultural backwardness, lack of democracy and the rule of law, suppression of human nature, poverty and backwardness, lifelong tenure in leadership positions, gambling, privileged thoughts, corruption, absolutism, three cardinal guides and five constant virtues in the feudal ethical code, Confucian tradition, God-making movement, obscurantism policy, personal worship, and patronage.
2. Kuomintang reactionaries	1946–1958	Civil War, old ideas, Party education, Americanization, embezzlement and waste, extortion, corruption, great nationalism, reactionary thought, reformist thought, counter-revolutionary thought, suspicion of communism, pro-American, and anti-Soviet.

3. imperialism	1949–1971	Selfishness, intrigue, enslaving education, war of aggression, social poverty, worshipping foreign things, counter-revolutionary ideas, unpatriotic thoughts, bourgeois ideas, war wounds, economic paralysis, anti-people scientific undertakings, suppression of national culture, comprador foreign slave philosophy.
4. capitalism	1949–1960, 1964–1976, 1979–1989	Individualism, bureaucracy, no distinction between the enemy and ourselves, waste of state property, fame and fortune, discrimination against Chinese medicine, idealism, Hu Shih's reactionary philosophy, lack of self-cultivation, Zhu Guangqian's aesthetic thought, free competition, right-wing thought, class exploitation, extortion, bad style, separation from labor, separation from the masses, yellow music, lack of overall situation, four old, counter-revolutionary economy, bourgeois dictatorship.
5. old society	1949–1974, 1979–1986, 1994	Speculation, dogmatism, buying and selling marriages, command thinking, reformism, bureaucracy, corruption and waste, favoritism, sectarian strife, despise labour and love ease, divorce from politics, disunity, wrong political line, hooligans/bad youth, formalism, low morality, contempt for labor, deforestation, individualism, right-wing thinking, selfishness and narrowness, being divorced from reality, professional hierarchy.
6. revisionism	1966–1979, 1968–1987, 2015–2017	The old tradition of exploiting class, specific individuals, black cultivation, black six theories, "three selves and one package", "four freedoms", "class struggle extinguishment", four spirits, "four men", black goods, black line of literature and art, revisionist military line, destruction of the Cultural Revolution, extravagance and waste, bourgeois medical and health line, backwardness of the masses, dignity of teachers' morality, and meticulous division of labor.
7. specific individual	1968–1976, 1977–1989, 2014–2019	The first stage: see "revisionism". The second stage: See Gang of Four. The third stage: See "Corruption/Unhealthy Party Conduct".
8. Gang of Four	1977–1989	Be fake Left but real Right, breaking the law and discipline, undermining modernization, setting up ideological forbidden zones and mental shackles, persecuting cadres, stereotyped writing style, formalism, anarchism, reactionary literary and artistic policies, false and arrogant, blind command, confusing truth with falsehood, deifying leaders, lifelong tenure of leading cadres, extreme left, right phobia, criticize and struggle, egalitarianism, pursuing privileged life, and bourgeois factionalism, the spiritual garden is deserted, intergenerational estrangement, rampant criminal offenses, black and white reversal, hegemony, slander, dictatorship, greed, ignorance, falsehood, Mao's quotation journalism.

(*Continued*)

Table 1.1 (Continued)

9. ultra-"Left" trend of thought	1979–2008	Being divorced from the masses, bureaucratic habits, right phobia, egalitarianism, discriminating against and suppressing intellectuals, rejecting professionals, not daring to rely on experts, resisting the party's line, single management restricting economic development, weeds in literary and artistic positions, disrespecting science and the masses, undermining the legal system, not acting according to objective laws, neglecting the production and circulation of commodities, imprisoning ideas, opposing labor to get rich, large in size and collective in nature, "big-pot" system, the Cultural Revolution.
10. Cultural Revolution	1980–2012	Personal bondage, unhealthy practices, illegal and criminal activities, neglecting wealth, turning black and white upside down, hindering the construction of spiritual civilization, evil practices, ideological confusion, hatred of the rich, leftism, personal worship, abuse of power, anarchism, guilty of speech, false accusations, infringement of civil liberties, unhealthy party conduct, contempt for education, feudal fascism, sectarianism, destruction of the legal system, and "rule of man".
11. religious extremism	1999–2000, 2018	Anti-science, Falungong, God-making movement and cults endanger society, psychotropic drugs, and religious issues.
12. corruption/ unhealthy party conduct	2014–2019	Zhou Yongkang, Su Rong, "Bo, Wang", Bai Enpei, Chou He, Huang Xingguo, corruption, unclear relationship between politics and business, serious violation of discipline and law, failure to observe political discipline and rules, damage to party spirit, party style and discipline, lack of serious political life within the party, and the party building work is empty, lazy and idle, not simplifying administration and decentralization, inaction and irresponsibility, irregular cadre selection procedures, and destruction of political ecology.

Generally speaking, the objects that become the source of "Pernicious-Vestiges" mainly include feudalism/feudal society/feudal thought, Kuomintang reactionaries, old society/old times/old system/old ideas, (bureaucrat) capitalism/bourgeoisie, imperialism, revisionism, Gang of Four, "extremely 'left' ideological trend", "Cultural Revolution/ten years of turmoil", and specific individuals. In the next part of this book, especially in Chapter 4, Chapter 5, and Chapter 6 when examining the social function of "us" and "them" created by "Pernicious-Vestiges" discourse, we will introduce and analyze these specific types of "Pernicious-Vestiges" discourse construction in a more detailed way in chronological order. Table 1.1 can also be used as a general picture for readers of this book to form a general impression of what memories contemporary China has opposed and how these opposed memories may contradict each other.

"Pernicious-Vestiges" reflects the modern China's view of history: Explanations and deficiencies

Through the brief analysis in the previous section, it can be seen that the "Pernicious-Vestiges" discourse constructed by *People's Daily* basically shows the process of reversal and re-reversal of the evaluation of contemporary Chinese historical events. The social consequences brought by the ideology that "Pernicious-Vestiges" discourse is constantly constructed and ceaselessly denied are the interruption of the historical paradigm of contemporary China (Dirlik, 1996). The dominant discourse of the narrative construction of "Pernicious-Vestiges" can not only reflect the historical track of the nation-state but is still in the process of constant change. The discourse practice of "Pernicious-Vestiges" will help us to understand the belief and common sense, social reality, changes of people's social relations, and social identities in China at present and reveal the hidden connections and reasons among them. The narrative practice of "Pernicious-Vestiges" embodies the memory view of power and official discourse construction, and it is also a reflection of China's contemporary historical view. Accompanying the ethical problems of memory of "Pernicious-Vestiges" discourse are the problems of historical justice caused by this discourse practice, and these problems will also respond to our re-understanding of the historical paradigm since the founding of New China.

As mentioned earlier, systematically portraying how the memories that contemporary China once opposed contradict each other, and how they cooperate with each other to jointly create the self-denial of China's history, is the first question this book is devoted to answering. But the curiosity of this book doesn't stop there. Besides describing the specific process of how the history of New China reversed repeatedly, we also hope to explain this phenomenon based on empirical evidence. In view of this, in this section, we will systematically sort out the current theoretical explanations about the historical self-denial of modern China and which "historical reversal" represented by "Pernicious-Vestiges" can be explained by the existing theoretical mechanism and which can't; we will further put forward the explanatory mechanism issues that this book hopes to systematically respond to.

For the self-reversal of contemporary China history, the current research on historical view and conceptual history has provided some powerful explanations, among which the post-colonial historical view driven by "revolution", the traditional cultural crisis in the conceptual field, and the legitimacy crisis of China's state governance are the representatives. For the phenomenon of "Pernicious-Vestiges" discourse constructed by the Central Committee of the Communist Party of China's official newspapers and the modern China historical view reflected in this book, these explanations either lack situational explanations focusing on specific cases, or it is difficult to consistently deal with the problem of contemporary China's historical view, which is constantly changing in its different stages. Next, we will briefly review the main viewpoints of these three explanations and their limitations when they are applied to the case study in this book.

The inevitable consequence of revolutionary power: The historical reversal of China from the perspective of post-colonialism

The intertwined relationship between China's cultural tradition and modernization was put forward as an important issue in Fairbank's book *The Great China Revolution* (Fairbank, 1986). Since then, many scholars, including Fairbank himself, have tried to discuss or explain this. Fairbank believes that China's thousand-year-old cultural tradition makes it face more obstacles in its reform: Modernization requires China to import technology from foreign countries, but this kind of introduction may arouse the conservative psychology of Chinese people, especially gentry and bureaucrats deeply influenced by Confucian culture, and make them more worried about the invasion of foreign forces. Therefore, China can only carry out modernization in its own cultural tradition, but the deep-rooted cultural tradition itself has great inertia, which makes it more difficult for China to complete modernization based on technological development on the basis of its unwillingness to change its social values, culture, and system (Fairbank, 1986, pp. 5–7). Indeed, as Fairbank said, when the Confucian tradition becomes the fetter of modernization, the state propaganda machine must be started, and any ideas and concepts that may become obstacles to modernity, no matter what social class they exist in, must be eradicated by constructing a specific past as a historical work of "Pernicious-Vestiges". This argument is reasonable to understand how modern China, whose general goal is reform and opening up after 1978, constructs the "Pernicious-Vestiges" discourse. But in fact, after the founding of New China, the modernization of the country has not always been the only priority development goal in different historical periods. At least in the years when it devoted itself to building favorable geopolitics and taking class struggle as the key goal, the priority of consolidating political power suppressed the goal of national modernization and even had an overwhelming advantage. In view of this, the tension between tradition and modernization seems difficult to provide a consistent explanation for the continuous production of "Pernicious-Vestiges" discourse. Although Fairbank also realized that the swing of major policies constituted a major feature of the historical process of contemporary China, that is, the part he called "from the extreme of one policy to the extreme of another" (Fairbank, 1986, p. 420), and he tried to give his own answer to the rapid and slow changes in China's modernization process, arguing that the impetus of China revolution came from the consensus between China and foreign countries formed in China's cultural complex. The driving force of modernization comes from foreign influences (Fairbank, 1986, p. 11), but this explanation can't respond to why there are still changes in the wrestling results of revolution and modernization in the period of constant external environment and foreign policy faced by New China, resulting in the repeated construction of "Pernicious-Vestiges" discourse.

Different from this explanation, Pei (2006) believed that the revolution was the permanent driving force for the formation of modern China history. This deep-rooted driving force was born together with the political power, and it penetrated into every corner of history everywhere, even the efforts to restore the modern order had a strong revolutionary color. This kind of "mastery and judging the situation" also comes from the inheritance and recreation of the "Pernicious-Vestiges" of "revolutionary authoritarianism": Various social contradictions are reinterpreted in the name of "class struggle". Only through the communist party's "divide-and-conquer" and "divide-and-rule" can it be resolved, thus forming "controlled polarization" (Chen, 1986). In essence, revolutionary authoritarianism needs to rely on revolutionary mobilization to save the underdeveloped economy, which is represented by a kind of "developmental autocracy" summarized by Pei (2006). "Returning to the revolution" is a kind of governance technique that divides society to make it obey the state. In the post-Mao era, the revolutionary creed became the source to prove the legitimacy of rule, such as many reappearances of the campaign modes like "revolutionary tradition", "mobilization", and "unity" in the official texts (Perry, 2006). However, such an explanation is highly focused on the social structure and can hardly be extended to the practice of why the Chinese Communist Party constructs a specific "thought" as a "Pernicious-Vestiges", especially when there is no clear one-to-one mapping relationship between class and "doctrine", and when "Pernicious-Vestiges" do not exist at that time and in the local area and cannot be simply summarized by "control" and "governance", the explanation of "returning to the revolution" becomes more and more impossible.

Similar to Perry (2006) view of "revolutionary heritage", Dirlik (1996) believes that the contemporary expression of China's history is characterized by its separation from the overall explanation. In the process of historical construction, the historical development of modern China is often interrupted by the purpose of time and space due to internal and external factors. Among them, interruption of temporaries for the purpose of time refers to refusing to carry out revolution in the name of modernization, especially capitalist modernization. Therefore, the China revolution has always denied its own historicity, that is, "historical aberration". The aberration of China's history is often marked by a reversal reevaluation of historical events and ideology. Revolution is a phenomenon in the center of modern China's history, which goes hand in hand with the revolution to reverse the evaluation of historical events. Similarly, due to its positive effect on the development of China, the Kuomintang's historical merits and demerits in China have been reevaluated, similar to the "bourgeoisie". The most noticeable thing is the reappraisal of imperialism and "tradition" in China's historical narrative. Among them, imperialism and the trading ports as its outposts have been reinterpreted as the driving force of China's modernization process, and Confucianism and Yan and Huang Emperors as the origin of the Chinese people have gradually become the representatives of the traditional revival. At the same time, the common changes of capitalism and socialism in China require that specific topics should be discussed to explain the history of China. What needs to be acknowledged is that Dirlik's (1996) conclusion that modernization may be a "re-revolution of revolution" seems that there is no way to fully explain the efforts made by the Chinese Communist regime to recover the economy after the Great Leap Forward and the Cultural Revolution, especially to develop the national economy by means of modernization because denying these two periods in the past can actually be done by other ways besides economic recovery, and the common trend after the two periods of history may not be accidental. This urges us to turn our attention to the other two possible explanations for the repeated reversal of the "Pernicious-Vestiges" discourse construction in the propaganda system of the Chinese Communist Party: The crisis of traditional culture and the crisis of legitimacy of the modern state.

The crisis of contemporary China traditional culture from the perspective of concept history

From the political and cultural point of view, China's monarchical governance in the past dynasties mainly focused on maintaining stability and prosperity, while the people's desire was also for national unity and long-term stability (Fairbank, 1986, p. 14), and the desire for multi-ethnic unity called for a unified ideology (Fairbank, 1986, p. 52). The imperial examination system for selecting bureaucrats emphasized the inheritance of classic books and the tempering of royal anthem. Intellectuals are more attached to the bureaucracy than independent, which makes better educated people lose the opportunity structure to put forward new political and philosophical views and criticize reality (Fairbank, 1986, p. 46). When intellectuals come out of the imperial examination system and its given bureaucracy and embrace the role of critics in the 20th century (Fairbank, 1986, p. 303), they also become "Pernicious-Vestiges". However, the follow-up and cooperation of the mass movement in the process of "ideological reform" shows that the fear of the monarch or the modern incarnation of the monarch and the hostility to the middle and upper classes of society have their own historical roots, including the egalitarian ideal accumulated in the agricultural society for thousands of years and the high degree of obedience to the authority of the monarch (Fairbank, 1986, pp. 355–357). In the process of the circulation of modern culture from the intellectual community to the public, it is not completely synchronized among different classes (Gao, 1996). To some extent, the confrontation and separation between the CPC and its dependent classes and intellectuals indicates that the infiltration of modern culture may be related to the internal crisis of China's traditional culture.

There are a lot of works in this field, especially the study of concept history. Scholars in this context believe that since the 20th century, many intellectuals in the West, especially in the United States, have been infected with two distinct characteristics, one of which is "the vision of the anointed": setting a picture of a perfect society to criticize the real society, thinking that they can provide a way out and a solution, and even thinking that they or a certain system or even a certain leader are individuals who are sanctified, which will lead the society out of ignorance and toward pure light (Sowell, 2010, pp. 95–96). The second is "rhetoric skills", that is, using one's own good speech or writing to beautify one's ideal picture, criticize others, filter facts, whitewash one's mistakes, and find out various rationalized excuses for oneself. This law is no exception for China culture because any culture is a system of the universe of meaning. When the traditional Confucian outlook on the universe and values were seriously challenged in the transitional era, the traditional meaning structure was shaken, which made Chinese people face some problems of life and the basic meaning of the universe that had settled in traditional culture. The emergence of these problems and the general confusion and anxiety caused by them gave rise to the spiritual orientation crisis of modern China intellectuals, which triggered the cultural identity crisis (Zhang, 1999). The abolition of imperial examination in 1905 and the New Culture movement in 1919 broke the cultural system pattern of the closed cycle of traditional culture in China. Scholars are also undergoing self-identity vicissitude in the transformation period, forming a group of intellectuals with new personality and new roles. Although the tradition of Shì 士 "scholar" has disappeared in the social structure of modern China, the ghost of "scholar" still haunts the intellectuals in modern China in various ways (Yu, 2003). Western thinkers were amazed at the spirit of "taking the world as their own duty" of Chinese intellectuals. They pointed out that intellectuals in China regard the realization of many modern values, including fairness, democracy, and the rule of law, as their exclusive responsibility, which is quite different from that in the United States and even in the whole West; the pursuit of these values is everyone's business, and intellectuals should not bear greater responsibility than others (Walzer, 1994, pp. 59–61).

Whether it is the era of "ism" formed by the emergence of various ideological trends at the end of the Qing Dynasty and the beginning of the Republic of China (Spira, 2015), or the discourse construction of "Pernicious-Vestiges" used in the first section of this chapter to break the old and create new ones for ideology, its spearhead points to a common root: Taking ideology and culture as the way to solve problems (Lin, 1979, p. 49). Under the interpretation of the crisis of China's traditional culture in the sense of concept history, the discourse construction of "Pernicious-Vestiges" may be similar to that of the New Culture movement, and it is an attempt by Chinese Communist Party propagandists, as intellectuals, to keep or discard traditional culture in a specific period according to the needs of the system and reality. However, in the actual operation process of the CCP's propaganda system, the ideological construction of "setting the tone for the policy" can only come from the orders of the CCP's top management, while the propaganda tools represented by *People's Daily* only have room for operation in the ideological interpretation of "serving the policy" and become the tools to rationalize the actual needs afterwards (Shambaugh, 2008, pp. 103–127). Although we can't rule out that there are intellectuals in the decision-making level of the Communist Party of China who need to make repeated attempts to delocalization and relocalization of ideology based on the crisis of traditional culture, since the May 4th movement, the premise that "new ideas are the source of change" presupposed by China intellectuals' firm belief in "humble words and righteous deeds" is dangerous (Lin, 1979, p. 49) because the relationship between ideas and institutions in human history has always been uncertain and changeable. In view of this, completely relying on the ideological transformation driven by cultural crisis to understand the driving force of historical change may also bring problems. We need to turn our perspective to the supplement of structure level and understand the complicated causal relationship between ideology and structure through the legitimacy crisis of contemporary China's state governance.

Fluctuation of legitimacy crisis: Interactive explanation of ideology and social structure

According to Fairbank's point of view, China's national governance depends on the ruler playing the authoritative role of the trinity of state, society, and culture at the same time (Fairbank, 1986, p. 9), representing and exercising totalism power covering all kinds of state functions and also needing to be a moral national model, thus continuing the rule of virtue instead of the rule of law (Fairbank, 1986, p. 52). In this sense, the initiation and termination of "Great Leap Forward" and Cultural Revolution are related to the scene changes of Mao Zedong's position and role in the Party and in China. In fact, as a state power forged in the social movement, looking at the actual situation of the establishment and construction of state power in China, charismatic authority has always played an important role in the process of constructing the legitimacy of state power. However, because charismatic authority is based on the leader's extraordinary endowment, how to continuously create achievements through economic construction and modernization, so as to show its extraordinary endowment and how to keep its followers' recognition and obedience to this endowment, has become the key to its legitimacy foundation and has induced the corresponding institutional arrangements.

However, no power can be permanently based on coercion or violence, but it must have its legal basis to be recognized and obeyed by the people. Therefore, the continuous operation of state power requires the strongest self-defense by resorting to the principle of its legitimacy. In this regard, Zhou (2017) demonstrated the relationship between the logic of state governance and its legitimacy in his book, and the so-called authority is the power based on legitimacy. Bureaucracy, as a specific organizational form, appears in China. Although there are a series of institutional mechanisms behind it, its legal basis and organizational operation characteristics are not independent but serve the institutional framework of the grand state system and obey the state-dominated form. The legitimacy of contemporary China is based on the mixed foundation of legal-rational authority but more on charismatic authority (Zhou, 2017, p. 69).

After the Cultural Revolution, the source of legitimacy of the Communist Party of China has changed from ideological legitimacy to economic development and governance (Perry, 2008), which is manifested in the development-oriented leaders, the rise of economic and technical bureaucrats, the promotion of private economic sectors by state power, the weakening of national autonomy and civil society, and the political legitimacy based on the achievements of rapid economic development (Johnson, 1999; Leftwich, 1995). However, on the other side of the legitimacy of political achievements, the shadow of ideological legitimacy is never far away, and the dependence of historical ways is strong. The existing institutional forces of organizations, interests, and ideas are still trying to fix the old framework, so many practices show efforts to strengthen charismatic authority, such as strengthening control in the ideological field and a series of efforts to strengthen political education. During the period of reform and opening up, the ruling party's efforts to bring order out of chaos were supported by the people, the performance of economic take-off, and the great improvement of people's living standards, all of which also guided the ruling party to follow the track of charismatic authority and rebuild its legitimacy foundation through its achievements. In the difficulty of not being able to build a new legitimacy foundation in a short period of time, the efforts to maintain and strengthen the authority of charisma seem to be the last choice of the ruling party, but it is also the strategy with high proficiency (Zhou, 2017, p. 80). The operation of charismatic authority needs to ensure the importance of the ruling party's ideology of governing, so as to prevent liberalization or diversification from questioning, weakening, or challenging the organizational system of charismatic authority. However, with the entry of a bureaucratic system into a charismatic authoritative country, the legitimacy of ideology may not only be strengthened by the infiltration of bureaucratic system into the political education of the people but also be challenged by the inconsistency between the legal-rational authority behind the system itself and the state form. Therefore, there is always a complicated relationship and dramatic tension between the factual legalization basis of economic development as the performance of state governance and ideology, which is the fundamental reason why the aforementioned judgment that the legal-rational authority is the basis of state legitimacy can be established.

In countries where the legitimacy is based on the authority of charisma and the extraordinary endowment of leaders, the mobilization of state governance through propaganda tools depends on the effectiveness of political mobilization as a party-state ideology, and the achievements of modernization or market economy development will also represent the legitimacy of state power under the domination of charismatic authority system, rather than the governance performance of social organizations or market institutions. Ideological bias not only partially constitutes the performance indicators of contemporary state governance but also affects the performance of other performance indicators of state governance, such as the stable performance related to the purpose of establishing state power and the material performance related to the economic ties between citizens and the state. However, it should be pointed out that if the latter happens in a country where ideology dominates, the performance of state governance should be regarded as a by-product of state rule in the secondary sense. Returning to a pair of competitive relationships investigated in this book, for China, the relationship between the legitimacy of ideology and the legitimacy of political achievements is usually rather tense. Both are closely related, and there has been a trade-off relationship in the historical context since 1949; the performance of state governance or "political achievements" measured by material performance indicators will decline with the degree that the state relies on ideology as a single driving force for governance (Ren & Zhu, 2018). Contrary to the "revolutionary motive force theory", the theoretical mechanism of a legitimacy crisis can provide an effective explanation for the return of the CPC's ideological work and the discourse construction of "Pernicious-Vestiges" after the reform and opening up, but it seems difficult to explain why the policy centered on ideological transformation was interrupted by the process of restoring economic order and modernization. It is also difficult to form an explanatory perspective of the persistent construction of "Pernicious-Vestiges" discourse and the persistent self-denial of China's history in isolation.

Generally speaking, these three perspectives can't consistently explain why the CPC's propaganda work continuously chooses new historical carriers for negation and re-negation through the discourse construction of "Pernicious-Vestiges". There are two main reasons. First, it seems that there is no effective consensus in the theoretical explanation mentioned earlier on how to treat and define the "revolution" of contemporary China. In order to avoid possible confusion, this book defines the continuous "revolution" trend reflected behind the "Pernicious-Vestiges" discourse in contemporary China as a social revolution (Zou, 2004) in which conflicts are resolved by "all wins and all loses". This is different from Mao Zedong's "Investigation Report on Hunan Peasant Movement", which emphasizes the characteristics of means in a narrow sense, "one class overthrows another" (Mao, 1969, p. 17). Even if the carrier of "Pernicious-Vestiges" once pointed to a specific individual, it was enough to be the beginning or signal of these specific individuals or groups' bad luck, but the discourse construction of memory work can never be equated with violence itself. At the same time, this kind of "revolution" is not a generalized "revolution" in Arendt's sense, which emphasizes results, that is, the complex of "seeking new things only" generated in pursuit of breaking away from the "going round and round" of the past (Arendt, 1965, pp. 21–52), because the carrier constructed by the "Pernicious-Vestiges" discourse itself is going round and round. Second, these theoretical perspectives seem to fail to discuss why the legitimacy of political power is closely related to the work of rebuilding memory. In view of this, it is necessary for this book to further clarify from the level of political system why it is possible to see the legitimacy of political power from memory work.

If the legitimacy in traditional politics is divided into three levels—political legitimacy of monarchies, political legitimacy of dynasties, and political legitimacy of monarchical power (Zhang, 2006)—then the legitimacy of monarchies belongs to the level of political ideology, while the legitimacy of monarchical power is the legitimacy argument of the relationship between emperors and political power (Liu, 1996, p. 103). The "legitimacy of regime" mentioned in this book is closer to the political legitimacy of dynasty regime, and it is a kind of social consciousness that members of society ask for the legitimacy and rationality of regime rule. There are two ways to form the sense of legitimacy of political power. One is the political memory of social members of history, that is, the values, positions, and beliefs formed during the reconstruction and writing of historical and political events. The other is the feeling and evaluation of social members on the ruling behavior of real political power. The awareness of regime legitimacy formed by the two ways influences each other, and the social awareness derived from political memory constitutes a theoretical frame of reference for evaluating the legitimacy and rationality of the current regime, while the feelings of social members about the regime's ruling behavior constantly modify and shape the "political memory" related to the legitimacy of the regime (Liu, 1996, pp. 4–5). In the view of memory researchers, memory is a citation of the present so-called previous presence, in which "citation" is a repetition of acquired knowledge, and "proof" is a creative activity of past knowledge. It has the special function of preserving experience and continuously injecting it into practice (Derrida, 1988, p. 69), while social memory is the sum total of social experiences of all members of a "larger self" group, including oral practice, routine historical documents, drawing or shooting pictures, collective memorial ceremonies, and geographical and social space. Therefore, whether it is a family, a certain social class, a professional group, or a nation-state, social groups will create their common traditions, interpret their essence, and maintain their cohesion by choosing, organizing, and retelling the "past". What this group orientation pursues is the mechanism that makes a certain stable order recognized and shapes the sense of legitimacy of the regime (Wang, 1997, p. 51).

It can be seen that memory is political, and some scholars even put forward the concept of "political memory" to emphasize the political function of social memory. Among them, the main body of memory is various groups with certain political and social power, which exists in a certain space-time framework. Its function mode is mainly to trace back and reconstruct history, and its main purpose is to express the political values held by this group (Wang, 2008, p. 21). The process of political memory production and reproduction can be divided into four stages: Arousal, reconstruction, solidification, and engraving, in which arousal is a large-scale convergent memory of the same time and space experience. In this process, political memory makes purposeful choices of memory content and memory objects, reconstructs the realistic significance of history through "forgetting" and "writing", and finally makes tradition continue and change in the framework of a society. Solidification is not only to maintain and consolidate the reconstructed political memory, but more importantly, to assimilate "dissent", reconstruct the legitimacy, strengthen the sense of identity, and accomplish its reproduction by engraving. There are three levels of information in the form of political memory: Ideology stores rules and reads traditions; what is stored is law, and what is read is morality; and what is stored is public opinion, and what is read is recognition. The difference between storing and reading information may be a false distortion, but the significance of these information functions in the scope of political memory are true to a large extent (Wang, 2008, p. 103). If we can solve the dilemma of political memory engraving in four aspects—the willingness to engrave, the choice of subjects, the choice of engraving objects, and the choice of engraving methods—political power will be able to successfully reconstruct not only society but also every individual in society by manipulating the production and reproduction of political memory (Wang, 2008, pp. 24–29).

To sum up, on the explanatory level, the mechanism question that this book tries to answer can be expressed as: What kind of political memory did the ideology that the Communist Party of China propaganda organization represented by *People's Daily* create when it constructed the carrier of "Pernicious-Vestiges" discourse in different contexts and social needs? What power will these political memories reflect to drive the historical changes of contemporary China? At the discourse level, the writing of political memory needs to be done by manipulating words like "Pernicious-Vestiges", and the ideological discourse illusion can be generated by the specific use of words in situations, so as to rewrite people's view of history. In the next section, we will specifically introduce the methodology system of ideology constructed by "Pernicious-Vestiges" narratives through the discourse practice of *People's Daily*.

Methodology: "Discourse illusion" as a theoretical and analytical framework

Based on the basic ideas of critical discourse analysis, this book will take the current domestic political "discourse events" framed by the word "Pernicious-Vestiges" in *People's Daily* as the "legal profile" of memory practice and examine it from the perspective of text, discourse practice, and social practice (Fairclough, 1993). Here, ideology is defined by Fairclough as different beliefs and thoughts that help to maintain or oppose the power relations in class society characterized by ruling relations (Fairclough, 1995, p. 82). With the passage of time, some ideological concepts eventually drifted away from their origins, seemingly forgotten; but in fact, they became naturalized and common sense through the reconstruction and reproduction of different languages and symbolic forms, making them more unpredictable. Groups condensed by individuals tend to hold a common ideological system. As time goes by, these systems will gradually be naturalized and integrated into the structure of social consciousness, resulting in discourse illusion.

To a certain extent, Fairclough's discourse analysis paradigm also anchors a suitable analytical perspective and conceptual framework for the research itself and holds that discourse is a projected, imaginary symbol construction that represents a possibility different from the real world and is often associated with projects that change the world in a specific direction (Fairclough, 2003, p. 124). Following this paradigm, discourse illusion proposed by Bhatia (2015), as an analytical framework, is not only a theory but also provides concrete aspects and process guidance to be analyzed. It advocates that through the use of metaphor and rhetoric in discourse, it examines how the ideological narrative constructed by discourse constructs the category of subjective concepts, so as to use the past to carry out historical attribution and serve to prove the present or predict the future discourse order. This analytical framework unlocks the mystery of ideological discourse by re-textualizing the past and conditioning the present. It advocates revealing the emergence of binary opposition categories through metaphorical rhetoric, allowing the critical analysis of public discourse events including revolution from multiple perspectives, and helping to transcend linguistic means and deconstructing the influence of social culture and historical emotions on argumentation in more detail (Ross & Bhatia, 2021). Especially when discourse illusion appears in a changing environment, it will be easier to recognize and become a problem that needs critical comment (Bhatia, 2015, p. 16). Therefore, the discourse illusion will also be applicable to the analysis of the historical reversal of contemporary China in the discourse construction of *People's Daily*.

As a methodology, the basic assumption of discourse illusion analysis is that the reality in people's eyes is not a complete process but a conceptualization of reality or a specific version of reality. The conceptualization of individual reality depends on Bourdieu's social and historical "habituation", that is, an individual and collective practice arising from socialization and historical experience (Bourdieu, 1990). People's understanding of reality is guided by their previous life experience, which in turn shapes the values, beliefs, and ideological positions of social actors. Illusion comes from the power to participate in the conceptualization of reality and form the subjective essence (Ross & Bhatia, 2019). For example, in political situations, powerful media gatekeepers can create illusions through public discourse with the help of authority, power struggle, hegemony, and the subordinate position of the public. The purpose is to resort to emotional weaknesses caused by people's lack of knowledge of power in their belief system, such as doubt, despair, laziness, and so on. Once the recipient of media discourse agrees with these versions of reality, and the individual is guided by ideology and generates subjective interpretation to become the only possibility or conclusion accepted by the society, the collective discourse illusion will be revealed. This "collective consensus" interpretation mechanism holds that once a subjective reality is agreed by many people, it can become a legitimate objective (Bhatia, 2015, p. 10). When people think that their subjective imagination and ideological understanding of the world is the only conclusion, it will lead to illusion, which will make discourse illusion begin to represent the "truth" and pose a challenge to the order of negative discourse construction. It is the integration of discourse illusion and social actors' habits that makes ideology and belief work smoothly. Studying ideology is the way to study meaning and maintain the ruling relationship because being considered legal helps to maintain the joy brought by the ruling itself (Thompson, 1984, pp. 130–131).

To sum up, discursive illusion is defined as the result of subjective representation of reality by groups. This illusion comes from the historical storage of experience, is embodied by language and symbolic behavior, and generates social and cultural categories of people and groups. The process of shaping collective illusion is dominated by the speaker of public discourse, and it is realized through persuasive efforts of mass media (Bhatia, 2015, pp. 15–16). The analysis using the framework of discourse illusion aims at revealing how the generation of history serves the current understanding and belief formation by comparing how different narratives of "truth" or realistic versions are constructed by discourse, how these beliefs are conveyed through powerful emotional metaphors, and how these narratives finally divide groups and individuals into divided categories (Ross & Bhatia, 2021). Discourse illusion, as an analytical framework, focuses on three aspects of the classification process of language text, visual rhetoric, and multimodal discourse shaping, which are (1) historicity, (2) linguistic and semiotic action of language and symbols, and (3) social impact. Among them, historicity mainly focuses on how discourse clearly evoke and reconstructs historical events; The function of language and symbols focuses on how discourse demonstrates the multimodal use of metaphor; Social influence focuses on how discourse clearly shows the classification of "us" and "them".

Specifically, in the discourse analysis steps of the "Pernicious-Vestiges" text constructed by *People's Daily*, first of all, the investigation of historical issues depends on the core concept of habituation. The collective habits formed by larger discourse entities such as newspapers and political parties, rather than individual habits, form the basis of discourse illusion, which reconstructs past experience into current reality. This book will examine how the "Pernicious-Vestiges" discourse constructed by *People's Daily* calls for or bids farewell to the past history through time reference, social and political history call and discourse-based re-textual, etc., and by referring to the past, put the current activities back into history.

Secondly, in terms of language and symbolic functions, writers create and spread specific intentions to represent metaphors through mixed cognitive and pragmatic perspectives. Therefore, metaphor is not only a linguistic phenomenon, but also a powerful tool of persuasion. Metaphor itself introduces the contradictory combination of clarity and vagueness into discourse illusion, which is necessary to present the world as a fair subjective representation, and can trigger an appropriate emotional response in the target audience. In view of this, this book will also fully consider what metaphors are used in the "Pernicious-Vestiges" narrative in *People's Daily* to construct a set of unfamiliar and abstract ideology with the help of familiar and concrete images, so as to serve the political goals, and what immediate emotions and lasting reactions are produced in the process.

Finally, in terms of social influence, ideological language usually leads to classification and stereotype. In this respect, the concept of categorization provides a useful tool for the content organization and in-depth analysis of this book. This concept mainly focuses on how people organize their moral positions and commitments around specific category identities (Jayyusi, 1984, p. 183). Categorization mainly covers three situations: (1) self-organized group united by common beliefs and goals; (2) type categorization, which is predicted to produce specific actions because of embedding specific classification features; and (3) assigning individual descriptor designers with ascriptive and descriptive functional labels to specific types of people (Jayyusi, 1984, p. 24). It is very important to understand the social and political classification and spread of contemporary China by analyzing the specific "Pernicious-Vestiges" directions and their fluctuation trends that *People's Daily* has constructed in different historical periods.

Research questions and content arrangement of this book

Derrida believes that memory is "the citation of the present so-called previous presence" (Derrida, 1988). Among them, "quoting" is a review of history, while "proving" is a creative activity based on history, which has the special function of preserving experience and continuously injecting it into practice. The narrative content of "Pernicious-Vestiges" contains a specific language style and standardization process and makes use of the metaphor of diseases to construct "moral exhortation" and "symbol of corruption" in the discourse, which plays a memory strategy of "memory domestication". Through discourse analysis and a historical comparison of the "Pernicious-Vestiges" narratives in the news texts of *People's Daily*, this book analyzes the rhetorical orientation and connotation of this discourse practice from the aspects of the memory object, memory subject, and its process constructed by the "Pernicious-Vestiges" narratives; devotes itself to revealing the main metaphors and political functions of China's "Pernicious-Vestiges" discourse construction in the past 76 years; and reflects on the social significance and ethical enlightenment of the memory subject and object constructed by the "Pernicious-Vestiges" discourse. By combing the time and social context of the rhetorical object of "Pernicious-Vestiges", this book gives a response to Dirlik's (1996) questions about the reversal, "aberration" and paradigm interruption in contemporary China's historical narrative.

To sum up, the core issues to be investigated in this book include the following three aspects: (1) Since 1946, when and under what social context did various rhetorical objects of "Pernicious-Vestiges" discourse in *People's Daily* appear? What kind of historical meaning did they have? (2) What metaphors are used in the construction of "Pernicious-Vestiges" discourse? What kind of social function does it intend to play on historical practice? (3) How does "Pernicious-Vestiges" discourse construct the subject and object of memory and the group classification of "us" and "them"? What is the social significance and ethical enlightenment? After the overall description and process analysis of these questions, we will also try to answer, what role did the discourse construction of "Pernicious-Vestiges" play in the process of generating and transforming modern China's view of history? What are the driving forces behind it? How helpful are these thoughts for understanding the Chinese Communist Party's national governance logic and propaganda logic?

The structure of this book is arranged in content and logically considered as follows. First, Chapter 1 defines the research object, theoretical framework, research methods, and research questions of this book. That is to say, this book will take *People's Daily*, the official newspaper of the Communist Party of China, as a typical case; take the construction of "Pernicious-Vestiges" discourse in this newspaper as the research object; take "discourse illusion" as the theoretical and analytical framework; and use the research methods of discourse analysis and historical analogy to explore the historical evolution of the narrative of "Pernicious-Vestiges" in *People's Daily*. Chapter 2 will specifically discuss the specific historical strategies adopted by *People's Daily* in constructing the "Pernicious-Vestiges" discourse and reveal the process of covering and domesticating the political memory behind the historical narrative of the "Pernicious-Vestiges" discourse by summarizing four groups of dualistic discourse and memory construction strategies adopted by the official media. Chapter 3 discusses the construction of "discourse illusion" by metaphorical rhetoric behind the "Pernicious-Vestiges" discourse and the direction behind the discourse rhetoric. Chapter 4 to Chapter 6 of this book will focus on the news texts of *People's Daily*, revealing the problems of historical writing and domestication of political memory behind the construction of discourse illusion of "Pernicious-Vestiges". Specifically, Chapter 4 will focus on the narrative tradition of feudal "Pernicious-Vestiges" in *People's Daily*, which has appeared the most and lasted the longest, from 1946 until now. Chapter 5 will focus on the historical transformation period of contemporary China from the founding of the People's Republic of China to the Cultural Revolution and systematically analyze the Kuomintang reactionaries, the old society, imperialism, and the "Pernicious-Vestiges" of capitalism. Chapter 6 will find out which historical events, social groups, or ideologies are defined as the sources of "Pernicious-Vestiges" through specific texts and explain the problem of discourse interruption and "re-narration". Chapter 7 will summarize and try to respond to many problems of contemporary historical paradigm and political memory construction in China by analyzing the discourse practice activities of typical cases.

References

Adorno, T. (1959/1986). What does coming to terms with the past mean? In G. Hartman (Eds.), *Bitburg in Moral and Political Perspective* (pp. 114–129). Bloomington: Indiana University Press.
Arendt, H. (1965). *On Revolution*. New York: The Viking Press.
Bhatia, A. (2015). *Discursive Illusions in Public Discourse: Theory and Practice*. New York: Routledge.
Bishop, R. L. (1989). *Qi Lai! Mobilizing One Billion Chinese: The Chinese Communication System*. Ames: Iowa State University Press.
Bourdieu, P. (1990). *The Logic of Practice*. Cambridge: Polity Press.
Chen, Y. (1986). *Making Revolution: The Communist Movement in Eastern and Central China, 1937–1945*. Berkeley: University of California Press.
Derrida, J. (1988). *Mémoires: Pour Paul de Man*. Paris: Galilée.
Dirlik, A. (1996). Reversals, ironies, hegemonies: Notes on the contemporary historiography of modern China. *Modern China*, *22*(3), 243–284. www.jstor.org/stable/189188.
Fairbank, J. K. (1986). *The Great Chinese Revolution, 1800–1985*. New York: Harper Collins.
Fairclough, N. (1993). *Discourse and Social Change*. Cambridge: Polity Press.
Fairclough, N. (1995). *Critical Discourse Analysis*. Singapore: Longman.
Fairclough, N. (2003). *Analyzing Discourse: Textual Analysis for Social Research*. London: Routledge.
Gao, B 高丙中. (1996). Jīngyīng wénhuà, dàzhòng wénhuà, mínjiān wénhuà: Zhōngguó wénhuà de qúntǐ chāyì jí qí biànqiān 精英文化、大众文化、民间文化：中国文化的群体差异及其变迁. *Social Science Front 社会科学战线*, *2*, 108–113.
Heywood, A. (2014). *Politics* (4th ed.). London: Palgrave Macmillan Ltd.
Jayyusi, L. (1984). *Categorization and the Moral Order*. Boston: Routledge and Keegan Paul.
Jia, C 贾春峰., & Teng, W 滕文生. (1980, October 9). Nǔlì kèfú 'háiwèi kèfú de y wù '— tántán sùqīng fēngjiànzhǔyì de cányú yǐngxiǎng wèntí 努力克服'还未克服的遗物'—谈谈肃清封建主义的残余影响问题. *Renmin Ribao 人民日报*, 5A.
Johnson, C. (1999). The developmental state: Odyssey of a concept. In M. Woo-Cumings (Eds.), *The Developmental State* (pp. 32–60). Ithaca: Cornell University Press.
Lakoff, G., & Johnson, M. (1980). *Metaphors We Live by*. Chicago: The University of Chicago Press.
Leftwich, A. (1995). Bringing politics back in: Towards a model of the developmental state. *Journal of Development Studies*, *31*(3), 400–427.
Lin, Yu-Sheng. (1979). *Crisis of Chinese Consciousness: Radical Antitraditionalism in the May Fourth Era*. Madison: University of Wisconsin Press.
Liu, Z 刘泽华. (1996). *Zhōngguó Ahèngzhì Sīxiǎngshǐ (Qínhàn Wèijìn Nánběicháo Juàn) 中国政治思想史(秦汉魏晋南北朝卷)*. Hangzhou: Zhejiang People's Publishing House.
Mao, Z 毛泽东. (1969). *Húnán Nóngmín Yùndòng Kǎochá Bàogào 湖南农民 运动考察报告*. Beijing: People's Publishing House.

Molden, B. (2016). Resistant pasts versus mnemonic hegemony: On the power relations of collective memory. *Memory Studies*, *9*(2), 125–142. https://doi.org/10.1177/1750698015596014.

Olick, J. K. (1998). What does it mean to normalize the past? Official memory in German politics since 1989. *Social Science History*, *22*(4), 547–571. https://doi.org/10.2307/1171575.

Olick, J. K., & Levy, D. (1997). Collective memory and cultural constraint: Holocaust myth and rationality in German politics. *American Sociological Review*, *62*(6), 921–936. https://doi.org/10.2307/2657347.

Olick, J. K., & Robbins, J. (1998). Social memory studies: From "collective memory" to the historical sociology of mnemonic practices. *Annual Review of Sociology*, *24*(1), 105–140. www.jstor.org/stable/223476.

Pei, M. (2006). *China's Trapped Transition: The Limits of Developmental Autocracy*. Cambridge, MA: Harvard University Press.

Perry, E. (2008). Chinese conception of right: From Mencius to Mao and now. *Perspective on Politics*, *6*(1), 137–147.

Perry, E. J. 裴宜理. (2006). Studying Chinese politics: Farewell to revolution?"告别革命"与中国政治研究 (trans. by P. Liu). *Thought and Words: Journal of the Humanities and Social Science* 思與言：人文與社會科學期刊, *44*(3), 231–291.

Ren, J 任剑涛., & Zhu, D 朱丹. (2018). Yìshíxíngtài yǔ guójiā zhìlǐ jìxiào 意识形态与国家治理绩效. *Academia Bimestris* 学海, *2*, 72–81.

Ross, A. S., & Bhatia, A. (2019). #secondcivilwarletters from the front: Discursive illusions in a trending twitter hashtag. *New Media & Society*, *21*(10), 2222–2241. https://doi.org/10.1177/1461444819843311.

Ross, A. S., & Bhatia, A. (2021). "Ruled Britannia": Metaphorical construction of the EU as enemy in UKIP campaign posters. *The International Journal of Press/Politics*, *26*(1), 188–209. https://doi.org/10.1177/1940161220935812.

Schwartz, B. (1991). Social change and collective memory: The democratization of George Washington. *American Sociological Review*, *56*(2), 221–236. https://doi.org/10.2307/2095781.

Scruton, R. (2007). *The Palgrave Macmillan Dictionary of Political thought* (3rd ed.). London: Palgrave Macmillan.

Shambaugh, D. (2008). *China's Communist Party: Atrophy and Adaptation*. Berkeley: University of California Press.

Sowell, T. (2010). *Intellectuals and Society*. New York: Basic Books.

Spira, I. (2015). *A Conceptual History of Chinese-Isms: The Modernization of Ideological Discourse, 1895–1925*. Boston: Brill Academic Pub.

The Works Compilation Bureau of Marx, Engels, Lenin and Stalin of the CPC Central Committee (Eds.) 中共中央马克思恩格斯列宁斯大林著作编译局编. (1972). *Selected Works of Marx and Engels*. (Volume II) 马克思恩格斯选集 (第二卷). Beijing: People's Publishing House.

Thompson, J. B. (1984). *Studies in the Theory of Ideology*. Cambridge: Polity Press.

Walzer, M. (1994). *Thick and Thin: Moral Argument at Home and Abroad*. Notre Dame: University of Notre Dame Press.

Wang, H 王海洲. (2008). *Héfǎxìng de Zhēngduó—Zhèngzhì Jìyì de Duōchóng Kèxiě* 合法性的争夺—政治记忆的多重刻写. Nanjing: Phoenix Publishing & Media, Inc.

Wang, M 王明珂. (1997). *Huáxià Biānyuán: Lìshǐ Jìyì yǔ Zúqún Rèntóng* 華夏邊緣：歷史記憶與族群認同. Taipei: Asian Culture Publishing Co., Ltd.

Wu, G. (1994). Command communication: The politics of editorial formulation in the people's daily. *China Quarterly*, *137*, 194–211. https://doi.org/10.1017/S0305741000034111.

Yu, Y 余英时. (2003). *Shì Yǔ Zhōngguó Wénhuà* 士与中国文化. Shanghai: Shanghai People's Publishing House.

Zhang, H 張灝. (1999). Zhōngguó jìndài sīxiǎngshǐ de zhuǎnxíng shídài 中國近代思想史的轉型時代. *Twenty-First Century* 二十一世紀, *52*, 29–39.

Zhang, X 张星久. (2006). Lùn dìzhì shíqī zhōngguó zhèngzhì zhèngdāngxìng de jīběn céngcì 论帝制时期中国政治正当性的基本层次. *CASS Journal of Political Science* 政治学研究, *4*, 99–106.

Zhou, X 周雪光. (2017). *The Logic of Governance in China: An Organizational Approach* 中国国家治理的制度逻辑——一个组织学研究. Beijing: Joint Publishing.

Zou, D 鄒讜. (2004). Gémìng yǔ gàobié gémìng—gěi 「gàobié gémìng」 zuòzhě de yīfēng xìn 革命與「告別革命」——給《告別革命》作者的一封信. In Z. Li 李澤厚 & Z. Liu 劉再復 (Eds.), *Lǐ Zéhòu Liú Zàifù Duìhuàlù： Gàobié Gémìng—Huíwàng Èrshíshìjì Zhōngguó* 李澤厚劉再復對話錄：告別革命——回望二十世紀中國 (pp. 3–20). Hong Kong: Cosmos Books Ltd.

2 Sheltering and domestication

Strategies, historicity, and memory politics in "Pernicious-Vestiges" discourse

People live in two realities; one is the subjective reality that is recognized and constructed through life experiences and thoughts, and the other is the real objective reality. According to the theory of social construction of reality, social environment is a kind of human product, which is institutionalized by individual's habitual behavior and finally becomes a part of external reality (Berger & Luckmann, 1966). Language plays a key role in the process of objectifying and proving the subjective concept of individuals embedded in objective facts. Although people's conceptual system can create the expression of objective reality, it is difficult for people to contact the objective reality directly. Therefore, the subjective reconstruction will be attributed based on discourse illusion mainly through various symbols and linguistic means. Illusion comes from complex and multifaceted phenomena, and its realization covers the intention of producers or actors, the power struggle in the social field, and the sociopolitical and historical background that affects the personal experience pool (Bhatia, 2015, p. 2). The principle of social confirmation further shows that the way of collective consent is helpful for people to affirm the truth of the outside world through the confirmation of others (Cialdini, 1997), especially when this confirmation comes from the fact that the more influential entities choose language to reproduce reality through privilege and objectify it through social hegemony (Bhatia, 2015, pp. 9–10).

The ideological construction process of "Pernicious-Vestiges" discourse first involves the key issues of how to deal with the past, present, and future of modern China. In the second chapter of the book, we will examine the strategies adopted by *People's Daily*'s "Pernicious-Vestiges" discourse to rebuild the history and then serve the politics of memory. As the basis of discourse illusion, the historical framework draws on the concept of "structured immediacy", holds that social actors will enrich their actions here and now by linking them with the past, and choose descriptions of people and activities to generate and provide the meaning of serving specific goals (Leudar & Nekvapil, 2011). Similarly, Bhatia (2015) also regards the historical framework in discourse illusion as the first aspect to be analyzed and thinks that it is a concrete example in which historical antecedents are re-recognized intentionally or unintentionally in discourse to locate and present the current reality, and its essence is to serve the future (p. 52). The common root of these theoretical resources comes from the time dimension of Bourdieu's

DOI: 10.4324/9781003409724-2

"habituation", that is, the past naturally becomes the basis of people's future actions (Schirato & Yell, 2000, p. 42). In other words, people are used to diagnosing new experiences in daily life by understanding the past.

On the concrete steps of analyzing the historicity of discourse, Wodak (2000) advocated that the historical tension and discourse illusion in the process of re-text should be revealed by presenting several binary opposites and their contradictory tendencies, including static and dynamic, simple and complex, precise and fuzzy, argumentation and statement, etc. In this chapter, we also choose four pairs of binary opposites, namely, forgetting and memory, injustice and justice, breaking old and creating new, and anthropophagic and anthropoemic. They frequently appear in the "Pernicious-Vestiges" discourse constructed by *People's Daily* and play a key role in reconstructing history. These contradictory trends show that every change of context will establish new meanings and convey new information. They will reflect the change of ideology through the power struggle within the community, and this ideology will also reveal the characteristics of the ruling relationship in class society (Fairclough, 1995, p. 82). Therefore, we will first pay attention to how the "Pernicious-Vestiges" discourse builders of *People's Daily* relate their intentions to the past to enrich their actions at that time and at present (Leudar & Nekvapil, 2011).

As a kind of social consciousness, political legitimacy is the social members' questioning of the legitimacy and rationality of regime rule. Political memory establishes and guarantees political legitimacy by selectively framing, continuing and strengthening the identity of social memory in the same historical period, or dissolving and assimilating heterogeneity. How does political memory show the selected information content? Some scholars believe that there are three corresponding levels of storing and reading information, namely, rules versus tradition, laws versus morality, and public opinion versus recognition (Wang, 2008, p. 103). The process of establishing new political legitimacy is often accompanied by the political subject's reconstruction of political memory and a series of memory strategies.

As a case of "legal brief introduction" in the historical narrative of New China, the discourse of "Pernicious-Vestiges" constructs a part of the political memory that continues from the past to the present. "Pernicious-Vestiges" has the same essence as other labels about "disease" and "harm". They all objectify, stigmatize people or their thoughts, and play the role of political mobilization, social mobilization, and moral exemption when eliminating "them" or become scapegoats of the denied past. In this process, the memory political strategies of "Pernicious-Vestiges" discourse mainly include forgetting and remembering, injustice and justice, breaking the old and creating the new, anthropophagic and anthropoemic, etc. In this chapter, we will analyze the new historicity constructed by these binary opposites in detail.

Forgetting/remembering

There is always a dichotomy between the concepts of "remembering" and "forgetting" in the research tradition of memory. On the one hand, it praises remembering; on the other hand, it belittles forgetting. In the research of memory, from the cognitive psychology paradigm of micro-perspective, to the media reappearance of specific historical events, to the discussion of ethnic boundaries and their recognition functions, and even to the ethical issues of memory, it seems to assume that remembering is naturally has higher justice than forgetting—"remembering is like a hero shining in the spotlight, while forgetting is a dark villain lurking behind the screen" (Brockmeier, 2002). The "Pernicious-Vestiges" discourse constructed by *People's Daily* also strengthened this logic. For example, in June 1946, *People's Daily* published an article entitled "Chóngqìng fójiàotú jīdūjiàotú qídǎo hépíng fǎnduì nèizhàn 重庆佛教徒基督教徒 祈祷和平反对内战 [Buddhists and Christians in Chongqing pray for peace and oppose the civil war]". In addition to serving as a wartime party newspaper to convey dissatisfaction with the Kuomintang government's persistence in the civil war, the article also constructed and emphasized the implied moral law that remembering is higher than forgetting:

> Huáng shì (mò hán) 黄氏 (墨涵) pointed out in his prayer: "There were a few ignorant leaders in the world who were aggressive and belligerent, and wanted to rule the world by violence. Although they were once prominent for a while, they eventually took their own lives. It can be seen that violence cannot defeat truth. However, although the culprit is removed, the Pernicious-Vestiges still exists. Although the organization is solved, the thought is not clean. To today's world, it is still in an uneasy state. Some people abandon the teachings of God the Father and make selfish plans; Some people forget the warning of the previous car and are still ready to kill. What a dangerous thing this is!?"
>
> (*People's Daily*, June 27, 1946, 1A)

Through the mouth of religious people, *People's Daily* compares Kuomintang leaders with fascist leaders, warning that if the former does not "learn from history" and give up violence and killing, it will surely become the heir of the latter's militaristic ideology and will have a similar tragic ending and fate. This kind of curse-like discourse strengthens the meaning and legitimacy of "don't forget" with a resolute and tough attitude.

So, is forgetting itself meaningless? Could it be accompanied by some kind of reflection? In order to eliminate the tension between remembering and forgetting, researchers have pointed out that forgetting may also be a form of memory and a constituent element of memory itself. "Remembering" and "forgetting", as two parallel paths, will dialectically affect the formation of memory (Terdiman, 1993, p. 250). For example, when changing the work style of grassroots cadres in the early days of New China through the words of "Pernicious-Vestiges", "must forget" replaced "don't forget" and became a powerful means to mobilize people to "draw a clear line" with the past:

> A few cadres are infected with the bad style of the rulers of the old society, and they want to ride on the heads of the masses and throws their weight around. They even think it's a shame to be a cadre who is not feared by the

masses. These cadres haven't distinguished the fundamental difference between revolutionary workers and the minions of the ruling class in the old society at all, so naturally they can't say their policy views. Many newly promoted workers and peasant cadres don't know the policy themselves, and because of the influence of their superiors' beating, they regard beating and swearing as a common occurrence, and they don't know that this is illegal. After analyzing these ideological situations, the leaders pointed out that this was the ideological Pernicious-Vestiges of the old society and dominated everyone's actions, and called on everyone to carry out the ideological revolutionary movement.

> ("Zhōnggòng Ānqìng dìwěi gànxiào zhěngfēng bān fēnxī pīpàn qiǎngpò mìnglìng sīxiǎng 中共安庆地委干校整风班 分析批判强迫命令思想 [The Rectification class of the Communist Party of China Anqing Prefectural Party Committee analyzes the thought of criticizing forced orders]", *People's Daily*, 3A, September 26, 1950)

In the minutes of this internal meeting, the cadres who carry out their work by forcing orders and beating people and swearing are interpreted as victims who are "dominated by the Pernicious-Vestiges of the old society's thoughts" and "infected with the bad style of the old society's rulers", and forgetting these old society's ruling ways becomes the only way out for them to avoid making further mistakes in the role of perpetrators. This kind of "forgetting" is not only ideological but also practical: Only by establishing a full understanding of why we want to "break with the past" in concept can we really show the new ways after the "break" in practice. Therefore, "don't forget" also constitutes the conceptual basis of "must forget".

There are also some more complicated questions about the discourse construction of "Pernicious-Vestiges", that is, the conditions of remembering and forgetting. Take an example: in 1956, after Chairman Mao formally put forward the policy of "letting a hundred flowers blossom and a hundred schools of thought contend", the ideological contention in academic circles extended to elementary schools, military units, and other places. On July 21st, *People's Daily* published a selected manuscript, entitled "Should we draw a circle?", the article writes like this:

> Some people think that there should be conditions for a hundred schools of thought to contend, that is, they can only be within the circle of Marxism–Leninism; Everything that conflicts with Marxism–Leninism should not be allowed to be heard . . . I think the academic debate can be a debate on different understandings of some issues under the Marxist principle, or a tit-for-tat debate with Marxism. In our society, both types of arguments should be allowed to exist. Only when idealism is wrong can materialism be correct . . . Some comrades think that if idealism is allowed to spread, it will poison the society and hinder socialist construction. Although it is well-intentioned, it is a kind of overblown . . . A hundred schools of thought contend just to find out which is right and which is wrong, and to find out what is beneficial to

the country and the people . . . It is bound to be beneficial to China's socialist construction to allow all kinds of academic opinions to contend.
("Dúzhě duì bǎijiāzhēngmíng de yìjiàn 读者对百家争鸣的意见 [Readers' opinions on a hundred schools of thought]", *People's Daily*, 7A, July 21, 1956, by Xiù Démíng 秀德明, from a unit of China People's Liberation Army)

Compared with simply arguing about which is the standard view of history, remembering or forgetting, the progress of this article is reflected in the fact that after adding the presupposition that opinions can compete with each other and the truth will become clearer and clearer, unreserved memory is no longer a historical concept worthy of worrying about the results. In this case, selective forgetting is no longer worthy of praise. Although the implementation of the "policy of a hundred schools of thought" is still a complete victory for Marxism and materialism, and the author's fate in the subsequent liquidation is unknown, the addition of such opinions still enhances the richness and complexity of the debate about which is higher, remembering or forgetting, in the discourse construction of "Pernicious-Vestiges" in *People's Daily*.

In *People's Daily*'s discussion of history and memory through the key word "Pernicious-Vestiges", some articles have also recorded that the intellectuals at that time questioned the way of thinking that all social problems were attributed to "Pernicious-Vestiges" of the "old society" ("Zhōngguó rénmín dàxué shīshēng bóchì Hè Ān de fǎn shèhuìzhǔyì gānglǐng 中国人民大学师生 驳斥贺安的反社会主义纲领 [Teachers and students of Renmin University of China refute He An's anti-socialist program]", *People's Daily*, 7A, August 13, 1957, written by Ma Dajun and Lu Yingfan, special envoys of this newspaper). But unfortunately, Hè Ān 贺安, a lecturer in the Department of Industrial Economics of Renmin University of China, who was a skeptic, appeared in this article as the object of criticism in the anti-rightist struggle. He could only appear in the para-text of the article as a "rightist" who was criticized and become the object of others' narration and criticism. He could not occupy a place at the *People's Daily* in 1957 and become a member of the "people" who were qualified to tell about themselves. It also makes such a position a rare voice in the "Pernicious-Vestiges" construction text examined in this book.

In addition, the threat to "real memory" includes not only what events are remembered but also how these events are remembered (Plate & Smelik, 2009). As a side of remembering, forgetting determines to some extent which events can't enter the frame of memory, and the process of forgetting reflects the hidden track of constructing memory. In 1961, a drama review published by *People's Daily* bluntly revealed that the illusion constructed by the words of "Pernicious-Vestiges" was the essence of keeping in line with the party's line without thinking:

If we can discover the most essential things, reflect the glorious victory of the general line, the Great Leap Forward and the People's Commune more profoundly and widely, and show the face of the great times, we will have greater ideological significance and educational function . . . What essential things does Wú Pèifāng 吴佩芳's deeds contain? . . . After analysis, we found that her thought was opposed and struggled with another thought from beginning to end . . . She thought that the urchin was caused by the Pernicious-Vestiges of the old society, and she was confident that she could reform him well, while the other thought assumed that it could not be reformed. The only way to deal with the urchin was to expel him . . . It strongly reflected the struggle between the two school-running ideas in the educational cause . . . Peifeng Lin broke through many difficulties, adhered to the party's educational policy, and finally won with more heroic spirit and advanced quality. This hero, though based on some real people, is still a character who combines the characteristics of advanced figures in the Great Leap Forward era.

("Cóng shēnghuó zhēnshí dào yìshù zhēnshí de tànsuǒ—tán hùjù Jīmáo fēishàngtiān de chuàngzuò 从生活真实到艺术真实的探索—谈沪剧《鸡毛飞上天》的创作 [Exploration from the reality of life to the reality of art—on the creation of Shanghai Opera chicken feather flying to the sky]", *People's Daily*, 7A, July 19, 1961, by Chén Rónglán 陈荣兰)

This drama review combines the conviction of "Pernicious-Vestiges of the old society" with the "excellent quality" of educators, and it constructs the binary opposition of suspecting that "Pernicious-Vestiges" is "another thought", thus closing the possible reflection space for the historical concept of the discourse construction of "Pernicious-Vestiges". Thus, power not only stipulates the justice of remembering rather than forgetting but also the way of remembering the past: Only by keeping in line with the illusion of discourse and remembering the "old society" as the root of any social problems can individuals have the possibility of moral recognition and legalization.

From 1966 to 1967, China experienced the catastrophe of the Cultural Revolution. After the farce, the *People's Daily* published an article at that time, which was used to break the situation that people dared not speak out against the Gang of Four which had long existed in society at that time. The article reads:

Up to now, some educators still have the band marks from the hats of the Gang of Four on their heads, and the wounds inflicted by the clubs of the Gang of Four on their bodies. The lingering fear itself, which is a painful experience, is a scar left by the Gang of Four on the spirit of some comrades . . . It's clear: the root of lingering fear lies in the Pernicious-Vestiges. The "Pernicious-Vestiges" is unclear, and the "lingering fear" is hard to disappear. The only way to turn a negative "lingering fear" into a positive and brave attack is to further eliminate the influence of Pernicious-Vestiges in the struggle!

("Yújì hé yúdú 余悸和余毒 [Lingering fear and Pernicious-Vestiges]", originally published in *Xinhua Daily*, reprinted by *People's Daily* on February 18, 1978, 2A, signed by Yù Huáng 毓璜 and Huái Dé 怀德)

This article points out that the obstacle to "eliminating the Pernicious-Vestiges" lies in people's lingering fear of the Cultural Revolution. Therefore, to forget this historical trauma, we must forget all the sufferings of the "past" and continue to "struggle". Referring to the historical process of China after 1978, it can be found that although calling for "courage and enterprising" may bring positive results after the end of the Cultural Revolution, such a proposition may not be established in other historical scenes because taking denying the past one by one as the social power and completely denying the neighboring past as the means of struggle can only make history and its creators enter a new endless cycle of "elimination" and "being eliminated". Therefore, it is better to eliminate the lingering fear than to eliminate the "Pernicious-Vestiges". Only by jumping out of the historical cycle of opposing and opposing again and breaking the fear caused by "the struggle between all people and all people", can we really establish an effective space for historical reflection.

In the transitional period between the end of the Cultural Revolution and the beginning of reform and opening up, the "Pernicious-Vestiges" of the Gang of Four was "forgotten". However, at other times, the "Pernicious-Vestiges of the Cultural Revolution" needs to be remembered and framing this particular memory is often done by setting up typical cases. For example, on September 23, 1983, *People's Daily* published three articles on the front page, reporting and commenting on the destruction of Yangluo Port in Hubei Province. Yangluo Port, located in the middle reaches of the Yangtze River, is an important water transport gateway in Hubei Province, which plays an important role in expanding the water transport capacity of Wuhan-Yangluo section of the Yangtze River and promoting the economic construction in eastern Hubei. However, the officials at the port's location "acted arrogantly, played power, and deliberately made things difficult", which caused the port construction to be severely damaged one after another and failed to be put into operation on schedule ("Yángluózhèn fùzérén chěng wēifēng shuǎ quánshì wéisuǒyùwéi chángjiāng yánluógǎng jiànshè lǚzāo pòhuài nán tóuchǎn huánggāng dìqū hé xīnzhōuxiàn duì yǒuguān rényuán jìnxíng le chǔlǐ 阳逻镇负责人逞威风耍权势为所欲为 长江阳逻港建设屡遭破坏难投产 黄冈地区和新洲县对有关人员进行了处理 [The head of Yangluo Town acted arrogantly and played power to do whatever he wanted, and the construction of Yangluo Port on the Yangtze River was repeatedly damaged, and the relevant personnel were dealt with in Huanggang and Xinzhou County]", *People's Daily*, 1A, September 23, 1983). In this regard, the official made important instructions, saying that this sabotage was "a serious incident of arrogance and power playing, and the result of vicious expansion of selfish departmentalism":

> The circular pointed out that some cadres, because of their ideological Pernicious-Vestiges of Lín Biāo 林彪 and the Gang of Four, impure party spirit and unhealthy style, used the power given by the party and the people as their own capital to dominate the world, and acted with arrogance and power. They were disorganized and undisciplined, and did whatever they wanted. Under the guise of safeguarding the interests of their departments and units, they disregard the overall situation, violate policies, set up obstacles to blackmail, deliberately make things difficult, and harm the interests of the state

and the people. Some even know the law, violate the law, engage in beating, smashing and looting, undermine national construction, and endanger stability and unity. Leaders at all levels must pay serious attention to this.

("Húběi yāoqiú quánshěng cóng yángluógǎng jiànshè zāo pòhuài shìjiàn zhōng xīqǔ jiàoxùn jiānjué shāzhù chěngwēifēng shuǎquánshì wāifēng 湖北要求全省从阳逻港建设遭破坏事件中吸取教训坚决刹住逞威风耍权势歪风 [Hubei requires the whole province to learn a lesson from the destruction of Yangluo Port and resolutely stop the abuse of power and arrogance]", *People's Daily*, September 23, 1983, 1A)

At the same time, *People's Daily* published a commentary on this incident, setting this local incident as a typical example, calling the abuse of power by local officials "the rebel's temper", rising to the height of "national interests" and "people's interests", and taking the "Pernicious-Vestiges" of the Cultural Revolution as its characterization:

It is an unhealthy trend to show arrogance and play power. In a sense, this wind is the sequela of the "Cultural Revolution". After bringing order out of chaos, in some places, they did not get the criticism they deserved, and the broad masses of cadres did not get the education they deserved. Therefore, in recent years, things like Yangluo Town have occurred from time to time, causing great losses to the party's cause and state property. All localities should seize some typical examples, organize cadres to discuss, raise awareness and clarify right and wrong. Let every cadre, especially the leading cadres, know that our power is given by the people and can only be used to serve the people. Whoever comes back to show his arrogance and power to the people will be taken back by the people.

("Zhèzhǒng rén zhǎngquán rénmín bù fàngxīn 这种人掌权人民不放心 [People are not at ease when such person are in power]", *People's Daily*, September 23, 1983, 1A)

In this commentary, the official propaganda organization used the local event of Yangluo Port to circulate a notice of criticism to strengthen the memory of the "Pernicious-Vestiges" of the Cultural Revolution. By setting a typical way to alert officials at all levels, in the period of social transformation and development, it is necessary to "remember" the source and scope of power and not to "forget" the "Pernicious-Vestiges" of the Cultural Revolution, so as to strengthen the legitimacy and stability of the power structure in the transitional period.

Historical and democratic nationalism can usually serve each other's purposes. If any mechanism wants to maintain good condition, it must control the memory of its members. Therefore, the state mechanism needs to make its members forget or change their experiences that are not in line with their image of justice and make them think of or produce events that can defend their self-flattering views (Douglas, 1986, p. 112). In essence, "Pernicious-Vestiges" should be the forgotten object. However, the construction of "Pernicious-Vestiges", as an appeal to forget the past or "break with it", is by no means to achieve real forgetting; on the contrary, this kind of mandatory "forgetting" actually just means the coercion of opposing memory. Through the writing practice of history in the dominant discourse, the "Pernicious-Vestiges" narrative evokes a series of "traditions" that either exist or have been invented (Hobsbawm, 1992), and members of the society counter this kind of memory marked as "wrong" with reverse physical practice, while the dominant discourse gives legitimacy to the social change and establish the power to define ideology, so that the construction of "Pernicious-Vestiges" performs a variety of social organization functions including historical attribution, emotional mobilization, and identity construction.

Injustice/justice

Compared with the "forgetting" of individuals or groups and the "covering" of words by power, the retention and writing of memory certainly reflects some legitimacy, but is the justice of memory itself inevitable? In response, the "Pernicious-Vestiges" discourse was originally a rhetoric used to reflect on the justice of memory, thus opening up a realistic possibility for "unjust memory". Since the late Qing Dynasty, the unprecedented changes experienced by modern China led to the bottom-up enlightenment movement in the whole society (Li, 2001, pp. 239–243), and the New Culture movement also took "reevaluating all values" as its anti-traditional slogan, which brought about a general awareness of "questioning" (Wang, 2015), all of which were closely related to the discourse origin of the "Pernicious-Vestiges" narrative. For example, the article "On the Theory" published in Ta Kung Pao 大公报 (Tianjin) on May 27, 1903 states:

> Since the theory of the three cardinal guides was created by corrupt Confucianism, later generations have attached benefits to it with these principles, driving the world into its cage and spreading its poison, resulting in an increasingly arrogant and firm heart, which leads to a world of arrogance, ignorance, and darkness.

Latter, Liang Qichao 梁启超's "Lessons from the past five years", published in the 2A of *Greater China Magazine* 大中华杂志 on October 20th, 1916, believed that "the evolution of the world civilization was incompatible, and half of them suffered from the Pernicious-Vestiges of the former Qing Dynasty and Yuan Shikai's adherents, and ate their evil retribution, which is an unforgettable lesson for us". The following can better reflect the general view of the intellectual community on how to use the word "Pernicious-Vestiges" at that time:

> Today's people have been inherited from four thousand years of authoritarian ideas, and they can't get rid of the Pernicious-Vestiges for a while, so everyone's minds are still authoritarian, because they have been under the authoritarian system for a long time, and they are only capable of arrogance and flattery,

and have no independence. All of the above are malice accumulated over thousands of years, but its power is so great that we should recognize and remove them one by one. The articles that have always attacked the old ideas and systems are not intended to be abusive, it is this detoxification. The country has become a republic in name, however, the political system is still the old style of the autocratic era, and the general people still can't get rid of the remnants of autocracy and stand out, showing their true life and value.

("Wǒmen zhèngzhì de shēngmìng 我们政治的生命 [The life of our politics]", *New Youth*, 5A, December 15th, 1918, by Táo Lǚgōng 陶履恭)

Although the direction of "Pernicious-Vestiges" has deviated since then, the main body of memory transformation in discourse practice has gradually evolved into a group of "victims". For example, the article Jǐngxíng jiāqiáng fùyùn gōngzuò zhìzhǐ qīnfàn fùnǚ quánlì 井陉加强妇运 工作 制止侵犯妇女权利 [Jingxing strengthening women's movement to stop infringement of women's rights] published in the 2A of *People's Daily* on March 8th, 1949, not only constructs women's pain as "Pernicious-Vestiges handed down from the old society", but also "mobilizes the masses and raising women's awareness" as an effective way to resolve this "Pernicious-Vestiges". However, it is undeniable that the proposal of "Pernicious-Vestiges" is based on the ethical assumption that not all memories have natural justice, but they need to be reconsidered.

More often than not, those who are constructed as "Pernicious-Vestiges" are often regarded as obstacles by power, so the justice of their modified objects is suspended or even inverted. For example, on July 24, 1953, *People's Daily* published an article written by Zēng Zhāolūn 曾昭抡, then vice chairman of the National College Admissions Committee. After listing in detail the specific proportion of 70,000 freshmen in engineering, normal education, health, science, and other fields in that year (see Table 2.1), it made a clear moral choice for senior high school graduates more directly through the discourse construction of "Pernicious-Vestiges":

When the great motherland began to enter a new period of planned construction of the national economy, you graduated from senior middle schools. In this new historical period, the Central Committee of the Communist Party of China put forward a new historical task to the people of the whole country, that is, to fight for the gradual industrialization of the country and the gradual transition to a socialist society . . . In order to accomplish this great and glorious historical task, our country needs to train thousands of technicians who are loyal to the people's revolutionary cause and have modern scientific knowledge and technology . . . Some students want to study medicine in order to "be a doctor, wear white clothes, have a good reputation, earn a lot of money, and seek medical attention for oneself rather than others." This idea of entering a higher school based on one's reputation, treatment and status is the Pernicious-Vestiges of capitalist "fame and fortune viewpoint" and should also be criticized. If students are infected with this bad idea, they are far from the lofty ambition of serving the people.

("Hé jīnnián gāozhōng bìyè de tóngxuémen tán shēngxué wèntí 和今年高中毕业的同学们谈升学问题 [Talking to students who graduated from high school this year about going to a higher school]", *People's Daily*, 3A, July 24, 1953)

Throughout the whole article, only studying medicine is constructed as the "Pernicious-Vestiges" of capitalism, while other disciplines do not have this rhetoric. As can be seen from Table 2.1, in the enrollment plan of 1953, the number of students enrolled in the "health" program corresponding to studying medicine was only a quarter of that of the engineering program with the largest enrollment in that year; so it is not difficult to understand such a language strategy. At this time, the "Pernicious-Vestiges" not only pointed to the origin of most doctors before liberation—the bourgeoisie—but also pointed to the idea of career choice that considered personal reputation, treatment, status, and even interests. The reason why these self-righteous personal interest considerations were criticized as "fame and fortune views" with "Pernicious-Vestiges" was closely related to the planned economic system and collectivist culture's high suppression of personal choice. Choosing a career according to one's personal interests, whether it needs to be inherited or comes from human rational instinct for the time being or whether this logic is just, is constructed by the words of "Pernicious-Vestiges" and has been firmly in the hands of state institutions and propaganda machines since then.

As a populist party that emphasizes the concept of "people", the propaganda strategy of the Chinese Communist Party and its official newspaper *People's Daily* also constructs the right to define justice in the hands of the "majority of the people". For example, a film review published by *People's Daily* in 1955 introduced the plot of the film like this:

Table 2.1 Number and proportion of enrollment subjects of colleges and universities in China in 1953

Higher school subjects	Enrollment	Enrollment ratio
field of engineering	29,600	42.3%
teacher-training	18,300	26.1%
health	7,200	10.3%
science	4,500	6.4%
agriculture and forestry	3,200	4.6%
liberal arts	3,000	4.3%
finance and economy	2,000	2.9%
politics and law (including diplomacy)	1,100	1.6%
sports	800	1.1%
art	300	0.4%
total	70,000	100%

Source: According to news texts.

Yáng Chūnméi 杨春梅, a newly-bred young generation, fought resolutely against the remnants of feudal consciousness of a few backward farmers in the village in order to strive for his own happy life. At last, with the help and support of the party, the government and the masses, they got rid of the influence of feudalism, got a happy life of freedom of marriage, and at the same time gave the masses meaningful education.

("Gèdì wénxué yìshù huódòng 各地文学艺术活动 [Literary and artistic activities in various places]", *People's Daily*, 3A, March 10, 1955)

This text constructs a democratic logic of "majority is justice": "Feudal Pernicious-Vestiges" does exist, but only a few backward farmers are infected; there is no way to know how individuals will fight against them, but what is certain is that this kind of struggle must rely on the help and support of the "party and government", and more importantly, the "homogeneous, virtuous and edifying people"—that is, the "masses" —in order to have a practical impact and realize a happy and free life. Through this view of justice, the political ideas of majoritarianism and even populism have been further consolidated and strengthened.

However, the framing of "justice" and "injustice" still rests on the nature and ideological attributes of the ruling party. In 1994, the Fourth Plenary Session of the 14th Central Committee of the Communist Party of China adopted "the Central Committee of the Communist Party of China's Decision on Several Major Issues of Strengthening Party Building" and focused on the construction of the Communist Party of China. They proposed to uphold and improve democratic centralism, strengthen and improve the construction of the party's grassroots organizations, and train and select leading cadres with both ability and political integrity ("Zhōnggòng shísì jiè sì zhōng quánhuì zài běijīng jǔxíng 中共十四届四中全会在北京举行 [The Fourth Plenary Session of the 14th Central Committee of the Communist Party of China was held in Beijing]", *People's Daily*, 1A, September 29, 1994), which laid a series of the most important foundations for the construction of political parties in the transitional period. After the meeting, the CCP decided to organize party member to learn from party constitution in 3 years. In this regard, Yè Dǔchū 叶笃初, a political scientist and party constitution research scholar, wrote a theoretical article in *People's Daily*, expounding the significance of studying party constitution:

> As a unified code of conduct of the whole party in party constitution, it is based on the general recognition and observance of party member. Abiding by party constitution means asking all party member and cadres to act in accordance with party constitution's overall will and interests in the collective activities and even personal lives of the party, and to make some partial or personal sacrifices when necessary. We can't think that a party member will naturally abide by party constitution and fulfill his obligations as soon as he joins the Party, nor can we think that a party member needs no education and management, and will always deal with all kinds of work and life problems according to party constitution. Communist party must adhere to the

principle of party spirit and remove ideological obstacles from two aspects: on the one hand, the influence of anarchism and bourgeois liberalization; On the other hand, it is the Pernicious-Vestiges of absolutism. We must fundamentally understand that it is our sacred duty to abide by party constitution's provisions on party member's rights and obligations, and truly understand party constitution's spirit and relevant obligations and rights provisions in essence; We must obey party constitution absolutely, truly understand the party's basic line and tasks, understand the overall situation of the party's work, have a good attitude of seeking truth from facts, calmly deal with problems, listen to the opinions of the masses, study new situations and problems, flexibly and creatively put party constitution's requirements into action, and make contributions to the reform and construction.

("Lùn guǎngfàn kāizhǎn dǎngzhāng xuéxí de yìyì 论广泛开展党章学习的意义 [On the significance of extensive study in party constitution]", *People's Daily*, February 23, 1995, 9A)

In this theoretical article, there is a clear definition of "justice" and "injustice" of a party member of the Communist Party of China. Among them, "injustice" refers to the political thought opposite to the socialist political system, including the "Pernicious-Vestiges" of absolutism; while "justice" includes all the restrictions imposed by party constitution on party member's behavior. This practice of shaping the ideology that may shake the ideological line of the ruling party into an "unjust" party by using "Pernicious-Vestiges" discourse is a propaganda discourse strategy to ensure the political attribute and legitimacy of the ruling party in the process of deepening reform.

From many social thoughts and ideologies that have been rhetorical by the word "Pernicious-Vestiges", we can piece together a number of tracks of memory systems that have been judged as "unjust" because of their social harm to the past or present, including the sources of various "Pernicious-Vestiges" and their main manifestations in the society at that time. It is not difficult to find that the memory of "Pernicious-Vestiges" is mainly based on the inheritance of the behavior of the power subject who used to be the "victimizer" in history, and the memory itself can be either the former perpetrator or the former victim. It can be the elite with power at present or the bottom of society under the control of power. Therefore, the memory that should be reflected is actually the self-empowerment imagination that everyone wants to be the owner and perpetrator of power, rather than reflecting and avoiding the recurrence of evil deeds.

When discussing memory ethics, the orientation of ethical relationship and moral relationship is different (Margali, 2002). Among them, the former emphasizes that when people share some specific collective memories, they need to make action choices at the level of shared ethical relations, while the latter elucidates the moral responsibility that people who lack the common memory base also need to share in order to meet the moral requirements of respecting human nature. For example, Takahashi (2008) put forward that the post-war generation of Japanese should bear the related "post-war responsibility" besides "war responsibility" (pp. 13–31). However, in the actual memory practice, *People's Daily*'s "Pernicious-Vestiges" discourse is often constructed in a vague way to deal with the subject who needs to reflect on history and take responsibility and even repeatedly reverses the identity of the victim and the victimizer, resulting in a "replaced memory subject". On the surface, the construction of "Pernicious-Vestiges" is often manifested as the collective memory of the victims carried by the broad "people" who can be united or reformed, as imagined by the mainstream discourse, while the historical and social roots of "Pernicious-Vestiges" are used to construct the "enemy" who is the perpetrator outside this collective. However, in this process, the narrative of "Pernicious-Vestiges" has repeatedly constructed "people" as the victimizer of "people" and "former people" as the "enemy" of "present people". In fact, the ideology of the "enemy" was unconsciously transformed into the historical memory of the physical practice of the "people", and the originally distinct identity boundaries and tensions between the victimizer and the victim shook hands in the memory, and all the aforementioned problems that should be tit-for-tat were resolved one by one in the construction of the evasive narrative of "Pernicious-Vestiges". The "class contradiction" and "contradiction between ourselves and the enemy", which are consistent with the revolutionary paradigm, have been absent many times or given way to "contradictions among the people", resulting in the weakness and ambiguity of revolutionary discourse.

Destruction/establishment

Apart from solving the inherent contradiction between remembering and forgetting and justice and injustice, the rhetoric of "Pernicious-Vestiges" also plays its preset role—"obsolescence" in the process of "establishing a new one". Different from the spontaneity of destroying old things behind the words of "Pernicious-Vestiges" in the late Qing Dynasty, the *People's Daily*'s construction of the words of "Pernicious-Vestiges" is organized and closely depends on realistic politics. They borrowed the "enlightenment tools" of the early 20th century to further serve the establishment and unification of a new country. For example:

> Digging roots from which? According to the specific situation at that time, we can adopt various methods, or start with class relations; or evolved from social history; or evolution from personal history; or from two different regimes ... cadres in progress to make a conclusion in time, so as to gradually improve. Many confused ideas of the masses' thoughts and long-term feudal "Pernicious-Vestiges" can be solved by rooting out the roots.
> ("Sīchóu chéng gōngfèn tuánjié jiān jiǎngjūn, bùduì sùkǔ wāgēn yùndòng jīngyàn jièshào 私仇成公愤团结歼蒋军，部队诉苦挖根运动经验介绍 [Personal enmity becomes public anger, unites and annihilates Chiang's army, and the army complains and digs roots]", *People's Daily*, 2A, August 11, 1947)

Moreover, the discourse construction of "Pernicious-Vestiges" with "old society" as the focus of discussion also shoulders the mission of reshaping personal life and carrying out women's liberation. For example, in January 1949, *People's Daily* published a question-and-answer column. In one article, the Ministry of Justice of the People's Government of North China responded to the question of "Comrade Xiāo Pèi 萧佩 of Shijiazhuang People's Court" as follows:

> Mercenary marriage is not legal at all, which is a Pernicious-Vestiges of the old society. We should try to stop it. Therefore, when dealing with this kind of problem, the "bride price" should not be regarded as the condition of divorce or not; If there are divorce conditions, the mediation method shall be applied, and according to the family economic status of both sides, the decision shall be made to refund completely, refund most, refund less or not refund at all. Women's liberation should not be affected because the woman is poor and can't get money.
> ("Jūnrén wèi bàn líhūn shǒuxù qīzi bùnéng qǔxiāo jūnshǔ dìwèi 军人未办离婚手续 妻子不能取消军属地位 [A soldier's wife can't cancel her military affiliation without divorce]",
> *People's Daily*, 4A, January 25, 1949)

Besides trying to establish a new marriage system through the binary opposition between "old" and "new", this kind of language pattern is more noteworthy. At the same time, in the last sentence of this response, it strengthens the social stratification order imagination that "old society" is equal to the suffering of the poor, and the "new order" should liberate the poor. This sentence also focuses on the core question asked by Comrade Xiāo Pèi: "Women from rich families can divorce, but if the poor can't pay back the money, they can't divorce, and women's liberation is adversely affected". It can be seen that the fundamental purpose of this "old" and "new" is to achieve "women's liberation" by means of justice for the poor, and its key task is still to reconstruct the class consciousness and social motivation serving the future social development goals through the innovation of marriage system and women's status.

However, in the process of breaking old and creating new ones through the words of "Pernicious-Vestiges", the carriers of "Pernicious-Vestiges" sometimes assume contradictory roles, and they are not only the victims of the old system, but also the actual obstructers of the new system. On December 29, 1949, *People's Daily* 5A published the article "Shuíshì shènglì gōngzhài de fùdānzhě 谁是胜利公债的负担者 [Who is the payer of victory bonds]" written by Wáng Xīnyuán 王新元, which said:

> In China, because this is the first time to raise bonds, and the general people's concept of bonds still retains some Pernicious-Vestiges of the reactionary era. Therefore, extensive publicity and explanation should be carried out beforehand, and it should be regarded as an important political task. Basically, we should break the old concept of public debt and build up our understanding of

new public debt. Especially the industrialists and businessmen, should show their progressive spirit and strength!

In anticipation of the difficulties that may be encountered in the issuance of the first bond, this article uses the title of "ordinary people" for those who may oppose the bond. First, it shows that opposing the bond is not a manifestation of a specific class or "ism" but a very universal and understandable concept. Then, it highlights the difference between the new regime and the "reactionaries" through the binary opposition between the old bond and the new bond. However, the income of the "new bond" is bound to be different from the tragic ending of the old bonds, and it will be a hopeful "victory bond", so as to mobilize the businessmen and businessmen to actively participate in the fund-raising and become a force trusted by the new regime, thus effectively promoting the completion of the "political task" of this fund-raising.

However, in other ambiguous "Pernicious-Vestiges" discourses, the emphasis on "obsolescence" does not mean that it is clear how to "establish a new one" but instead expands the "new one" into a more uncertain and dangerous open field. For example, on February 25th, 1951, the 5A of *People's Daily* published an article written by Hóu Jīnjìng 侯金镜, a literary critic, entitled "Yánsù zhǔnquè de chuàngzào zhànshì xíngxiàng 严肃准确地创造战士形象 [Creating fighter images seriously and accurately]". This article criticizes the creation of the opera "Wòjǐn shǒuzhòng qiāng 握紧手中枪 [Holding a gun in your hand]" at the viewing party of literary works in the capital to resist U.S. aggression and aid Korea, and it thinks that it is a blind pursuit of theater effect and drama by portraying ordinary soldiers as "vulgar in taste, low in language and lacking in education", which is rooted in the "Pernicious-Vestiges" of formalism. Then, where does this "formalism Pernicious-Vestiges" come from and how should it be avoided? At first, the author suggested that literary and art workers should abide by the "realistic creative method" and then summed up the disadvantages of this creative style as "not improving the audience's appreciation level from positive aspects, mechanically imitating life, and not analyzing, concentrating and refining it". This self-contradictory logic can't hide the author's true aesthetic standard and his constantly emphasized "class viewpoint" in the article. The author quotes the original text of Chairman Mao's speech at the Yan'an Literature and Art Symposium and tells the true target served by the "Pernicious-Vestiges" discourse: "We should certainly praise the people's army and the people's political party". If readers only understand the real purpose of this article as the pursuit of realistic creative ideas, their works may fall into the category of literary and artistic creation that fails to "abide by Chairman Mao's teaching". Another example is the article published in the 6A on September 30th, 1954, which created the image of a people's juror who has both working strategies and initiative:

Shijingshan District People's Court accepted a divorce in May this year . . . This case was attended by people's jurors Lǐ Guìzhēn 李桂珍 and Chǔ Zhìhóng 褚志宏 . . . But there was a difficult problem: When mentioned divorce, the wife would commit suicide, saying that she would "come in in a sedan chair and go out in a coffin" and resolutely refused to divorce . . . Lǐ Guìzhēn said: "As long as we educate the wife well, break her feudal thoughts and point out her bright future, she won't seek death". She patiently explained to the wife the harm of feudal Pernicious-Vestiges to people, and explained that our country is carrying out socialist construction, and everyone has a bright and beautiful future . . . After in-depth ideological education, the woman finally understood the truth and agreed to divorce.

("Rénmín qúnzhòng cānjiā le guójiā shěnpàn gōngzuò 人民群众参加了国家审判工作 [People participated in the national judicial work]", *People's Daily*, 6A, September 30, 1954)

As a typical text that is "old" but not "new", this report, through the mouth of juror Lǐ Guìzhēn, tells another strategy of this kind of "Pernicious-Vestiges" construction, that is, through the opposition between the ethereal "new" and the concrete "old", constructs a utopia for people to imagine at will. But in fact, as the opposite of feudal "Pernicious-Vestiges", what will happen after divorce? In the "bright and beautiful future" mentioned twice, there is no sufficient and specific explanation. What is certain is that the "newness" of a socialist country makes it easier to fill it as an omnipotent sacred space at will; as long as "the motherland is carrying out socialist construction", the individual's "bright future" will be firmly and steadily guaranteed.

The purpose of "breaking old" and "establishing new" can also play a role at the same time through the construction of "Pernicious-Vestiges" discourse. For example, in the aftermath of criticizing Wǔ Xùn zhuàn 《武训传》 in 1951, Chén Hèqín 陈鹤琴, a famous educator, published "Wǒ duì 'huó jiàoyù' de chūbù jiǎntǎo 我对'活教育'的初步检讨 [My preliminary review of 'Living Education']" in the 3A of *People's Daily* on October 8th.

As the initiator of the theory of "living education", Chén Hèqín called his educational theory of "being a human being, being a native of China, being a native of the world", "nature and the big society are all living textbooks", and "teaching by doing, learning by doing, and striving for progress by doing" as "the Pernicious-Vestiges of reformist educational thought". This expressed his recognition of "present is right and past was wrong", and more importantly, of the class, politics, and its representation of enemies and friends to make it serve the "vigorous resistance to the United States and aid Korea, suppression of counter revolution and land reform", and "resolute struggle against American imperialism, feudalism, and Kuomintang counter revolutionaries". In order to strengthen and solidify the efforts to define "living education" as "Pernicious-Vestiges", *People's Daily* published a letter from readers of Áo Hǎiruì 敖海瑞 in Yichun Middle School, Jiangxi Province, on October 27th, with the title "Wǒ rènshí le 'huó jiàoyù' de běnzhì 我认识了'活教育'的本质 [I know the essence of 'Living Education']". This intellectual who "studied in the Education Department of Beijing Normal University one year before liberation" declared in his article that the theory of "living education" was so arrogant that he was obsessed with "saving the nation through education" and instead "became a propaganda tool for the reactionary rulers to anesthetize the people", so that "the ideological Pernicious-Vestiges of this 'super-political' and 'super-class' reformist educational thought must be cleared away" in order to "implement the policy and task of new-democratic edification in educational work".

"Breaking the old" and "establishing the new" are reflected in the revolutionary discourse in the reform narrative and are most often used to emphasize its subversive nature of constantly breaking the old order that is the possibility of restoring the modern order by denying the past. In dealing with the contradiction between "new" and "old", the autocratic behavior in the old power allocation left over from the fanatical worship of leaders during the Cultural Revolution is regarded as the old feudal thought and classified as the "Pernicious-Vestiges" in political life:

> The key to a leading group's adherence to democratic centralism lies in how well the secretary works. There is no such thing as a "big secretary" or a "small member" in the leading group. The secretary is a "monitor", not a parent, and should consciously put himself in the collective as an equal. In addition, the secretary should have a good democratic style, actively create an atmosphere of discussion and liveliness in the team, and encourage every comrade to dare to speak. At the same time, we should listen to different opinions attentively, be good at concentrating correct opinions, accept good advice and make decisions. The phenomenon of being used to "one-man" and "paternalism", even being self-centered, bossy and suppressing different opinions, is the Pernicious-Vestiges of feudal autocracy in our party's political life. We must get rid of this bad style. As a "monitor", you should have a broad mind and an open-minded temperament. You should not be petty and haggle over personal grievances. Be generous to comrades, and be good at unity. Comrades who disagree with themselves or even oppose themselves should work together. Be able to take responsibility for problems at work. The "monitor" should have a high coordination ability. Like a good band conductor, he can accurately identify the pronunciation of each instrument in complex performances, and give timely guidance to some players to make the band's performance successful.
> ("Biàn gèrén yōushì wéi jítǐ yōushì—Tán jiāqiáng lǐngdǎo bānzǐ mínzhǔjízhōngzhì jiànshè 变个人优势为集体优势—谈加强领导班子民主集中制建设 [Turning individual advantage into collective advantage—on strengthening the construction of democratic centralism of leading groups]", *People's Daily*, 5A, September 30, 1986)

In this way, not only did the Cultural Revolution and the Gang of Four lose the opportunity to be defined as "the second revolution" and "revolutionaries", but the revolutionary characteristics of the institutional revolution almost overwhelmingly shifted to the historical movement law of "breaking the old and establishing a new one".

"Enlightenment" plays the role of a bridge between "old" and "new". Since the May 4th movement, the propaganda and action in the name of "enlightenment" has always been a sharp weapon to break the old and create the new. In 1989, *People's Daily* published an article on the dialogue and interaction between CCTV's "Half-Hour at Noon" column and the audience. According to the article, the enlightenment in the 1980s surpassed the May 4th period in general, and besides Mr. De 德先生and Mr. Sai 赛先生, there was another Mr. Kang 康先生 (commodity): "For Mr. Kang, the intellectuals and the public are equally ignorant, and sometimes those farmers and self-employed people who are not covered by the socialist 'big-pot' system and iron rice bowl have more say than the intellectuals". Based on this, this paper cites a group of interesting games between "the masses" and "enlightenment". One case is the problem of "majority and minority". It tells the story of the accusation of the old feudal "Pernicious-Vestiges" and the desire for "new" knowledge by the child laborers who dropped out of school in a mountainous area in a "corner forgotten by civilization":

Poor and backward mountain villages, shortage of talents, lack of knowledge, deep feudal Pernicious-Vestiges, a lot of boys drop out of school, and only about 10% of girls go to school. Can it not make people sad! I want to shout loudly to the society: please care for us, and don't let the illiterate hat be put on our heads, so that everyone will drink bitter wine!
("Ràng qǐméng zǒuxiàng dàzhòng 让启蒙走向大众
[Let enlightenment reach the public]", *People's Daily*, 5A, May 13, 1989)

In the aforementioned dialogue between the audience and the official media, the feudal "Pernicious-Vestiges" that neglects education and the concept of scientific democracy form a set of bright old and new opposites, highlighting the great harm of this ignorant and backward feudal "Pernicious-Vestiges". If left unchecked, it will drown the kindling ignited by "enlightenment".

To sum up, behind the "old" and "new" lies a specific language style and its standardization process. Once this "regulated past" begins to enter political rituals and routine, it can be regarded as a kind of "domestication" of history (Olick, 1998). Therefore, the significance of the construction of "Pernicious-Vestiges" is not so much to inspire the public to reflect on and resist the old things but rather to encourage people to directly embrace "new things" without thinking or judging—the ideology advocated by official discourse. However, what the official discourse does not reveal is that the old things that are opposed are usually noticeable and detectable, while the new society promised by the "blueprint" is not; it actually exists in people's imagination in different forms according to people's various needs. Nevertheless, the discourse construction of "Pernicious-Vestiges" and the accompanying social discourse practice process—especially the public discourse practice in which people lack the necessary struggle for the established order—will also breed a series of social consequences, including if those ideas and traditions that have not yet been denied can fill the spiritual space after the "old things" are deconstructed, if it will lead to new belief vacuum and nihilism, etc., and become another official "Pernicious-Vestiges".

Anthropoemic/anthropophagic

As to how to deal with the differences of others, Lévi-Strauss (1955/1992) put forward two strategies, namely, "anthropoemic strategy" and "anthropophagic strategy" (anthropoemia from the Greek *emein*, to vomit): The former means cutting off social contacts, imprisonment, exile, or slaughter, thoroughly eliminating the absolute alien, and the latter assimilates the opposite other by accommodating, absorbing, and engulfing, so as to end or eliminate the difference of the other (pp. 386–387). If the goal of the first strategy is to completely eliminate dissidents, then the goal of the second strategy is to eliminate the differences of others. Relatively speaking, anthropoemic strategy is more suitable for eliminating specific individuals or political power with sufficient moral defects, while anthropophagic strategy is more practical for abstract and experimental system construction. It is also in this sense that anthropophagic strategy can be distinguished from anthropoemic strategy.

In the example of adopting anthropophagic strategy to "Pernicious-Vestiges", the practice of accommodating and absorbing differences is mainly used to "establish new". For example, on the eve of the founding of People's Republic of China, *People's Daily* reprinted the speech made by President Mao Zedong at the people's congresses of all walks of life in Beiping on August 13th, 1949. The article discusses the people's congresses as follows:

> Facts have proved that people's congresses from all walks of life are the best organizational form for the people's government to keep in touch with the masses during the period of military control after the liberation of a city. This form of organization is much better than the provisional Senate. It can more widely and effectively connect with the masses, wash away the Pernicious-Vestiges of bureaucracy of the old regime, and make the people's regime look new among the masses. However, the establishment of a temporary Senate can easily remind people of the Senate held in the era of Kuomintang rule, resulting in a bad impression. And because it is an advisory body, and its composition is often not easy to be broadly representative, it is impossible to establish close ties with the masses.
>
> ("Xùnsù zhàokāi gèjiè rénmín dàibiǎo huìyì 迅速召开各界人民代表会议 [Quickly convene People's Congresses from all walks of life]", *People's Daily*, 3A, September 17, 1949)

This speech portrays the provisional Senate under the Kuomintang as "old" and "bureaucratic Pernicious-Vestiges", and its purpose is to oppose the advisory bodies with limited representation, so as to construct the representative meetings of "people's representatives from all walks of life" and "extensive contact with the masses" into a better participation system with sufficient reasons to replace the provisional parliament of the Kuomintang, thus excluding the provisional parliament from potential political space rather than completely destroying the founder of the system in physical or corporeal existence. Coincidentally, in an article signed by

Gāo Wànchūn 高万春 published in *People's Daily* on November 12th of the same year, a similar discourse strategy was used to pave the way for the new concept of middle school education:

> Stuff on dogmatic formulas, be ambitious, and read big books and famous works. This dogmatic learning attitude and method is the Pernicious-Vestiges of exploiters who train intellectuals to serve them. Therefore, in the past, a popular saying "what you learn is not what you use, and what you use is not what you learn" is a portrayal of the old education. Today's education has fundamentally changed. Our education must be good in speaking, better in doing, and capable of speaking and doing. Everything is for and beneficial to the people. We must change the dogmatic learning attitude and method, proceed from reality, to reform our own thoughts and solve practical problems . . . Nowadays, physical and chemical natural history experiments are not enough. Many daily natural phenomena, problems in China's natural science circles or agricultural, medical and scientific fields are too little related to achievements. As a result, students often can't explain a very common natural phenomenon or feel hopeless about China's construction after they have studied natural science . . . In middle schools, Teachers' guiding role is so important for students' study, so we must first ask teachers to change their attitude of selling knowledge in the past, and establish an attitude of being responsible to the people and the new-democratic revolution and construction. This requires teachers to first reform their own learning and further reform their students' learning.
>
> ("Shùlì xīnde jiàoxué tàidù—Jì Sānzhōng shīshēng dàibiǎo zuòtán 树立新的教学态度—记三中师生代表座谈 [Establishing a new teaching attitude—a discussion between teachers and students in No.3 middle school]",
> *People's Daily*, November 12, 5A)

In this reflection on the natural science education in Beijing No.3 Middle School, the "Pernicious-Vestiges" of the old education includes not only the dogmatism and knowledge selling mentioned earlier but also the context of "simply satisfying the thirst for knowledge, hoping to tell a big story in front of others". Therefore, the educational goals of "doing well is better than saying well" and "having confidence in China's construction through natural science study" are shaped into "new democracy".

In 1952, the Communist Party of China launched the ideological reform of teachers and the "三反" 运动 "three antis" movement in colleges and universities, calling for learning advanced science from the Soviet Union. In this movement, as the opposite of Michurin's genetics, "Mendel's and Morgan's thoughts" were constructed as "reactionary" "bourgeois academic thoughts", and the biological science viewpoint that inherited this thought became "the Pernicious-Vestiges of bourgeois idealism" ("Guànchè shēngwù kēxué de mǐqiūlín lù xiàn, sùqīng fǎndòng de wéixīnzhǔyì de yǐngxiǎng—Běijīng nóngyè dàxué mǐqiūlín yíchuánxué jiàoyánzǔ sānniánlái de gōngzuò zǒngjié 贯彻生物科学的米丘林

46 Sheltering and domestication

路线, 肃清反动的唯心主义的影响—北京农业大学米丘林遗传学教研组三年来的工作总结 [Implementing the Michurin line of biological science, eliminating the influence of reactionary idealism—a summary of the work of Michurin's genetics teaching and research group of Beijing Agricultural University in the past three years]", *People's Daily*, December 26, 1952, 3A). Reading through the full text, we can find that, as a value-neutral biological science theory, the fundamental crime of Mendel's and Morgan's thoughts becoming "Pernicious-Vestiges" lies in "hypocrisy and uselessness". On the contrary, Michurin's genetics is "a weapon for human beings to transform nature". Through the competition between pragmatism and scientism, this report has become a typical text that uses anthropophagic strategy and replaces the systematization of scientific theory with "route" science. Two years later, under the guidance of Michurin's Science, universities such as Zhejiang Agricultural College, South China Agricultural College and Beijing Agricultural University successively obtained asexual hybrids, which marked that "the Pernicious-Vestiges of Mendel-Morgan pseudoscience" was swept away in one fell swoop ("Wǒguó yùnyòng mǐqiūlín xuéshuō huòdé de chūbù chéngjiù 我国 运用米丘林学说获得的初步成就 [Preliminary achievements of China's application of Michurin theory]", *People's Daily*, 3A, October 28, 1955). Also, in this report, academician Lysenko, who was criticized by later generations for politicizing scientific issues, appeared as a firm supporter of Michurin's theory. It is not difficult to understand that in the attitude of the Chinese Communist Party toward science and technology, it has always been technological pragmatism that has swallowed up the original appearance of science and has long held the upper hand.

It is worth considering, if the anthropophagic strategy is applied to the field of thought, especially culture, sometimes it is basically difficult to replace the old things because the latter has been deeply rooted in the soil of social culture. For example, in April 1958, *People's Daily* reported the "Shíwǔwàn rén sān gē yùndòng 十五万人三歌运动 [Three-Song movement of 150,000 people]" in Kunming. Its purpose is to replace the long popular folk song tradition of courtship between men and women in Yunnan with the song "healthy and enthusiastic lyrics and tune" to "sing out the heroism of people of all ethnic groups in the Great Leap Forward". These folk songs are regarded as "yellow songs" that run counter to the spirit of the "Great Leap Forward" movement, are decadent in enjoyment, and are not conducive to production and construction ("Gǔwǔ qúnzhòng gémìng gànjìn, sùqīng huángsè gēqǔ yúdú 鼓舞群众革命干劲 肃清黄色歌曲余毒 [Inspire the masses to make revolutionary efforts to eliminate the Pernicious-Vestiges of yellow songs]", *People's Daily*, 2A, April 13, 1958). However, the problem is that even if the "new songs" are successfully implemented, it will not hinder the continued singing of "yellow songs", and it will be difficult to "eliminate" the "Pernicious-Vestiges", because these folk songs reflect the eternal steps and internal needs that people must take to get into marriage and family life.

Another typical application of anthropophagic strategy is concentrated in the "reform and opening up" period of Chinese society after 1978. The proposal of socialist market economic system is essentially a typical anthropophagic strategy, that is, it does not completely deny other forms of economic system outside the socialist system but absorbs and accommodates the parts of the "alien" system that can be used for reference and turns them into own use. The editorial article on the front page of *People's Daily* on July 8, 1981 explained the commercial circulation and services in the economic development as follows:

> In old China, agriculture was the foundation, and the commodity economy was very underdeveloped, which formed the traditional concept of attaching importance to agriculture and neglecting commerce. After liberation, we paid attention to the development of industry, but linked the commodity economy with capitalism, forming the idea of heavy industry over commerce. It should be said that despising and even discriminating against circulation has a far-reaching historical origin in China . . . In 1958, we dreamed of transforming China into a pure and pure country owned by the whole people in one morning or evening. Chén Bódá 陈伯达 and others even advocated banning commodities and adopting a communist supply system. Although this reactionary viewpoint was criticized by Comrade Mao Zedong, the Pernicious-Vestiges of neglecting commodity production and circulation has not been eliminated. As a result of the large-scale dismantling of collective ownership of commercial service outlets in the circulation field, and the large-scale cutting down of individual traders, a state-owned commercial service industry has become an exclusive business, which makes the circulation channels narrower and narrower, with fewer outlets, and brings great difficulties to people's lives. After suffering enough, people began to realize that the national economy and people's livelihood would suffer great misfortune if they didn't recognize the important role of socialist circulation.
>
> ("Zhèngquè rènshí liútōng de zuòyòng, dàlì xīngbàn shāngyè fúwùyè 正确认识流通的作用 大力兴办商业服务业 [Correctly understanding the role of circulation and vigorously establishing commercial service industry]", *People's Daily*, July 8, 1981, 1A)

The editorial article is a typical case of adopting anthropophagic strategy. First of all, the editorial attributed the current economic development situation of belittling or discriminating against commercial circulation to the "Pernicious-Vestiges" of the traditional concept of attaching importance to agriculture and neglecting commerce in old China. Then the article adopts the anthropophagic strategy to separate the commodity economy from capitalism, so as to absorb and integrate this economic model, become an integral part of China's socialist system, and transform it into "socialist circulation". Then the article implicitly admits that the Great Leap Forward launched by the Chinese Communist Party in 1958 attempted to build a purely socialist country owned by the whole people at the early stage of national construction, which was an rash and unrealistic approach in terms of economic development. Subsequently, the article points out the importance of socialist commercial circulation and the harmfulness of narrowing circulation channels and services. Through the discussion of advancing layer by layer, the official propaganda skillfully blends the market economy with the socialist system, emphasizing its importance to the country's development, while on the key opposition issues, it still adheres to the most basic principle, that is, the opposition between the socialist system and the capitalist system.

In the economic transformation period of reform and opening up, such discourse strategies are common. The following is the speech made by Wàn Lǐ 万里, vice premier of the State Council, at the National Conference on Economic and Technical Cooperation and Counterpart Support in 1984. In this speech, "Left" thought, "feudal thought", and "small peasant economy thought" were all classified as "Pernicious-Vestiges" on the road of economic development, while the development mode of international economic and technical cooperation became the mode with the ability to "swallowed up":

> For a long time, due to our lack of advanced economic management experience, the influence of "Left", feudal Pernicious-Vestiges and small-scale peasant economic thought, the economic system has been compartmentalized and blocked. We don't know enough about the importance of economic and technological cooperation, and we realize it too late, so its development is slow. International economic and technical cooperation is needed, and of course, this kind of cooperation is also needed among various regions and departments in China . . . In any case, this alliance must be voluntary, otherwise nothing can be done. In short, we should see that this is a big trend, and whoever closes the door will suffer. Economic and technological exchanges between countries, mutual assistance and mutual benefit are beneficial to all countries.
>
> ("Jīngjì jìshù xiézuò yě shìgè dàde gǎigé 经济技术协作也是个大的改革 [Economic and technical cooperation is also a big reform]", *People's Daily*, 2A, October 6, 1984)

The speech also revealed an important message, that is, in the process of economic development, the state functional departments only need to do a good job of bridging the gap between different regions. "Do not force, do not do everything, be a matchmaker, not a mother-in-law." This means that the concession of state power to market economy has also laid the foundation of China's regional economic development model.

Unlike anthropophagic strategy, which serves the historical reconstruction of the new system, anthropoemic strategy is mainly combined with the social goal of destroy the "old". For example, since the outbreak of the War to Resist U.S. Aggression and Aid Korea in October 1950, *People's Daily* has carried out a series of discourse practices of constructing "American imperialism" as a "Pernicious-Vestiges" in order to make people completely break with American culture. From the article titled "Xuéxí sūlián diànyǐng de dòuzhēngxìng, sǎoqīng měiguó yǐngpiàn de yídú 学习苏联电影的斗争性 扫清美国影片的遗毒 [Learn from the struggle of Soviet films and eliminate the Pernicious-Vestiges of American films]" published in the 1A of *People's Daily* on March 4, 1951, we can see that the key way to "clean up the Pernicious-Vestiges of American imperialist films to China people" lies in "learning from the fighting spirit of Soviet films" because Soviet film art has been with bourgeois art for 30 years. Therefore, under certain circumstances, after the initial implementation of anthropoemic strategy, it can also serve the subsequent anthropophagic purpose.

There are also some texts that advocate prohibition through "Pernicious-Vestiges" discourse, but instead of giving a way out after prohibition, they emphasize the importance of ending or destroying the other, including the class and thought that is regarded as the other. For example, corruption, as a "Pernicious-Vestiges" of the old society, directly harms the interests of the people's country and will never be allowed to continue ("Quánguó tiělù cáiliào làngfèi xiànxiàng yánzhòng, cái liào bùmén hé shēngchǎn bùmén yīng mìqiè jiéhé jiāqiáng zhěngtǐ guānniàn 全国铁路材料浪费现象严重 材料部门和生产部门应密切结合加强整体观念 [There is a serious waste of materials in national railways. Material departments and production departments should combine closely to strengthen the overall concept]", *People's Daily*, 2A, August 13, 1951). Another example is the construction of "bureaucracy" and "the Pernicious-Vestiges left by the old decaying Yá Mén 衙门 style" (Fǎnduì wéndú zhǔyì 反对文牍主义 [Anti-officialism], *People's Daily*, November 30, 1951, 1A). As the latter said in the article, the anthropoemic strategy of this kind of discourse is embodied in its function, which shows that "we must thoroughly eliminate all old and decadent work styles". A similar situation also occurred in the process of "anti-corruption, anti-waste, anti-bureaucracy" in 1952. The author cited the "common program" and skillfully transferred the objects that might be eliminated from the class itself to the class's thoughts:

> Corruption has been prevalent for too long and too common in the past history. I think that in order to thoroughly eliminate the Pernicious-Vestiges of the old society, we must carry out ideological transformation, especially the ideological transformation of the bourgeoisie . . . To transform bourgeois ideology is not to abolish the bourgeoisie, nor to immediately implement socialism. The preface of the common program states that the bourgeoisie is one of the four classes of the people's democratic united front. Because it is the same people's democratic united front, ideas must be worthy. If it is still the old democratic ideology, it will not conform to the common program. All ideas that do not conform to the common program cannot be allowed to exist.
> ("Zīchǎnjiējí sīxiǎng bìxū gǎizào 资产阶级思想必须改造 [Bourgeois thought must be reformed]", *People's Daily*, 3A, January 29, 1952, by Yú Huánchéng 俞寰澄)

Through the construction of the "Pernicious-Vestiges" of the "old society", the author shows his position as a bourgeois, that is, he approves of banning certain ideas as a solution to eliminate the "Pernicious-Vestiges": if the transformation of ideas can prevent the class and even the flesh from being wiped out, then the statement in words and the submission of ideas will be acceptable compromise solutions.

Therefore, in the official propaganda discourse, the anthropoemic strategy is more manifested on the issues of absolute position and absolute difference, including the indisputable aspects of absolute power such as national sovereignty, social system, and fundamental values. The most typical cases are reflected in issues involving national sovereignty and socialist system. The following article is a commentary published by *People's Daily* on the Hong Kong issue, which sharply criticized the adversarial role played by the United States in the Hong Kong issue, while "American democracy" and "American ideological trend" interfering in China's internal affairs have become "ideological Pernicious-Vestiges" that needs to be completely banned and eliminated:

> The reaction of some American politicians shows that they are increasingly frustrated and even desperate. They are unwilling to see that those anti-China-Hong Kong rebels who have been carefully supported for many years have no chance to be used by them. They are unwilling to see that Hong Kong's national security law shows more and more strong vitality in the process of implementation, and they are unwilling to see that the anti-China-Hong Kong rebels' space for insurrection is gradually zeroed out. Over and over again, they interfered with the rule of law in Hong Kong and grossly interfered in China's internal affairs with the rhetoric of reversing black and white. Today, through these sinister performances, the world can see more chaos and tragedy that happened at Kabul International Airport in Afghanistan not long ago. In that place that was "illuminated" by the American democratic lighthouse, the Afghan people deeply learned what "American arrogance", "American trampling" and "American abandonment" are. It is the general consensus of Hong Kong society to safeguard sovereignty and dignity, improve the rule of law and ensure order. In the comparison between the past and the present, and the international comparison, Hong Kong people have a deeper understanding of this. The Hong Kong Special Administrative Region government and the police will continue to conduct in-depth investigations into the suspected illegal acts of the "Hong Kong Alliance in Support of Patriotic Democratic Movements of China" and investigate the legal responsibility of its ringleaders according to law, which will help eliminate the ideological Pernicious-Vestiges of all kinds of fallacies and defend the authority of Hong Kong's national security law and the dignity of the rule of law.
>
> ("Měi yīng zhèngkè bìxū shōuqǐ gānyù xiānggǎng shìwù de hēshǒu 美英政客必须收起干预香港事务的黑手 [American and British politicians must put away their black hands in interfering in Hong Kong affairs]", *People's Daily*, 17A, September 10, 2021)

In a word, whether it is exclusion or absorption, anthropoemic and anthropophagic strategies have the same purpose: To eliminate the existence of the other, which is a hidden "domestication" process behind memory. True memory can make people feel nervous, but by reducing memory into content, establishing a phenomenal counterpart for the source of "Pernicious-Vestiges", and then explaining it, the discourse practice of "Pernicious-Vestiges" completes the "taming" of memory, making it "obedient and controllable" (Songtag, 1966, pp. 6–10). The domestication process of memory usually contains a specific purpose, and the official discourse hopes to unify people's understanding of the past in order to achieve a specific social function, reflecting the primary goal and dominant logic of the discourse construction of "Pernicious-Vestiges": Serving the present, building the enemy and identity, and laying a legitimate foundation for the upcoming war, and regime establishment.

Before the formal discussion of metaphorical forms in the discourse construction of "Pernicious-Vestiges" in Chapter 3, we first observed the importance of metonymy in this chapter, that is, people's understanding of a large number of meanings came into being in the form of "in terms of"—"realizing that A is B" (Burke, 1989, p. 5). In the process of continuous metonymy, people's daily life world gets its appearance and form. The mode of consciousness helps people organize their daily life experience and makes the strange and chaotic world understandable, especially the mutual metonymy between part and whole and the mutual metonymy between cause and result, which is very common in the rhetoric of "Pernicious-Vestiges". At the same time, the discourse construction of "Pernicious-Vestiges" can also be regarded as an interpretation, because at the beginning of its generation, the discourse of "Pernicious-Vestiges" has reserved a great discourse space for the interpretation of itself and a series of related phenomena in different social situations. That is to say, the narrative of "Pernicious-Vestiges" can not only construct a specific ideology, individual, or group as the hostile object of the mainstream society through metaphorical rhetoric, but it can also explain the social phenomenon that needs to be opposed as the social consequence that the aforementioned "Pernicious-Vestiges" has not been eradicated, that is, "historical reasoning". As a "conscious psychological behavior aimed at clarifying a certain rule", the interpretation of "Pernicious-Vestiges" will redescribe social phenomena and find new equivalents for them (for example, "A is actually/means B"), thus establishing understanding and meaning.

Songtag (1966, p. 8) holds that the interpretation system can be used to express respect or aggressively construct hostility or contempt, and most contemporary interpretation behaviors come from the latter. Therefore, interpretation needs to be re-embedded into historical situations for understanding. According to the conclusion of social psychology research, people often need to explain the "negative past" most because major public events accompanied by emotional responses such as loss or shock can not only make individuals produce more profound and vivid memories (Liu et al., 2009) but also make people have a deeper and more urgent understanding of their generation (Klein, 2013; Van Prooijen & Douglas, 2017). Whether from the cultural level or the historical level, the occurrence of these events needs to be attributed historically, even if it is "counterfactual reasoning". Although this attribution has been disputed and opposed by historians (Fischer, 1970), it still has universal significance for understanding historical events (Bruckmüller et al., 2017; Tetlock & Lebow, 2001), and different historical representations and interpretations also reflect different rational bases of public discourse (Knights, 2005).

As far as the attribution of historical events is concerned, the traditional attribution paradigm holds that when historical events are unexpected, accompanied by trauma, or closely related to other events, discourse will be induced to explain historical attribution, especially some self-relevant attribution based on individual behaviors in daily life (Weiner, 1985). Under the paradigm of normative theory, when an event is characterized by conflict with the background of the times, public discourse and historical narration will resort to changes of differences and norms, including trends, associations, and contingencies. Among them, norms mean that people will gradually establish their spiritual principles that can explain specific events in negative events and then establish explanations by comparing the differences according to the normative expectations generated by other similar events (Kahneman & Miller, 1986). However, normative theory or counterfactual attribution theory hold that when an event does not conform to the spiritual norms of the times, counterfactual interpretation, reconstruction of the spirit of the times, and alternative event interpretation will be produced (Roese, 1997), and they are constructed as "abnormal", man-made, controllable, and a link in the historical causal chain. Usually alternative explanations are more related to later events, and people rarely doubt the historical attribution of early events (Teigen, 2004). In a fractured historical period, discourse often focuses on the beginning of a historical event rather than the end of a event, constructs the end of an event as the beginning of another event (Teigen et al., 2017; Zerubavel, 2010), or re-standardizes the attribution of previous historical events according to the current spirit of the times (Klein et al., 2017).

However, historians point out that understanding historical attribution can't only rely on individual cognitive process. More importantly, we need to examine the dialogic background in which historical explanations are generated, including the interpersonal relationship and discourse rules, as a "common principle" of self-certifiable knowledge. For new events that are frequently discussed but not yet defined, common ground will be sought to establish a background social consensus and even a new social norm foundation (Hilton, 1990). On this basis, the discourse research paradigm holds that historical attribution is not only to fulfill the explanatory purpose of individuals or groups, but more importantly, it can become a social action with a clear direction. It is inextricably linked with social dynamics and changes in social relations, and it will have a close interaction with social situations and social consequences (Bruckmüller et al., 2017). The explanation of the event will serve a specific purpose in a special situation and will be appealed to its emotional, personal, or group interests, including competing for and defining ownership, blaming, shirking responsibility, apologizing, etc (Edwards & Potter, 1993). This phenomenon will be reflected in the historical period when there is a great conflict of interests among social groups. During this period, historical attribution is not only reflective but also "performative" (Woolf, 2011). Its purpose is for politicians and historians to apply historical attribution to the present representation of the past and create a suitable political or policy agenda on this basis.

The so-called "consensus" can also be regarded as the result of the dynamic game of political forces of all parties.

What's more, people's conceptual system is metaphorical in nature, and it is necessary to use metaphor to understand and classify the experience of social life. Accordingly, human explanations of events and individuals are often metaphorical. Therefore, the reference system of human language is composed of attribution illusion (Robins & Mayer, 2000). Metaphor also plays an important role in historical attribution, and its fundamental goal is to serve the strategy of recontextualization of discourse illusion. Recontextualization is a discourse practice that puts the old experience in a new context and redefines language expression, concepts and propositions, "facts", arguments, values and ideologies, knowledge and theoretical structures, ways of looking at and treating things, and ways of behavior, thinking, and speech (Linell, 1998). It plays the role of co-constructor in the process of meaning generation that helps to create different meanings and experiences the possible world (Fairclough, 2003) and reveals the speaker's intention and ideology.

Recontextualization reorganizes texts according to different contexts, resulting in intertextuality and interdisciplinarity between texts, which leads to specific mixing of genre, style interdiscursive (Fairclough, 2003; Bhatia, 2004, 2010), which reconstructs the relationship between the accentuation and the text by emphasizing or elimination specific semantics, thus realizing the transformation of meaning and perspective (Linell, 1998). Metaphorical recontextualization uses language to activate unconscious emotional associations, manipulates language and other symbolic patterns to create subtle persuasive premises, and creates presence or absence, sympathy, or hostility (Spivey, 1997, pp. 126–127), which can influence people's beliefs, attitudes, and values as well as the measure of good and evil (Charteris-Black, 2005, p. 13). Next, in Chapter 3 of this book, we will examine the specific reflection of the metaphorical system created by the discourse practice of *People's Daily* through the word "Pernicious-Vestiges" in text.

References

Berger, P. L., & Luckmann, T. (1966). *The Social Construction of Reality*. London: Penguin Books.
Bhatia, A. (2015). *Discursive Illusions in Public Discourse: Theory and Practice*. New York: Routledge.
Bhatia, V. K. (2004). *Worlds of Written Discourse: A Genre-Based View*. London: Continuum International.
Bhatia, V. K. (2010). Interdiscursivity in professional communication. *Discourse & Communication, 21*(1), 32–50. https://doi.org/10.1177/1750481309351208.
Brockmeier, J. (2002). Remembering and forgetting: Narrative as cultural memory. *Culture & Psychology, 8*(1), 15–43. https://doi.org/10.1177/1354067X0281002.
Bruckmüller, S., Hegarty, P., Teigen, K. H., Böhm, G., & Luminet, O. (2017). When do past events require explanation? Insights from social psychology. *Memory Studies, 10*(3), 261–273. https://doi.org/10.1177/1750698017701607.
Burke, K. (1989). *On Symbols and Society*. Chicago: University of Chicago Press.

Charteris-Black, J. (2005). *Politicians and Rhetoric: The Persuasive Power of Metaphor*. New York: Palgrave Macmillan.
Cialdini, R. B. (1997). Interpersonal influence. In S. Shavitt & T. C. Brock (Eds.), *Persuasion: Psychological Insights and Perspectives* (pp. 195–217). Boston: Allyn & Bacon.
Douglas, M. (1986). *How Institutions Think*. New York: Syracuse University Press.
Edwards, D., & Potter, J. (1993). Language and causation: A discursive action model of description and attribution. *Psychological Review*, *100*(1), 23–41. https://doi.org/10.1037/0033-295X.100.1.23.
Fairclough, N. (1995). *Critical Discourse Analysis*. Singapore: Longman.
Fairclough, N. (2003). *Analyzing Discourse: Textual Analysis for Social Research*. London: Routledge.
Fischer, D. H. (1970). *Historian's Fallacies: Toward a Logic of Historical Thought*. New York: Harper & Row Publishers.
Hilton, D. J. (1990). Conversational processes and causal explanation. *Psychological Bulletin*, *107*(1), 65–81. https://doi.org/10.1037/0033-2909.107.1.65.
Hobsbawm, E. (1992). Mass-producing traditions: Europe 1870–1914. In E. Hobsbawm & T. Ranger (Eds.), *The Invention of Tradition* (pp. 263–307). Cambridge: Cambridge University Press.
Kahneman, D., & Miller, D. T. (1986). Norm theory: Comparing reality to its alternatives. *Psychological Review*, *93*(2), 136–153. https://doi.org/10.1037/0033-295X.93.2.136.
Klein, O. (2013). The lay historian: How ordinary people think about history. In R. Cabecinhas & L. Abadia (Eds.), *Narratives and Social Memory: Theoretical and Methodological Approaches* (pp. 25–45). Braga: University of Minho.
Klein, O., Hegarty, P., & Fischhoff, B. (2017). Hindsight 40 years on: An interview with Baruch Fischhoff. *Memory Studies*, *10*(3), 249–260. https://doi.org/10.1177/1750698017701.
Knights, M. (2005). *Representation and Misrepresentation in Later Stuart Britain: Partisanship and Political Culture*. Oxford: Oxford University Press.
Leudar, I., & Nekvapil, J. (2011). Practical historians and adversaries: 9/11 revisited. *Discourse & Society*, *22*(1), 66–85. www.jstor.org/stable/42889721.
Lévi-Strauss, Claude. (1955/1992). *Tristes Tropiques*. New York: Penguin.
Li, H 李孝悌. (2001). *Qīngmò de Xiàcéng Shèhuì Qǐméng Yùndòng: 1901–1911* 清末的下层社会启蒙运动: *1901–1911*. Shijiazhuang: Hebei Education Press.
Linell, P. (1998). Discourse across boundaries: On recontextualizations and the blending of voices in professional discourse. *Text*, *18*(2), 143–157. https://doi.org/10.1515/text.1.1998.18.2.143.
Liu, J. H., Paez, D., Slawuta, P., Cabecinhas, R., Techio, E., Kokdemir, D., Sen, R., Vincze, O., Muluk, H., Wang, F., & Zlobina, A. (2009). Representing world history in the 21st century: The impact of 9/11, the Iraq war, and the nation-state on dynamics of collective remembering. *Journal of Cross-Cultural Psychology*, *40*(4), 667–692. https://doi.org/10.1177/0022022109335557.
Margalit, A. (2002). *The Ethics of Memory*. Cambridge, MA: Harvard University Press.
Olick, J. K., & Robbins, J. (1998). Social memory studies: From "collective memory" to the historical sociology of mnemonic practices. *Annual Review of Sociology*, *24*(1), 105–140. https://doi.org/10.1146/annurev.soc.24.1.105.
Plate, L., & Smelik, A. (2009). Technologies of memory in the arts: An introduction. In L. Plate & A. Smelik (Eds.), *Technologies of Memory in the Arts* (pp. 1–17). Basingstoke: Palgrave.
Robins, S., & Mayer, R. E. (2000). The metaphor framing effect: Metaphorical reasoning about text-based dilemmas. *Discourse Processes*, *30*(1), 57–86. https://doi.org/10.1207/S15326950dp3001_03.

Roese, N. J. (1997). Counterfactual thinking. *Psychological Bulletin, 121*(1), 133–148. https://doi.org/10.1037/0033-2909.121.1.133.
Schirato, T., & Yell, S. (2000). *Communication and Culture*. London: Sage.
Songtag, S. (1966). *Against Interpretation and Other Essays*. New York: Farrar, Straus & Giroux.
Spivey, N. N. (1997). *The Constructivist Metaphor: Reading, Writing and the Making of Meaning*. San Diego: Academic Press.
Takahashi, T. (2008). *On Postwar Responsibility* (trans. by X. Man). Beijing: Social Sciences Academic Press.
Teigen, K. H. (2004). When the past becomes history: Effects of temporal order on explanations of trends. *European Journal of Social Psychology, 34*(2), 191–206. https://doi.org/10.1002/ejsp.191.
Teigen, K. H., Böhm, G., Bruckmüller, S., Hegarty, P., & Luminet, O. (2017). Long live the king! Beginnings loom larger than endings of past and recurrent events. *Cognition, 163*, 26–41. https://doi.org/10.1016/j.cognition.2017.02.013.
Terdiman, R. (1993). *Present Pasts: Modernity and the Memory Crisis*. Ithaca: Cornell University Press.
Tetlock, P. E., & Lebow, R. N. (2001). Poking counterfactual holes in covering laws: Cognitive styles and historical reasoning. *American Political Science Review, 95*(4), 829–843. https://doi.org/10.1017/S0003055400400043.
Van Prooijen, J. W., & Douglas, K. M. (2017). Conspiracy theories as part of history: The role of societal crisis situations. *Memory Studies, 10*(3), 323–333. https://doi.org/10.1177/1750698017701615.
Wang, F 王汎森. (2015). "Fánmèn" de běnzhì shì shénme—"Zhǔyì" yǔ zhōngguó jìndài sīrén lǐngyù de zhèngzhìhuà "烦闷"的本质是什么—"主义"与中国近代私人领域的政治化. *Forum of Intellectuals* 知识分子论丛, *1*, 263–304.
Wang, H 王海洲. (2008). *Héfǎxìng de Zhēngduó—Zhèngzhì Jìyì de Duōchóng Kèxiě 合法性的 争夺—政治记忆的多重刻写*. Nanjing: Phoenix Publishing & Media, Inc.
Weiner, B. (1985). "Spontaneous" causal thinking. *Psychological Bulletin, 97*(1), 74–84. https://doi.org/10.1037/0033-2909.97.1.74.
Wodak, R. (2000). Recontextualization and the transformation of meanings: A critical discourse analysis of decision-making in EU meetings about employment policies. In S. Sarangi & M. Coulthard (Eds.), *Discourse and Social Life* (pp. 185–206). Essex: Pearson Education.
Woolf, D. (2011). *A Global History of History*. Cambridge: Cambridge University Press.
Zerubavel, E. (2010). In the beginning: Notes on the social construction of historical discontinuity. *Sociological Inquiry, 63*(4), 457–459. https://doi.org/10.1111/j.1475-682X.1993.tb00324.x.

3 Body and politics

Moral responsibility and authority construction of "Pernicious-Vestiges" metaphors

Most of our daily conceptual systems are metaphorical, and "Pernicious-Vestiges" is no exception. Here, metaphor is defined as a figure of speech (Sontag, 1990, p. 83) of "naming this thing in the name of something else", which is generally accompanied by explanatory structure from the familiar field to other fields, enabling people to establish structural similarity through the experience of a certain kind of thing, so as to understand it (Krippendorff, 1993; Lakoff & Johnson, 1980, pp. 4–5). Because people often lack the necessary intuitive perception and imagination for the abstract ideology and political events that are constructed as "Pernicious-Vestiges", such abstract concepts have similar characteristics, namely "comparability", with other counterparts in the human world. Therefore, the biological metaphor of "Pernicious-Vestiges" is used to have an analogy relationship with it, and its main purpose is to help people understand strange things through their relatively familiar phenomena and social scenes.

Metaphor analysis draws on the key elements and ideas of critical discourse analysis, focusing on the intention of the generation and dissemination of discourse metaphor structure (Bhatia, 2015, p. 2). Critical metaphor analysis from the perspective of constructivism holds that the subjective conceptualization of reality is usually expressed by concrete metaphor. The subjective representation of the world has produced important metaphorical rhetoric (Charteris-Black, 2004). Through metaphorical analysis, it is possible to identify how a specific discourse frame reveals its intention and ideology through the use of language (Charteris-Black, 2005, p. 26). Metaphor is not only a kind of "renaming", but it is also a kind of "reconceptualization" to create a new representation of reality. It is not only the surface decoration of language but also the key phenomenon in the process of human thinking (Cameron, 1999). This book regards metaphor as a social cognitive process, and its function is to create new meanings by juxtaposing references in language, so as to prevent human language from falling into a static state, thus expanding human knowledge into unknown areas (Mac Cormac, 1990, p. 50). This rhetorical device simultaneously introduces a combination of clear and vague contradictions to create discourse illusion, which is also needed to construct the world as a just and objective ideology (Bhatia, 2015, p. 20).

Conceptual metaphor is a common figure of speech. In Lakoff's definition (1993), this is a way to conceptualize an ideological field with another mental domain, so

DOI: 10.4324/9781003409724-3

as to transfer the language from the source domain to the target domain. Metaphor activates unconscious emotional associations, including direct fears, threats, and defenses (Charteris-Black, 2005, p. 13), and generates associations through multimodal connotations of words, symbols, colors, and their combinations, enabling people to explain social, cultural, and political experiences. Metaphor is a useful tool in persuasive discourse, which can negotiate between conscious cognition and unconscious emotion and trigger emotional connotation (Bhatia, 2015, p. 22). The mass media has unequal discourse volume and intellectual power to the audience. Therefore, metaphor concepts are mostly created by speakers with power and authority, and followers can only accept subjective metaphors provided by speakers naturally and institutionally. Theoretical metaphors try to extract ideas and situations from their familiar and orthodox backgrounds, manipulate them in more unconventional and unfamiliar contexts, and encourage the reconceptualization of experience, thus revealing the creativity of the speaker (Goatly, 1997).

Metaphor is not evenly distributed in conversations and texts, but it plays the most important role in providing understanding for little-known phenomena (Zinken, 2003). Especially when dealing with complex problems, it is easy to appear in groups and cluster at specific points in the discourse. It helps discourse producers to carry out "main discourse work" and "out of the ordinary" (Cameron & Stelma, 2004) and provides an understanding of the connection that is not feasible or needs over-imagination to be feasible. One of its functions is to make the complex development of the social and political world acceptable (Bhatia, 2015, p. 19). In particular, new and creative metaphors can effectively grasp the meaning in a chaotic environment and create new realities instead of strengthening existing ones, thus creating a coherent structure and highlighting some things and hiding others, so as to sanction actions, prove the rationality of inferences, and set goals (Lakoff & Johnson, 1980, pp. 139–142). In this chapter, we will discuss several main metaphors constructed by the word "Pernicious-Vestiges" in *People's Daily* and their specific functions in different social scenes.

"Pernicious-Vestiges" and STD

The narrative of "Pernicious-Vestiges" is a typical normative discourse. It takes the official discourse as the memory construction method, anchors the nature of specific historical events as "Pernicious-Vestiges" to define and explain an idea that needs to be opposed, so as to arouse the hatred of "the surviving enemy", take "eliminating Pernicious-Vestiges" as a part of the revolutionary legitimacy and social mobilization, or blame the historical suffering on the abstract "past" and realize the division between the current regime and the old regime. On the level of "transitivity", the rhetoric of "Pernicious-Vestiges" has some commonness; through metaphor and its interpretation, the connection of conceptual meaning is established, and this choice has ideological significance (Fairclough, 2003), which involves the transformation process of synonyms or implied relationships (Harris, 1963).

The difficulty in the formation of a modern political community in China lies in the fact that each social group has its own special tendency or trend. No social

58 Body and politics

structure can integrate the huge professional groups with growing self-awareness into a whole with common interests, and the final arbiter of disputes between groups can only be strength. In other words, the rise of different groups, and even the emergence of new social strata, is bound to be full of conflicts. Stigma is just a result of competition between them; it is necessary to create new stigmas to belittle the opposing party and limit its development opportunities, so as to strengthen the control over this group. Therefore, the opposite interest groups will use media propaganda to label each other as poisonous and dirty "Pernicious-Vestiges" and regard each other as a target, whether it is harmful or harmless. This kind of propaganda method, which stigmatizes opposing groups by "labeling" and "hitting targets", has been extended to the propaganda system of the communist party from this period. With "Pernicious-Vestiges" as the key word, it was searched in the full-text database of the journals of the late Qing Dynasty and the Republic of China in the Shanghai Library. From 1876 to 1949, the frequency of relevant articles is shown in Figure 3.1.

In China, the word "Pernicious-Vestiges" was once used in the field of medicine. According to the records of Wúyī huìjiǎng 吴医汇讲 in 1799, as early as the Tóng Zhì 同治 period, the medical community in China had a relatively systematic discussion on "Pernicious-Vestiges": "Those who infected with Pernicious-Vestiges, leave it behind, that is, the remaining evil remains in the meridians, so that blood and breath does not follow, contrary to the flesh principle, and it is carbuncle and swelling" (Yídú yízì biàn 颐毒颐字辩 by Zhū Yīngjiē 朱应皆, recorded in 清乾隆唐氏《问心草堂》刻本 Inscription of Tang's "Heart Enquiry Thatched Cottage" in Qianlong of the Qing Dynasty). In China at the end of the Qing Dynasty and the beginning of the Republic of China, for a long time, the term "Pernicious-Vestiges" used to refer exclusively to highly contagious sexually

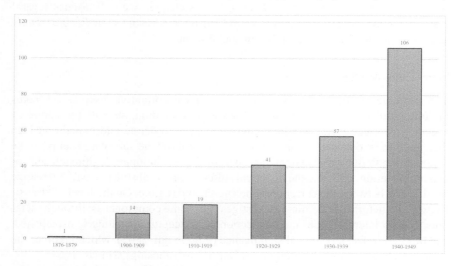

Figure 3.1 Narrative distribution of "Pernicious-Vestiges" discourse before the founding of the People's Republic of China

transmitted diseases (STDs), implying that people infected with "Pernicious-Vestiges" were often notorious, scandalous, lacking in self-restraint ability or personal achievements, and had some moral flaws. In the same year, the following commentary appeared in *Shēn Bào* 申报:

> If you don't behave properly, the obscenity will be very serious, either outside or inside. First, it is easy to be infected with this kind of disease in close contact with it. The cause of sores is Pernicious-Vestiges. If you are seriously ill, you will perish. If you are slightly ill, you will damage your appearance, infect your wife with Pernicious-Vestiges, and cause life-long illness.
> ("Huā yānguǎn kēngrén lùn 花烟馆坑人论
> [How the house of prostitution and opium harm people]",
> by Yǎnshān Yìsǒu 弇山逸叟, *Shēn Bào* 申报, October 5, 1872).

In the historical period from the end of the Qing Dynasty to the founding of the People's Republic of China, the narration of "Pernicious-Vestiges" was mostly attached to "diseases", stigmatizing "groups" and "dissent" in order to construct the opposition between the new and the old. This kind of "Pernicious-Vestiges" discourse topics include "Pernicious-Vestiges" of imperial examination, procuress, superstition, concession, Japan and autocracy, etc. The objects possessed by "Pernicious-Vestiges" range from concrete bad habits that endanger public order and good customs, such as pimping, smoking opium, and gambling, to abstract cultural system and political system, and they cover all levels of society. For example, there are "Pernicious-Vestiges" about the social vices such as opium, gambling, and prostitution in the old society, which are mostly described as "parasitic" viruses in the society. To eradicate these "Pernicious-Vestiges", it is necessary to perform "surgery" on the society to diagnose and treat social chronic diseases:

> It's been more than two months since the victory, and there are still a few bad habits left in Shanghai society. First, campfire boys curled up in the road, still counting upon a piece of tinfoil and a pipe, rubbing matches and hissing; Secondly, there are many hookers at the gate of the Great World, Zhongzheng Road, just like dung maggots in the pit, which are grotesque and force passers-by; Third, when the store is in business hours, you may as well swing mahjong dice in the counter, and make hubbub of gambling, so you can take care of your business customers. At present, although the authorities are vigorous and vigorous in cracking down on opiophagy, gambling and prostitution, Shanghainese have been used to follow this habit for many years, thinking that these things are like daily life, which is not surprising. Even though a ban has been enacted, they temporarily take shelter from the trouble and remain indifferent afterwards. Although half of the reason is the result of the poisoning policy implemented by the enemy and puppet troops in the past eight years, the other half is the Pernicious-Vestiges of the past "concession" era. Now, the word "concession" has been cancelled. If these abnormal bad habits continue to be parasitic, it will be tantamount to apply a remedy worse

than the ailment. How can we still engage in the construction? Therefore, in order to clear the root of the problem, I boldly shouted the slogan of "eliminating the Pernicious-Vestiges of concession".

("Sùqīng "zū jiè" yídú 肃清"租界"遗毒 [Eliminating the Pernicious-Vestiges of the concession]", 神州日报 *Shenzhou Daily*, December 9, 1947, by Qián Jiāngcháo 钱江潮)

During the period of alternation of old and new systems and ideas, the opinion leaders who implemented the new system identified the old ideas and systems in the name of "Pernicious-Vestiges", or the opposite party to their own opinions, as the source of diseases that poisoned the society. Overthrowing this opposing target has become a powerful means for new ideas and new systems to gain legitimacy in order to flourish in society. In 1947, *Peace Daily*, a newspaper of the Kuomintang military system, published the article "Eradicating the Pernicious-Vestiges of unequal treaties: the Pernicious-Vestiges of ideology and legal system should be eradicated", criticizing the "Pernicious-Vestiges" of ideology and legal system and holding that social and military forces should be used to jointly eradicate this "root cause":

> Because the root of ideology has not been removed, the Pernicious-Vestiges of the legal system still exists, which is reflected in the society. Up to now, the bad forces in Shanghai during the concession period are still rampant. We should know that this kind of social evil forces, as well as the pernicious influence of opiophagy, gambling, and prostitution, are all left over from the concession period, and can also be said to be the "Pernicious-Vestiges" of unequal treaties. This evil force can be said to be deeply rooted in Shanghai, and it is necessary to use social forces and cooperate with various political and military measures to achieve results.

("Chǎnchú bùpíngděng tiáoyuē yídú: yìshíxíngtài jí fǎzhì shàng de liúdú jūn yīng chǎnchú 铲除不平等条约遗毒：意识形态及法制上的流毒均应铲除 [Eradicate the Pernicious-Vestiges of unequal treaties: ideological and legal Pernicious-Vestiges should be eradicated]", 和平日报 *Peace Daily*, April 14, 1947)

Another typical "Pernicious-Vestiges" is the "imperial examination system" that has existed for more than 1,000 years in the history of China. This system of selecting officials through examinations has been criticized by new intellectuals and political groups. In one article, the author set the "imperial examination system" as the target of "Pernicious-Vestiges" and knocked down this feudal examination system in order to promote the development of the new system:

> From the official establishment of the Sui and Tang Dynasties to the abolition of the imperial examination system in the late Qing Dynasty, it has existed for more than 1,300 years. On the surface, the function of the imperial

examination system is an institution that cherishes talents and respects knowledge, but it is a wonderful trap to anesthetize, win over and lure intellectuals into the arms of the rulers, and help the ruler control and oppress the people. At that time, intellectuals buried themselves in old books all day long, worked tirelessly, indefatigably, wasted years and energy, and never had any dissimilar ideas. Taming and accepting the "Pernicious-Vestiges" left over from the imperial examination system controlled by the rulers plays an important role in our intellectuals' consciousness. It often drags us, forbids us, or leads us into a wrong path in the course of our progress. Today, under the surging tide of new democracy, we want to move on and make further progress. We must summon up courage to thoroughly eliminate these "Pernicious-Vestiges" before we can move forward smoothly.

("Qīngchú kējǔ zhìdù de yídú 清除科举制度的遗毒 [Eliminating the Pernicious-Vestiges of the imperial examination system]", 时论周刊 *Times Weekly*, No.4, 1949, by Níng Yùxiáng 宁裕详)

In a word, the narrative of "Pernicious-Vestiges" is often expressed as a metaphor of illness (Sontag, 1990), and as a kind of "judgment to the loser", the rhetoric of "Pernicious-Vestiges" is mostly derogatory and vehement in terms of emotional color. Another tradition that can't be ignored in incorporating "Pernicious-Vestiges" into disease metaphors comes from Bolshevik debates. According to Deutscher (1963/1998), on March 21, 1938, Trotsky wrote in a letter to Philip Rahv, a Jewish intellectual in New York and one of the founders of *Party Review*:

Trotsky talked about "Stalinist syphilis" or "a cancer that should be burned off from the workers' movement with a red-hot soldering iron", and believed that he was giving life to an organization (p. 458). Some means are necessary to fight against wrong theories, while the other is necessary to fight against cholera epidemic. Stalin undoubtedly belongs to the category of cholera, not the category of erroneous theories. The struggle should be intense, fierce, and ruthless. The element of "fanaticism" is beneficial to health.

(p. 464)

Not only that, the spiritual implication of "Pernicious-Vestiges" is also linked with rape in a subtle way. In June 1950, the Korean War broke out. On October 25th of the same year, the Chinese People's Volunteer Army went to North Korea to fight, which opened the prelude to the Korean War. On July 23rd, *People's Daily* published a group of poems by the poet Biàn Zhīlín 卞之琳 on 5A entitled "Salute to the heroic North Korean People's Army!", including a poem called "Salute to the North Korean People", which wrote:

In order to clean up the Pernicious-Vestiges of fascism/The 38th parallel, I had to gird up at your waist/Upper body was clean, with unprecedented vitality and uniformity/Lower body was wrapped in fascist aprons

The magic hands not only continue to paralyze you/but also turn on your aprons to cover your eyes/You are very alert to stop them from fooling around/You take advantage of the opportunity to untie your aprons

As soon as the apron is torn, its claws are exposed under it/You are not afraid, you must cut it off and destroy it/People all over the world thank you for your bravery/We are ready in full battle array

This poem is intended to praise the bravery of the North Korean people, but it is compared to a woman wearing an apron who was molested. The reason for the split between North and South Korea is interpreted as a helpless move to "clean up the fascist Pernicious-Vestiges". The reason is to prevent the "fascist Pernicious-Vestiges" from spreading from the south of the "lower body" symbol of the Republic of Korea supported by the United States to the north of the "upper body" symbol. This double metaphor of STD and rape shapes division into a symbol of chastity, and by emphasizing "the upper body is clean", it further strengthens the classification and comparison between the moral purity of socialist camp and the filth of the United States and South Korea.

Following this rhetorical tradition, *People's Daily*'s "Pernicious-Vestiges" narrative uses the metaphor of disease and simultaneously constructs "moral exhortation" and "symbol of corruption" in its discourse (Sontag, 1990, pp. 53–54). In March 1952, in an article published in *People's Daily*, the discourse construction "subject" signed "All women workers in Beijing Jiefang Weaving Factory" made the following expression:

We studied in the women's production reformatory or Huaxing Factory after we closed the brothel. After the liberation, we female workers returned to the Jiefang Weaving Factory last November. We were rescued from the fire pit where we could not live or die, but we still had "Pernicious-Vestiges" and worries in our minds. After the anti-corruption campaign began, we reported 27 corrupt elements, and six sisters reported the tax evasion or corruption of our husbands. No matter who he is, even our husbands, we will resolutely report him as long as he is corrupt. During the anti-corruption campaign, we found that the remnants of the corrupt thoughts of the bourgeoisie, especially the most vicious brothel owners in the bourgeoisie, also eroded us, and we had shortcomings in our work, life, style and feelings. The government loves and trains us, and the anti-corruption campaign has cured our diseases. Without hesitation, we boldly exposed the vicious scars left by our brothel owners. Our slogan is that you can't cure a disease if you don't hurt. It took us half a month to get rid of these scars, and we changed our wrong position of regarding the enemy as kith and kin and not being able to distinguish between ourselves and the enemy. We uprooted the rotten thought of getting something for nothing and corruption. Previously, the brothel owners taught us how to steal and cheat. Later, we became a habit, and we couldn't live without stealing. Under their leadership, we have never said a word of truth, and we are always trying to cheat money and dress up. Under the abuse of these of tigers and wolves, we are not like humans! If we had not been liberated, we wouldn't know what it would be like now. We like a bottle pouring out smelly water and pouring it into clear water. After the peace of mind, our production would have improved with the improvement of consciousness.

> ("Běijīng jiěfàng zhībù gōngchǎng nǚgōng xiěxìn gěi Péng Zhēn shìzhǎng 北京解放织布工厂女工写信给彭真市长 [The women workers in Beijing Jiefang Weaving Factory wrote to Mayor Peng Zhen]", *People's Daily*, March 19, 1952, 6A)

Such words are spoken in the first person through the mouth of sex workers before liberation, thus trying to establish some connection between STD and occupation to strengthen the persuasiveness of the text, then during the War to Resist U.S. Aggression and Aid Korea, in order to illustrate that the American "PUMC" invested in Peking Union Medical College and left many "Pernicious-Vestiges of American imperialism". In contrast, another article in *People's Daily*, quoted a professional medical term mentioned by an ordinary worker, wrote this:

> Lián Qīngkuí 连清奎, the guide at the exhibition, was a laundry worker in the hospital. He was affected and accused those devil human clothing of crimes on the spot. Peiers, an "expert of dermatology", once tested trypanosomiasis on a large number of black people in Africa. After arriving at PUMC, he inoculated the patients with live Treponema pallidum for "immune test". A photo of a patient with chancre is the evidence of this experiment ...
> In the movement to resist U.S. aggression and aid Korea, many teachers, students and employees of PUMC took part in volunteer surgical medical teams and blood transfusion teams. In the movement against the three evils, especially in the current stage of ideological construction, they also cleaned up the "Pernicious-Vestiges" left by American imperialism. On May 16 this year, at the prosecution meeting of the hospital, they saw the bloody evidence of the crime, and the audience burst into tears. Wiping their tears, they made angry complaints and painful self-examination, determined to use the practical work of serving the motherland and the people and the practical actions of resisting U.S. aggression and aiding Korea to wash away the shame given to them by U.S. imperialism. All the conspiracies and deadly tricks carried out by American imperialism in PUMC for decades went bankrupt. With infinite happiness, we celebrate the new life of PUMC, and with infinite hope, we pray that PUMC will continue to advance on a new road!

> ("Chùmùjīngxīn de zuìzhèng—jì zhōngguó xiéhé yīxuéyuàn kòngsù měi dìguózhǔyì zuìxíng zhǎnlǎnhuì 怵目惊心的罪证—记中国协和医学院控诉美帝国主义罪行展览会 [Shocking evidence-record of exhibition of Chinese Union Medical College accusing American imperialist crimes]", *People's Daily*, June 10, 1952, 3A)

This article tells the "fact" that the experts inoculated Treponema pallidum to the patients by using the mouth of the laundry workers in hospitals. This unclean metaphor of sexually transmitted diseases is told through the story of in vivo experiments, which further deepens the moral stain of "American imperialism" that funded China to set up hospitals.

The mapping relationship between STD and "Pernicious-Vestiges" extended to Tibet after liberation. In a report in 1959, "the wounds and 'Pernicious-Vestiges' left by the former local government of Tibet" were very rich, and the measures to "clean up the 'Pernicious-Vestiges'" also included effective treatment of sexually transmitted diseases:

> Into the Yūgá Gǎng 迂噶岗, there are disasters everywhere. There are only sixty-five households here, but there are twelve casinos, four pubs, a big smokehouse and three prostitutes. Thirty-eight households are forced by life to become hooligans, thieves and beggars. Nobles, Tibetan troops, gamblers and drunkards come in and out here, gambling and drinking, raping women, fighting and robbing, everything, and it has become "hell on earth". Around the Yūgá Gǎng, the sewage becomes a lake, the garbage becomes a mound, and it stinks . . . As soon as the rebellion in Lhasa subsided, the Lhasa Municipal Committee of the Communist Party of China and the Municipal Military Management Committee set up residents' committees and working groups in various urban areas according to the requirements of the citizens, and sent many Tibetan and Han cadres and citizens together to thoroughly eradicate the trauma and "Pernicious-Vestiges" left by the former Tibetan local government. Under the leadership of the Military Management Committee of Lhasa City, Yūgá Gǎng quickly changed its appearance. All the residents organized themselves, cleared up the accumulated garbage, eliminated the smelly pond, built many sewers, and set up public toilets . . . More than 50 households and 42 orphans and disabled people received relief from the people's government, and received Zanba, tea, ghee and clothes. Many of them now had houses to live in. More than 70 people suffering from syphilis and venereal diseases have received free treatment, and many have found proper jobs with the help of the Municipal Military Management Committee.
>
> ("Guòqù ré jiān dìyù, jīnrì xìngfú lèyuán, lāsà Yūgá gǎng miànmào wánquán gǎiguān 过去人间地狱 今日幸福乐园 拉萨迂噶岗 面貌完全改观 [Past hell on earth, today happiness paradise, Yugagang, Lhasa, has completely changed its appearance]", *People's Daily*, November 21, 1959, 4A)

Although metaphors such as sexually transmitted diseases and rape are no longer common in the central and eastern parts of New China after liberation, they can still be used in the construction discourse of "Pernicious-Vestiges" that reflects the progress of ethnic minorities and remote areas. Through the juxtaposition of "prostitution", "rape", "garbage", "syphilis" and "venereal disease", the stale and dirty of the "former local government" and the cleanliness, health, and warmth brought by the "people's government" form a sharp contrast. The latter also easily obtained self-evident legitimacy from it.

In the aforementioned cases, through the mutual innuendo of "diseases" in the sexual and political fields, the metaphor of "Pernicious-Vestiges" not only extends its argument field from "body" to personal moral level but also establishes the rationality of all-round transformation of private life field. Similar or even more typical to "metaphor of disease", a major feature of the discourse system of "Pernicious-Vestiges" is that it constructs the metaphorical object "moral infectivity". The discrimination and resistance of "Pernicious-Vestiges" is equivalent to the prevention responsibility of "plague" and becomes a powerful force for individuals to regulate their own behavior. As a result, "Pernicious-Vestiges" has become a moral evaluation standard. Individuals carrying "Pernicious-Vestiges" are not only morally inferior to others, but they also become the object of being "disinfected" or even destroyed. By using the ultimate value judgment of "life above all else" and eliminating the source and infected person of "Pernicious-Vestiges", it will naturally have unquestionable legitimacy.

Extension from body to morality

As a kind of "anxiety about social order", the metaphorical system of "Pernicious-Vestiges" compares the ideal of a sound society to "physical health", while opposing the old politics and calling for a new political order; "disease" represents social disorder to some extent (Sontag, 1990, pp. 65–69). As "every deviation from the social convention can be regarded as a disease" (p. 51), the metaphor of "Pernicious-Vestiges" also bears the narrative function of defining the social convention. To compare a political event or a political situation to a disease is to regard it as an out-and-out and unchangeable evil and blame it for the evil, and the only "prescription" for it is punishment (p. 73). The "Pernicious-Vestiges" construction in the national narrative often comes from the intolerance of the chaotic social order in the transitional period of the regime, which reflects the hidden worry of the new regime about the possibility of the overthrown old regime or forces "coming back"; so it has to be "wiped out". Especially after 1948, this kind of consolidated discourse construction of "Pernicious-Vestiges" was frequently seen in newspapers. On June 8th, 2008, *People's Daily* reprinted a notice from the northeast of Xinhua News Agency, saying:

> Since the land reform in Northeast China, the feudal system has been completely destroyed politically and economically . . . However, it has recently been found that some loafers around the country have been infected with the "Pernicious-Vestiges" of the feudal class and become parasites of the new society . . . In the future, loafers who never take part in production must be forced to take part in labor production. Those who steal gambling for a living and take opium drugs but don't quit, or use the slogan of "democracy" to be unruly and harmful, should be punished according to law. All those who waste their land due to idleness shall temporarily stop issuing their land licenses.
>
> ("Dōngběi xíngzhèng wěiyuánhuì bānfā bùgào, qiángzhì èrliúzi lǎnhàn shēngchǎn 东北行政委员会颁发布告 强制二流子懒汉生产 [Notices issued by the Northeast Administrative Committee to force loafers and idlers to produce]", *People's Daily*, 2nd edition, June 8, 1948)

In the announcement published in this report, although it was declared that "the feudal system was completely destroyed", "doing nothing to produce" was constructed as a lazy individual's "habit is hard to return", and his occupation before the land reform was not mentioned at all, which was called "loafer (lazy man)", while his non-participation in labor production was collectively referred to as "the Pernicious-Vestiges of feudal class". Since then, "not being productive", together with "taking drugs", has become the pronoun of "feudal Pernicious-Vestiges" and personal decay from body to morality, and the moral metaphor of "Pernicious-Vestiges" has been established.

The metaphor of "Pernicious-Vestiges" is optimistic at the whole social level. As most diseases can be cured or alleviated, metaphors of infectious diseases often carry a timeliness (Sontag, 1990, p. 14). Although being infected with the "Pernicious-Vestiges" means that the social organism as the "body" is weakened, disordered, and lost, this "disease" can be cured, and the current efforts of the whole social organism are also "practical and effective". For example, in a signed article, the author Zhāng Zhìràng 张志让 constructed the marriage non freedom, including marriage divorce non freedom, as the "Pernicious-Vestiges" of the feudal marriage system and pointed out:

> The widespread existence of feudal marriage is an undeniable fact. My Marriage Law abolished all arranged and forced feudal marriage systems, forbidding anyone to ask for property through marital relations, making sure that both men and women must be completely willing to get married, forbidding any third party to interfere, and clearly stipulating that those who violate this law will be punished according to law. It is really a powerful medicine for clearing away the "Pernicious-Vestiges" left over by the society in the past.
> ("Qièhé xūyào de hūnyīnfǎ 切合需要的婚姻法 [Marriage law meeting needs]", *People's Daily*, 3A, April 17th, 1950)

In this passage, the reason why the official discourse construction is called "Pernicious-Vestiges" or "residual poison" is that such a judgment can show that the most important "treatment" work has been completed. As a "social cell", individuals don't need subjectivity. As long as they actively cooperate, winning the final "battle" will be the inevitable result just around the corner.

Apart from the metaphor of a "medicine-clearing agent", "operating a surgery" is also a common rhetorical device to solve the pain of social change in the metaphor of the body with "Pernicious-Vestiges". On May 5, 1950, the 5A of *People's Daily* published an article written by Zhāng Nǎiqì 章乃器, a patriotic democratic personage, in which there were many metaphors of "operating a surgery" to solve the "Pernicious-Vestiges":

> Today's difficulties and sufferings are the Pernicious-Vestiges of years of plundering by the enemy, not created by the people's government. Once the pustules that have grown for more than ten years are treated by surgery, the pain will be greater for a while, but to be a healthy person, it is inevitable

to bear the pain for a while. This is the pain of victory, and we can only make persistent efforts to move forward in order to achieve the final and greater victory ... If your industry is speculative, then today, without a plan for industry transformation, you have to close the door early. Speculation is harmful to the people; It is pus in pustules, which must be removed and disinfected before the disease can be cured ... The question is whether these measures are reasonable and basically beneficial to industry and commerce. If so, some pains and sacrifices should be endured. Just like cutting a cancer, it's impossible without damaging any good flesh or without bloodshed. Businesses should know that after this period of pain, there will be no more pain, but a situation of steady development.

("Bìzhì wěndìng hòu sīyíng gōngshāngyè zěnme bàn? 币制稳定后私营工商业怎么办？[What about private industry and commerce after the monetary system is stable?]", *People's Daily*, 5A, May 5, 1950)

In this article, the author first constructed the difficulties faced by the private industry and commerce in Shanghai since the Spring Festival in 1950 as "the Pernicious-Vestiges of years of plunder by the enemy", rather than the responsibility of the people's government. Later, as an economist, Zhāng Nǎiqì anticipated the tightening process that the upcoming "inflation to stability" must go through and the difficulties that it might bring to private industry and commerce. Therefore, he used the metaphor of "operating a surgery to cure pustules" to give an early warning of the degree of pain in this process, and at the same time, he brought confidence to the business owners that "they will recover after operating a surgery" and further pointed out that "this kind of pain is equally suffered by government agencies and state-owned enterprises". In a deeper narrative, the way to stabilize inflation includes, in addition to "shifting from speculation to commerce", changing the industrial and commercial undertakings that "serve imperialism, feudalism and bureaucratic capitalism" into those that "serve the people" to avoid being eliminated, so as to establish the general direction of future development of private industry and commerce that "faces the people" and "faces the countryside". Zhāng Nǎiqì was wrongly classified as a "rightist" in 1957 and was persecuted during the Cultural Revolution. He died in May 1977.

In addition, as Olick (1998) pointed out, the importance of memory domestication is not only to standardize the expression but also to legalize the accompanying emotions. A weak "body" susceptible to "Pernicious-Vestiges" implies that people were in a backward social situation that made them poor and ill. With such a narrative, the memories of former sufferings are recalled again, which is in sharp contrast with the vision of "new life" in sight, such as "defeating Pernicious-Vestiges" as a narrative strategy of socialist construction achievements. In addition, for overcoming the "Pernicious-Vestiges", the positive personal emotions full of fighting spirit are obviously more conducive to the "healing" of the whole social organism than the depressed mentality (Sontag, 1990, pp. 49–50). Therefore, from the perspective of social mobilization, the metaphorical system of "Pernicious-Vestiges" plays an inspiring role (Lincoln, 1989). But the modern disease metaphor of "Pernicious-Vestiges" is very pessimistic on the personal level. Just as patients will never know more about their illness than doctors who are professional groups and discourse authorities, the metaphor of infectious diseases with "Pernicious-Vestiges" also secretly presupposes the great possibility that people will become infected: They lack discrimination between "history" and "social reality" and their relationship, and they have no resistance. If they are a little careless, they will unfortunately be infected with "Pernicious-Vestiges"; at the least, they will be shunned by the whole society. At worst, they will seriously endanger personal health and even lose their lives. Thus, the "Pernicious-Vestiges" discourse constructs the "qualification of the accuser". For example, Lǎo Shě 老舍 had a typical discussion at the opening ceremony of the Beijing Literature and Art Work Congress held in May 1950:

> Among the two million people, many of them have lived under the emperor's feet for a long time, so they need some laxatives to clean up the feudal Pernicious-Vestiges in their stomachs. At the same time, they also need a little tonic to nourish their hearts and strengthen their brains, so that they can become healthy citizens of the people's government. This kind of elixir can only be processed by literary and artistic workers, and it neither causes severe diarrhea nor excessive nutrition. Moreover, it uses entertainment, persuasion, affection, and beauty as its attractors.
> ("Běijīng shì wénxué yìshù gōngzuòzhě dàibiǎo dàhuì shàng, zhǔxí Lǎo Shě kāimùcí quánwén 北京市文学艺术工作者代表大会上，主席老舍开幕词全文 [The full text of the opening speech of Chairman Lǎo Shě at the Beijing Literature and Art Workers Congress]", *People's Daily*, 3A, May 30, 1950)

It can be seen that in the face of the "Pernicious-Vestiges" that needs to rely on "expert" technology and discourse to give an exact judgment, people no longer need basic rationality but can only trust and follow the dominant authoritative discourse adopted by the state institutions. The discourse stipulates what thoughts may be "harmful", what phenomena are contagious, how to deal with them, and how to make aesthetic judgments about beauty and ugliness, cleanliness, and impure, familiarity, and strangeness (Sontag, 1990, p. 115). From 1954 to 1955, the CCP advocated pro-Soviet and anti-American culture. As "the depraved behavior of young people and teenagers is inseparable from the seduction of the Pernicious-Vestiges of the old society" ("Jìxù guànchè duì qīngnián de dàodé pǐnzhì jiàoyù 继续贯彻对青年的道德品质教育 [Continuing to carry out the moral quality education of youth]", *People's Daily*, 3A, April 12, 1955), it is necessary to "transform the old entertainment places and sell the old book stalls of pornographic books and periodicals" in the external environment to further eliminate the "Pernicious-Vestiges" of the old society ("Guǎngzhōu gè xuéxiào zěnyàng jìnxíng gòngchǎnzhǔyì dàodé jiàoyù de 广州各学校怎样进行共产主义道德教育的 [How do schools in Guangzhou carry out communist moral education?]", *People's Daily*, 3A, April 6, 1955). In internal self-transformation and moral remolding, *People's Daily* directly stipulated a moral lifestyle for young people with the help of the poison metaphor of "Pernicious-Vestiges":

> As our country is still in a transitional period, the Pernicious-Vestiges of the old society, especially hooligans, has not been completely eliminated, and it also endangers the physical and mental development of some young people . . . In this way, make some young people grow selfish, lazy and so on . . . As a part of the decadent bourgeois culture, the old book stalls and dirty entertainment places that rent and sell pornographic books and periodicals are still spreading toxins that corrupt young people's morality . . . This kind of enjoyment can only make a vigorous young man lose his lofty ambition, turn his eyes from the boiling struggle to the decadent life, and become a morally corrupt person.
> ("Nǔlì péiyǎng qīngnián yīdài de gòngchǎnzhǔyì dàodé pǐnzhì 努力培养青年一代的共产主义道德品质 [Strive to cultivate the communist moral quality of the young generation]", *People's Daily*, 1955)

Only by participating in the "boiling struggle" can the young people achieve the moral lifestyle, and can they become physically and mentally healthy people. However, who to fight against, how to fight against, and if all struggles are ethical are often left to the individual to explain at will.

In order to depict the possibility that "Pernicious-Vestiges" may delay the outbreak, and to gain time for attributing the current social problems to the accumulated disadvantages of earlier regimes, body metaphors also play an irreplaceable unique role. In the article "Report on the Work of the People's Court" published in the 1A on June 21, 1950, this official document adopted a similar strategy to explain the growth of civil and criminal cases after the founding of the People's Republic of China:

> At present, there are quite a few people's criminal cases in local courts, generally speaking. The biggest reason is that the feudal Pernicious-Vestiges and the reactionary rule of the Kuomintang for more than 20 years caused numerous pustules in the society. After liberation, they gradually broke out and asked the people's court for solutions.
> ("Report on the Work of the People's Court [Report at the Second Session of the National Committee of the Chinese People's Political Consultative Conference on June 17th, 1950]", *People's Daily*, June 21, 1950, 1A)

Through this metaphor, the increase in the number of cases in various places in 1950 is no longer related to the establishment of the New China and the governance of the new regime but to the "Pernicious-Vestiges" of the Kuomintang's "reactionary rule" over the past 20 years. They are just like pustules, which will not immediately erode the social body but will need a slow process of "gradual outbreak" and will emerge intensively under the new regime. With the help of the slow-release "pustule" rhetoric, the "Pernicious-Vestiges" can be completely blamed on the feudal regime and the Kuomintang rule, and this rhetoric further strengthens the morality and purity of the new regime in comparison.

On November 28, 1950, when the War to Resist U.S. Aggression and Aid Korea was in full swing, Warren Austin, the U.S. representative to the United Nations Security Council, emphasized in the Security Council the U.S. investment in China's cultural undertakings and church institutions since 1835 and the friendship between the two countries, which aroused the dissatisfaction of Beijing church organizations, schools, hospitals, and students studying in the United States. On December 14th, the *People's Daily* published an editorial entitled "Jìnyībù kāizhǎn fǎndì àiguó yùndòng 进一步开展反帝爱国运动 [Further launching the anti-imperialist patriotic movement]" in its 1A, which read,

> Now, we should not only cut off the 'cultural' chains that bind the souls of the people of China, but also thoroughly eliminate all the ideological toxins that you spread, so that you can no longer breed aggressive bacteria on the soil of China.

This metaphor contrasts the "filth" of American culture with the purity of China's land, and at the same time, it emphasizes the vulnerability of foreign cultures, which is easy to reproduce but still fragile after being transplanted to other countries' soil through "bacteria". Similarly, in the "three evils" movement in 1952, corruption, waste and bureaucracy were constructed as "the Pernicious-Vestiges of the old society". Yú Huánchéng 俞寰澄, a well-known industrialist, constructed a metaphor in an article published in *People's Daily*, arguing that although these three ethos proliferate rapidly in social organisms, they are actually only a superficial layer of "dirt" and "bacteria". As long as they are "washed away" and people's awareness and actions are "thorough", there is nothing to worry about, and the party representing "cleanliness" and morality will surely win. The article reads:

> For more than two years, under the leadership of communist party, political clarity has been achieved. However, there are still many poisons left by the old society. In this campaign, many facts of corruption, waste and bureaucracy were discovered. This is the Pernicious-Vestiges of China's old society for thousands of years. In the past, the ruling class, which exploited and oppressed the people, lived a corrupt life for a long time, learning from each other and taking root in it. In the era of Kuomintang reactionaries' rule, this poisonous fungus spread even more, which made the society rottener. This anti-corruption, anti-waste, anti-bureaucracy campaign is a thorough washing of the filth left by the old society, and its revolutionary significance is very monumental. In this campaign, all cadres who are steadfast can be praised; And sneaky and evil things have to show their true colors and have nowhere to hide. It's really something that has never happened before in history. This is the victory of the next revolution under the leadership of the great communist party and Chairman Mao, and it has overcome the bad ethos left over from thousands of years.
>
> ("Zīchǎn jiējí sīxiǎng bìxū gǎizào 资产阶级思想必须改造 [Bourgeois thought must be transformed]", *People's Daily*, 3A, January 29, 1952)

Similarly, the bureaucratic habit of "being an official without doing anything" is called "the Pernicious-Vestiges of the old society" and "the decadent habit", implying that such officials' manners are like old materials in terms of system and morality and eventually eroded and ruined by years ("Cóng yīfēng dǎngyuán láixìn shuōqǐ 从一封党员来信说起 [Starting from a letter from party member]", *People's Daily*, July 16, 1956, 1A). At this stage, since "poison" is fragile, "curing diseases and saving people" has potential possibility. In a commentary published by *People's Daily* in June 1957, a discourse strategy was constructed to separate the "Pernicious-Vestiges" from its carrier and divide and rule the two:

> Today's bureaucracy is not the inevitable product of today's social system, but the Pernicious-Vestiges of the old society and system . . . We must pay attention to the method of "beating" to achieve the goal of killing bureaucracy and saving "comrades who committed bureaucracy". Is a simple and rude stick better, or repeated reasoning, gradually sterilized criticism and self-criticism? While killing bureaucracy with a stick, "we should treat and save people for comrades who have committed bureaucracy". Bureaucracy and comrades who have committed bureaucracy are different and related, and the former is the "disease" of the latter. Kill the former, in order to save the latter, how about a stick? Even if one dose of "one stick" medicine can really kill all germs at once, can the patient stand it? What's more, today's bureaucratic disease is a chronic ideological disease. Can a stick kill?
> ("Guānyú 'yī gùnzi dǎsǐ guānliáozhǔyì' 关于'一棍子打死官僚主义' [On 'A Stick Killing Bureaucracy']", *People's Daily*, 8A, June 4, 1957)

This passage constructs "Pernicious-Vestiges" as a fragile "germ" but reduces its carrier from "nonhuman" to human beings, emphasizing that officials who may be at fault in their behavior are also "sick bodies" that need to be protected. Therefore, it is only necessary to "prescribe the right medicine" for ideological problems, without completely destroying people or classes, and not to be impatient because "Pernicious-Vestiges of the old society" means that this is a kind of disease that lasts for thousands of years. Such a humanitarian concept was rare calm in the social atmosphere at that time. Unfortunately, such calm quickly gave way to the fanatical anti-rightist movement since then.

In January 1958, when the anti-rightist movement was in full swing, *People's Daily* published an article written by poet, playwright, and the "Yellow River Cantata" lyricist Zhāng Guāngnián 张光年 (pen name: Guāng Wèirán 光未然). This article refers to individualism as the "Pernicious-Vestiges" of "exploiting class" and "bourgeoisie" and compares it to "brain cancer". Under the medical conditions at that time, this "brain cancer" was not only hidden and difficult to cure, but it even caused people's thoughts to change and get out of control:

> The terrible thing about cancer is that it lurks deeply. When the right time comes, it will develop liberally, disorganized and undisciplined until a person's body tissues are completely destroyed. And the greed of individualism

is endless ... Individualism is the Pernicious-Vestiges of the exploiting class. Explorers always try their best to beautify their thoughts of exploitation, and try their best to prove the justice of their exploitation, in order to convince the exploited, and willing to stretch out their necks to bear the master's slaughter ... In the new socialist society, the Pernicious-Vestiges of the bourgeoisie in one's mind actually represents the interests of the old system, and it desperately misses the old system and class that have been or are being eliminated, while showing instinctive resistance to the new system and class ... If he doesn't have a relationship with the old system. Encountered, these yeasts will swell up greatly, desperately crowding out new factors that are neutral and unstable in his mind ... The current socialist revolution in political thinking is aimed at solving the problem of who wins over who in the whole ideological field, and at pushing each and every one of us to solve this problem quickly and uproot the cancer of individualism from our minds.

("Zàitán gèrénzhǔyì yǔ ái 再谈个人主义与癌
[Rethinking individualism and cancer]", *People's Daily*,
8A, January 21, 1958)

Judging from the previous reports of "cancer" in *People's Daily*, the popularity of specific "cancer" in modern health concepts in New China is quite limited. In order to better explain the infinite expansion of cancer cells to readers, the author compares the cancer in the brain to the yeast that can be seen everywhere in people's daily life. Because the volume of the brain is constant, this metaphor presupposes a zero-sum relationship between individualism and new socialist ideas. Therefore, it is necessary to completely uproot the "Pernicious-Vestiges" of this idea as soon as possible.

The disease metaphor of "Pernicious-Vestiges" gives great legitimacy to "treating diseases", and at the same time it expands the boundary of who is qualified to be a "doctor". At the end of 1959, an article reprinted in *People's Daily* that criticized intellectuals for "building a car behind closed doors" as "Pernicious-Vestiges" used this metaphor of "taboo against diseases and medical treatment". Its purpose was to gain more space and rights for the masses to criticize intellectuals:

> Correction equals cure. Changing one's mistakes rather than exposing them is equal to treating a disease without telling the truth. Logically, how can this make sense! The only way to make mistakes and prove that there is something wrong with your thoughts and positions is to expose them and analyze and criticize them yourself. At the same time, ask the party and the masses to help you analyze and criticize them, dig out the root of the mistakes, and point out the nature of the mistakes, so as to raise your awareness and make up your mind to correct them. Otherwise, it would be too weak to fight against diseases with unhealthy bodies alone ... You must think about opening the door, combining self-criticism with mutual criticism, and thoroughly exposing your wrong words and deeds. This is like treating a disease,

paying attention to exercise, and paying attention to daily life. It is really important, but once you are ill in bed, the more important thing is to take an injection and take medicine, and rely on the doctor.

("'Bìmén s guò' sāncuò '闭门思过' 三错 [Three mistakes of 'Thinking Behind Closed Doors']", *People's Daily*, 8A, December 15, 1959, by Mò Guīrú 莫圭如)

This metaphor constructs the binary opposition between doctors and patients. Paradoxically, when thinking about the specific "diseases" and their manifestations in vague terms, the professionally trained intellectuals have been constructed into "patients" irresponsibly. Instead, the main force acting as the professional role of "doctors" is the masses, and the only evidence for the rationality of their opinions is the numerical advantage of "collective supervision". More importantly, intellectuals have become "unhealthy bodies" who are "sick in bed" and naturally lose the right to self-diagnosis. In this way, the masses' criticism of intellectuals has not only become the only life-saving straw and reliable object for intellectuals to "save themselves", but the exercise of this "right" is also concealed by the professional and goodwill of "medical qualification", which hides the real purpose of seizing "power".

During the Great Leap Forward, the legitimacy of the mass movement also bred the metaphor of "killing" as a means. This metaphor compares the "Pernicious-Vestiges" of unknown origin to an "infectious disease" that will blossom everywhere once infected, and mass criticism becomes a "spray" that can effectively curb this infection. For example,

Whenever an evil wind strikes, it expands its position everywhere, and some people who lack immunity will be infected. Therefore, we must timely organize mass criticism of unhealthy tendencies, combine positive education and thoroughly eliminate the Pernicious-Vestiges, so as to safeguard the socialist cause from damage.

("Rènqīng dàhǎo xíngshì, qiānfāngbǎijì de wèi shíxiàn jīnnián de gèngdà yuèjìn ér fèndòu 认清大好形势，千方百计地为实现今年的更大跃进而奋斗 [Recognize the good situation and do everything possible to strive for the greater leap forward this year]", *People's Daily*, 7A, January 6, 1960, by Céng Xīshèng 曾希圣, first secretary of Anhui Provincial Committee of the Communist Party of China)

The "unhealthy trend" here not only refers to the sugar-coated cannonball corrupting cadres, but it also refers to a special form of opinion expression in the Great Leap Forward, which is the suspicion of the truth that "production can be increased even if disaster strikes". Thus, in the face of the severe drought from 1959 to 1961, the Great Leap Forward movement continued to emphasize and continuously amplify people's agency. Together, the two finally brought a nationwide food shortage crisis for 3 years to China.

On this basis, the metaphor of "Pernicious-Vestiges" further adopts its internal classification system to distinguish two parts that may threaten people's health: the source of "Pernicious-Vestiges" and its "infected person". It is worth noting that although "infected people" were originally the objects with hope of cure, in the construction of "Pernicious-Vestiges" discourse, both "infectious people" and "infected people" were deprived of their group membership, thus being stigmatized and finally excluded from the organism of human society. Moreover, once the power of the two forces grows, the "non-us" part of the social body will gradually devour the "self" (Sontag, 1990, p. 61). This is precisely the implication of choosing "plague" as its analogy object in the discourse practice of "Pernicious-Vestiges" among many diseases, which makes people not only regard "Pernicious-Vestiges" as a disaster caused by the fragile "other" themselves but also as a disease that everyone may suffer from (Sontag, 1990, p. 135). In addition, the possibility and harm of "Pernicious-Vestiges" are unknown, and people don't know how to act, so they can only wait and die, leaving only the fear of losing their lives and ugly appearance. Furthermore, this metaphorical system has further deepened people's sense of rejection of "the other" and the sense of panic that almost everyone is in danger.

"Poisonous weeds" and "seeds": Metaphors of land and production

Undeniably, health and public hygiene have always been an unfamiliar modern discourse for contemporary China. If the metaphor of diseases in the sense of personal body is not enough to arouse the general attention of people in China with limited public health conditions at that time, then, in the process of constructing "Pernicious-Vestiges", *People's Daily* will often use agricultural production scenes that farmers are more familiar with, and they use the "poison" and "harm" to compare the "Pernicious-Vestiges" of feudal superstition as ideological resources. For example, on July 26, 1949, the 4A of *People's Daily* published an article entitled "Zhànshí nóngcūn zhōng de kēxué pǔjí gōngzuò 战时农村中的科学普及工作 [Popularization of science in rural areas during wartime]", sharing the achievements and experiences of popularization of scientific knowledge in the old liberated areas of North China. This article narrates the process of locust extermination in this area in 1944. By stimulating readers' memories of crop diseases such as diseased plants, sphacelotheca reiliana, white disease, puccinia striiformis, and honey ear disease, the traditional practices such as "praying for rain" and "worshipping the gods" are constructed as "the Pernicious-Vestiges of thousands of years of feudal superstition and backwardness", and modern agricultural knowledge naturally becomes a double effective way to solve crop diseases and get rid of ideological "Pernicious-Vestiges".

Not only that, the metaphors of "seed" and "toxin" will also be used in the texts of intellectuals explaining abstract theories to the public and will even be called again when mobilizing the masses to resist such theories. For example, in the criticism of Hu Shih's philosophy and his teacher, John Dewey, at the end of 1954, the land metaphor in *Collected Essays of Hu Shih*《胡适文存》was quoted to mobilize people to better understand why they should "draw a line" with Hu Shih himself:

Dewey, the leader of pragmatism, Hu Shih's teacher and the executor of American imperialism's policy of cultural aggression against China, came to China on a visit in May 1919, traveling around ten provinces for two years, selling his reactionary theories, and his five lectures in Beijing were the most notorious. Hu Shih said, "Mr. Dewey really loves China and China people. He is our good teacher and friend." [Mr. Dewey and China] After returning to the United States, Dewey also declared: "Our concern for China is not economic, but the kind of concern parents have for their children" [America and Far East]. The two men sang a pragmatic duet, one "recognizing a thief as a father" and the other "insincere", which can be regarded as the best footnote of the true theory of pragmatism. During Dewey's trip, in the ideological circle of old China, "seeds of toxins have indeed spread a lot", and they have also "blossomed and borne fruit" [Collected Essays of Hu Shih II]. Today, it's time for us to thoroughly disinfect and uproot pragmatism.

("Chèdǐ sùqīng fǎndòng zhéxué sīxiǎng shíyòngzhǔyì de yǐngxiǎng 彻底肃清反动哲学思想实用主义的影响 [Thoroughly eliminating the influence of pragmatism in reactionary philosophy]", *People's Daily*, 3A, December 20, 1954, by Yáng Zhèngdiǎn 杨正典)

One of the great conveniences of citing land metaphor is that as long as the author skillfully stigmatizes the crops that can grow from "seeds" and depicts "seeds" as "seeds with toxins", he can easily use the words of "lingering poison" and call on people to "uproot" them. Although it is more difficult to ban the mind than the body and capital, when the mind is constructed as a crop, it is as difficult as weeding in the field. With enough determination and vigilance, the working people can easily accomplish it, and its effectiveness will be immediate.

In 1955, *People's Daily* published an article on children's issues written by Kāng Kèqīng 康克清, then Secretary-General of the Chinese National Committee for the Defence of Children. This article not only constructs "feudal and superstitious customs that harm children's health" and "ways to pray to God and worship Buddha, burn incense and call souls when children are ill" as "Pernicious-Vestiges of the old society", but it also uses metaphors of land and planting to urge parents to better understand the importance of adult roles in children's growth:

> The blossoming orchard depends on the cultivation of gardeners, the sound growth of children, and the patient education of adults. Today, the Pernicious-Vestiges of the old society and the decadent ideas of the bourgeoisie will affect children directly or indirectly in many ways ... We should study hard the knowledge and methods of raising children and educate them with socialist ideas. Only in this way can the good moral character that has sprouted in children today be developed and consolidated through the correct cultivation of families, schools and society, so that they can grow into active builders and defenders of the communist cause.

("Zǔguó jiànshè zhōng de értóng 祖国建设中的儿童 [Children in the construction of the Motherland]", *People's Daily*, 3A, October 1, 1955)

76 Body and politics

It is not uncommon to compare children to "flowers of the motherland" and children's growth to "buds" in the official discourse system of contemporary China. However, when this kind of metaphor and "Pernicious-Vestiges" appear at the same time, people will naturally understand how much harm this "pest" will cause to young plants that are still in the bud, and they will be particularly able to accept the discourse framework that caring for children carefully is crucial to their growth. Children's scientific parenting concept is determined through the joint action of land metaphor and "Pernicious-Vestiges".

In 1963, after the People's Commune movement suffered setbacks, *People's Daily* quoted the scenes and common sayings of agricultural production and criticized the "Pernicious-Vestiges of the old society" of farmers "sweeping the snow in front of their own doors":

> There used to be a saying in the countryside of Hunan: "Drought makes poison". But this year, news of new people and new things spread in some areas during the drought . . . In fact, the poisonous people were not created by nature, but showed their poison during drought. Therefore, it is necessary to specifically analyze what class and thought people are and how they behave poison. In the past, the exploiting class did everything possible to harm farmers and enrich themselves. When the drought is urgent, they are extremely toxic, and their vicious nature is particularly conspicuous. These two ponds in Liangxinwu used to be occupied by landlords. Usually, farmers who had to pick up some water to irrigate vegetables would also be severely beaten. Drought is even a "good opportunity" for the landlord to bully people. Another landlord would rather discharge water into the river than into the farmer's field. In the past, landlords in rural areas all over the world made farmers shed countless blood and tears by occupying land and water sources . . . The principle of our new work can't be "I can only take care of myself", and it can't be "poisonous people" harming others' self-interest. Instead, we should focus on the whole revolution and construction, the friendship of the revolutionary class, and the common fundamental interests . . . The more serious and effective we are in removing the Pernicious-Vestiges of the old society, the faster the new people and new ethos will grow in the new society.
>
> ("Yīchǎng zhēnglùn 一场争论 [An argument]", *People's Daily*, 6A, September 19, 1963, by Yáng Kěnfū 杨垦夫)

Combining with the specific social scenes published in this article, it is not difficult to find that the discourse construction of "Pernicious-Vestiges" in this article is to encourage farmers to regain their confidence in public ownership, especially after they have suffered from the double blows of system failure and food shortage, and to re-believe that "common ownership" is not "damaging private interests and fattening public interests" but is "ownership by everyone" in another sense. In order to avoid this concept being too abstract, the author specifically cites the poison of "poisoning people" in the common saying, constructs this self-interest tendency to be unique to "landlords", and mobilizes farmers to update their own public and private ideas in a more concrete and visible way by sketching out a "new atmosphere" such as a bumper harvest of crops growing on healthy land after "removing the poison".

Since then, this discourse mode, which was originally used to publicize new ideas to readers familiar with agricultural production, was acquired by Kē Qìngshī 柯庆施, a hot figure during the Anti-Right movement and who almost replaced Zhou Enlai's position. He used this metaphor in the call for dramatists with certain writing skills:

> China's feudal culture and art have experienced thousands of years of ups and downs; The development of capitalist culture and art in western Europe has been going on for hundreds of years since the Renaissance. In China, as a socialist culture and art, it has only a short history of fifteen years. Socialist drama art is, after all, a new sprout. The drama of building socialism is itself a great and profound revolution. To make the socialist drama firmly occupy the position and completely exclude the drama that spreads the toxin of feudalism and capitalism from the stage, it needs our screenwriter, director, actor and stage workers to work together and make long-term and arduous efforts and struggles. We must not be discouraged or afraid to advance when we encounter difficulties. As long as we make continuous efforts in the right direction and constantly improve the ideological and artistic quality of socialist drama, we can create dramas worthy of our great era, and blossom infinitely brilliant artistic flowers on the stage.
> ("Dàlì fāzhǎn hé fánróng shèhuìzhǔyì xìjù, gènghǎo de wèi shèhuìzhǔyì de jīngjì jīchǔ fúwù 大力发展和繁荣社会主义戏剧,更好地为社会主义的经济基础服务 [Vigorously develop and prosper socialist drama to better serve the socialist economic foundation]", *People's Daily*, 2nd Edition, August 16, 1964)

In this article, Kē Qìngshī put forward some suggestions on the development of China's drama work in difficult times. He not only compared the socialist drama with a history of 15 years to a new sprout but also took it for granted that its strength was insufficient compared with the feudal art of 1,000 years and the capitalist art of 100 years, thus preparing for the challenges that the development of socialist drama might face; he also emphasized feudalism and capitalism. Therefore, we must work hard to cultivate the shoots of "socialist drama" and make them "occupy the position". In this way, feudal drama and capitalist drama will be squeezed out of the historical stage instead of coexisting with socialist drama, and the "flowers" of socialist drama will always bloom undefeated. Born in a peasant family, Mao Zedong was quite appreciated Kē Qìngshī in 1950s and 1960s, who used this set of words well, until Kē's death in 1965.

In 1965, in order to promote the concept of public ownership established by the People's Commune movement, the documentary literary work published by *People's Daily* also used a more familiar agricultural production scene, comparing "Pernicious-Vestiges" to "poisonous grass". To prevent the spread of poisonous thoughts, we must thoroughly eliminate them by "digging roots":

Check our thoughts, it is completely contrary to the spirit of being selfless and dedicated to others as stated in the article "In Memory of Bethune". It's the Pernicious-Vestiges of capitalist thought, and we must root it out in the future.
("一匹马 [A horse]", *People's Daily*, 2A, July 25, 1965, by Táng Guǎngyì 唐广益 and Wáng Rénhòu 王仁厚)

Although in this historical period, the meaning of "bourgeoisie" has been quite different from that in 1939 when Mao Zedong wrote "In Memory of Bethune". Compared with the idea carried forward in 1939's "In Memory of Bethune"—no matter whether it is a socialist country or a capitalist country, the proletariat needs to form an internationalist alliance that transcends the state—the "Pernicious-Vestiges of the bourgeoisie" in 1965 has completely become synonymous with the weak concept of public ownership and the pursuit of personal interests. However, under the powerful rhetoric of "digging the root of poison", no one is willing to pursue such a mistake, making it a silent but solid part of the discourse illusion.

After the Cultural Revolution began, the contrast between "poisonous weeds" and "flowers" was widely used in the criticism of literary critics Zhōu Yáng 周扬 and others. For example, the fauvism art of Matisse and Picasso is regarded as the expression of "bourgeois liberalization", and the appearance of these arts is related to Zhōu Yáng's personal educational philosophy. "All poisonous weeds that were afraid to take out in the past are regarded as flowers" ("Zhōu Yáng de 'zìyóuhuà' dúhuà le zhōngyāng měishù xuéyuàn 周扬的'自由化'毒化了中央美术学院 [Zhōu Yáng's 'liberalization' poisoned the Central Academy of Fine Arts]", *People's Daily*, 3A, July 16, 1966). Under the influence of the increasingly unimaginative revolutionary language, the "sweeping" of "sweeping away the Pernicious-Vestiges" also has a designated tool: "Proletarian revolutionaries should bravely take up the iron broom of revolution and thoroughly eliminate the Pernicious-Vestiges of capitalism and revisionism in all fields" ("Bùduàn gémìng, yǒngyuǎn qiánjìn 不断革命，永远前进 [Constantly revoluting and advancing forever]", *People's Daily*, 3A, June 14, 1967, by Rèn Lìxīn 任立新). This discourse pattern was repeated for years during the Cultural Revolution, so that after the end of the Cultural Revolution, people who had suffered from it still adopted this discourse framework to prove their innocence:

> The discussion of restoring the reputation of "Jiafeng Style" in Shanghai No.33 Cotton Textile Factory reflects a situation worthy of attention: it has been more than a year since the Gang of Four was smashed, but the remnants of the counter-revolutionary revisionist line of the Gang of Four, like invisible hoops, still bind some comrades' thoughts and make them feel scared . . . Is "Jiafeng Style" the fragrant flower of socialism or the poisonous weed of revisionism? Is it the fine tradition of the proletariat to run enterprises, or is it the product of "bourgeois masters' pressure on management"? . . . "Jiafeng Style" is the product of the production of political commanders. There are many processes and machines in the textile factory, and it takes thousands of hands from cotton

entering the factory to finished products leaving the factory. If there is no in-depth and meticulous political and ideological work and a high sense of political responsibility of thousands of people, how can we be strict and meticulous, and how can our products meet the inspection-free export standards?

("Wéi 'jiāfēng fēnggé' huīfù míngyù 为'嘉丰风格'恢复名誉 [Restoring the reputation of Jiafeng Style]", *People's Daily*, 3A, March 18, 1978)

The strong discourse inertia and thinking inertia can be seen in this text: Even though the discourse illusion that dominated in the previous historical period lost its power, this logically constructed historical view, metaphor, and the boundary between the friend and the enemy still shaped people's thinking mode. Even in the scene of industrialized production and in the era of breaking the pan-politicization myth, people still rely heavily on the framework of agricultural production and "politics in command" to understand the outside and defend themselves.

"Metabolism" of social organisms

The disease metaphor of "Pernicious-Vestiges" also constructs the organic characteristics of society as "body". Using narrative techniques similar to "plague", the metaphorical system of "Pernicious-Vestiges" maintains the relationship between social individuals and further clarifies the collectivity and sociality of the social phenomenon it depicts. At the same time, it quickly completes the collectivism "ideological persuasion" whose overall value is higher than that of individuals (Lincoln, 1989). That is to say, once the health of the whole "body" is threatened, the life of the individual will cease to exist. Therefore, in order to ensure the survival and operation of a social organism as a "body", individuals who are part of the organism can and must make sacrifices, which are not only "inevitable" but also completely "legitimate" (Sontag, 1990, p. 60), such as the discourse pattern of "in order to wipe away the Pernicious-Vestiges". In October 1950, around the first National Day, *People's Daily* published a large number of lyrical literary works, including a poem by Wú Yán 吴岩, which reads:

> The people have turned over/Chang'an Street has also turned over/the sewers have been turned over/the Pernicious-Vestiges of feudalism for thousands of years/the sewages of imperialism, bureaucracy and capitalism for hundreds of years/it's completely clean/it's discharged, it's discharged, . . ./Chang'an Street has a new life/it's long/wide/it's an open and honest People's Avenue!
>
> ("Gēchàng zhōngguó rénmín de shènglì 歌唱中国人民的胜利 [Singing in praises of the victory of China people]", *People's Daily*, 3A, October 5, 1950)

The image of this poem not only regards the society as an organism, but it further compares the infrastructure of municipal engineering to the "body" that needs to be polluted. Through the intertextuality of "Pernicious-Vestiges" and "sewage", the "three mountains" of feudalism, imperialism, and bureaucratic capitalism are constructed into urban waste landscapes that can be seen everywhere, thus strengthening the opposition between the present "cleanliness" and "magnanimity" and the past filth and reminding people that the "old forces" may fight back at any time.

With the struggle object of the discourse construction of "Pernicious-Vestiges" shifting from class to thought, sometimes the body metaphor of "Pernicious-Vestiges" will adopt the discourse strategy related to the brain in order to link the abstract conceptual domain with the specific body organs. For example, in the article "Wǒmen yào chèdǐ de wéi fǎntānwū fǎnlàngfèi fǎnguānliáozhǔyì ér dòuzhēng 我们要彻底地为反贪污反浪费反官僚主义而斗争 [We must fight against corruption, waste and bureaucracy thoroughly]" published in the 1A of *People's Daily* on December 30, 1951, the "Pernicious-Vestiges of feudalism, imperialism and bureaucratic capitalism" was constructed as "the toxin left by the enemy that some people have not yet knocked down". Although this kind of "thought" represented by corruption and waste has not shown tangible concrete performance for the time being, it still lurks dangerously in people's minds, and its unexplored harm can't be underestimated. Therefore, "only by thoroughly eliminating all kinds of toxins left over from the general old society" can we "completely reverse the ethos".

At the end of 1954, China cultural circles criticized the Yú Píngbó 俞平伯's textual research of "Dream of Red Mansions" and constructed it as "the Pernicious-Vestiges of bourgeois idealism" of Hu Shih's "reactionary philosophy of experimentalism" (for the cause and effect of this discussion, please refer to the section of Chapter 6 of this book entitled "Cultural 'Pernicious-Vestiges' of Intellectuals"). As the participants in the discussion covered the important figures in China's literary world at that time, everyone in these literary circles also produced more in-depth discussions, explanations, and understandings around the "Pernicious-Vestiges". Guō Mòruò 郭沫若, then chairman of the China Federation of Literary and Art Circles, published the "Trademark Theory", which is a rather subtle example:

> Take the criticism of this study of A Dream of Red Mansions for example. Mr. Yú Píngbó has been studying "Dream of Red Mansions" for 30 years. According to himself, the more he studies, the more confused he becomes. Comrade Li and Comrade Lan are only young people in their twenties. It is said that they have only studied "Dream of Red Mansions" for two years, but they hit the target with an arrow . . . Shouldn't such young people be especially cared for? I feel that many of our elderly people are really brain degenerated. Our cerebral cortex, like the suitcase of a world traveler, is full of hotel logos on various docks. Such a person, it can really be said to be a mess, and there is little room for accepting new things . . . Old things occupy our brains and refuse to give way . . . Metabolism is absolutely necessary, both physiologically and socially. Old people should clear the way for young people . . . There are some bad elements among young people. Although this is the Pernicious-Vestiges of the old society, we can't ignore it . . . Our age is an era of youth, and it is an era of ever-rising youth.
>
> ("Sāndiǎn jiànyì 三点建议 [Three suggestions]",
> *People's Daily*, December 9, 1954, 1A)

With the help of the social organism, the connection between "brain" and "heart" and the metaphor of "Pernicious-Vestiges of the old society" mentioned earlier, this passage creatively adds the image of "suitcases plastered with hotel trademarks all over the world" and constructs a new binary opposition relationship—the relationship between youth and the elderly. The elderly are relatively knowledgeable, but they are slow and have accumulated too much knowledge, so they are full of doubts about new things. On the contrary, young people, like a blank sheet of paper, are better at learning "new ideas". Even if they have shortcomings, they are caused by the old people and the "old society". With the "metabolism" of generations, the organism of society will naturally "metabolize", and the current "new ideas" will surely win all-round victories in both physical and conceptual aspects. Under this premise, no matter how knowledgeable and high-ranking the elderly are, they will not be a worry for the regime because in the linear development historical view presupposed by the existence of the natural law of "metabolism"; in any case, the times will "rise forever".

Then, in the *People's Daily* published the next day, Máo Dùn 茅盾, a famous writer, sublimated Guō Mòruò's "trademark theory" and further expounded in his speech the specific measures to eliminate the "trademark Pernicious-Vestiges of various countries":

> Now I'm going to extend his meaning and make a little metaphor. I think that we didn't learn Marxism–Leninism well, as if we had pasted some slogans of Marxism–Leninism on the cerebral cortex covered with various hotel trademarks; On the surface, it's a bit Marxism–Leninism, but it can't stand the test; Once tested, those messy trademarks behind the slogan will come out . . . The most dangerous thing is that it comes out with the slogan of Marxism–Leninism, which is called selling dog meat with sheep's head, pretending to be a Marxist, enough to cheat the world and steal the name! I think: We must have the courage to reflect on ourselves. From now on, we must study honestly and study hard. We must use Marxism–Leninism as an ideological weapon to eliminate the toxic hotel trademarks on our cerebral cortex, instead of sticking Marxism–Leninism's slogan on these hotel trademarks. We must get rid of that self-deception style.
>
> ("Liánghǎo de kāiduān 良好的开端 [A good start]", *People's Daily*, December 9, 1954, 3A)

Such a move not only reminded the literary circles of China at that time to be wary of slogan formalism but also placed the importance of the strategy of banning unpopular ideas on the strategy by replacing old ideas with Marxism–Leninism (see "Anthropoemic/anthropophagic" in Chapter 2 of this book for details), arguing that the promotion of new ideas must be based on the premise of "eliminating those toxins in our cerebral cortex", and only when Marxism–Leninism was also constructed as an "ideological weapon" here, which made Máo Dùn's speech full of the highly respected "fighting style" at that time. The specific role of this military term in "cleaning up" the "Pernicious-Vestiges" will be further discussed in the next section.

However, if we constantly emphasize that society, as an organism, has the nature of the alternation of the old and the new, "Pernicious-Vestiges" will be automatically replaced by new things without any concern, and people's vigilance and fighting spirit in the face of "Pernicious-Vestiges" will inevitably decrease, which will fundamentally weaken the mobilization and influence of "Pernicious-Vestiges" discourse. In order to avoid this kind of situation, this kind of metaphor has been patched for itself in time. On March 19, 1957, *People's Daily* published the article "Fàngxià kōng jiàzi 放下空架子 [Relinquishing haughty airs]" by Péng Bótōng 彭伯通 in 8A, in which the word "blood relationship" was used, thus completing the self-repair of the discourse framework of social organism: "It can't be said that the current intellectuals' lack of knowledge, ignorance of pretense and nonsense have no blood relationship with the Pernicious-Vestiges of the old society". In this way, even if "metabolism" helps to clean up the "Pernicious-Vestiges", this "symptom" may be passed down from generation to generation through genes, so people still need to pay enough attention to it and carefully keep a distance from it.

In 1958, at the white-hot stage of the anti-Rightist struggle, there was a text that used the words of "Pernicious-Vestiges" to explain why the mass movement was used to achieve the goal of otherization. On the 7A of January 18, *People's Daily* published an article written by Hán Míng 韩明, which wrote:

> If the mass movement is not adopted, it will be impossible to mobilize the masses to win the movement, and it will be impossible to thoroughly eliminate the Pernicious-Vestiges of the three enemies thought. It will be difficult to basically draw a clear line between the revolutionary and counter-revolutionary, and it will be difficult for teachers' awareness level to rise rapidly, and it will be impossible for them to accept such a broad and profound socialist revolution in China. All this shows that it was absolutely necessary to carry out ideological transformation by mass movement at that time.
> ("Zài gāoděng xuéxiào zhíxíng zhīshífènzǐ zhèngcè de wèntí 《在高等学校执行知识分子政策的问题》 [Problems of implementing intellectuals policies in colleges and universities]", *People's Daily*, 7A, January 18, 1958)

The so-called "three enemies thought", namely "imperialism, feudalism, and bureaucratic capitalism", uses the metaphor of social organism to construct the binary opposition between "infected minority" and "clean majority" and make them form a strong power contrast, thus completing the myth that the uninfected cells in the organism can devour infected cells to achieve complete "health". In fact, the justice of the society can't be simply judged by the majority or minority forces.

The metabolic metaphor of organism also presupposes the rationality of the pain that the process of "clearing away the Pernicious-Vestiges" may bring to people. Different from the surgical metaphor of "operating a surgery", which introduces external forces, "metabolism" strengthens the self-purification process of a social organism and naturalizes it. As another text in the Great Leap Forward period said,

While setting up a new atmosphere and forming a new style, we must thoroughly eliminate the Pernicious-Vestiges of the old society . . . This seems to be the process of peeling off the old scabs and growing new flesh for skin patients once they are treated, which is a good thing.

("Dǎdiào jiāoqì 打掉娇气 [Beat the pettish]", *People's Daily*, 4A, May 18, 1958, by Yè Wén 叶雯)

As a result, the value judgment that the new ethos replaces the old one and that the pain in the process belongs to "good things" has also been brought into a larger discourse space without thinking about it.

After that, because the Great Leap Forward was eager to announce the success and past tense of the previous New China's elimination of all kinds of "Pernicious-Vestiges", with the arrival of the Cultural Revolution, the metaphor of metabolism also needed to be updated. In 1967, when the Cultural Revolution was in full swing, a new form of organism metaphor was created—the body metaphor of the carrier of "Pernicious-Vestiges poison": Although certain social classes have been declared extinct, if the "remains" of these classes or even countries cannot be cleaned up in time, their remains will still breed more toxins. For example, *People's Daily* quoted from Xinhua News Agency, claiming that an article written by India's *Progressive Journal* stated that "the goal of the cultural revolution is to wipe out another powerful enemy, that is, old ideas, old culture, old customs and habits—the Pernicious-Vestiges of the old feudal class and bourgeoisie and their ideology that are now dead" ("Yìndù jìnbù kānwù zànyáng wǒguó wénhuà dàgémìng shēnyuǎn yǐngxiǎng 印度进步刊物赞扬我国文化大革命深远影响 [Indian progressive publications praise China's Cultural Revolution for its profound influence]", *People's Daily*, February 13, 1967, 4A). An article in 1971 also quoted Lenin's similar assertion and wrote:

The leading members of the district committees and revolutionary committees also learned Lenin's wise judgment: "When the old society perished, its dead bodies could not be put into coffins and buried in graves. It rots and stinks among us and poisons us. "They said that the remnants of the counter-revolutionary revisionist line, the old traditional ideas and the old habitual forces still exist in us, and the class struggle in society is bound to be reflected in the Party. We must work harder to learn and apply Marxism, Leninism and Mao Zedong Thought, consciously transform the world outlook, study and transform all our lives, and strive for the implementation and defense of Chairman Mao's revolutionary line all our lives.

("Shànghǎi pǔtuó qūwěi hé qū géwěihuì lǐngdǎo chéngyuán zūnzhào máozhǔxí de jiàodǎo jiānchí rènzhēn dúshū 上海普陀区委和区革委会领导成员遵照毛主席的教导坚持认真读书 [The leading members of Shanghai Putuo District Committee and District Revolutionary Committee adhere to Chairman Mao's teaching and study hard]", *People's Daily*, 1A, May 9, 1971)

Although we have no way of verifying who wrote these articles, the metaphor of social organism constructed in them is still very clever; it is consistent with the previous conclusion that "clearing away the Pernicious-Vestiges" has declared victory, and it also builds a new imaginary enemy for launching a new mass movement, so that this motivation can be continuously passed on.

"Pernicious-Vestiges" and military terminology

"Metaphor of disease" carries a lot of military terms (Sontag, 1990, p. 59). This metaphorical system has set a clear action goal: to overcome the "Pernicious-Vestiges" and eliminate its sources, such as inspection, annihilating, and so on. For example, on November 20, 1950, after the War to Resist U.S. Aggression and Aid Korea began, the 3A of *People's Daily* published the article "Rénmín de zhèngyì yāoqiú 人民的正义要求 [People's just demands]" written by Yáng Huì 杨晦, a professor in the Chinese Department of Peking University. The article praised the boycott of the Shanghai newspapers to stop advertising American films and the cinemas to stop showing American films. The article regarded it as an organic part of the War to Resist U.S. Aggression and Aid Korea and called on people to take this opportunity to "eliminate the 'Pernicious-Vestiges' of Americanization in the past." The article also quotes the folk saying that "a thief bites a bite, and a pain goes deep into the bone" as an analogy to how long it takes to dilute the "Pernicious-Vestiges" of foreign culture, but it doesn't explain in detail why American movies are culturally toxic. Similarly, the author also quotes Mencius' famous saying, "A villain's glory is cut for the fifth generations", which is intended to construct American culture as the opposite of "a gentleman" but ignores the first half of Mencius' famous saying, "A gentleman's glory is cut for the fifth generations". Therefore, this text, which constructs American culture as "Pernicious-Vestiges", uses the military term "elimination" to resist a specific culture. The real function of this seemingly paradoxical combination is to serve the military purpose of resisting U.S. aggression and aiding Korea. Even though the means to prevent the "Pernicious-Vestiges" from spreading are mild measures such as "studying hard . . . strengthening our national self-confidence, self-esteem, loving the motherland and the people, and actively participating in the country's construction", in the expression of the purpose of action, this kind of discourse still chooses such fierce military vocabulary as "thoroughly wipe out" ("Běijīngshì tiānzhǔjiào géxīn yùndòng zhōng de jǐgè wèntí 北京市天主教革新运动中的几个问题 [Several issues in the Catholic Reform movement in Beijing]", *People's Daily*, 1999).

Moreover, even in peaceful times, the "legacy" narrative of the *People's Daily* also borrows the military style. It not only constructs the "relationship between ourselves and the enemy" caused by conflicts of interest, but it also constructs the absolute authority of the official discourse as the "commander" and the absolute obedience of the people in the battle against "legacy". By highlighting the achievements of "heroes", it further demonize or dehumanize the image of the enemy (Pan, 1997). At the same time, when the social phenomenon caused by the "legacy" is a malignant, terrible, uncontrollable, or a treatable "disease", the social organism enters a state of emergency. The state has the power to suppress and for violence, and people can only choose to wipe out the "legacy", while the violent revolution and authoritarian politics have legitimacy, and people have fallen into "non-historical revolutionary optimism" again and again (p. 72–76). In addition, war metaphor is also crucial to the generation of space concept and boundary of modern countries. In the narrative of "legacy", the spatial meaning of "limitation, fragmentation, and containerization" is also related to the construction of social reality and social identity. This kind of war metaphor construction was concentrated during the Cultural Revolution. For example, in September 1966, the *People's Daily* published an article that used the military vocabulary of "sweeping" and even more hateful verbs such as "extinction" and "cut off". But behind the "shouting and killing", these young Red Guards were evasive about what they were going to exterminate:

> Young revolutionaries, for the remnants of feudalism, the germs of capitalism, and the bane of revisionism, it is to eliminate, exterminate, and cut off. Only by thoroughly destroying all kinds of old traditions of the exploiting class can we inherit and carry forward the revolutionary tradition of the proletariat.
> ("Hóngwèibīng zàn 红卫兵赞 [Praise of the Red Guards]", *People's Daily*, 2nd edition, September 19, 1966, by commentator of *Red Flag*《红旗》*Magazine*)

At the same time, as Foucault said, disciplinarian power is often produced by highlighting the disciplined individuals, while shielding the joint action of the exercise process of disciplinarian power (Foucault, 1975/1995). Similarly, the narrative of "Pernicious-Vestiges" spends a lot of ink to construct the crimes of "source of infection" and "infected person" and their social role in fighting against them, but it often makes no mention of the essence of their "being born as human beings" and their pain in the process of being "destroyed", and it further makes them "otherized". Similarly, Yang (2006) also believes that labels such as poison, virus, bedbugs, and pests are inherently similar in nature, and they all otherize, objectify, and stigmatize people or their thoughts, thus making them play the role of "scapegoats"; then they play the role of political mobilization, social mobilization, and moral exemption when eliminating them. This shows that the legitimacy of the regime not only needs to be proved by the ability of converging external forces to fight, but it also needs to fix such emotions through political ceremonies. With the help of the metaphor that bacteria are "the symbol of imperialism", the universal epidemic prevention has become an important ritual behavior, and this ritual behavior has the effect of the so-called "Rite of Intensiveness"—through repeated operations year after year, the daily relationship of the masses can be strengthened and reconfirmed through periodic rituals, although the intensification of this ritual has nothing to do with "germ warfare". This can also be shown in people's use of Mao Zedong's inscriptions. During the anti-germ warfare period, Mao Zedong's earliest inscription was: "Mobilize, pay attention to hygiene, reduce diseases and improve people's health. Prevent the Bacteriological warfare launched by imperialism". Since 1953, every time the slogan "Patriotic Health Campaign" launched, it periodically has been used again, only the first sentence is always kept and the last sentence is removed. This shows that "Patriotic Health Campaigns", as a ritual, have the nature of cross-regional collective cooperation. They have surpassed the restriction of the original "symbolic community" and constantly confirmed the new cooperative relationship of "socialism". With the establishment of the People's Commune system, and even with other types of political movements, it has the effect of supporting operation and mutual echo (pp. 424–425).

In the face of this "random, unreasonable, and unknown source" pollution (Sontag, 1990, p. 36), the reason for the "Pernicious-Vestiges" contamination has been mystified. More specifically, similar to the metaphor of "plague", "Pernicious-Vestiges" also "all comes from other places" in its root (p. 121). However, the official discourse still blames individuals for the contamination of "Pernicious-Vestiges"; "patients create their own diseases" (p. 43): These people either "contaminated/kept the Pernicious-Vestiges" or "the Pernicious-Vestiges still exists", implying that people should be responsible for their own health and life. In addition, the narrative of "Pernicious-Vestiges" skillfully bypasses the guilt and punishment of its source and phenomenon in the legal domain and turns to the moral domain, so that the rejection of "infected people" is only regarded as a "helpless action" by social organisms to protect themselves, which is only contrary to morality; its essential "no treatment" also escapes the possibility of being tried at the legal level. The value of "Pernicious-Vestiges" is devalued, and the possibility of being prevented and saved is always absent, which constitutes a simple and fanatical way of thinking that does not reflect on "Pernicious-Vestiges" and directly sublets it (p. 75).

The framework of discursive illusion holds that language and symbolic actions represented by metaphorical rhetoric have specific social consequences, and the ultimate purpose of analyzing these metaphors is to reveal the emotions and ideologies created by them, especially the social classification and stereotypes created by ideology (Ross & Bhatia, 2021). As Lakoff and Johnson (1980) said, reason involves at least classification, implication, and inference, and only imagination involves seeing one thing with another: metaphorical thinking. Therefore, metaphor is an imaginary reason (p. 193). Next, in Chapter 4 to Chapter 6, this book will make a concrete analysis of the social impact of the "Pernicious-Vestiges" discourse of *People's Daily* through group classification.

References

Bhatia, A. (2015). *Discursive Illusions in Public Discourse: Theory and Practice*. New York: Routledge.

Cameron, L. (1999). Operationalizing "metaphor" for applied linguistics research. In L. Cameron & G. Low (Eds.), *Researching and Applying Metaphor* (pp. 3–28). Cambridge: Cambridge University Press.

Cameron, L., & Stelma, J. H. (2004). Metaphor clusters in discourse. *Journal of Applied Linguistics*, *1*(2), 107–136. https://doi.org/10.1558/japl.2004.1.2.107.

Charteris-Black, J. (2004). *Corpus Approaches to Critical Metaphor Analysis*. Winchester: Palgrave Macmillan.
Charteris-Black, J. (2005). *Politicians and Rhetoric: The Persuasive Power of Metaphor*. New York: Palgrave Macmillan.
Deutscher, I. (1963/1998). *The Prophet Outcast: Trotsky, 1929–1940* (trans. by Y. Shi, B. Zhang & H. Liu). Beijing: Central Compilation & Translation Press.
Fairclough, N. (2003). *Analyzing Discourse: Textual Analysis for Social Research*. London: Routledge.
Foucault, M. (1975/1995). D*iscipline and Punish: The Birth of the Prison* (trans. by A. Sheridan). New York: Vintage Books.
Goatly, A. (1997). *The Language of Metaphors*. London: Routledge.
Harris, Z. (1963). *Discourse Analysis*. La Haye: Mouton and Company.
Krippendorff, K. (1993). Major metaphors of communication and some constructivist reflections on their use. *Cybernetics & Human Knowing*, *2*(1), 3–25.
Lakoff, G. (1993). The contemporary theory of metaphor. In A. Ortony (Eds.), *Metaphor and Thought* (pp. 202–251). Cambridge: University of Cambridge Press.
Lakoff, G., & Johnson, M. (1980). *Metaphors We Live by*. Chicago: University of Chicago Press.
Lincoln, B. (1989). *Discourse and the Construction of Society: Comparative Studies of Myth, Ritual, and Classification*. New York: Oxford University Press.
Linell, P. (1998). Discourse across boundaries: On recontextualizations and the blending of voices in professional discourse. *Text*, *18*(2), 143–157. https://doi.org/10.1515/text.1.1998.18.2.143.
Mac Cormac, E. R. (1990). *A Cognitive Theory of Metaphor*. Boston: MIT Press.
Olick, J. K. (1998). What does it mean to normalize the past? Official memory in German politics since 1989. *Social Science History*, *22*(4), 547–571. https://doi.org/10.2307/1171575.
Pan Zhongdang. (1997). "War" as metaphor in discourse. In W. Mingming & P. Zhongdang (Eds.), *Symbol and Society: A Probe into Chinese Folk Culture* (pp. 64–88). Tianjin: Tianjin People's Press.
Robins, S., & Mayer, R. E. (2000). The metaphor framing effect: Metaphorical reasoning about text-based dilemmas. *Discourse Processes*, *30*(1), 57–86. https://doi.org/10.1207/S15326950dp3001_03.
Ross, A. S., & Bhatia, A. (2021). "Ruled Britannia": Metaphorical construction of the EU as enemy in UKIP campaign posters. *The International Journal of Press/Politics*, *26*(1), 188–209. https://doi.org/10.1177/1940161220935812.
Sontag, S. (1990). *Illness as Metaphor and AIDS and Its Metaphors*. New York: Anchor Books.
Yang, N. (2006). *Re-creating the "Patient"-Space Politics under the Conflict between Chinese and Western Medicine (1832–1985)*. Beijing: Renmin University of China Press.
Zinken, J. (2003). Ideological imagination: Intertextual and correlational metaphors in political discourse. *Discourse & Society*, *14*(4), 507–523. https://doi.org/10.1177/0957926503014004005.

4 Developing from nothing

The evolution of feudal "Pernicious-Vestiges" discourse

People's Daily generates social influence and new social classification through the discourse construction of "Pernicious-Vestiges", thus serving different hidden ideologies. As mentioned earlier, the concept of categorization focuses on how people organize their moral positions and commitments around specific categories of identities (Jayyusi, 1984, p. 183), which mainly covers three situations: (1) self-organized group united by common beliefs and goals; (2) type categorization, which is predicted to produce specific actions because of embedding specific classification features; and (3) assigning individual descriptor designers with ascriptive and descriptive functional labels to specific types of people (Jayyusi, 1984, p. 24). Similarly, the categories and stereotypes produced by the language and behavior of individuals or groups can also be examined by the method of membership category analysis (MCA) (Sacks, 1992), which explains how people organize their moral positions and commitments around the identities of specific categories.

Categorization is an important aspect of understanding meaning in various fields of dialogue and social life (Makitalo & Saljo, 2002). It is also a kind of "filter" (Sarangi & Candlin, 2003) through which people intentionally or unintentionally understand events and experiences, usually with a purpose (Sacks, 1992). By emphasizing the negative aspects of external groups and describing it as the enemy of essence and homogenization or alien others (Gal & Irvine, 1995), the actors of discourse construction try to establish a new social classification to serve the unity within the imaginary group (Ross & Bhatia, 2021). The social impact of this discourse pattern may cause individuals and groups to set themselves against others, build new communal relationships, and construct this practice of social calibration as the organic integration of human experience and imagination, perception and culture, and metaphor, synonyms, and mental images (Lakoff, 1987, p. 8).

Another main function of categorization is to help people understand the present or predict the future according to past experience. As a kind of "situation definition", it provides a memory framework for changing details and adapting to reality according to needs (Linell & Thunqvist, 2003; Minsky, 1977). When people lose order and control in their lives and face incomprehensible situations, discourse illusion will come into effect, making discourse frame begin to act as a structure in human memory that can be selected or retrieved at any time according to needs (Bednarek, 2005) and helping people to use classification as a concrete way to

DOI: 10.4324/9781003409724-4

define and deal with social problems. Therefore, classification refers to the past experience through the framework process (Bhatia, 2015, p. 27).

Generally speaking, the basic function of ideology is also realized through classification, which responds to the questions of who we are, what we stand for, what our values are, and what our relationship with others is. "We" and "they" are characterized as social groups, maximizing the similarities within categories and differences between categories (Oktar, 2001), positioning the status and relationship of individuals in society. It proves the effective way of "scapegoating" and defending the label of "victim", and the practice of reclassification (or restructure) shows that categorization has the potential of explanation (Sarangi & Candlin, 2003), which also echoes the internal motivation that the society with changing membership needs to frequently use classified discourse.

When dealing with controversial structures and concepts that are more common in daily life, such as democracy, freedom, revolution, poverty, and terrorism, reclassification will continue to influence the actions and decisions of members of society. The classified discourse ideology will eventually be reflected in the stereotypes formed by people, and its important function is to reorganize the reality and experience faced by people; supplement the ever-changing social roles, group conflicts, power distribution and retention; rationalize and maintain the status quo; and provide a sense of identity (Hilton & von Hippel, 1996). By inspiring the public's feelings; making them believe in their moral, political, economic, social, and professional advantages; and encouraging people to judge others, the elite constantly reaffirms the boundaries between "self" and "others" while strengthening group unity. It excludes those who exceed the boundaries of "normative" behavior, thus maintaining the existing power structure of society through prescriptive nature (Bhatia, 2015).

According to Dirlik (1996), feudalism is the object of common opposition between a revolutionary paradigm and modernization paradigm. Consistent with the basic assumption of this view, feudal "Pernicious-Vestiges" has also become the narrative tradition of *People's Daily*. Feudal "Pernicious-Vestiges" has appeared the most and lasted the longest, and it has not been cut off since 1946. The most recent one appeared in the article "Resolutely Preventing and Opposing Dock Culture" on March 29, 2018, and all sectarianism, circle culture, and dock culture were included in the feudal "Pernicious-Vestiges". In this chapter, we will systematically discuss the different manifestations and stages of *People's Daily* in the construction of feudal "Pernicious-Vestiges" and reflect on which specific social classifications have been generated to determine its unique discourse function and social influence. It is thought-provoking that the feudal "Pernicious-Vestiges" appeared in different historical periods in the discourse practice of *People's Daily*. Its main contents and manifestations are as follows:

1 The stage of feudal "Pernicious-Vestiges" as an accomplice in class struggle (March 1947–September 1959): From the discourse point of view, feudalism in this stage is basically equated with "old society", and the concept connotation and extension of its opposition overlap, including bureaucracy, formalism,

sectarian disputes, male superiority to female inferiority, imperial examination system, and scholar bureaucrat education. At the same time, in the discourse system of "Three Mountains", it defines the meaning of some "old customs" together with "Pernicious-Vestiges of imperialism" and "Pernicious-Vestiges of (bureaucratic) capitalism".

2. The feudal "Pernicious-Vestiges" stage as a tool of "breaking the old and creating a new one" (June 1964–July 1974): As mentioned earlier, in this stage, feudal "Pernicious-Vestiges" became the derivative and foil of capitalist "Pernicious-Vestiges" and revisionist "Pernicious-Vestiges", and its content involved religion, four old things, the tradition of the exploiting class, following the beaten track and "The Way of Confucius and Mencius".

3. The feudal "Pernicious-Vestiges" as a substitute for the "Pernicious-Vestiges" of the Cultural Revolution (May 1978–April 1991): During the period of "bringing things right", there was a consensus between the "Pernicious-Vestiges" of feudalism, the "Pernicious-Vestiges" of the Cultural Revolution, the "Pernicious-Vestiges" of the Gang of Four, and even the "Pernicious-Vestiges" of the extreme "Left"'s thoughts. Relatively speaking, this stage is also the period when the connotation of feudal "Pernicious-Vestiges" has been fully explained. Its contents include the feudal fascist dictatorship, privileged thought, deciding everything by one man's say, paternalism, lifelong system, personal attachment, ignorance of the people, usurping the party and stealing the country, forming gangs, pretending to be crazy and self-sufficient, destroying the legal system, denying social division of labor, the idea of "great unification", the idea that officials are expensive and the people are cheap, the idea of imperial power/theocracy, blind exclusion, and seclusion. Since 1984, feudal "Pernicious-Vestiges" has gradually changed from co-appearing with the aforementioned three "Pernicious-Vestiges" narratives to a metonymic form that directly refers to social phenomena during the Cultural Revolution.

4. The period of feudal "Pernicious-Vestiges" in which revolution and "de-revolutionization" coexisted (February 1995–October 2012): After a short period of interruption, on February 23, 1995, *People's Daily* published an article entitled "On the Significance of Extensive Study in party constitution", which started with opposing "absolutism" and revived the feudal "Pernicious-Vestiges". At this stage, although the frequency of feudal "Pernicious-Vestiges" has decreased, its performance is full of internal tension. The object of the criticism of feudal "Pernicious-Vestiges" not only refers to the discourse direction of absolutism, absolute power, and personal worship, but it also includes the three cardinal principles and five permanent rules, Confucian tradition, male superiority over female inferiority, and father is superior to son; it also covers the personal moral field mentioned earlier.

5. Remodeling and redefining the discourse practice stage of feudal "Pernicious-Vestiges" (2012–present): Since the 18th National Congress of the Communist Party of China, anti-corruption has become the most important work in the Communist Party of China. At this stage, *People's Daily* published a total of 28 narrative articles about "Pernicious-Vestiges", of which 22 articles were

used to describe the far-reaching harm to the party discipline and the society caused by high-ranking officials and corruption cases. The factionalism is called "the Pernicious-Vestiges of feudal dock culture", and "corruption" is defined as "the cancer and maggot carbuncle that breed on the Party's body. If you don't have the courage to 'use the scalpel to yourself', it will be endless, nourishing carbuncle, and cause fatal harm to the Party" ("Fǎn fǔ bài: jué xīn hé yǒng qì bù kě huò quē 反腐败：决心和勇气不可或缺 [Anti-corruption: determination and courage are indispensable]", *People's Daily*, March 12, 2014, 07A). At this stage, on the one hand, the discourse of "legacy" continues the discourse direction of "feudal legacy"; on the other hand, it constructs China's current political discourse system.

It can be seen that the discourse of feudal "Pernicious-Vestiges" is constructed in the current stage of the times, and it has become one of the key areas in which many narrative modes and discourse strategies compete. Moreover, throughout the narration of feudal "Pernicious-Vestiges" in *People's Daily* since 1946, almost at every stage, there are other "Pernicious-Vestiges" discourses with similar meanings and expressions as narrative types. It can be judged that feudalism has gradually become an all-encompassing source of "Pernicious-Vestiges" because of its long history and protracted nature, and any social reality and ideology that is opposed can find the historical trace that the dominant discourse hopes to construct. Because of the all-inclusive of its ideographic system, not only does Dirlik (1996) claim that "revolutionary paradigm becomes specious", but we can't judge if the suppression of traditional "revival" by the narrative of feudal "Pernicious-Vestiges" can better serve the modernization process. Feudalism has become a time and space dimension that is almost "lost" in contemporary China historical discourse. As mentioned earlier, in this chapter we will make a detailed analysis of so-called feudalism, which has consistently played the role of "Pernicious-Vestiges" in the history of contemporary China, and the flowing group boundaries constructed by it.

Object and conspiracy of "class struggle" (1947–1959)

In the early days of *People's Daily*'s discourse of "Pernicious-Vestiges", the reason why feudal "Pernicious-Vestiges" became the most frequently used type of "Pernicious-Vestiges" was mainly due to its huge social mobilization potential contained in its seemingly all-encompassing meaning space. For example, in August 1947, *People's Daily* published an article signed as "Reference Room of this newspaper", which introduced the experience and achievements of the Chinese Communist Party's grievance movement during the civil war between the Kuomintang and the Communist Party. The "feudal remnants" further became a discourse resource to dig at the root and strengthen the fighting will of the troops:

> Make up your mind to dig at the root, find a way, and take revenge. This stage is an important key to turn grief into strength and raise personal animosity to public outrage . . . Where do you start to dig the root? Either start with class

relations, or evolved from social history; either start with the evolution from personal history, or from two different regimes . . . Many confused ideas of the masses' thoughts, and long-term feudal remnants, can be solved by uprooting and sweeping away . . . How can the enemy find revenge? After digging the roots, we must summarize these materials, hold a general meeting to inspire and mobilize revenge, and make up our minds to make plans . . . The movement can be further transferred to meritorious service competition. ("Sī chóu chéng gōng fèn tuán jié jiān jiǎng jūn, bù duì sù kǔ wā gēn yùn dòng jīng yàn jiè shào 私仇成公愤团结歼蒋军部队诉苦挖根运动经验介绍 [Personal enmity becomes public outrage, uniting and wiping out the Chiang army's troops to grievance and root out movement]", *People's Daily*, 2A, August 11, 1947)

By breaking the boundary between personal enmity and public anger, among the Chinese Communist Party troops, the fighting will of certain individuals who are "poor and exploited" has been further strengthened through the mobilization of "revenging personal enmity", while the "backward elements" who are middle peasants, small businessmen, young people who think they are not bitter, or who are not bitter compared with others, all began to cry at the first complaint. Whether it is this kind of clearly pointed "class suffering" or the "love suffering" of "how many young men and women suffer from marriage problems and even commit suicide" constructed by the article "Hūn yīn wèn tí de sān zhǒng cuò wù lùn diǎn 婚姻问题的三种错误论点 [Three wrong arguments about marriage problems]" published in the 4A of *People's Daily* on March 31, 1949, they are all classified as the result of the "Pernicious-Vestiges" of the feudal society. It also further shows that constructing the suffering "people" with a human discourse strategy, which makes them humanized and compassionate through tragic victim stories (Steimel, 2010), may trigger readers' empathy reactions such as guilt and betrayal and also give the "people" the opportunity to share their own stories, so as to gain listening and empowerment.

The discourse extension of "feudal remnants" can not only strengthens the boundary and mutual hatred between different economic classes during wartime propaganda, but it also lifts the solidarity based on class status at the bottom when grassroots democracy contradicts the "selfless" CPC inner-party discipline. In other words, the bottom-level unity that is not allowed will also become a kind of feudal "Pernicious-Vestiges". An article in *People's Daily* tells the experience of grassroots democracy construction in Handan, Hebei Province, China in April 1948:

In every concrete action, we should pay attention to breaking up various sectarian groups among farmers caused by the clan and neighborhood relations left over from the feudal society in the past. For example, when Zhao Zhuang elected members of the peasant association and the village government in order to break the "piecemeal doctrine", he broke the boundaries of the streets and cut in seats respectively; However, when compiling agricultural representative groups, they are not restricted by the past streets, and they are mixed. In the practice of pumping, filling, and evaluating the output, the method of disrupting the establishment and division of labor and cooperation was also adopted, and the remnants of "we share the same surname", "we share this place" and "we share this group" in feudal society were swept away.

("Jiàn lì jiàn quán mín zhǔ shēng huó, zhào zhuāng zhù yì chāi sàn zōng pài 建立健全民主生活 赵庄注意拆散宗派 [Establishing and perfecting democratic life Zhaozhuang pay attention to breaking up sects]", *People's Daily*, 1A, April 7, 1948)

From such a passage, it is not difficult to see that before the founding of New China in 1949, the meaning of "feudal remnants" was quite rich, and its purpose was to reorganize the society according to the CPC's idea. When necessary, the social classification boundaries of classes, clans, and communities should obey the boundaries stipulated by the ideal social order. As stated in this *People's Daily* article mentioned previously, "groups of the masses cannot be used to oppose groups of cadres in party member". Similarly, the article "Wěi bā zhǔ yì zhù zhǎng zōng pài jiū fēn, qīng yān sì gōng zuò zǔ jiǎn tǎo jīng yàn jiào xùn 尾巴主义助长宗派纠纷 青烟寺工作组检讨经验教训 [Lessons from the Review of Qingyansi Working Group on Tailism Contributing to Clanish Disputes]" published in the 1A on April 7, 1948, also attributed the elimination of the "clannish rift" to the establishment of the democratic government of the Communist Party of China and blamed the sectarian struggle between farmers in the upper and lower streets of Qingyansi Village, Wu'an District, Handan, on "bad cadres . . . stained with the Pernicious-Vestiges of feudal rulers" and reused the clannish sentiments of farmers in order to "consolidate their own position", thus completely reorganize the social unity in the liberated areas according to the design of social engineering.

After the founding of New China in October 1949, some subtle changes have taken place in the objects of feudal "Pernicious-Vestiges". For example, in an article published in the 1A of *People's Daily* on October 29th, there appeared such a statement:

> Shanghai is the area with the largest concentration of female workers, with light industry female workers accounting for almost 75% of the national light industry female workers. Therefore, to do a good job of female workers in Shanghai means to do a good job of most of the national female workers. The key to doing a good job in female workers' work is to carry out class education and equality education among male and female workers at first, and to break the patriarchal ideology reflected in the workers for thousands of years and the idea of relying on men to run trade unions reflected in female workers' minds. And gradually improve and organize worker welfare undertakings such as factory nurseries, laundry, workers' dormitories, public canteens, etc., so as to reduce the burden of female workers' housework and child-rearing; And train a large number of female cadres and activists to

participate in trade union work, and persuade and solicit a large number of even all female workers to join trade unions.

("Shàng hǎi fù dài huì tōng guò jīn hòu shàng hǎi fù nǚ gōng zuò de jué yì 上海妇代会通过今后上海妇女工作的决议 [Shanghai Women's Congress passes resolution on future women's work in Shanghai]", *People's Daily*, October 29, 1949, 1A)

According to the basic occupational composition of Shanghai women, this resolution discusses several different aspects of Shanghai women's work, including female workers, rural women in the suburbs, intellectual women, housewives, and unemployed and out-of-school women. However, it is worth noting that, as a kind of feudal "Pernicious-Vestiges", the preference for sons over daughters only appeared in the discussion on the work of female light industry workers. It seems that in Shanghai, China in 1949, there was no such way of thinking among farmers, intellectuals, and housewives, and these groups seem to have widely accepted the idea of equality between men and women. Combined with the context, it can be found that the feudal "Pernicious-Vestiges", which emphasizes that women workers prefer boys to girls and rely on men, actually serves the purpose of the Shanghai Women's Movement, which is "based on women workers, launching and organizing working women freely, striving for intellectual women, and uniting women from all walks of life". As an important indicator of the development of women's work, the number of women workers participating in trade unions is very important. Women's representative conferences from all walks of life in Shanghai will not hesitate to construct workers who hold the idea of "valuing men over women" and women workers who rely on men to run trade unions as carriers of feudal "Pernicious-Vestiges", and the divide the workers, who have long been the main solidarity force in the new democratic society, again to achieve the goal of "persuading and soliciting a large number of women workers to join trade unions".

As a part of achieving class equality, a major proposition of gender equality is that women participate in labor, which is highly consistent with the realistic task of requiring a large number of labor force to participate in construction at the beginning of the founding of New China. On October 23, 1950, *Hé Xiāngníng* 何香凝 published the article "Wèi le jiàn kāng de dì èr dài 为了健康的第二代 [For the second generation of health]" in the 3A of *People's Daily*, arguing that only by taking part in practical production work in the fields can women "get reasonable maintenance for their children", while opposing women's participation in production is the "Pernicious-Vestiges" of feudal bondage. An article published in the special edition of *Women's Day* in 1956 pointed out that "belittling the remnants of feudal thoughts of women" would bring more difficulties for women to be advanced than men. At the same time, this article pointed out the key purpose of advocating the elimination of feudal remnants at this point in time: "Strive to fulfill the individual workload stipulated in the national plan ahead of schedule and exceed the targets of the first five-year plan"; by stimulating individual initiative, make labor and self-realization serve the national planning and number management of the planned economic system ("Nǚ zhí gōng men, xiàng xiān jìn zhě kàn qí 女职工们，向先进者看齐 [Women workers, keep up with the advanced]", *People's Daily*, March 8, 1956, 3A).

The early days of the founding of the People's Republic of China were a period of concentrated promotion of women's status. Therefore, feudal "Pernicious-Vestiges" was frequently used to describe the concepts of valuing sons over daughters and suppressing freedom of marriage. Except for the article titled "Yī jù hūn yīn fǎ zhēng qǔ hūn yīn zì yóu 依据婚姻法争取婚姻自由 [Fighting for freedom of marriage according to marriage law]" published in the 3A of *People's Daily* on May 22, 1950, which once clearly defined the carrier of this "Pernicious-Vestiges" as "some cadres" who "led to the phenomenon of women being forced to commit suicide", the perpetrators of the "Pernicious-Vestiges of arranged marriage" mentioned in most articles may be husbands, in-laws, or even others. For example, on September 22, 1950, the 3A published the article "Jiāng xī pó yáng yī gè yuè qī gè fù nǚ bèi nüè dài zhì sǐ 江西鄱阳一个月七个妇女被虐待致死 [Seven women were abused to death in Poyang, Jiangxi Province in a month]" that tells a story where all four news elements are unclear. The author clearly stated in the article that the purpose of writing this article is "now I'll tell you some of the worst facts to attract everyone's attention". On October 22nd, the 3A published "Fēng jiàn hūn yīn zhì dù de yí dú! Liǎng fēng bào gào nüè shā tóng yǎng xí de lái xìn 封建婚姻制度的遗毒！两封报告虐杀童养媳的来信 ['Pernicious-Vestiges' of Feudal Marriage System! The two letters reporting the killing of child brides]". This article not only describe the killing of the daughter-in-law by her mother-in-law's beating and scolding, but it also explains the "Pernicious-Vestiges" of the feudal marriage system as "women are slaves and cattle and horses of feudal families". In the discourse construction of these feudal "Pernicious-Vestiges", it can be clearly observed that its function of appealing to emotion and mobilizing society takes precedence over verifying and reporting specific facts. As for the 3A of *People's Daily* published on October 15, 1951, the article "Zuì gāo rén mín fǎ yuan, sī fǎ bù guān yú jiǎn chá sī fǎ gàn bù sī xiǎng zuò fēng jí duì gān shè hūn yīn zì yóu shā hài fù nǚ de fàn zuì xíng wéi zhǎn kāi qún zhòng xìng sī fǎ dòu zhēng de zhǐ shì 最高人民法院，司法部 关于检查司法干部思想作风及对干涉婚姻自由杀害妇女的犯罪行为展开群众性司法斗争的指示 [Instructions of the Supreme People's Court and the Ministry of Justice on examining the thought and style of judicial cadres and launching mass judicial struggle against the crime of interfering with the freedom of marriage and killing women]" made the mass movement against this "Pernicious-Vestiges" reasonable by constructing "feudalism and its marriage system" instead of solving it through the construction of the rule of law, so as to make the efforts to cultivate modern citizens' awareness of the rule of law temporarily give way. This idea of using the discourse construction of "Pernicious-Vestiges" as a means of emotional mobilization and publicity is explained in the following:

> All parts of the country, except ethnic minority areas and areas where land reform has not yet been completed, should take March 1953 as the campaign month to publicize and implement the Marriage Law, regardless of cities or

villages. Within this month, we must fully mobilize the masses of men and women, especially women, to launch a mass movement with great momentum and scale, so as to make the Marriage Law a household name, deeply rooted in people's hearts and play a great role in changing customs. To this end, all localities should mobilize all propaganda forces and use various means to set off an upsurge of publicizing the Marriage Law in all factories, rural areas, institutions, schools and streets... In order to promote the movement, counties should be taken as units to select typical criminals who abuse women or interfere with the freedom of marriage, causing serious consequences and causing great public anger. After full preparation, people's courts are organized, public trial meetings are held, and public convictions are made according to law.

("Zhōng yāng rén mín zhèng fǔ zhèng wù yuàn guān yú guàn chè hūn yīn fǎ de zhǐ shì 中央人民政府政务院 关于贯彻婚姻法的指示 [Instructions of the Government Council of the Central People's Government on implementing the marriage law]", *People's Daily*, February 2, 1953, 1A)

It can be seen that the legal system construction of freedom of marriage in the early days of the People's Republic of China is also inseparable from the propaganda work and is even confused with it. It is also for this reason that "Pernicious-Vestiges" is frequently used as a rhetorical strategy that lacks strong evidence and only resorts to typical cases, emotions, and discourse illusions. It has long served the mobilized national governance and the construction of charismatic authority, thus gradually drifting away from the establishment of legal authority led by state institutions.

Another theme that has been strengthened by the discourse of feudal "Pernicious-Vestiges" is the pro-Soviet and anti-American movement that began in 1953, which is mainly manifested in the emphasis on engineering technology and its education in the intellectual circles. For example:

> Our national construction requires engineers who have graduated from universities to creatively solve practical problems. Our country's past education was colonial and semi-colonial education, and engineering education was no exception... Plus the Pernicious-Vestiges left to us by the scholar-bureaucrat education in feudal society, the education in the past institute of technology made a serious problem of being divorced from reality. But in the Soviet Union's teaching plan, theoretical study and practical work are closely combined... The Soviet Union has 35 years of experience in advanced socialist construction. Education in the Soviet Union meets the requirements of socialist countries. Chairman Mao called on us to learn from the Soviet Union... We believe that in the future work and study, we will gradually realize the essence and spirit of the Soviet academic system and apply it to our cause of cultivating talents.

("Zài xiū gǎi jiào xué jì huà guò chéng zhōng xué xí le xiē shén me 在修改教学计划过程中学习了些什么 [What I learned in the process of revising the teaching plan]", *People's Daily*, 3A, April 27, 1953, by Zhāng Wéi 张维, director of Tsinghua University Civil Engineering Department)

After the elimination of Yenching University's "Pernicious-Vestiges of American imperialism", Tsinghua University, another top university in China, was chosen as the object of discourse construction and transformation. What's different is that the source of funds used by the United States "Gengzi Refund" to build the predecessor of Tsinghua University has not been emphasized, but the historical background of running a school by the Qing government has been selectively intercepted. As a result, the expression of "Pernicious-Vestiges" has suddenly changed, and the "separation from reality" of engineering college education has become a bad influence of "education of scholars in feudal society". The key purpose of this discourse construction also serves a specific social function to be "pro-Soviet" in disciplines with application prospects, including biology and civil engineering. It is necessary to make the function of theoretical education in Chinese universities serve the actual construction of socialist countries like the Soviet Union.

In the efforts to change the dependent class, feudal "Pernicious-Vestiges" occasionally appears in the form of a more intuitive "exploiting class thought". For example, according to the 2A of *People's Daily* on May 16, 1957, Hú Yàobāng 胡耀邦, then the first secretary of the Central Committee of the Communist Youth League of China, on behalf of the 2nd Central Committee of the China New Democratic Youth League, made a report to the Third National Congress. The report said:

> For thousands of years, due to the influence of the exploiting class's contempt for labor, less than two years after the socialist transformation of our country was basically completed, and many young people in our country came from exploiting class families, the mentality of despising labor, especially physical labor, still exists among many young people in our country. We must further strengthen labor education for young people, continue to work hard to eliminate the ideological Pernicious-Vestiges of the exploiting class, and make this work a long-term task for us.
>
> ("Tuán jié quán guó qīng nián jiàn shè shè huì zhǔ yì de xīn zhōng guó 团结全国青年建设社会主义的新中国 [Unites the youth of the whole country to build a socialist New China]", *People's Daily*, 2A, May 16, 1957)

This report not only attributed "contempt for manual labor" to "the ideological Pernicious-Vestiges of the exploiting class", but it also constructed mental labor and manual labor as a watershed to divide the exploiting class from the exploited class. It also compared the time gap between feudal thought lasting for thousands of years and socialist transformation completed in less than 2 years, and it constructed a powerful mobilization force by resorting to sympathy, encouraging people to stand on the side of young but hopeful socialism by getting close to manual labor.

After years of calling for the elimination of feudal "Pernicious-Vestiges", this term even began to become a vocabulary consciously used by intellectuals. For example, Yè Gōngchuò 叶恭绰 was a scholar, calligrapher, and painter who had been widely involved in the fields of literature, history, and philosophy after the Qing Dynasty, the Beiyang Government, the National Government and the New China era. Yè Gōngchuò called Cantonese opera, which was despised by the cultural circles as a local style village opera but not studied, "a flaw in the drama circle" and attributed this phenomenon to "the Pernicious-Vestiges of feudalism, which hinders all progress, and drama is no exception" ("Lüè tán cháo hàn qióng jù de yuān yuan 略谈潮汉琼剧的渊源 [On the origin of Chaohan Qiong Opera]", *People's Daily*, May 30, 1957, 8A). Yè Gōngchuò was wrongly classified as a rightist in 1958, suffered persecution during the Cultural Revolution, and died of illness in 1968, although he donated a large number of calligraphy and painting cultural relics to the museum.

Tools for breaking old and creating new (1964–1974)

After the Great Leap Forward movement and the People's Commutation movement started around 1958, the criticism of the feudal "Pernicious-Vestiges" temporarily gave way to the construction and criticism of the private concept of a "Pernicious-Vestiges" of the bourgeoisie or the old society. This concept became the key obstacle to the establishment of the public system, resulting in a brief silence of the "Pernicious-Vestiges" discourse (see the corresponding section in Chapter 5 about the discourse direction of "Pernicious-Vestiges" from 1958–1963). In 1964, the discourse of feudal "Pernicious-Vestiges" began to recover gradually, and its typical application scenarios included normalizing the shop windows with feudal "Pernicious-Vestiges" in Beijing ("Shāng diàn chú chuāng bù kě xiǎo shì 商店橱窗不可小视 [Shop windows can't be neglected]", *People's Daily*, 2A, October 27, 1964). There are also articles that believe that Buddhism in Chinese history needs to be called upon to "dispel the evils of Buddhism in the Tang Dynasty" because it serves the "exploiting class" and has a "religious Pernicious-Vestiges" ("Fàn wén lán lùn shù táng cháo fó jiào de huò hài 范文澜论述唐朝佛教的祸害 [Fan Wenlan discusses the evils of Buddhism in the Tang Dynasty]", *People's Daily*, 5A, December 7, 1965, by Zhāng Zhìyàn 张智彦). These highly symbolic rather than structured "Pernicious-Vestiges" words also laid the groundwork for the upcoming Cultural Revolution.

In the early and middle period of the Cultural Revolution, the narrative of feudal "Pernicious-Vestiges" in *People's Daily* has been serving "dòu sī pī xiū 斗私批修 [Fight selfishness and criticize revisionism]" for a long time, and it was only abstracted as the expressions of "muddy water in the past" and "four old things". It was not until the late period of the Cultural Revolution that feudal "Pernicious-Vestiges" was added with "criticizing Lin and criticizing Confucius" as its discourse connotation. In 1966, the word "Pernicious-Vestiges", which had already become a common practice, and its discourse mobilization function were eagerly used in the initiation of the Cultural Revolution. The frequency and critical objects of "Pernicious-Vestiges" in *People's Daily* were basically faithfully reproduced and reflected the trend of the Cultural Revolution. Continuing the discussion about "Hǎi ruì bà guān 海瑞罢官 [Hai Rui's dismissal from office]" in the early period of the Cultural Revolution, on April 22, 1966, *People's Daily* published an article entitled "Nóng mín kàn tòu le 'qīng guān' de fǎn dòng běn zhì 农民看透了'清官'的反动本质 [Peasants see through the reactionary essence of 'honest officials']" reprinted from *Shaanxi Daily* on April 19th, 1966. The author was from 西北大学

半耕半读历史系 "the Department of Half-time Farming and Half-time Studying History of Northwest University" and signed Shǐ gēng 史耕. The article reads:

> Some peasants watched the play and listened to the story of "honest officials" and thought that there were honest officials who worked for peasants in feudal society . . . There was a vague understanding of the problem of "honest officials" among peasants, which reflected class struggle in the ideological field and a Pernicious-Vestiges of deception and propaganda by the exploiting class.

Consistent with the fuse of the Cultural Revolution, the order that this article tries to establish is also the eternal absolute opposition between the "exploiting class" and the "exploited class". Therefore, "there are good and bad officials" is constructed as "the Pernicious-Vestiges of feudal rule", thus opening up a space for the upcoming movement to be criticized by both officials and people.

In addition, the performance of feudal "Pernicious-Vestiges" is compared with the present, and it is also attributed by the Cultural Revolution culture to the achievement of becoming "Mao Zedong Thought". An article recounting the farmers' "learning and using the achievements of Chairman Mao's works" in Huangshandong, Boluo County, Guangdong Province, wrote:

> Now, in Huangshandong, it has become a common thing to "not pocket the money one picks up". In the past, it was common for husbands to beat their wives and worship God and believe in ghosts. Now, the remnants of "patriarchal power" and "divine power" left by these feudal patriarchal systems have been swept away. The elderly were gratified to see a memorial meeting and wreaths given to the dead in the village. Singing yellow folk songs and talking dirty words has become a "vulgar taste" that everyone resists. What is exciting now is reading red books and singing red songs. The revolutionary songs are loud everywhere in mountain villages. Don't underestimate these things. All old ideas, old culture, old customs and habits are drugs used by the exploiting class to deceive the people. Now, thanks to Mao Zedong Thought, a cultural revolution that wiped out the Pernicious-Vestiges of class society for thousands of years has begun in Huangshandong!
> ("Máo zé dōng sī xiǎng wēi lì wú qióng—guǎng dōng shěng bó luó xiàn huáng shān dòng nóng mín zài gé mìng huà de dào lù shàng fèn yǒng qián jìn 毛泽东思想威力无穷—广东省博罗县黄山洞农民在革命化的道路上奋勇前进 [Mao Zedong Thought's endless power—farmers in Huangshandong, Boluo County, Guangdong Province march forward bravely on the road of revolutionization]", *People's Daily*, 2A, August 27, 1966, the original edition of *Nanfang Daily*, with some deletions)

This article constructs the complete opposition between "new" and "old". All the old ones have become "Pernicious-Vestiges", while all the new ones are attributed to "Mao Zedong Thought", which presupposes the complete mutually exclusive relationship between socialist ideas and class society. This "contrast between the old and the new" made it necessary for the Cultural Revolution to oppose all the "old" that are different from a few "new" while opposing the feudal "Pernicious-Vestiges". For example,

> The Red Guards are trying to destroy the tradition of the landlord and bourgeoisie. Young revolutionaries, for the remnants of feudalism, the germs of capitalism, and the bane of revisionism, it is to eliminate, exterminate, and cut off. Only by thoroughly destroying all kinds of old traditions of the exploiting class can we inherit and carry forward the revolutionary tradition of the proletariat.
> ("Hóng wèi bīng zàn 红卫兵赞 [Praise of the Red Guards]", 2A of *People's Daily*, September 19, 1966, signed by the commentator of *Red Flag Magazine*).

Here, feudalism, capitalism, and revisionism have formed an intertextual relationship. They are all the concrete manifestations of residual poison, germs, and bane, and they all need to be thoroughly solved. Red guards not only need to oppose all "traditions", but they also need to oppose what is defined as the opposite of what they defend. If, as this article says, "Chairman Mao is our red commander, and we are Chairman Mao's little red soldiers," then, what they need to oppose is the whole world except Chairman Mao.

In the practice of the feudal "Pernicious-Vestiges" discourse of the Cultural Revolution, the scope of the object that was constructed to be opposed gradually expanded from the "tradition of landlord and bourgeoisie" to all traditions. An article in the *People's Daily*, which narrates how people in a commune in Ningxiang, Hunan Province learned from Chairman Mao's works, wrote:

> Mao Zedong Thought is deeply rooted in the hearts of the people, and the farmers in Hetang are determined to sweep away the Pernicious-Vestiges of the old society and build a new socialist countryside. In many members' homes, appraisal columns have been set up and merit books have been hung up. They use Mao Zedong Thought as the standard to measure all people. Now, everyone reads red books and sings revolutionary songs. Those old place names and names with feudal and bourgeois colors have been changed in batches. Feudal superstition, which has been poisoned for thousands of years, is being spurned by farmers. As early as the Spring Festival, the members learned "Where does the correct thought of man come from?" After that, the commune members automatically rose up and destroyed the statue of Bodhisattva and ancestral tablet.
> ("Diē qīn niáng qīn bù rú máo zhǔ xí qīn qiān hǎo wàn hǎo máo zhǔ xí zhù zuò dì yī hǎo—hé táng dà duì nóng mín huó xué huó yòng máo zhǔ xí zhù zuò jīng shén miàn mào huàn rán yī xīn 爹亲娘亲不如毛主席亲 千好万好毛主席著作第一好—荷塘大队农民活学活用毛主席著作精神面貌焕然一新 [Father and Mother are not as good as Chairman Mao's works—The Hetang Brigade farmers learn and use Chairman Mao's works to take on a new look]", *People's Daily*, 3A, September 22, 1966)

Here, if it is not certain that a certain cultural product is consistent with "Mao Zedong Thought", it seems that people should completely destroy it as "the pernicious influence of feudal superstition", including books, songs, place names, ancestors, and even their own names.

All these seemingly crazy actions are related to the slogan of "breaking the four old things" put forward in the Cultural Revolution in June 1966: "Completely breaking the old ideas, old cultures, old customs and habits that have poisoned the people for thousands of years caused by all the exploiting classes". It is this kind of "everything" that makes people regard the tradition in Chinese society as a scourge and avoid it. Literally, "breaking the four old things" and "establishing four new things" depend on each other, but the absence of how to "establish new things" makes people have to focus on the four old things, and the vague meaning of the four old things forces people to make enemies with all imaginary past things in a hurry. To avoid possible panic, in February 1967, *People's Daily* reprinted the news of Xinhua News Agency, saying that *Hú mǎ yún* 胡马云 *Homayoun*, an Urdu progressive monthly magazine published in New Delhi, India, published an article praising China's Cultural Revolution because "the goal of the cultural revolution is to eliminate another powerful enemy, that is, old ideas, old culture, old customs, and old habits—the Pernicious-Vestiges of the old feudal class and bourgeoisie and their ideology that are now dead" ("Yìn dù jìn bù kān wù zàn yáng wǒ guó wén huà dà gé mìng shēn yuǎn yǐng xiǎng 印度进步刊物赞扬我国文化大革命深远影响 [Indian progressive publications praised the far-reaching impact of China's Cultural Revolution]", *People's Daily*, 4A, February 13, 1967). Although this passage is familiar to people, under the restriction of international communication conditions at that time, we can hear the affirmation of this "Pernicious-Vestiges" from foreign countries, which is undoubtedly for. As to whether the situation is true or not, Chinese readers at that time would not and could not verify it.

In 1968, the Standing Committee of the Congress of Poor and Lower Middle Peasants in Tong County, Beijing, made a very naked statement with the help of "Pernicious-Vestiges", which seemed to be "breaking the old and establishing a new one", but the more practical purpose was to draw a clear line with the "old Beijing Municipal Committee", which was the first to be criticized during the Cultural Revolution:

> In 1965, the old Beijing Municipal Committee engaged in the illusion of "prosperity" of clubs in rural areas of our county, and dispatched a group of professional literary and art workers to squat in several villages to cultivate "top-notch". They also use literature and art to serve the workers, peasants and soldiers verbally, but in essence they use the "red flag" to counter the red flag. They didn't make a single pilot. The masses said, "Counseling, counseling, help and fall". After their so-called "counseling", there are no benefits, but many Pernicious-Vestiges. The old and bad plays of emperors and princes, talented people and beautiful women are even more powerful in ruling the rural cultural positions and poisoning the masses.
> ("Fā dòng qún zhòng miàn xiàng qún zhòng 发动群众 面向群众 [Mobilizing the masses to face the masses]", *People's Daily*,
> 4A, May 23, 1968)

The discourse style constructed by "Pernicious-Vestiges", which is completely separated from the past, is very suitable for the dichotomy between the enemy and the friend and the logic of loyalty in the Cultural Revolution, so it is common in *People's Daily* at this stage. Since then, the vocabulary of "Pernicious-Vestiges" has been used to serve the overwhelming "counter-revolutionary revisionist line", except for the minority areas, which are subject to poor information channels, the Pernicious-Vestiges of feudalism, capitalism, and revisionism is still being used ("Lái zì shǎo shù mín zú dì qū de yì jiàn 来自少数民族地区的意见 [Opinions from minority areas]", *People's Daily*, 3A, June 21, 1969, signed by the Education of the Revolutionary Committee of Qiandongnan Miao and Dong Autonomous Prefecture, Guizhou Province), as well as a few unthinking, empty, and even absurd slogans (such as "educational thoughts of closing, funding and cultivating for thousands of years", "Jiào yù gé mìng shì yī chǎng shēn kè de shè huì dà gé mìng 教育革命是一场深刻的社会大革命 [Educational Revolution is a profound social revolution]", *People's Daily*, 3A, November 8, 1969, by the Revolutionary Committee of Qinyang County, Henan Province). The word feudal "Pernicious-Vestiges" was used between 1969 and 1976. It wasn't until 1978, after the Cultural Revolution, that *People's Daily* resumed the construction of anti-feudal "Pernicious-Vestiges" discourse that had been interrupted for 10 years ("Science and democracy", *People's Daily*, 2A, May 4, 1978). In this article, not only did the long-lost words "Pernicious-Vestiges of feudal society and semi-feudal and semi-colonial society" reappear, but what's even more commendable is that the monopoly of "Pernicious-Vestiges" was different than before.

Substitutes for the Cultural Revolution "Pernicious-Vestiges" (1978–2012)

After the end of the Cultural Revolution, modern China entered a more difficult stage of reevaluating history. This is because the manipulation of ideology during the Cultural Revolution reached a crazy level. Accordingly, restoring the order before this farce and reconstructing "them" as "us" will inevitably require a high degree of reliance on previously established ideas and verbal inertia. Otherwise such efforts will not succeed. Thus, since 1978, we have seen a strange picture in *People's Daily*. The propaganda workers used the construction of "Pernicious-Vestiges", which was as strong as the wording during the Cultural Revolution, and persistently reshaped the initiator of the Cultural Revolution as "Pernicious-Vestiges" itself. As the "enemy"–"counter-revolutionary revisionist line" set up in the Cultural Revolution is almost all-encompassing, the propagandists can only look for the ideas that the current "enemy" has not mentioned or rarely mentioned as the concrete manifestation of the ideological illegitimacy of the initiators of the Cultural Revolution. At this time, feudal "Pernicious-Vestiges" has become one of the few words to choose from. At the same time, efforts against the "Pernicious-Vestiges" of the Cultural Revolution and the "Pernicious-Vestiges" of feudalism began.

On November 13, 1978, *People's Daily* reprinted an article published in the third issue of 1978 of 《中国青年》 *China Youth Magazine*, the central organ of the China Communist Youth League, with the title of "Promoting Democracy and Strengthening the Legal System". Although the title and diction still carry the discourse style of the Cultural Revolution, the authors Lín chūn 林春 and Lǐ yín hé 李银河 boldly put forward the equivalent relationship that the "Pernicious-Vestiges" of the Gang of Four is the "Pernicious-Vestiges" of feudalism:

> China's feudal ideology is so tenacious, not only because it has a history of more than 2,000 years, but also because the imperial power has not been profaned and arrogated as in Europe, and not only because the new social system was directly born out of a semi-colonial and semi-feudal country with extremely low productivity, but also because the conditions for its survival still exist in the real society. At present, China's social productive forces are still very backward, with a large amount of manual labor, a low commodity rate of agricultural production, and a low degree of socialization, division of labor and specialization of industrial production. This makes the majority of the people still stay in the backward material and cultural life, and makes the feudal ideology often appear as "socialism", and continue to smell like a corpse. Don't the "theories" and policies promoted by Lin Biao and the Gang of Four have a strong color of feudal socialism? Up to now, people's consciousness is still widespread, that is, when they hear the words "democracy" and "freedom", they become silent and regard them as "heresy". Therefore, it is necessary to start a new enlightenment and ideological emancipation movement and make a thorough liquidation of the feudal tradition and ideology. Chinese nation had great abilities originally! Following the epoch-making victory of the China Revolution in 1949, the world-famous victory of smashing the Gang of Four also has epoch-making significance, and China has thus entered a new period of historical development. Although socialist democracy and legal system have gone through a tortuous road, they have an infinite bright future.
>
> ("Yào dà dà fā yáng mín zhǔ hé jiā qiáng fǎ zhì 要大大发扬民主和加强法制 [To greatly promote democracy and strengthen the legal system]", *People's Daily*, 3A, November 13, 1978, with some modifications)

Combined with the full text, the meaning of "feudal ideology" is interpreted as "autocracy", "oligarchy", and "dictatorship". Not only that, but this article also points out that the reason why China could not get rid of feudalism or "autocracy" in all historical periods, including the Cultural Revolution, is China's industrialization degree, professional division of labor, and accumulation of social wealth were always insufficient. Besides continuing to develop social productive forces and people's material and cultural life, the solution needed "new enlightenment and ideological emancipation movement", and it needed "socialist democracy and legal system" to guarantee the system level to avoid the recurrence of the "Cultural

Revolution" tragedy. These candid warnings were not only applicable to China in 1978, but at the time when this book was written, the echo of history was still ringing.

Generally speaking, the discourse construction of feudal "Pernicious-Vestiges" in the early period of reform and opening up is mainly used to "break the old" rather than "create new ones". Some texts further reveal why Cultural Revolution "Pernicious-Vestiges" is equivalent to feudal "Pernicious-Vestiges". For example, in the Cultural Revolution, a large number of "unjust, false and wrong cases" that affected family members, relatives, and friends were called the influence of "the Pernicious-Vestiges of the feudal Zhulian law" ("'Zhū lián' xiǎo yì '株连' 小议 [On Zhulian]", *People's Daily*, 3A, January 26, 1979, by Suí xǐ wén 隋喜文). The "theory of blood lineage" is called the "feudal Pernicious-Vestiges" and the "evil wind of Lin Biao and the Gang of Four" ("Wéi rào xuè tǒng lùn wèn tí de yī cì tán huà 围绕血统论问题的一次谈话 [A talk about the problem of blood lineage]", *People's Daily*, 3A, February 19, 1979, by Hú sī shēng 胡思升). During the Cultural Revolution, "it was not allowed to address leaders as 'comrades', and all the titles of presidents except the chairman of the CPC Central Committee were abolished" was called "engage in modern superstition and deify leaders". It is compared with the "taboo" habit of forbidding monarchs, sages, and elders to call them by their first names or comment on their faults in the feudal dynasty of China, which is called "obvious feudal Pernicious-Vestiges" ("Shuō "huì" 说"讳" [On taboo]", *People's Daily*, 3A, December 11, 1979, by Zhōu xiū qiáng 周修强), and so on. The creativity of these articles in establishing the connection between concepts reflects the profound change of people's historical attribution thinking in the early days of reform and opening up.

What needs to be acknowledged is that some articles have constructed the return of feudal "Pernicious-Vestiges" as the crime of the Cultural Revolution destroying the social atmosphere, such as:

> Marriage is the Pernicious-Vestiges of feudal landlords and bourgeoisie. After liberation, through a large-scale campaign to publicize the Marriage Law and the joint efforts of all sectors of society, this unhealthy trend has basically stopped. Due to the destruction of Lin Biao and the Gang of Four, the social atmosphere deteriorated, the "four old things" revived, and sales and arranged marriages grew.
> ("Yī dìng yào zá suì mǎi mài hūn yīn de jiā suǒ 一定要砸碎买卖婚姻的枷锁 [We must break the shackles of mercenary marriage]",
> *People's Daily*, February 13, 1979, 4A)

In fact, as an important task in the Cultural Revolution, "breaking the four old things" can only be implemented poorly, but there is no suggestion that the Gang of Four deliberately resumed buying and mercenary marriage. Although the article is committed to restoring the order before the Cultural Revolution, such a fabrication of "crime" is no different from the Gang of Four, and it also lacks solid evidence.

This shows that the restoration of social order may take a longer time and more patience than destructive events.

Dirlik (1996) once criticized the view of mainstream American historians that "the modernization paradigm won in China in the competition with the revolutionary paradigm in 1970s" was inaccurate. He pointed out sharply that the modernization paradigm did not really win an overwhelming victory, otherwise, this victory would not be replaced by the temporary "teleology" again and again. The discovery in this book also confirms Dirlik's judgment on the whole. If the "revolution" is the continuous reconstruction of social stratum distribution, then until the end of the Cultural Revolution, this motive force remains in the efforts to mold the Cultural Revolution into a feudal "Pernicious-Vestiges", especially in the discourse construction of anti-political privileged class in the name of anti-feudalism. For example:

> On top of the fascism of the Gang of Four, the word "feudalism" is very characteristic of "national legacy". The remnants and stench of feudalism are often prominent in the education of cadres' children. For example, some people seek to show off their family status, some people hope that their relatives and followers can be promoted after they become senior officials, some people work hard and hope that their children and grandchildren will not work hard, some people seek benefits for future generations in order to get back more money, and some people want family members to become officials so as to protect each other. What class do these ideas belong to? Are these ideas imported? I don't think so. It's more like "ancestral". The central idea of the above manifestations is nothing more than this word: hereditary. Although the next generation cannot inherit status, rank and salary, for some people with privileged thoughts, property power can be hereditary as much as possible. This is undoubtedly their wish-other means of subsistence, housing, money, etc., and it is best to pass it down from generation to generation . . . The hereditary thought of feudal privilege invaded the fighting communist party. It is not strange to say that this is a pile of heavy historical dross.
>
> ("Jiào zǐ piān—dú Jìng gào fù mǔ men bù yào yí wù zǐ nǚ qián túyǒu gǎn 教子篇—读《敬告父母们不要贻误子女前途》有感 [Thoughts on teaching children—reading 'warn parents not to mislead their children's future']", *People's Daily*, 4A, May 8, 1979, by Shū zhǎn 舒展)

In fact, since 1979, the society of China has been faced with the anti-"Pernicious-Vestiges" project, which is much richer than that in the early stage of the socialist revolution. The objects that need to be reflected include feudalism and the "old society" that have existed for a long time, and efforts should be made to eliminate the influence of the Gang of Four, the Cultural Revolution, and extreme "Left" thoughts that have just been experienced. At the same time, the seemingly paradoxical ideological landscape of persevering in the struggle against "revisionism" and capitalism seems to have given the answer to the choice of the historical paradigm of modern China: It may be either still dominated by the revolution or a "post-revolutionary history" in which revolution and modernization coexist. But one thing is certain; the historical view reflected by the discourse practice of "Pernicious-Vestiges" not only did not oppose the revolution, but it even inherited the discourse construction and "thought work" mode of "Pernicious-Vestiges" from the beginning to the end. Naturally, it was more in line with the revolutionary paradigm, and it also reflected from the side that the judgment of "modern historical paradigm" represented by the "two 30-year" argument was completely defeated. On the whole, although the appearance of feudal "Pernicious-Vestiges" has become ambiguous at this stage, its performance is full of internal tension. The objects of its criticism not only involve the cultural and political fields but also the personal moral fields, and it ultimately point to the political system.

Part of the discourse construction of feudal "Pernicious-Vestiges" also focuses on "establishing a new foundation". In the field of rule of law, after reviewing the decline of law and discipline caused by the Cultural Revolution for 10 years, an article pointed out that we should "resolutely implement equality before the law", thoroughly criticize, and eliminate "the feudal Pernicious-Vestiges that human feelings are greater than the king's law and officials protect each other" ("Xióng yī fú de sǐ gěi wǒ men de jiào xùn 熊一福的死给我们的教训 [Lessons from Xiong Yifu's death]", People's Daily, 3A, October 27, 1979). In the field of literature and art, there are articles that compare the cause of the Cultural Revolution to "the rulers of feudal society like flattery and listen to the words of treacherous officials and eunuchs and empresses". To eliminate the remnants of Lin Biao and the Gang of Four's ultra-left line, we should "vigorously eliminate the remnants of feudal society", which shows that we should avoid "using bold letters in newspapers and magazines in large quantities and quoting quotations in a distorted way . . . asking for instructions and dancing loyalty dance. Never describe a flaw", so as to "truly reflect people's life and express people's joys and sorrows" ("Fán róng wén yì bì xū sù qīng fēng jiàn liú dú 繁荣文艺必须肃清封建流毒 [To prosper literature and art, we must eliminate feudal Pernicious-Vestiges influence]", People's Daily, 3A, December 17, 1979, by Ài wú 艾芜). In the field of enterprise management, some articles refer to "the blind command of leading cadres that violates the principle of scientific management" as "the Pernicious-Vestiges of feudal paternalistic leadership" and advocate that socialist enterprises should implement democratic management. Through the conclusion that democratic management itself is a kind of scientific management, democracy and science are regarded as social ideals after the "Pernicious-Vestiges" has been eliminated ("Qǐ yè mín zhǔ guǎn lǐ de wèn tí 企业民主管理的问题 [Problems of democratic management of enterprises]", People's Daily, 5A, January 14, 1980, by Lín pī 林丕). In the field of political life, some articles further clarify the "democracy" that we hope to pursue as "socialist democracy" to distinguish it from "bourgeois democracy" and define healing the wounds caused by the "ten-year catastrophe" as a major task of cleaning up the remnants of feudal autocracy. Otherwise, people will "have doubts about the party and the socialist system, and make bourgeois democratic thoughts take advantage of it". By "establishing a new foundation", it is emphasized that "dilapidated" needs firm determination and policy repetition must be avoided ("Jiān chí shè huì zhǔ yì mín zhǔ de zhèng què fāng xiàng 坚持社会主义民主的正确方向 [Adhering to the correct direction of socialist democracy]", *People's Daily*, January 21, 1980, 1A). The reflection and criticism on the "Pernicious-Vestiges" of feudalism has gradually revived in all fields of social life in China and gradually stepped out of the routine of slogan and formulaic, which has a clear realistic direction. The discourse construction of "Pernicious-Vestiges" has gradually enriched and become full.

After the reform and opening up, Chinese society inevitably began to face such problems as how to view its relationship with the outside world and how to rethink the similarities and differences between the Chinese and western cultures. This adds more diverse connotations to the feudal "Pernicious-Vestiges". It has been pointed out that blind arrogance and inferiority are not conducive to national self-esteem and modernization reform. These two ideas are the remnants of the feudal patriarchal society and the Cultural Revolution and should be discarded ("Zǒu chū "wèi zhuāng" zhī hòu 走出"末庄"之后 [After going out of the Wei village]", *People's Daily*, June 17, 1980, 8A, by Sòng zhì jiān 宋志坚). This kind of articles that construct the discourse of feudal "Pernicious-Vestiges" have the commonness in that they not only take "developing productive forces" as the goal to break the feudal "Pernicious-Vestiges" but also regard it as a means: "Only when the social productive forces are highly developed, the people's scientific and cultural level is greatly improved, and the socialist system is more perfect, can the feudal ideological Pernicious-Vestiges be completely eradicated from our party and our society" ("Fēng jiàn zhǔ yì sī xiǎng yí dú yīng gāi sù qīng 封建主义思想遗毒应该肃清 [The feudalism Pernicious-Vestiges should be eliminated]", *People's Daily*, 5A, July 18, 1980). The elimination of feudal "Pernicious-Vestiges" and the development of social productive forces have become a set of fixed conceptual relationships that frequently appear in China after the reform and opening up.

On the broad cultural level, feudalism is a contradiction. The history of China, which stretches for more than 2,000 years, determines the deep influence of feudal culture. Stratification of culture has become one of the important issues of all the revolutions in modern China. Promoting the modernization process of China will inevitably involve the choice of new and old cultures. Therefore, from the Westernization movement of 19th century, to the Revolution of 1911, the May 4th movement, and the Socialist Revolutionary movement, including the Cultural Revolution after the founding of the People's Republic of China, all involved the judgment and choice of traditional feudal cultural values. Among them, the Cultural Revolution is different from other movements in that it even carried out large-scale destruction and elimination of feudal culture. The reality is that traditional culture has become an important part of Chinese society, including interpersonal relationship, social ideological trend, literary and artistic development, and so on. Therefore, it is a solution to take the essence and discard the dross. The judgment of "essence" and "dross" becomes the key to distinguish if it is feudal "Pernicious-Vestiges". This idea is reflected in the discourse construction of feudal "Pernicious-Vestiges" in *People's Daily* after the reform and opening up, in a more specialized social field, is used to advocate "a new style of funeral through thrift" ("Jiě fàng jūn bào Fā biǎo píng lùn yuán wén zhāng, biǎo yáng wáng jiàn ān tóng zhì jí qí jiā shǔ zàn jié yuē cóng jiǎn bàn sāng shì de xīn fēng《解放军报》发表评论员文章表扬王建安同志及其家属 赞节约从俭办丧事的新风 [People's Liberation Army Daily published a commentator's article praising Comrade Wang Jian' an and his family for the new style of funeral through thrift]", *People's Daily*, 1A, August 5, 1980). Sometimes, it calls on people to reduce their criticism of lawyers, so as to promote the institutionalization of lawyers' defense work ("Guān yú zhōng huá rén mín gòng hé guó lǜ shī zàn xíng tiáo lì de jǐ diǎn shuō míng 关于《中华人民共和国律师暂行条例》的几点说明 [Notes on the provisional regulations of People's Republic of China lawyers]", *People's Daily*, 4A, August 29, 1980, by Lǐ yùn chāng 李运昌, the first deputy minister of the Ministry of Justice of the People's Republic of China). The distinction between "essence" and "dross" also advocates the restoration of social division of labor by criticizing the phenomenon of "monopolizing power" as "the Pernicious-Vestiges of feudal autocracy's 'unification' ideology" ("Quán lì bù néng guò fèn jí zhōng 权力不能过分集中 [Power cannot be excessively concentrated]", *People's Daily*, 5A, Nov. 14, 1980). In other situation, it may cite Lysenkoism's harm to scientific research in the Soviet political movement and academic criticism, considered that "interfering in scientific academic issues by administrative means alone" was a kind of "feudal Pernicious-Vestiges", and advocated that the right to judge scientific achievements should be returned to the intellectual community itself ("Kē xué gōng zuò zhě zuò tán kē xué chéng guǒ píng jià hé rén cái kǎo hé wèn tí 科学工作者座谈科学成果评价和人才考核问题 [Scientific Workers' Symposium on Scientific Achievement Evaluation and Talent Assessment]", *People's Daily*, December 18, 1980, 3A).

In the larger field of social life, the discourse of feudal "Pernicious-Vestiges" can be used to coordinate the internal consistent relationship between "eliminating feudal Pernicious-Vestiges" and "opposing bourgeois ideology" because "feudal ideology is the backer of China's bourgeois ideology" and, if "opposing hypothetical capitalism with feudal practices", it will actually protect real capitalism and damage socialism ("Sī xiǎng zhàn xiàn yī gè zhòng yào de rèn wù 思想战线一个重要的任务 [An important task of the ideological front]", *People's Daily*, 5A, August 28, 1980). Another article pointed out that "the contention of a hundred schools of thought is only attributed to the contention of the proletariat and the bourgeoisie" is actually a kind of feudal "Pernicious-Vestiges", thus further broadening the space for multiple expressions ("Bǎi jiā zhēng míng shí jì shàng shì 'liǎng jiā zhēng míng' ma? 百家争鸣实际上是'两家争鸣'吗? [The contention of a hundred schools of thought is actually 'the contention of two schools'?]", *People's Daily*, 5A, October 24, 1980). It even more bluntly criticized the defense that the superstition and blind obedience in the Cultural Revolution were interpreted as "simple class feelings", arguing that the so-called "simple class feelings" also had feudal color and were also the remnants of feudalism in the mind ("'Pǔ sù gǎn qíng' bù yī dìng pǔ sù' 朴素感情'不一定朴素 ['Simple feelings' are not necessarily simple]", *People's Daily*, October 27, 1980, 5A, by Wáng gōng xī 王功熹) and put forward that "the task of eliminating the Pernicious-Vestiges of feudalism" lies in "abolishing the lifelong system of leading posts of cadres" ("Dǎng hé guó jiā lǐng dǎo zhì dù de yī xiàng zhòng yào gǎi gé 党和国家领导制度的一项重要改革 [An important reform of the party and state leadership system]", *People's Daily*, 5A, October 28, 1980). Since then, the discourse construction of feudal "Pernicious-Vestiges" has actually appeared and served in various scenes of China's reconstruction of modern order.

In the revolutionary era, Mao Zedong put forward a similar solution of the principle of "making the past serve the present". The so-called "making the past serve the present" is a general formulation of critically transforming and inheriting excellent traditions from the viewpoint of historical materialism to promote revolutionary culture and literary and artistic development. It contains the unity of opposites of two interrelated aspects. On the one hand, it is necessary to admit the most basic fact: "Today's China is a development of historical China; We are Marxist historians, and we should not cut off history", while our nation has thousands of years of history, its characteristics and many valuable things, and we must learn from and inherit this heritage seriously; on the other hand, our learning and inheritance should never be bogged down, but "give a critical summary with Marxist methods" (Mao, 1938/1991, pp. 533–534). This judgment principle has been used up until now; the theoretical article of *People's Daily* stated that "the principle of 'making the past serve the present' put forward by Comrade Mao Zedong is still the only correct principle for us to treat traditional culture and literature and art", and combined with the current situation, it was explained:

> China is a country with more than 2,000 years of feudal tradition. The influence of feudalism is almost everywhere and deeply rooted. The victory of the revolution in 1949, though politically overthrowing the three mountains that had been weighing on the people of China for a long time, was not so easy to eliminate the feudal Pernicious-Vestiges of thousands of years. Today, all kinds of backward feudal stereotypes and bad habits are flooding again in the land of China, which forms a strong contrast and sharp contrast with our ever-changing modernization process, which cannot but arouse our due attention and vigilance. This fact also poses a severe challenge to our cultural workers, that is, in the study and inheritance of traditional culture, we must unswervingly criticize the pernicious influence of feudalism and adhere to the principle of making the past serve the present. We must not absorb the dross and the essence, distinguish the good from the bad, or even turn right from wrong, thus contributing to the growth of feudal backward thoughts. In recent years, with the promotion of traditional culture, while adhering to historical materialism and the principle of "making the past serve the present", in a few studies, there has been a phenomenon that should not be seen:

instead of taking its essence and discarding its dross, it is doing the opposite, beautifying and eulogizing the feudal and backward dross in the name of "carrying forward". In the recent upsurge of Confucianism and Chinese studies, people have seen this kind of situation more than once, and even the feudal superstition of "fortune telling" has become the object of "carrying forward", which echoes the spread of feudal stereotypes and bad habits in society. We have to face up to this reality.

("Guān yú 'gǔ wéi jīn yòng' de wèn tí 关于'古为今用'的问题 [On 'Making the Past Serve the Present']", *People's Daily*, October 17, 1995, 10A)

In this theoretical article, the author returns the critical perspective to the period of socialist revolution and thinks that the victory of revolution is a political victory, while it is an unfinished project in the revolutionary era to overcome and eliminate the feudal "Pernicious-Vestiges" of thousands of years. Therefore, the solution is to return to Marx's dialectical materialism and adopt Mao Zedong's revolutionary cultural guiding principle of "making the past serve the present" to selectively clean up the "pernicious influence" of feudalism.

Another thing worthy of attention is the continuation of the discussion on "truth standard". The third plenary session of the eleventh central committee of the CPC held at the end of 1978 decided to shift the work center of the Party from taking class struggle as the key link to socialist modernization. The meeting affirmed:

> Only when the comrades of the whole party and the people of the whole country emancipate their minds under the guidance of Marxism–Leninism and Mao Zedong Thought, make efforts to study new situations, new things and new problems, and adhere to the principle of seeking truth from facts, proceeding from reality and integrating theory with practice, can our party successfully realize the transformation of its work center, correctly solve the specific road, principles, methods and measures for realizing the four modernizations, and correctly reform the production relations and superstructure that are incompatible with the rapid development of productive forces.

As to the essence of the discussion on the criterion of truth, Deng Xiaoping pointed out in his article "Emancipating the mind, seeking truth from facts, uniting and looking forward" that this discussion "is actually a debate on whether to emancipate the mind" and "is an ideological line issue, a political issue, and a problem related to the future and destiny of the party and the country" (Deng, 1978/1994, p. 143).

It can be seen from this that the discussion of truth standard is a phased project of reflection and reconstruction; through this discussion, Chinese society can face up to the mistakes in the Cultural Revolution and realize the reflective work of "de-revolutionizing" social thought. At the same time, adjusting the CPC's line and policy through ideological discussion is essentially a new revolution, a revolution of socialist modernization. This new wave of constructive revolution continues to this day, extending to the nationalist revolution of the "Chinese dream" and "realizing the great rejuvenation of the Chinese nation". At the same time, the debate at the ideological level ultimately points to bringing order out of chaos at the institutional level while the wrong route is still classified as the "Pernicious-Vestiges" of feudal absolutism:

> Practice is authoritative. However, it is far from enough to adhere to the practice standard in work and only rely on people's ideological understanding to guarantee it. It is weak and must be guaranteed by the authority of system and law. China is a country with a long feudal history. It is not easy to eliminate the ideological and political Pernicious-Vestiges of long-term feudal absolutism. In the past, one of the fundamental reasons for our party's deviation from the correct ideological line in the overall situation, which led to the wrong political line, was that we failed to institutionalize and legalize the democracy within the party and the democracy in the political and social life of the country, or that although laws were enacted, they did not have due authority. In order to implement the practice standard, besides advocating the democratic spirit, it is more important to work hard on the system construction, and truly establish an authoritative mechanism that can ensure the scientific and democratic decision-making. Besides the operational mechanism that can be operated, there should also be a mechanism to supervise the implementation, so that what has been proved to be wrong by practice can be found, put forward, and corrected, and what has been proved to be correct by practice can be adhered to, maintained, and continued to be implemented, so as to achieve the state of "not changing due to the change of leaders, not changing due to the change of leaders' attention and views". This is the task of political system reform and the construction of socialist democracy and legal system.
>
> ("Zhēn lǐ biāo zhǔn tǎo lùn de yì yì hé qǐ shì 真理标准讨论的意义和启示 [The significance and enlightenment of the discussion of truth standards]", *People's Daily*, 10A, May 14, 1998)

In the aforementioned article, the "Pernicious-Vestiges" of "feudal absolutism" implies that during the Cultural Revolution, Mao Zedong enlarged and absolutized the class struggle in socialist society and criticized many correct things as capitalism and that subjectivism and personal arbitrariness became increasingly serious. In other words, the autocratic behavior of political leaders during the Cultural Revolution was classified as "the Pernicious-Vestiges of feudal autocracy" when the road was re-planned in the new period. Calling the words of "Pernicious-Vestiges" is a strategy of de-revolutionizing. At the same time, the "system construction" mentioned in this paper is considered as the task of political system reform and socialist democracy and legal system construction, and its essence is the embodiment of rebuilding new system and road revolution.

112 *Developing from nothing*

Therefore, the debate on the ideological level essentially rests on the political level of system construction. Here, the ambiguous area between "de-revolutionization" and revolutionization of the reorganization of the political line program—how to face the mistakes in the past revolution and open the present and the future on the premise of the past—has become the key to the official discourse propaganda strategy. In 1980, Deng Xiaoping pointed out in his speech at the enlarged meeting of the Political Bureau of the Central Committee that it was necessary to draw a clear line between socialism and feudalism, the "Pernicious-Vestiges of feudalism", and the past mistakes of the ruling party, which also provided a plan for how to "de-revolutionise" on the premise of ensuring the absolute authority and legitimacy of the socialist system and the ruling party:

> First of all, it is necessary to draw a clear line between socialism and feudalism, and it is absolutely not allowed to oppose socialism in the name of anti-feudalism, nor to engage in feudalism with the false socialism advocated by the Gang of Four. Secondly, we should draw a clear line between the democratic essence and feudal dross in cultural heritage. It is also necessary to draw a clear line between the Pernicious-Vestiges of feudalism and some unscientific methods and unsound systems arising from lack of experience in our work. Don't be a gust of wind again, and describe everything as feudalism without analysis.
> ("Dǎng hé guó jiā lǐng dǎo zhì dù de gǎi gé 党和国家领导制度的改革 [Reform of the leadership system of the Party and the State]", *People's Daily*, August 18, 1980, 1A, by Deng Xiaoping)

In 2004, *People's Daily* published a theoretical article ("Xué xí dèng xiǎo píng mín zhǔ fǎ zhì sī xiǎng fā zhǎn shè huì zhǔ yì mín zhǔ zhèng zhì 学习邓小平民主法制思想 发展社会主义民主政治 [Learning Deng Xiaoping's thought of democracy and legal system to develop socialist democratic politics]", *People's Daily*, September 13, 2004), which reiterated Deng Xiaoping's viewpoint on how to define feudalism and feudal "Pernicious-Vestiges". The following is also one of the typical official strategies—affirming the whole, denying the parts, and attributing the partial mistakes to the "Pernicious-Vestiges" of feudal culture, so that the past can bear the mistakes:

> In the past 29 years, our party has rich and precious experience and profound and painful lessons. For the latter, the reasons are multiple and complicated. Specifically, there are the following points: First, our party has been in power for a short time, lacks the experience and ideological and theoretical preparation of governing the country and large-scale socialist construction, and has not correctly understood and grasped its objective laws. We don't fully understand what socialism is and how to build it. Second, the democratic system within the Party is imperfect, the principle of democratic centralism is

gradually being destroyed, and there are some phenomena in the Party, such as excessive concentration of power, paternalism, tenure of leading positions of cadres, personal arbitrariness, and personal worship. Our country's legal system is not perfect, and some feudal ideological Pernicious-Vestiges has not been eliminated. Third, after the victory of the revolution, the party and some of its leaders developed a sense of pride and complacency to a certain extent, and appeared to be divorced from the masses. Fourth, the pressure caused by the external unfavorable environment made us make inaccurate judgments and overreactions to the international situation for a period of time, and so on. Lessons learned from the past can guide one in the future. We should firmly remember and always remember the experience and lessons gained through 29 years' heavy cost.

("Cóng dǎng de lì shǐ zhōng jí qǔ qián jìn de zhì huì hé lì liàng—dú 《 zhōng guó gòng chǎn dǎng lì shǐ 》 dì èr juàn (1949–1978) 从党的历史中汲取前进的智慧和力量—读《中国共产党历史》第二卷 (1949–1978) [Drawing forward wisdom and strength from the history of the Party-Reading the History of communist party, China, Volume II (1949–1978)]", *People's Daily*, 11A, January 18, 2011)

Although since 1989, the public opinion volume of "Pernicious-Vestiges" has gradually decreased in the official discourse system represented by *People's Daily*, its narrative strategy of "opposing the past" is still the inheritance of the revolutionary discourse system. As summarized by Dirlik (1996), "even if the revolution is rejected, the historical Pernicious-Vestiges of the revolution will shape the historical work". As a kind of cultural hegemonic structure, the narrative of "Pernicious-Vestiges" remains in the official discourse and even enters the bottom of society, becoming "common sense in the daily life of human relations" (Adamson, 1980, pp. 140–162), which reflects from another aspect that the revolutionary domination has really been deeply rooted in the hearts of the people. That is to say, the "Pernicious-Vestiges" discourse that was originally used to reflect on the justice of memory, on the contrary, dispelled the historical justice of contemporary China, and it will inevitably dispel the justice of memory itself. As a kind of tradition or heritage, the meaning of "Pernicious-Vestiges" rhetoric has been constantly questioned. The "Pernicious-Vestiges" rhetoric itself, which is used to reflect on the justice of memory, has become a discourse system that should be reflected again; "Pernicious-Vestiges poison" eventually became something that was opposed by itself at first.

However, historical research can't easily deny the possibility of anti-paradigm historiography and "alternative modernity". The revolutionary paradigm has not completely broken with the modernization paradigm, and the two may work together again. That is to say, modernization and revolution are not completely opposite, but they need each other under specific historical conditions. Therefore, the memory of the revolution is preserved and becomes a part of the modernization narrative (Dirlik, 1996).

Rebirth in the fight against corruption (2012–present)

Since the 18th National Congress of the Communist Party of China in 2012, the Communist Party of China has launched an unprecedented anti-corruption struggle. In the past 10 years, China has investigated and dealt with more than 761,000 violations of the eight central regulations, including 553 middle management cadres who have been examined and investigated by the national discipline inspection and supervision organs. Xi Jinping, General Secretary of the Central Committee of the Chinese Communist Party, has repeatedly emphasized the importance of anti-corruption to the ruling party and the country. He compared "corruption" to "cancer" and claimed that to ensure "the CPC's physical health", we must fight against it:

> We must persist in using the system to manage people, pay close attention to forming an effective mechanism that doesn't want to corrupt, can't corrupt or dare not to corrupt, let the people supervise power, let it run in the sun, and put it in the cage of the system. We must persist in fighting "tigers" and "flies" together, persist in combating and eliminating corruption, make every effort to solve the problem of corruption, strive to create a clean and upright social atmosphere of party style and politics, and constantly win the trust of the people with new achievements in combating corruption and promoting honesty.
> ("Zài qìng zhù quán guó rén mín dài biǎo dà huì chéng lì liù shí zhōu nián dà huì shàng de jiǎng huà 在庆祝全国人民代表大会成立六十周年大会上的讲话 [Speech at the 60th Anniversary of the National People's Congress]", *People's Daily*, September 6, 2014, 1A, by Xi Jinping)

Here, Xi Jinping put forward "putting power in the cage of the system", which means that the CCP's anti-corruption work is mainly aimed at party officials, while "tiger" and "fly" respectively refer to central-level cadres and local small officials. The anti-corruption work mainly deals with formalism, bureaucracy, hedonism, and extravagance in the CCP system. Therefore, the presentation of anti-corruption discourse mainly revolves around typical individual and specific group styles. In the huge anti-corruption struggle in the new era, the feudal "Pernicious-Vestiges" belonging to the past has been widely used again. Feudalism is no longer a theoretical form of social form but a synonym for those who have more resources in any hierarchical society, giving people more room to imagine and practice a utopian society where there is no inequality at all.

In modern China, since 2012, the individuals who have been established as "Pernicious-Vestiges" of corruption that needs to be eliminated are mostly former high-level officials of the CPC, with Bo Xilai, Zhou Yongkang, Su Rong, and others as typical representatives. In this regard, the commentary in *People's Daily* believes that problems in political discipline and rules are even more harmful to the party than corruption. Therefore,

We must draw a clear line with Zhou Yongkang and others in ideological and political actions, eliminate their residual poison, be brave in being a guard, a warrior and a soldier, and dare to fight against those who do not observe political discipline and rules.

("Sī xiǎng zuò fēng dǎng xìng de jí zhōng 'bǔ gài' 'jiā yóu' 思想作风党性的集中'补钙' '加油' [Concentrate on 'supplementing calcium' and 'refueling' for ideological style and party spirit]", *People's Daily*, 1A, December 29, 2015)

The typical establishment of this kind of corrupt "Pernicious-Vestiges" is the warning and removal of opposing factions by the new leadership of the CPC, and it has played an alert role for officials within the political system of the CPC. The purpose is to grasp the "key minority" by both breaking and establishing, so as to "trace the source".

On the one hand, we must thoroughly and thoroughly eliminate Sun Zhengcai's bad influence and the Pernicious-Vestiges of "Bo and Wang", and ensure that all actions of the cadres in party member obey the command of the CPC Central Committee; On the other hand, we should give full play to the demonstration of leading cadres, set up correct thinking, fine style, good orientation and positive examples, and resolutely prevent the resurgence of wrong thoughts and behaviors.

("Zhèng fēng sù jì yōu huà zhèng zhì shēng tài 正风肃纪优化政治生态 [Upholding the right wind and discipline to optimize the political ecology]", *People's Daily*, March 20, 2018)

The aversion to "corrupt officials" and the shaping of honest official images are the simplest moral feelings and good wishes that have remained in the hearts of Chinese people since feudal times. Therefore, sanctified official images such as "Bāo qīng tiān 包青天" have been shaped. In a commentary in *People's Daily*, the story of an honest official Niú sēng rú 牛僧孺 who refused to accept bribes in the Tang Dynasty in China was cited as an example, and the style of officials in communist party was compared:

If in feudal society, it is impossible to expect all officials to be like Niú sēng rú in not accepting gifts, so that they can be "upright and incorruptible", then today, as communist party people, they should do better than feudal officials. Admittedly, most of our leading cadres are clean officials who satisfy the masses, and they can keep their words and deeds in line with their deeds. However, we must finally see that some leading cadres, especially in places where cadres, the masses and organizations can't supervise them, are bold and lawless, repeatedly reaching out and taking risks.

("Jīn tái suí gǎn: xiǎng qǐ xiè jìn de yī xí huà 金台随感：想起谢晋的一席话 [Impression of Jintai: remembering Xie Jin's words]", *People's Daily*, August 9, 2014)

In the passage, the author compares officials in feudal times with those in modern China, affirms the behavior of ancient officials, and thinks that communist party people should do better than them. At the same time, the corrupt behavior is blamed on feudal "Pernicious-Vestiges". This gives rise to such an interesting phenomenon; when talking about anti-corruption, the commentary articles of *People's Daily* are often in the same article, which not only praises and affirms the incorruptible officials in the feudal era but also attributes the current corrupt behavior in China to feudal "Pernicious-Vestiges" and criticizes it greatly.

> Honesty and integrity are the traditional political virtues of China. All previous dynasties have regarded honesty and integrity as the key to politics and the foundation of being an official, and the common people also regard it as an important criterion for judging officials' virtues. People are familiar with Di Renjie, Bao Zheng, Yu Qian, Hai Rui, Yu Chenglong, who is honest, honest and upright, and so on. They are all models of honest and upright officials in people's minds. Because of their honesty, these honest officials are immortal and widely praised . . . In the long-term practice, our party has formed a good political culture. However, it should also be noted that China has a history of more than 2,000 years of feudal society, which has inertia, and the influence of the remnants of feudal decadent culture cannot be underestimated. For example, larded learning, unspoken rules, circle hilltops, friendship with friends, habits of Jianghu, personal attachment, cronyism, seeking fairy worship, and divination, and so on. Although these decadent and dross things can't be put on the table in a fair and square way, they are taken for granted in some people's minds, and some places are covered with scum. Moreover, the erosion of western values and decadent lifestyles in recent years has also been shown in some party member and cadres, who have been poisoned by money worship, hedonism and extreme individualism. At the same time, the erosion of the principle of commodity exchange to the political life of the party, the erosion of the political ecology of the party and the damage to the ruling foundation of the party cannot be ignored.
> ("Fēng qīng qì zhèng pǔ xīn piān—rú hé bǎo chí qīng zhèng lián jié de zhèng zhì běn sè 风清气正谱新篇—如何保持清正廉洁的政治本色 [A new chapter of integrity—how to keep honest and clean politics]", *People's Daily*, 9A, May 2, 2017)

From these examples, it can be seen that the official propaganda organization of the Communist Party of China adopted a selective strategy of affirming the individual and the part and denying the whole for feudalism when propagating the anti-corruption struggle, so that it can make full use of the "Pernicious-Vestiges" of feudalism from both sides. At the same time, the criticism and cleaning up of the typical individual "Pernicious-Vestiges" of anti-corruption often ends up in the officialdom, the power system of the Chinese Communist Party itself. Here, the political ecology of officialdom is often compared to the natural ecology. The slogan of environmentalism, "Green Mountain", is used in the political ecology, which means the incorruptible style of officials. The typical personal and corrupt "Pernicious-Vestiges" is the ecological "pollution source":

> If one or two fish die in the river, it may be the problem of the fish itself; But if all the fish die, it's likely that there is something wrong with the ecosystem of this river. Only by rooting out the soil where corruption breeds and spreads at the source can we really improve the political ecology.
> ("Hán yǎng zhèng zhì shēng tài de lǜ shuǐ qīng shān—lái zì bù fèn shěng shì yíng zào liáng hǎo zhèng zhì shēng tài de diào yán zhī yī 涵养政治生态的绿水青山——来自部分省市营造良好政治生态的调研之一 [Green river and green mountains that cultivate political ecology—one of the investigations from some provinces and cities to create a good political ecology]", *People's Daily*, October 12, 2018).

From corrupt high-ranking officials to political ecology, the CCP's anti-corruption struggle classified the corruption within the power system and believed that the rise of corruption had the characteristics of group. In the history of China, Niú lǐ dǎng zhēng 牛李党争, Niu-Li factional struggles in the Tang Dynasty, the struggle between the old and new parties in the Northern Song Dynasty, Dōng lín dǎng zhēng 东林党争, Donglin faction fighting in the late Ming Dynasty, and the struggle between the emperor and the queen in the late Qing Dynasty all lost their development opportunities in the struggle for internal friction. More importantly, they shook the legitimacy of centralization and deepened the ruling crisis. China's ruling class has always been wary and hostile to "party struggle". In the CCP's anti-corruption struggle, the "circle culture" with the meaning of cronies' rivalries are also a strategy of strict prevention and elimination. At the end of 2014, the Politburo meeting of the Chinese Communist Party once reiterated that "the party will never tolerate engaging in group gangs, forming a party for personal gain, and forming gangs". The commentary in *People's Daily* also pointed out, "To purify the political ecology and straighten out the official atmosphere, we must get rid of the negative influence of 'circle culture' and eliminate the pernicious harm of political hilltops and sectarianism." ("Qīng zhèng guān chǎng xū yuǎn lí quān zi wén huà 清正官场须远离圈子文化 [Honest officialdom must stay away from circle culture]", *People's Daily*, 5A, January 5, 2015). Therefore, local corruption, cronyism, and other behaviors are classified as the embodiment of feudal "Pernicious-Vestiges" with the nature of "party struggle". They are the remnants of poisons in feudal culture and the poison and threat of the old system to the new power system.

The dock culture in the political sense refers to the feudal gang culture with sectarianism and regionalism. The traditional dock culture of the society has a long history, and there are many scourges such as "forming a party for private gain", "fighting between cronies and gangs" and "playing with power to trick the party" throughout the dynasties. People who believe in wharf culture intersect their interests and try their best to safeguard the interests of a few people. Or they cultivate private forces, raise "retainers", pull gangs, and engage in personal attachment; Or visit the docks and look for backers everywhere. The emergence of dock culture in our party is, to a certain extent, the product of the interaction between the feudal "cronies" and "gangs" culture and the negative effects of market economy. Our party led the people to build a new China, but the Pernicious-Vestiges of feudal wharf culture still exists in the minds of some party member and cadres. After the reform and opening-up, the changes in the interest pattern brought about by the rapid development of the market economy have eroded the ideals and beliefs of a small number of party member and cadres, and worshipping the dock, looking for a backer, and engaging in attachment have become their "cheats for promotion", and the loyalty of Jianghu and political unspoken rules have become their "way to be an official". At the same time, the impetuous trend in the period of social transformation and the imperfection of related systems have also provided social soil and opened the door to convenience for the growth of dock culture.

("Pò huài tuán jié tǒng yī, wū rǎn zhèng zhì shēng tài, jiān jué fáng zhǐ hé fǎn duì mǎ tou wén huà 破坏团结统一 污染政治生态 坚决防止和反对码头文化 [Destroy the unity and unity, pollute the political ecology, resolutely prevent and oppose the dock culture]", *People's Daily*, 7A, March 29, 2018)

The original intention of dock culture refers to the culture of a group of people who focus on riverside freight transportation. It often takes the word "profit" as its slogan and the word "righteousness" as its slogan, with a strong flavor of Jianghu (Feng, 2017, p. 40). One of the biggest characteristics of this Jianghu culture is its awareness of absorption. In this commentary, the author will use metonymy to divert the folk "dock culture" into the political culture—the behavior of ganging, playing politics, and seeking personal gain in the officialdom. This connection between loyalty in Jianghu and political unspoken rules was accomplished through feudal "Pernicious-Vestiges" —the author attributed the bad habits of officialdom and the corrupt behavior of officials to feudal "Pernicious-Vestiges", thus clearing the political system of modern China. At the same time, the strict defense of "circle culture" and "dock culture" is the consolidation of the absolute authority of the ruling party, and it also implies a deep fear of party strife or political crisis and legitimacy shake.

As for the kinds of corruption phenomena in Chinese society, such as eating, drinking, and having fun with public funds; traveling abroad at public expense; and seeking personal gain with public power, the argument that "public ownership is the root of corruption" has emerged. In this regard, feudal "Pernicious-Vestiges" is used to refute this view:

> As a historical phenomenon, corruption is essentially the product of the exploiting system and exploiting class. Corruption in the economy is still

rooted in the decadent ideas of the exploiting class, and at the same time, there are specific practical reasons. In the process of establishing the socialist market economic system, the Pernicious-Vestiges of feudalism and other exploiting classes will continue to exist; Opening to the outside world, the decadent ideas and lifestyles of capitalism will take the opportunity to enter; The weakness and negative effects of the market itself will have an impact; There will be gaps and some disorder in the process of system transition; In addition, the transformation and management of the realization form of the public ownership economy can't keep up, some localities and units are lax in administering the party, and some party member and cadres grow money worship, hedonism and individualism, etc., all of which make corruption breed or spread. Therefore, it is wrong to attribute the root of corruption to public ownership itself.

("Yǒu zhōng guó tè sè shè huì zhǔ yì yǔ fǎn fǔ bài lǐ lùn yán tǎo huì zōng shù 有中国特色社会主义与反腐败理论研讨会综述 [Summary of the Seminar on Socialism with Chinese characteristics and anti-corruption theory]", *People's Daily*, 9A, August 19, 1997)

The solution to this phenomenon is to "put power in the cage of the system", that is, the official believes that promoting the reform of the political system will help to form a mechanism to curb power corruption: "Deepening the reform of the political system should take carrying forward inner-party democracy and people's democracy, improving the socialist legal system, standardizing power behavior and strengthening the supervision and restriction of power as a basic content". This explanation of the official propaganda organization not only clears up the relationship between the existing system and corruption but also blames it on "problems left over from history" and feudal "Pernicious-Vestiges" to defend the existing ideology and political system. At the same time, it also puts forward a convincing solution—deepening reform and restricting power.

Generally speaking, the basic function of ideology is realized through classification, which responds to the questions of who we are, what we stand for, what our values are, and what our relationship with others is. We and they are characterized as social groups, maximizing the similarities within categories and differences between categories (Oktar, 2001) and positioning the status and relationship of individuals in society. It proves the effective way of "scapegoating" and defending the label of "victim", and the practice of reclassification (or restructure) shows that categorization has the potential of explanation (Sarangi & Candlin, 2003), which also echoes the internal motivation that the society with changing membership needs to frequently use classified discourse. When dealing with controversial structures and concepts that are more common in daily life, such as democracy, freedom, revolution, poverty, and terrorism, reclassification will continue to influence the actions and decisions of members of society. The classified discourse ideology will eventually be reflected in the stereotypes formed by people, and its important function is to reorganize the reality and experience faced by people; supplement the ever-changing social roles, group conflicts, power distribution, and retention; rationalize and maintain the status quo; and provide a sense of identity (Hilton & von Hippel, 1996); inspire the public's feelings; make them believe in their moral, political, economic, social, and professional advantages; and encourage people to judge others, the elite constantly reaffirms the boundaries between "self" and "others" while strengthening group unity. It excludes those who exceed the boundaries of "normative" behavior, thus maintaining the existing power structure of society through prescriptive nature (Bhatia, 2015, p. 31). In Chapter 5, we will analyze the "Pernicious-Vestiges" of some more abstract and uncertain vocabularies, focusing on how these vocabularies were used in the meaning formation stage from the early days of the founding of New China to the beginning of the Cultural Revolution and how they were used to construct the boundaries of the opposed groups, including "old society", Kuomintang reactionaries, imperialism, and capitalism.

References

Adamson, W. L. (1980). *Hegemony and Revolution: A Study of Antonio Gramsci's Political and Cultural Theory*. Berkeley: University of California Press.

Bednarek, M. A. (2005). Frames revisited: The coherence-inducing function of frames. *Journal of Pragmatics, 37*(5), 685–705. https://doi.org/10.1016/j.pragma.2004.09.007.

Bhatia, A. (2015). *Discursive Illusions in Public Discourse: Theory and Practice*. New York: Routledge.

Deng, X. (1978/1994). *Selected Writings of Deng Xiaoping-Volume 2*. Beijing: People's Publishing House.

Dirlik, A. (1996). Reversals, ironies, hegemonies: Notes on the contemporary historiography of modern China. *Modern China, 22*(3), 243–284.

Feng, W. B. (2017). *Chongqing Dwellings: Traditional Settlements*. Chongqing: Chongqing University Press.

Gal, S., & Irvine, J. T. (1995). The boundaries of languages and disciplines: How ideologies construct difference. *Social Research, 62*(4), 967–1001.

Hilton, J. L., & von Hippel, W. (1996). Stereotypes. *Annual Review of Psychology, 47*(1), 237–271. https://doi.org/10.1146/annurev.psych.47.1.237.

Jayyusi, L. (1984). *Categorization and the Moral Order*. Boston: Routledge and Keegan Paul.

Lakoff, G. (1987). *Women, Fire, and Dangerous Things: What Categories Reveal about the Mind*. Chicago: University of Chicago Press.

Linell, P., & Thunqvist, D. P. (2003). Moving in and out of framings: Activity contexts in talks with young unemployed people within a training project. *Journal of Pragmatics, 35*(3), 409–434. https://doi.org/10.1016/S0378-2166(02)00143-1.

Makitalo, A., & Saljo, R. (2002). Talk in institutional context and institutional context in talk: Categories as situated practices. *Text, 22*(1), 57–82. https://doi.org/10.1515/text.2002.005.

Mao, Z. (1938/1991). *Selected Works of Mao Zedong—Volume 2*. Beijing: People's Publishing House.

Minsky, M. (1977). Frame-system theory. In P. Johnson-Laird & P. C. Watson (Eds.), *Thinking: Readings in Cognitive Science* (pp. 355–376). Cambridge: Cambridge University Press.

Oktar, L. (2001). The ideological organization of representational processes in the presentation of us and them. *Discourse & Society, 12*(3), 313–346. https://doi.org/10.1177/0957926501012003003.

Ross, A. S., & Bhatia, A. (2021). "Ruled Britannia": Metaphorical construction of the EU as enemy in UKIP campaign posters. *The International Journal of Press/Politics, 26*(1), 188–209. https://doi.org/10.1177/1940161220935812.

Sacks, H. (1992). *Lectures on Conversation Volume I & II*. Oxford: Blackwell.

Sarangi, S., & Candlin, C. N. (2003). Categorization and explanation of risk: A discourse analytical perspective. *Health, Risk & Society, 5*(2), 115–124. https://doi.org/10.1080/1369857031000123902.

Steimel, S. J. (2010). Refugees as people: The portrayal of refugees in American human interest stories. *Journal of Refugee Studies, 23*(2), 219–237. https://doi.org/10.1093/jrs/feq019.

5 From prosperity to decline
Historical aberration and mnemonic silence

Through the analysis in Chapter 4, it can be seen that feudal "Pernicious-Vestiges" is the most typical embodiment of re-narration and historical interruption of modern China's historical evaluation. In addition, imperialism, feudalism, and (bureaucratic) capitalism have produced the expression of "re-narrativization", a historical interruption type, in the process of "Pernicious-Vestiges" discourse practice, from the corresponding social reality. In this chapter, we will make a more systematic analysis of the Kuomintang reactionaries, the "old society", the "Pernicious-Vestiges" of imperialism, and capitalism.

The obscure "old society" (1949–1966)

In the narrative of "Pernicious-Vestiges" in *People's Daily*, some historical events or ideologies are constructed as the rise and fall of "Pernicious-Vestiges" words or their complete disappearance, which is actually similar to "mnemonic silence". By suppressing the "Pernicious-Vestiges" words of specific historical events, the association with "Pernicious-Vestiges" is gradually lifted by "inducing" forgetting (Stone & Hirst, 2014). First of all, this feature is vividly reflected in the "Pernicious-Vestiges" narrative and discourse strategies against the "old society".

Relatively speaking, it seems that it takes a longer historical process to dissipate the "Pernicious-Vestiges" of the old society. From the time point of view, the "Pernicious-Vestiges" narrative of the "old society" was divided into two stages: before and after the reform and opening up. The first stage started in January 1949 and lasted until January 1974, and its manifestations were all-encompassing, covering almost all fields from social reality to ideology—including mercenary marriages, bureaucracy, corruption and waste, feudal hierarchy, contempt for labor, formalism, individualism, reformism, right-wing thinking, individual economy, separation from politics, hooligans/bad youth, low morality, forest destruction, etc.—which almost embodies all the revolutionary determination of a new socialist country to eliminate all "unhealthy practices" and set a precedent for social atmosphere. But interestingly, in the second stage of the narrative of "Pernicious-Vestiges" of the "old society", from June 1979 to May 1986 and then again in March 1994, when the narrative of "Pernicious-Vestiges" of the "old society" appeared alone, the "Pernicious-Vestiges" of "Pernicious-Vestiges" of the "old society" began to

DOI: 10.4324/9781003409724-5

become dark and unclear, usually appearing in a style lacking concrete images, such as unsatisfactory social conditions and unclear "Pernicious-Vestiges". It can be seen that the ideological shock from 1974–1979 not only became a milestone event to divide the "Pernicious-Vestiges" of the "old society" in the two stages, but it also reflected that, at the time, China's time imagination of the "old society" showed a fault-like change. To some extent, the second revival of the "Pernicious-Vestiges" of the "old society" after intermittent interruption shared a part of time and phenomenon with the modern narrative of Chinese history, which became the discourse evidence different from the traditional revolutionary paradigm. In this section, we will discuss the "Pernicious-Vestiges" of the "old society" from the founding of New China in 1949 to the beginning of the Cultural Revolution in 1966. For the discourse construction of the "Pernicious-Vestiges" of the "old society" during the Cultural Revolution and after the reform and opening up, please refer to the relevant contents in Chapter 6, "The Gang of Four and the Cultural Revolution: From criticizing to becoming 'Pernicious-Vestiges'".

In the first stage of the narrative of the "Pernicious-Vestiges" of the "old society", this vocabulary is highly isomorphic to the "Pernicious-Vestiges" of feudalism. For example, on Women's Day, the eve of the founding of New China, *People's Daily* published a column titled "cóng mín yáo zhōng kàn jiù shè huì fù nǚ de tòng kǔ 从民谣中看旧社会妇女的痛苦 [Looking at the pain of women in the old society from folk songs]" in the 4A of March 8, 1949. This article enumerated the lyrics of folk songs in the liberated areas of North China related to patriarchal attitudes, the child bride system, polygamy, etc., as evidence of the existence of "Pernicious-Vestiges of feudal society" and then called on women to actively participate in the front line of production support. The hidden feature of this kind of rhetoric lies is that compared with literal categories, metaphorical categories are more likely to cause discourse illusion, especially traditional metaphorical categories. Compared with the original metaphorical categories influenced by changing social conditions, the traditional metaphorical categories are usually stable, and the longer they are implemented, the more people will understand them literally, thus firmly believing in discourse illusion (Bhatia, 2015, p. 30).

However, traditional sayings are sometimes regarded as the embodiment of the "Pernicious-Vestiges" of the "old society" and become the object of criticism. In 1956, when the national wage reform was carried out, an article published in *People's Daily* used this rhetoric in reverse:

> It is not surprising that there are complaints such as "ten years of hardship, still one hundred and fifty". In the old society, there was a saying, "You can't be a master until you have suffered through hardships." This was a dose of poison given by the master to others at that time. People suffer from hardships. Although they don't see any signs of success, some people do like to comfort or even encourage themselves with this sentence. Being bullied by others and trying to squeeze into the ranks of others is where the poison lies. Nowadays, there are few masters here, but there is a difference in salary. People with the above thoughts have tasted "ten years of hardship", and feel that they have

124 *From prosperity to decline*

suffered through all the hardships, so how can they not complain about "one hundred and fifty" because they are not good enough? In the old society, there was another saying, "to be a scholar is to be the top of society". Those who have this kind of thoughts have tasted "ten years of hardship" and think they are superior to others, but of course they are not willing to be "one hundred and fifty". So it's not surprising that there are such complaints.

("'shí nián hán chuāng kǔ' '十年寒窗苦' ['Ten years of hardship and bitter learning']", *People's Daily*, 2A, July 7, 1956, by Fan Rongkang)

According to the background information introduced at the beginning of the article, "one hundred and fifty" here refers to a fixed salary, not a salary of 150 yuan. The author criticized the well-educated workers who failed to occupy a dominant position in the wage reform and the leaders who sympathized with this kind of workers. The purpose was not to smooth out the wage difference but to try to make people reverse the education flow concept of China in ancient times and accept the concept of "distribution according to work" adopted by New China, so as to clear the obstacles for the wage reform. By comparison, it can be found that when proverbs will be constructed as solid evidence of the existence of "Pernicious-Vestiges", and when they will become loose and changeable conceptual objects mainly depends on the social needs and propaganda policies at that time, and they will not be institutionalized and treated as constant or internally consistent discourse elements.

In more cases, the "Pernicious-Vestiges" of the "old society" lacks specific content and fixed sources. For example, according to the article "sù qīng tóu jī huó dòng fā zhǎn zhèng dāng jīn róng rén mín yín háng jīng fēn háng zhào jí yín qián yè zuò tán 肃清投机活动发展正当金融 人民银行京分行 召集银钱业座谈 [Eliminating speculation, developing legitimate finance, Beijing branch of People's Bank of China convenes a forum on banking and money industry]" in the 2A of *People's Daily* on November 10th, when the Beijing branch of People's Bank of China convened a forum on banking and money industry, Liang Zhengfu, general manager of Qianxing Qianzhuang made a self-examination of its illegal behavior, saying,

> This kind of mistake is the ideological Pernicious-Vestiges of the old society for thousands of years, and the business is only based on personal interests. Today, we should think about ourselves. In this discourse construction, the business logic of pursuing interests is equated with "speculative psychology" and has become synonymous with "the Pernicious-Vestiges of old social thoughts", thus prompting the whole financial industry to "contribute its own strength in the climax of economic construction.

For another instance of the 10th anniversary of Dr. Bethune's death on November 12, 2008, in the article "bái qiú ēn dài fū shì xīn zhōng guó yī wù gōng zuò zhě de fāng xiàng 白求恩大夫是新中国医务工作者的方向 [Dr. Bethune is the direction of medical workers in New China]" published in the 4A of *People's Daily*, the "Pernicious-Vestiges" of the "old society" was used to refer to "irresponsible to the people, irrelevant, empty talk about theory, copy foreign experience mechanically, use patients as experimental subjects, traffic technology, and earn money from people's health, all for one's own sake." Although this "Pernicious-Vestiges" may be specifically targeted at "capitalist individualists" and "selfish and hypocritical humanists" according to the context, the main purpose of this discourse is to praise Bethune's revolutionary quality and scientific spirit, thus placing too many opposed elements in the framework of "Pernicious-Vestiges", which constitutes the huge opposite of those who are praised. On July 2, 1951, Hua Luogeng, a famous mathematician, published a signed article in the 3A of *People's Daily* entitled "zài gòng chǎn dǎng de shēng rì xiàng dǎng bǎo zhèng 在共产党的生日向党保证 [Assuring the party on communist party's birthday]". In this article, he constructed "scholars despise each other" as the "Pernicious-Vestiges" of the "old society", thus demonstrating his determination to "overcome prejudice such as factionalism" in New China. In this article, Hua Luogeng called "the tradition of serving the people . . . the only tradition of new China" but failed to give his own explanation for the possible inconsistency between the "tradition" and the new regime.

It is also because of the ambiguity of the direction of "old society" that the "Pernicious-Vestiges" of "old society" is sometimes used to strengthen the conflict and opposition between "relying on the masses" and "working class" and "bureaucracy". On January 25, 1950, *People's Daily*, 2A, published the article "quán miàn kāi zhǎn gōng zuò dà jiǎn chá，yī kào gōng rén jiē jí shí xíng mín zhǔ gǎi gé 全面开展工作大检查，依靠工人阶级实行民主改革 [Carrying out the general inspection in an all-round way and relying on the working class to carry out democratic reform]", which is a typical case. This article not only directly uses the subtitle of "Tangshan Branch relies on workers to overcome flood disasters, Beijing Branch keeps breaking away from the masses", which reflects each other and forms a sharp contrast, but it also attributes "not knowing the following situations, causing many unnecessary losses at work" to "the residual poison left by the old enterprise organization" and turns the mechanical accidents in power plants into a new set of narratives to strengthen class struggle. On February 21, 1951, the article "jì zhōng yāng jiān wěi huì guān yú lín jié àn jiàn de zuò tán huì 记中央监委会关于林洁案件的座谈会 [The Symposium of the Central Supervisory Commission on Lin Jie's case]" was published in the 6A of *People's Daily*. Not surprisingly, although this article referred to the "corruption" of former Beijing Coal and Iron branch manager Lin Jie and others who used their powers for personal gain, it was special that this vocabulary was spoken by Chu Yuanxi, a professor at an engineering school in Zhangjiakou. This time, the Central Supervisory Commission discussed the handling of Lin Jie's case precisely because the newspaper reading group of Chu Yuanxi's school and other readers wrote *People's Daily*, which was specially organized by the Central Supervisory Commission after receiving letters from readers. Therefore, the double direction of the "Pernicious-Vestiges" of the "old society" not only includes the corruption in Lin Jie's case, but more importantly, it points out that "the reactionary Kuomintang government" can't be as serious and responsible to the people as "today's government". Even Chen Zhining, a cadre of the Beijing Film Studio, who dismantled tenants' water, electricity, and toilets and threatened tenants to move has became a part of the "Pernicious-Vestiges" of the "old society", no matter how long the history of owning electric meters, pressurized water machines, and toilets occupied in the process of Beijing's municipal construction ("Běi jīng diàn yǐng zhì piàn chǎng jiē shòu pī píng chǔ fèn chén zhì níng, bìng jué dìng jiāng suǒ gòu fáng wū yí jiāo qīng guǎn jú 北京电影制片厂接受批评处分陈治宁，并决定将所购房屋移交清管局, [Beijing Film Studio accepted criticism and punished Chen Zhining, and decided to hand over the purchased house to Pigging Bureau]", *People's Daily*, December 7, 1951, 2A).

After the rectification movement began in 1952, "anti-corruption, anti-waste, anti-bureaucracy" were constantly emphasized. Corruption, waste, and bureaucracy became the "Pernicious-Vestiges" of the "old society" that contradicted the "morality of the new society", and the solution was to resort to years of mobilized moral governance ("rén mín zhèng xié quán guó wěi yuán huì cháng wù wěi yuán huì jué dìng zhǎn kāi sī xiǎng gǎi zào de xué xí yùn dòng, mù qián yǐ fǎn tān wū làng fèi fǎn guān liáo zhǔ yì wèi xué xí nèi róng 人民政协全国委员会常务委员会决定展开思想改造的学习运动，目前以反贪污浪费反官僚主义为学习内容 [The Standing Committee of the National Committee of the Chinese People's Political Consultative Conference decided to launch a study campaign of ideological reform, which currently takes anti-corruption and waste and anti-bureaucracy as its learning content]", *People's Daily*, 1A, January 8, 1952). "The Pernicious-Vestiges of the old society" has become a political slogan, which has been endlessly used in the self-examination of the reformed object (such as "duì rén mín yín háng shì chá tuán pū zhāng làng fèi de zì wǒ jiǎn tǎo 对人民银行视察团铺张浪费的自我检讨 [Self-examination of the extravagance and waste of the inspection team of the People's Bank of China]", *People's Daily*, 1A, January 14, 1952, by Hu Jinglian, deputy governor of the People's Bank of China), the statements of political institutions (such as "yíng jiē sī xiǎng gǎi zào yùn dòng, guàn chè fǎn tān wū, fǎn làng fèi, fǎn guān liáo zhǔ yì dòu zhēngfl 迎接思想改造运动，贯彻反贪污，反浪费，反官僚主义斗争 [Meeting the ideological reform movement, implementing anti-corruption, anti-waste], etc." *People's Daily*, 3A, January 14, 1952, by Chen Shutong, vice chairman of the National Committee of the People's Political Consultative Conference of China), and the drum call for the movement ("zī chǎn jiē jí sī xiǎng bì xū gǎi zào 资产阶级思想必须改造 [Bourgeois thought must be reformed]", 3A, January 29, 1952, by Yu Huancheng). Since then, in order to encourage the enthusiasm of the masses to participate in mobilized governance, the 2A published on March 15, 1952, "yōng hù zhōng nán jú duì zhōu jì fāng sòng yīng děng yīn móu xiàn hài àn de zhèng què chǔ lǐ—dú zhě lái xìn zōng shù 拥护中南局对周季方宋瑛等阴谋陷害案的正确处理—读者来信综述 [Supporting the Central South Bureau's correct handling of the conspiracy and frame up cases of Zhou Jifang and Song Ying—a summary of readers' letters]", which discussed the Ji Kaifu case that was overturned twice in the next 30 years, and it constructed two parallel "Pernicious-Vestiges" of the "old society" in it, one is the corruption itself and the other is "dare not report corrupt elements". This discourse construction, combined with the power of letters from readers of *People's Daily*, further promoted the struggle consciousness of the masses, and at the same time, it continuously expanded its scope of power.

What needs to be emphasized is that although the direction of "Pernicious-Vestiges" of the "old society" is relatively vague, in the almost simultaneous movements against Three Evils and Five Evils, this rhetoric is only used by the former for the staff of the party and government organs, while the latter for the private industry and commerce rarely appears, except what nuclear physicist Zhao Zhongyao put in his article "qìng zhù guó qìng jié 庆祝国庆节 [Celebrating National Day]" in the 3A of *People's Daily* on September 30, 1952. The *People's Daily*, published on June 25, 1952, in its 3A, "wèi quán miàn zhǎn kāi gōng yè ài guó zēng chǎn jié yuē dà jìng sài yùn dòng ér nǔ lì—yī jiǔ wǔ èr nián liù yuè shí èr rì zài huá běi gōng yè shēng chǎn jìng sài huì yì shàng de bào gào 为全面展开工业爱国增产节约大竞赛运动而努力——一九五二年六月十二日在华北工业生产竞赛会议上的报告 [Made great efforts to launch a nationwide industrial patriotic competition to increase production and save money—a report at the North China Industrial Production Competition Conference on June 12, 1952]", especially emphasized this point. After the victory of the movements against Three Evils and Five Evils, it was put forward that the former one "prominently carried out the anti-waste movement. . . . . . . Their ideas, styles, technicalism views and Pernicious-Vestiges of the old society of the European and American bourgeoisie have been strongly criticized by the masses and self-examined", thus laying a favorable foundation for "popularizing the advanced experience created by the Soviet Union and its employees". This also shows that, as the official newspaper of the Central Committee of the Communist Party of China, *People's Daily*'s discourse construction of "Pernicious-Vestiges" needs to be faithful to the tone set by the decision-making department, and there is less room for language creativity.

In 1955, the internal and external pressure of "sweeping away the Pernicious-Vestiges" was relatively small, and the transformation object of this discourse construction was extended to primary and secondary school students. For primary and secondary school students,

> Our country is in a transitional period, the Pernicious-Vestiges of the old society has not been completely eliminated, and the decadent ideas of the bourgeoisie have directly and indirectly influenced and corrupted the children and the younger generation in many aspects.
> ("jiā qiáng duì zhōng xiǎo xué xué shēng de zì jué jì lù jiào yù 加强对中小学学生的自觉纪律教育 [Strengthening the conscious discipline education for primary and secondary school students]", *People's Daily*, June 15, 1955, 1A)

The moral requirement for primary and secondary school students is very simple, direct, and clear: "observe discipline". As long as discipline is observed, it is possible to "cultivate the moral qualities of children and young people and make them all-round talents" ("jiā qiáng duì zhōng xiǎo xué xué shēng de zì jué jì lù jiào yù 加强对中小学学生的自觉纪律教育 [Strengthening the conscious discipline education for primary and secondary school students]", *People's Daily*, June 15, 1955, 1A). Part of the reason for this circular argument also comes from the ambiguity of the specific direction of "Pernicious-Vestiges" of the "old society".

The phenomenon that we are trying to change is collectively referred to as "Pernicious-Vestiges of the old society", and any model that we may wish to set up is shaped as the opposite of "Pernicious-Vestiges". The more obvious purpose of this vague generalization construction of "Pernicious-Vestiges of the old society" is to carry out the new social transformation plan on the basis of lack of rationality demonstration. This inference was verified in a report in *People's Daily* on February 6, 1953, by Zhang Daye, the engineer and design director of Dihua Cement Plant:

> Why is the Pernicious-Vestiges of old ideas so deep? He said: "In the past, we kept saying that politics was important, but we didn't seriously implement it in practical work; Learning from the advanced experience of the Soviet Union is only verbal, but not concrete. Lack of practical spirit". Therefore, he believes that "it can't be the same as before, and we should fully understand the national policies; Otherwise, the design work will lose its way and cause losses to the country".
>
> ("zhòng gōng yè bù jiàn zhù cái liào gōng yè guǎn lǐ jú shè jì rén yuán lián xì shí jì jiǎn chá shè jì sī xiǎng xī qǔ dōng běi dì yī táo cí chǎng jiào xùn jiē fā dí huà shuǐ ní chǎng de cuò wù shè jì 重工业部建筑材料工业管理局设计人员联系实际检查设计思想 吸取东北第一陶瓷厂教训揭发迪化水泥厂的错误设计 [Designers of Building Materials Industry Administration of the Ministry of Heavy Industry check the design ideas with practice, draw lessons from Northeast No.1 Ceramic Factory and expose the wrong design of Dihua Cement Plant]",
> *People's Daily*, February 6, 1953, 1A)

From this passage, it can be seen that any ideas and practices different from "national policies" can be included in the "Pernicious-Vestiges" of "old ideas". Therefore, "fully understanding" or even "accurately guessing" the trend of national policies has become the only way for people to understand and avoid "Pernicious-Vestiges" of "old ideas". In this increasingly vague discourse direction, the category of "Pernicious-Vestiges of the old society" has gradually expanded and even cattle dealers have become the object of cleaning up "Pernicious-Vestiges". When the normal price of livestock in the market law rises beyond the planned economic system of New China, and "the breeding of farm animals can't keep up with the needs", it will be blamed on the cattle dealers the "reform their ideological style slowly". The reason for the change of supply and demand is that livestock traders are "deeply influenced by the Pernicious-Vestiges of the old society" ("jiā qiáng duì gēng chù fàn yùn shāng hé jiāo yì yuán de gǎi zào 加强对耕畜贩运商和交易员的改造 [Strengthening the transformation of livestock traffickers and traders]", *People's Daily*, 2A, June 30, 1954). Social problems that should resort to economic laws are constantly being placed in the category of moral governance and ideological transformation to try to solve.

At other times, "old ideas" are not only the source of "Pernicious-Vestiges", but they are also the weapon against "Pernicious-Vestiges". This self-contradictory argument shows that the propaganda work of New China still inherits the tradition of "allusion" of the Chinese literati rather than sublating it. For example, in a commentary entitled "zūn zhòng yī wù rén yuán 尊重医务人员 [Respect for medical staff]" (*People's Daily*, 7A, April 5, 1957), the author signed as "Commentator of this newspaper" talked about the phenomenon that doctors and nurses were beaten and insulted by government cadres who were hospitalized due to illness and called for "forming an atmosphere of opposing the Pernicious-Vestiges of old ideas in society, so that people can have a correct understanding of the work of medical staff and respect their labor". Then the author quoted the admonition of the ancients in China that "doctors should be benevolent" to advise people to continue the China tradition of "respecting medical staff" from ancient times to the present, completely ignoring that the previous article had blamed beating and scolding medical care as "the privileged thought of the rulers of the old society to treat laborers", which reflected the vacillation within the discourse pedigree of "Pernicious-Vestiges". Similarly, "belittling labor, especially the labor of service workers" was constructed as the "Pernicious-Vestiges" of the "old society" because the old class that caused "contempt" had been "wiped out" and it was impossible to reform the perpetrators. Therefore, the way to eliminate this "Pernicious-Vestiges" was absurdly changed into enhancing "the feelings, sense of responsibility and dedication of service workers" and strengthening "the political and ideological education of trade unions, provide timely help to workers' misconceptions" as a series of further transformation of "victims" ("shè huì fú wù yè zhí gōng de guāng róng rèn wù—zài běi jīng shì fú wù yè zhí gōng dài biǎo huì yì shàng de bào gào 社会服务业职工的光荣任务—在北京市服务业职工代表会议上的报告 [The glorious task of social service workers—report at Beijing Service Workers' Congress]", *People's Daily*, 4A, May 31, 1957, by Wang Jiong, Chairman of Beijing Federation of Trade Unions).

Thanks to the openness of the word "old society", the "Pernicious-Vestiges" of the "old society" can sometimes even be used to shape a new environmental concept. On March 15, 1958, *People's Daily* published a commentator's article entitled "yòng zhǔ rén wēng tài dù duì dài sēn lín 用主人翁态度对待森林 [Treating forest with the attitude of master]" in the 2A, in which "paying no attention to forest fire prevention" and "seeing this phenomenon and not stopping it" were constructed as the "Pernicious-Vestiges of the old times" because "in the old society, the exploiting class always plundered all natural and artificially created resources recklessly". But in the new era, "the people are the masters of the land" and "the masters of the forest". Therefore, "the decisive factor is people's attitude towards forest resources". What the author didn't realize was that in what he called the "old society", the "exploiting class", didn't have the natural predatory ability of modern industrialization, and the argument that "attitude" decided everything and exaggerated human initiative was deeply influenced and inspired by the Great Leap Forward movement at that time. Even though this appeal seemed to serve a natural view of "harmonious coexistence between man and nature", in fact, it was the same as the anthropocentrism perspective of "man will conquer nature".

The Great Leap Forward movement also calls for the transformation of gender temperament, especially the reshaping of femininity. This urgent demand for labor and productivity is reflected in *People's Daily*, which is concentrated in shaping the aesthetic identity and standardization of socialist working women. If it is said that the discourse construction of feudal "Pernicious-Vestiges" at the beginning of the founding of New China serves the liberation of both sexes, especially women's independent choices, then "labor beauty" in the Great Leap Forward period strongly advocated replacing femininity with masculinity, thus compressing rather than expanding women's choice space for aesthetics and even morality. For example, an article entitled "xué xí mù guì yīng 学习穆桂英 [Learning from Mu Guiying]" reads:

> A handful of female comrades... some of them are still admiring the morbid beauty of Xi Shi, while others are as weak as Lin Daiyu... These weaknesses and shortcomings can be seen at a glance now, but they are appreciated and praised by the literati and ruling class in the old days, and are regarded as models for women. This kind of fallacy spreads, leaving a lasting Pernicious-Vestiges. Today, the Pernicious-Vestiges must be eliminated. We don't want these pale beauty and unhealthy feelings. If anyone is still so delicate, there is a cure: go to work and exercise!
>
> ("xué xí mù guì yīng 学习穆桂英 [Learning from Mu Guiying]",
> *People's Daily*, 4A, April 27, 1958, by Zhou Cheng)

In this article, the author calls on women to learn from Mu Guiying, a fictional character of China's history and literature, to actively participate in production and construction and to become a moral model for women in the "new era". They are either digging in the future Dongfeng Lake outside Jianguomen, Beijing, or "expressing their determination through loudspeaker to compete with the heroes of the whole construction site", which is completely different from the feminine aesthetic standards such as "femininity". By constructing femininity as a "pale" and "unhealthy" "Pernicious-Vestiges of the old times", the author gives a way to get rid of this "Pernicious-Vestiges" by encouraging women to participate in labor and "take the lead" like Mu Guiying. But, Mu Guiying, like historical and literary characters such as Xi Shi and Lin Daiyu, also comes from the construction and admiration of the "old literati and ruling class". Another similarity between Xi Shi and Mu Guiying is that they are all female representatives who complete the defense of the national interests of the feudal dynasty through self-sacrifice.

Whether or not this contradiction is obvious enough, the Great Leap Forward movement can't wait to declare its victory. On September 15, 1958, *People's Daily* published an editorial entitled "gèng dà yuè jìn de qǐ diǎn 更大跃进的起点 [The starting point of Greater Leap]" in its 5A. The editorial pointed out:

> The leap in industrial production and construction is also the result of the victory of the nationwide rectification movement. In the rectification movement, under the leadership of the Party, the people of the whole country not only smashed the attack of the bourgeois Rightists, but also swept through the

bureaucratic airs, lethargy, extravagance, arrogance and femininity among the cadres and the masses, further eliminating the Pernicious-Vestiges of the old system, old habits and old ideas in society.

However, although the *People's Daily* declared the "elimination" of the "Pernicious-Vestiges" at this historical event, such language construction and the mass movement initiated in the name of "Pernicious-Vestiges" will not stop.

Words such as "old society/old times/old system/old ideas" that have existed for a long time in *People's Daily*'s "Pernicious-Vestiges" narrative point to an empty and ambiguous "era", and the time period of their reference is not clear. The result of this "evasion of interpretation" is revealed by Songtag (1966/2003): "Without content, there is no explanation, so that the discourse itself cannot be explained" (pp. 12–13), and then it becomes a kind of "memory politics". "Memory politics" mainly emphasizes the "usefulness" or "availability" of memory—to what extent or scope memory can be used. With regard to the ethical issues pointed out by the narrative of "Pernicious-Vestiges" represented by "ism" and "old times", some scholars have pointed out sharply that it blurs the clear boundary between historical ontology and epistemology and tries to replace the storage memory with the functionality of functional memory through the construction of "validity" rather than "reliability" of people's memory (Assmann & Assmann, 2012). There may be three motivations for memory, including legalization motivation, non-legalization motivation, and tribute. Among them, the legalization motivation of memory domestication means that the regime needs to look back on the past and look forward to the future by re-expressing the memory, and the motivation of paying tribute is often manifested in the process of memory domestication by using the past and solidifying it in social memory, which is a symbolic expression for shaping collective identity. This approach, on the surface, seems to call on people to pay attention to the construction of reality, deepen their reflection on history, and enhance their thinking on human conscience and social morality. However, in fact, a more critical issue has been ignored—how to approach the historical truth as much as possible and restore the original features of history. When the dominant discourse of historical narration is more and more focused on "validity" rather than "reliability", the value position and moral judgment of the subject of discourse practice will invade the internal space of memory; rewrite the subject, object, and memory behavior of memory; and influence or even change the nature of the memorized object, which makes it possible to change from true to false or from good to bad and to accelerate the ethical crisis of "memory distortion" (Zhao, 2013, 2015). In fact, as collective memory is usually diverse and contradictory, it is not only very difficult but also full of danger to generalize the collective memory of the whole society of an era (Olick & Robbins, 1998). The content entered into the official memory through the "Pernicious-Vestiges" narrative is not equal to the collective memory but is the imagination, "reflection", and even stigmatization of the collective memory by political institutions including the official media, aimed at shaping, domesticating, and strengthening the memory and "hostility" of specific historical events through the aforementioned means, so that the "Pernicious-Vestiges" narrative can play a series of different functions including identity construction and social mobilization in a specific historical stage.

Narrative of the "Pernicious-Vestiges" of Kuomintang reactionaries (1946–1958)

Similar to the discourse construction of "Pernicious-Vestiges" in "old society", the narrative of "Pernicious-Vestiges" of Kuomintang reactionaries has also experienced a process from prosperity to decline. In 1946, the term "Pernicious-Vestiges of Kuomintang reactionaries" first appeared in *People's Daily*. On June 8, *People's Daily*, the newspaper of the Central Bureau of the CPC in Shanxi, Hebei, Shandong, and Henan, published the news with the narrative theme of "eliminating the Pernicious-Vestiges" for the first time in its 2A. This article, entitled "sù qīng dà hàn zú zhǔ yì yí dú, duō lún méng hàn huí róng qià kōng qián, chá shěng zhèng fǔ bō liáng jiù jì shòu zāi méng mín 肃清大汉族主义遗毒，多伦蒙汉回融洽空前，察省政府拨粮救济受灾蒙民 [Eliminating the Pernicious-Vestiges of Han chauvinism, bringing back unprecedented harmony to ethnic groups in Duolun, the Chahar provincial government has allocated grain to relieve the affected Mongolians]", has a hidden theme, and its criticism is directed at the "Han chauvinism" regime of the local government of the Republic of China. According to the records of Xilin Gol League (锡林郭勒盟志 xī lín guō lè méng zhì), since 1914, Yuan Shikai allowed imperialist businessmen and capitalists to live and do business in Duolun, and Duolun Naoer became Japan's commodity market and raw material base. In May 1931, the Japanese secret service was established in Duolun County. In April 1933, Duolun County was occupied by Japanese invaders. From July 12– August 8 of the same year, the National Revolutionary Army led by Ji Hongchang captured Duolun for a short time. On August 11, the puppet Mongols supported by the Japanese Puppet Army reoccupied Duolun, and the Chahar provincial government and Mongolian officials reorganized by the government of the Republic of China and Duolun County quickly fell into the hands of the Japanese secret service in the name of "national autonomy". Until August 15, 1945, when Xilin Gol League and Chahar League were liberated for the first time, the "Mengjiang United Autonomous Government" took refuge in the Kuomintang. In September 1945, the puppet Mongolian government announced the establishment of the "Interim Government of the Inner Mongolia Republic"; The CPC Duolun County Committee was established. This article seems to be devoted to criticizing a certain doctrine, but in fact, it praises Duolun City "under the leadership of the correct ethnic policy of the Chinese Communist Party, the phenomenon of estrangement and exclusion caused by Han chauvinism has been changed, and the mutual relationship has reached unprecedented harmony and unity", which has expanded the discourse space for realizing the political goal of building a new regime and deterring the old forces.

In March 1947, this newspaper excerpted the second half of the article "dú zhèng jūn yǔn jūn gǔ chuī zhèng zhì de xīn lǐ wèi shēng dú hòu 读郑君允钧鼓吹

政治的心理卫生读后 [After reading Zheng Junyun's advocacy of political mental health]" published by Zhang Gang Bo, a famous Shanghai democrat, in the joint publication of Volume 14, Issue 5 of *Shanghai Mass Magazine* (published on February 4th) and republished it with the title "Justice in the Communist Party of China", which was intended to emphasize that "ordinary people today" were represented by "national capitalists" such as Zhang Gang Bo. Connecting the Kuomintang "dictator" with the feudal "Pernicious-Vestiges", it constructed a sharp opposition between the past Republic of China and the future democracy, but only the current regime is reactionary, which also reflected a clear linear view of history:

> Since the Republic of China, it has been bustling for thirty-five years, inspired by the wisdom of the people, and the wind has spread widely. From feudalism to capitalism, it has gradually degenerated into socialism. In the transitional period, there must be a hard process to remove the old and replace the new, and to improve it. At present, all kinds of chaotic situations and dark phenomena are the remnants of feudalism and autocracy, which are bound to decline. Reactionary dictatorship, outdated times, will be destroyed and demolished, and will be overthrown. Justice, conforming to the trend, is like the rising sun, and will surely rise. Before dawn, is it midnight? Before spring comes, winter comes first. Metabolism, human evolution is endless.
> ("zhèng yì zài zhōng gòng fāng miàn 正义在中共方面 [Justice in the Communist Party of China]", *People's Daily*, 4A, March 4, 1947)

Although this excerpt from *Shanghai Mass Magazine* was published in *People's Daily* because it revealed the true aspiration and official position of the Chinese Communist Party in the civil war between the Kuomintang and the Communist Party, "the Kuomintang and the Communist Party should not be treated equally, and it is necessary to distinguish right from wrong (standing on the side of the Chinese Communist Party–the author's note), otherwise it will help the dictator". But as the editor's note of this article said, Mr. Zhang, as a famous democrat in Shanghai, represented progressivism as a general society at that time. However, this concept of linear progress can't explain why the Kuomintang regime has a retrogressive social reality compared with that of the people's country. At this time, constructing it as feudal "Pernicious-Vestiges" can realize the inherent logical self-consistency of the progressive historical view. As a rhetorical device, "Pernicious-Vestiges" builds and strengthens the discourse illusion of progressivism, and through the categorization process of "the darker the present, the brighter the future", it creates an illusory hope for people in the civil war.

In addition, in the process of constructing a new order of "new democratic society", "the Pernicious-Vestiges" of the Kuomintang is equated with "the Pernicious-Vestiges" of the "old society", and it is constructed in a labeling way of reactionary forces. For example, the *People's Daily* published an article on Women's Day in 1949, "Recording the Experimental Nursery School", and at the same time, with the help of the binary opposition between "pure children" and "poisoned adults", it constructed a virtue to be pursued by citizens in a "new society" with clear love and hate:

Once, a Chiang bandit plane attacked our peaceful residents, and a child pointed at the bandit plane as he walked, and bitterly scolded him . . . We should educate the children in the new democratic society to be brave and strong, so as to take on the construction of a new society. We must eradicate the old society which taught our children to behave, be timid, be weak, and be afraid of being bullied by the strong . . . These little comrades are much purer than some of our adults who were poisoned by the old society.

("jì shí yàn bǎo yù yuàn 记实验保育院 [Record the experimental nursery school]", *People's Daily*, 4A, March 8, 1949)

Therefore, observing social order has become a product of "poisoning" education, while subverting social order has potential rationality, which is regarded as a virtue to be praised. Through the implicit classification relationships between children and adults, new world and old society, purity and pollution, *People's Daily* has established a set of moral models and codes of conduct for the new regime to be established by the Chinese Communist Party, which regards revolution as a lasting driving force for social development and looks forward to the future.

Compared with other narrative types, *People's Daily* took the shortest time to construct Kuomintang reactionaries as "Pernicious-Vestiges" and only made concentrated statements in the two periods from May 1949–October 1951 and April 1955–January 1958, which was basically consistent with the judgment of Assmann and Assmann (2012). That is to say, in modern times, the deeper the social memory involved in the political field, the shorter its validity period. Among them, the remnants of Kuomintang reactionaries in the previous period were mainly manifested in economic activities and social life fields such as civil war, party education, corruption and waste, extorting and extorting, and corruption, while in the latter period, they resorted to grand nationalism, reformism, counter-revolution, suspicion of communism, pro-America and anti-Soviet. This also coincides with the basic goal that China's socialist revolution is different and related to each other in each period.

Specifically, the construction of the "Pernicious-Vestiges" of the Kuomintang in the first stage mainly serves the establishment and consolidation of the Chinese Communist regime. On April 24, 1949, the People's Liberation Army occupied Nanjing, the center of Kuomintang rule. On June 10, 1949, Nanjing Xinhua Daily published an editorial entitled "wèi jiàn shè xīn nán jīng ér fèn dòu—nán jīng rén mín dāng qián de rèn wù yǔ nǔ lì de fāng xiàng 为建设新南京而奋斗—南京人民当前的任务与努力的方向 [Struggle for building a new Nanjing—the current task and direction of Nanjing people's efforts]", which was reprinted by Xinhua News Agency Nanjing and *People's Daily* on June 15th and June 16th, respectively. This editorial pointed out that the construction of People's Nanjing should start with four tasks, including restoring and developing production, destroying the remnants of the Kuomintang reactionaries, and resettling Kuomintang public servants and their families. The fourth important task of the editorial is to "eliminate the Pernicious-Vestiges of the propaganda of the feudal fascist culture of the Kuomintang reactionaries and strive to build a national, scientific and popular culture", which shows that the problems of the propaganda work of the Kuomintang reactionaries mainly come from the influence of feudal culture and western culture. Therefore, it is necessary to replace western culture with national culture and defeat feudalism through science. Correspondingly, the cultural problems of the Kuomintang reactionaries themselves will be constructed to deviations from "the masses". This hidden mapping relationship lays the foundation for the connotation of the "Pernicious-Vestiges" of the Kuomintang, and the isomorphism between the bureaucratic bourgeoisie represented by the Kuomintang and the "Pernicious-Vestiges" of imperialism will be further discussed in the third section of this chapter, "Imperialism and the "Pernicious-Vestiges" capitalism (1949–1959).

Besides the isomorphism with imperialism and bourgeoisie, the Kuomintang's own "Pernicious-Vestiges" is more concentrated in the social strata that it occupied and united before 1949. On August 21, 1949, Lin Feng, chairman of the Northeast Administrative Committee, reported to the Northeast People's Congress on the work of the Northeast People's Government in the past 3 years. Xinhua News Agency Shenyang and *People's Daily* reprinted this report on the August 26th and August 29th of that month, respectively. In this paper, "the Pernicious-Vestiges of the education of the Kuomintang Party" is discussed as follows:

> In terms of education, in the past three years, the Pernicious-Vestiges of the enslavement education of the enemy and puppet troops and the education of the Kuomintang Party has been preliminarily eliminated, and the policy of new-democratic education has been established. At present, the number of primary schools, middle schools and institutions of higher learning and the number of students have exceeded those before September 18th or any period under the puppet Manchuria and Kuomintang rule. The proportion of students and children of working people has increased dramatically. Adult education has been carried out through winter education in the last year after the land reform. For the political and cultural education of workers, except Northeast Workers' Political University, many schools or short-term training courses have been set up in major cities. Attention should also be paid to the development of education for ethnic minorities. All primary, middle and primary schools in ethnic minority areas use their own languages for teaching.
> ("dōng běi rén mín dài biǎo dà huì shàng lín fēng zhǔ xí bào gào zhèng fǔ gōng zuò 东北人民代表大会上林枫主席报告政府工作 [Chairman Lin Feng's report on government work at the Northeast People's Congress]",
> *People's Daily*, August 29, 1949, 2A)

From this text, it can be seen that the "Pernicious-Vestiges" of Kuomintang means the suppressed proportion of working people's children, adults, workers, and minority students in the educational policy, while "new democratic education" will be the opposite. A similar situation also appeared in the article "zhōng xué dì lǐ jiào běn zhōng de jǐ gè zhèng zhì sī xiǎng wèn tí 中学地理教本中的几个政治思想问题 [Several political and ideological problems in middle school geography textbook]" written by Jin Canran and published in the 5A book review column on

May 3, 1950. In this article, stereotypes and even contemptuous words used to describe ethnic minorities in the revised edition of *Enlightened New Primary Geography of Our Country* ("kāi míng xīn biān chū jí běn guó dì lǐ 开明新编初级本国地理") were regarded as the concrete manifestation of "the Pernicious-Vestiges of great nationalism instilled in their thoughts by reactionary Kuomintang rulers". Although most of the social classifications in the aforementioned texts are projected in an idealized discourse of educational equity, their roots are closely related to the CCP's mobilization and dependence on the bottom rather than the elite at that time.

From October 20–24, 1949, People's Congresses from all walks of life were held in Fuzhou. On November 2nd, the 1A of *People's Daily* published the article "fú zhōu zhào kāi gè jiè rén mín dài biǎo huì yì tuán jié sān shí liù wàn shì mín jiàn shè xīn fú zhōu 福州召开各界人民代表会议 团结三十六万市民建设新福州 [Fuzhou holds people's congresses from all walks of life to unite 360,000 citizens to build a new Fuzhou]", which recorded the report made by Wei Guoqing, then director of Fuzhou Military Control Commission and mayor of Fuzhou, on the takeover work in the past 2 months and the future policy. The report said:

> Fuzhou is a consumer city. Due to the long-term raids by Kuomintang gangs, the national industry is shrinking day by day, and the handicraft industry is on the verge of complete bankruptcy . . . But there are many difficulties in turning Fuzhou, a city of consumption, into a city of production. To overcome these difficulties, the people of the whole city must do everything possible to support the People's Liberation Army to quickly eliminate the bandits; Restore land and water transportation and strengthen material exchange between urban and rural areas and regions; Resume industrial production and maintain the continuous production of some handicrafts as much as possible; Continue to mobilize and organize unemployed and unemployed people to return to their hometowns for production; Build a new-democratic culture and thoroughly eliminate the reactionary cultural remnants; Implement strict simplification and economy to reduce unnecessary expenses.

From the excerpt of this report, it can be seen that during the ruling period, "Kuomintang gangs", as exploiters and saboteurs of the local economy, also spread out the "reactionary cultural Pernicious-Vestiges" of extravagance and waste. These two major faults are closely related to the fact that the Kuomintang used to occupy more political and economic capital, thus constructing it as an integral part of the "old order" that must be destroyed when creating a new social structure.

Besides, the "Pernicious-Vestiges" of the Kuomintang can also be expressed in a more flexible form. For example, *People's Daily*, 3A, March 2, 1950, reprinted the Beijing message of Xinhua News Agency on February 28, the same year, entitled "shì yìng xīn de jiàn shè shí qī xū yào huá běi jú zhào kāi gè shěng shì xuān chuán bù zhǎng huì yì 适应新的建设时期需要 华北局召开各省市宣传部长会议 [Meeting of Propaganda Ministers of Provinces and Cities Held by North China Bureau to meet the needs of new construction period]". This paper analyzes the situation of the propaganda work of the North China Party, including that "the

From prosperity to decline 137

Pernicious-Vestiges of the Kuomintang's long-term reactionary propaganda still remains among some intellectuals and other people", but it does not explain its specific performance. But in more cases, the "Pernicious-Vestiges" of the Kuomintang is mainly used to change the social class structure and avoid the loss of state-owned assets. For example:

> Now, a few employees have been poisoned by the corrupt ideology and style of the reactionary Kuomintang rule era, and mistakenly treat the railways after liberation with the same attitude they used to treat the railways under Kuomintang rule. Now, our railway is no longer a tool used by reactionaries to exploit and oppress the people, but a tool to faithfully serve the people . . . Our working class is in a leading position in the people's democratic country, and in all state-owned enterprises, the working class is completely in the position of masters. Can we take irresponsible and stealing actions against our own cause? It is not only a shame, but also a criminal act that must be punished for people's own cause to take irresponsible and theft and other destructive acts. All employees of Beijing-Suiyuan Railway should resolutely fight against this wrong idea.
> ("tí gāo jué wù xìng yǔ jì lǜ xìng—píng jīng suí tiě lù dà jiǎn chá 提高觉悟性与纪律性—评京绥铁路大检查 [Improving awareness and discipline—comment on Beijing–Suiyuan Railway inspection"], *People's Daily*, March 4, 1950, 1A)

Without talking about the income of railway workers and how to improve it, "Pernicious-Vestiges" can be understood as a discourse resource of moral governance in this passage. It not only constructs the possible "corruption, theft, smuggling, irresponsible and other wrong behaviors" as the "Pernicious-Vestiges of corruption" that the higher social class can enjoy through privilege, but it also implicitly creates a fear that "theft is the Kuomintang", and the real purpose is to "generally establish a sense of discipline among employees" to avoid "the loss of national transportation". Similarly, the article "chá běi cūn cái zhèng qíng kuàng hùn luàn cūn gàn bù tān wū xiàn xiàng yán zhòng xiàn qū lǐng dǎo yīng jiān chí guàn chè tǒng yī cái zhèng zhèng cè 察北村财政情况混乱 村干部贪污现象严重 县区领导应坚持贯彻统一财政政策 [Chabei Village's financial situation is chaotic, village cadres' corruption is serious, county and district leaders should adhere to the unified financial policy]" was reprinted in the 2A of *Hal Daily* on March 22, 1950. This article also attributed the problem of village cadres' style to "the Pernicious-Vestiges of corruption, waste and extorting by village office workers during the puppet rule", avoiding the specific process of how the former "victims" became today's "victimizers", thus blurring the boundaries between dominant and subordinate class.

Although Kuomintang reactionaries are a relatively specific carrier of "Pernicious-Vestiges", they also lack a clear direction in specific situations, thus constructing an empty and ineffective historical attribution. For example, on March 16, 1957, the 4A of *People's Daily* published the speech made by Sangre Gyatso at the 3rd plenary session of the Second National Committee of the Chinese People's

Political Consultative Conference on "qīng hǎi shǎo shù mín zú jiào yù yǐ yǒu hěn dà fā zhǎn 青海少数民族教育已有很大发展 [Education of ethnic minorities in Qinghai has made great progress]", in which it was mentioned that "the Pernicious-Vestiges left by reactionaries in this respect is very deep, and many parents have all kinds of doubts before or even after their children have enrolled in school". Qinghai Province, located in the northwest of China, was set up by the Kuomintang before the founding of New China. It never suffered from wars waged by other countries, and its economy was dominated by self-sufficient animal husbandry. Therefore, the current problem of "low enrollment rate in minority areas" can only be attributed to "the Pernicious-Vestiges of reactionaries". However, what concerns parents and students have, and how these concerns are related to the "old government", have been vaguely skipped in their speeches, which makes people wonder. However, people are mobilized in such discourse construction, constantly fighting against the shadow of the "past".

In January 1958, "the long-term reactionary propaganda of the Kuomintang gangs" became the last "Pernicious-Vestiges" of the Kuomintang in *People's Daily* ("wǒ men lái yíng jiē xīn de yī nián 我们来迎接新的一年 [Let's welcome the New Year]", *People's Daily*, January 1, 1958, 7A, by Duan Xuefu) and gradually faded out of the historical stage. This article mainly served the "anti-rightist struggle" at that time, and the attack on the "Pernicious-Vestiges" of the Kuomintang was actually an aid to the opposition to "American imperialism" (for a detailed introduction of this article, please refer to section of this chapter entitled "Imperialism and the 'Pernicious-Vestiges' and capitalism [1949–1959]"). But does the short duration of the "Pernicious-Vestiges" of the Kuomintang mean that its influence on the Kuomintang government and the society under its rule has really disappeared completely in the Chinese mainland? Of course, the answer is no. What is certain is that the efforts made by the propaganda organizations of the Chinese Communist Party to clear and "liquidate" the memory of the Kuomintang came to an end temporarily in early 1958. When this effort stopped and if it will be resumed will not change because of the fading or reversion of memory, but it will depend on the CPC's regulations and judgments on realistic social goals. The transformation of memory becomes a highly standardized verbal action that can override social facts.

Imperialism and the "Pernicious-Vestiges" of capitalism (1949–1959)

Different from the two "Pernicious-Vestiges" narratives of the Kuomintang's "Pernicious-Vestiges" and the "old society's" "Pernicious-Vestiges", which changed from prosperity to decline or even disappeared completely, there are some subtle common changing trends among the discourse practices of feudalism, imperialism, and capitalism. First of all, as the "three mountains" oppressed by the "New China people", the narratives are the most typical ideological construction of the revolutionary historical paradigm. For a long period of time, at least from May 1949–October 1971, the intertextuality and symbiotic relationship between imperialism, feudalism, and (bureaucratic) capitalism has always existed. The social reality and ideological problems caused by the three together include years of wars, economic paralysis, social poverty, lack of patriotism, corruption of social atmosphere, exploitation and oppression, and separation from labor and the masses. Besides, the "Pernicious-Vestiges" of imperialism also breeds selfish conservatism, intrigue, worshipping foreign things, and fawning on foreigners, while the "Pernicious-Vestiges" of capitalism has become synonymous with individualism, bureaucracy, wasting state property, fame and fortune, lack of self-cultivation, and obscenity. The aforementioned "Pernicious-Vestiges" narrative, together with its phenomena, has become a discourse resource to define the new socialist state form and the main social contradictions, and it has also become the source of legitimacy and the most powerful revolutionary mobilization method in the early socialist revolution.

Dirlik (1996) pointed out in particular that the concept of imperialism still plays an important role in understanding the history of China at present, but its connotation is completely different from that of the early period. For example, after the short-term interruption of the aforementioned narrative of "Pernicious-Vestiges", since 1966, the "Pernicious-Vestiges" of imperialism began to be expressed as "non-people's scientific undertakings", "art of suppressing national culture", "comprador foreign slave philosophy", "bourgeois theory of human nature", etc., and together with the bourgeoisie, it was incorporated into revisionism.

The "Pernicious-Vestiges" of imperialism appeared in *People's Daily* earlier, in an article entitled "Nightingales in China liberated area" published in the 4A on May 12, 1949. Although this article regards "factionalism, conservatism, selfishness and mutual exclusion" as the concrete manifestation of "the Pernicious-Vestiges of China enslaved by imperialism", these manifestations seem to be the same as the "Pernicious-Vestiges" of feudalism in the same period (see the analysis in "Object and conspiracy of 'class struggle' [1947–1959] of Chapter 4). So, why is the same performance constructed as "Pernicious-Vestiges" from different sources? Other paragraphs of this article provide some clues to the answer:

> Nurses in urban hospitals in liberated areas are generally highly educated, have received special education, have a stable working environment and complete hospital facilities, which is beneficial and necessary for the regular progress of medical and health care. However, some people, especially nurses in private hospitals, must change their views and styles. Since health work is a social welfare undertaking, it is necessary to realize that the present society belongs to the masses of the people, and all modern scientific conditions must be spontaneously dedicated to the masses of the people, so as to overcome the remaining money worship and serve only the minority bourgeoisie. In the past, the attitude of hating the "dirty" working people should be changed, and more consideration should be given to the great contributions of the working people to the society and their suffering from the cruel exploitation of imperialist, feudal and bureaucratic capitalism. More attention should be paid to the fact that science and culture in the vast rural areas of China are not yet popular, and it should not be confined to cities only for pictures. It is even more necessary to oppose those people who use technology as a commodity, and advocate the popularization of science and technology in rural areas, so

as to save the epidemic disasters and the difficulty of lack of medicine in rural areas. Actively consider the health of the people, so as to develop production and support the people's revolutionary war.

(zhōng guó jiě fàng qū de nán dīng gé ěr men 中国解放区的南丁格尔们 [Nightingales in the Liberated Areas of China], *People's Daily*, 4A, May 12, 1949)

It can be seen from this passage that "factionalism, conservatism, selfishness and mutual exclusion" may be regarded as a concrete representation of feudal thought if they appear in rural areas, but when they appear among well-educated medical staff in urban areas, they can only be constructed as the result of actually existing and understandable "imperialist" education, whose fundamental purpose is to completely equate the working people with "dirty" and urban money and goods with "clean". A similar situation also appeared in the report of the "June 6th" Teacher's Day in the same year. In the 1A of *People's Daily* published on June 7, 1949, in the article "Píng shì jiào zhí yuán huān qìng jiào shī jié 平市教职员欢庆教师节 [Teachers' Day celebration in Beiping City]", the author Bai Sheng quoted the speech of Deng Tuo, then the propaganda minister of the CPC Beiping Municipal Committee: "thoroughly eliminate the feudal remnants and fascist remnants, build new people's education, serve the production and construction, and cultivate a large number of new construction talents". Here the author does not elaborate on the performance of these two kinds of "Pernicious-Vestiges". However, what can be seen from the text is that it is not only the need of "cultural and educational work" but also the need for the members of the teaching staff to break away from the higher social strata symbolizing wealth and good education and reunite with the bottom.

Different from the intuitive and concrete "Pernicious-Vestiges" of the "old society", the discourse of "Pernicious-Vestiges" of imperialism and "Pernicious-Vestiges" of capitalism have a clearer range of potential readers, often focusing on those individuals who have really felt this kind of abstract social structure, such as social groups who once lived in cities, had a high socio-economic status and education level, and had close contact with western civilization and capital. Therefore, the "Pernicious-Vestiges" discourse construction of imperialism and capitalism is more theoretical and abstract because of the higher education level of their target readers, and they appear as a discourse mode of social ideological trend. For example, from July 15–16, 1949, *People's Daily* serialized the full text of Guo Moruo's opening speech at the sponsor's meeting of China Social Science Workers' Congress held in Peiping on the July 14th and systematically discussed the "Pernicious-Vestiges" in this article:

Imperialism, feudalism and bureaucrat-capitalism have been defeated at present, but they won't give up for a while. They still have to engage in various conspiracies to disrupt our construction. And their Pernicious-Vestiges is deep, and sometimes those toxins may lurk in our own hearts. Therefore, in the process of building a new democratic new China, we can't help but carry out a sharp ideological struggle to eliminate all the Pernicious-Vestiges of the old times, resist all possible intrigues, and completely eliminate all possible invisible enemies.

("guō mò ruò zài shè huì kē xué gōng zuò zhě dài biǎo huì fā qǐ rén huì shàng de kāi mù cí 郭沫若在社会科学工作者代表会发起人会上的开幕词 [Guo Moruo's opening speech at the Initiator's Meeting of the Social Science Workers' Congress]", *People's Daily*, July 16, 1949, 3A)

In this opening speech, "imperialism, feudalism and bureaucrat-capitalism" appeared at the same time, which almost faithfully carried out the "three mountains" discussion of the CPC's policy, which is the understanding of the "main contradictions" from which the people needed to be liberated in the early days of the establishment of People's Republic of China (PRC) regime. This passage not only constructs a long-term and arduous nature of "clearing away the Pernicious-Vestiges", but also "predicts" the difficulty of opposing the three doctrines at the same time and the inherent logical difficulties that may arise from it. It is attributed to the personal reason that "toxins lurk in our hearts" and requires "sharp ideological struggle" to complete it. If the "Pernicious-Vestiges of the old times" points to changing the inequality between the rich and the poor brought about by feudalism, and "intrigue" indicates the need to prevent the counterattack of bureaucratic capitalism represented by Kuomintang reactionaries, then "the possible invisible enemy" corresponds to the imperialists' "death-fighting" in order to reject all possible material and ideological exchanges with the West when it is difficult to identify the development and intention of external forces around the world.

A similar juxtaposition of "three mountains" also appeared in the opening ceremony of the preparatory meeting for the first national educators' congress reprinted in the 1A of *People's Daily* on July 28, 1949, in the abstracts of speeches by Lu Dingyi, Li Jishen, Shen Junru, Xu Teli, Guo Moruo, Wu Yuzhang, Ma Xulun, and Li Dequan. In the article, Lu Dingyi, then minister of Propaganda Department of the CPC Central Committee, explained in his speech, "the difference between colonial education, semi-colonial and semi-feudal education in Kuomintang areas and new-democratic education in liberated areas" and stressed that "we are determined to wipe away the Pernicious-Vestiges of imperialism, feudalism and bureaucratic capitalism! Our people's cultural and educational undertakings must have an infinitely bright future." On September 24, 1949, the 2A of *People's Daily* published the article "zhōng guó rén mín zhèng zhì xié shāng huì yì dì yī jiè quán tǐ huì yì gè dān wèi dài biǎo zhǔ yào fā yán 中国人民政治协商会议第一届全体会议 各单位代表主要发言 [Main speech by representatives of all units in the First Plenary Session of China People's Political Consultative Conference]". It also recorded the speech of Liang Xi, the chief representative of natural science workers:

> The culture and education in New China is scientific, and we must resolutely fight against reactionary ideas such as feudalism and fascism that violate science . . . The remnants of feudalism are just like weeds growing on the road in people's minds, and we have to use more and more efforts to eradicate the weeds.

142 *From prosperity to decline*

On December 26, 1949, the 3A of *People's Daily* published the article "chóng qìng xué sheng, wén jiào jiè, fù nǚ fēn bié jǔ xíng zuò tán huì, liú bó chéng jiāng jūn qīn lín zhǐ shì 重庆学生，文教界，妇女分别举行座谈会，刘伯承将军亲临指示 [Chongqing students, cultural and educational circles, and women held symposiums, with General Liu Bocheng attending and giving instructions]", which took "checking and eliminating the Pernicious-Vestiges of imperialist and feudal bureaucrat-capitalist education" as one of the purposes of Chongqing's "new democratic cultural and educational policy". It can be seen that this abstract socialist-style discourse construction is mainly aimed at intellectuals and cultural and educational undertakings, rather than being applied to propaganda scenes targeting workers and peasants. Its significance has gradually solidified in the programmatic discussions of the CPC. The educational policy of new democracy should be national, scientific, and popular, and they will also become powerful magic weapons for cleaning up imperialism/fascism, feudal forces, and comprador/bureaucratic capitalism, respectively.

After the establishment of People's Republic of China regime on October 1, 1949, the discourse construction mode of "three mountains" juxtaposing "Pernicious-Vestiges" gradually changed. For example, in the *People's Daily*, October 4, 1949, the 6A published an article entitled "Captain Kurishenko—Remembering the Soviet Air Force Volunteer Team in War of Resistance against Japan", which began to construct the "Pernicious-Vestiges" of imperialism as the "Pernicious-Vestiges" of capitalism in the West:

> At that time, the two biggest problems of China pilots were the residual poison left by German and British and American instructors before and after the Anti-Japanese War—they didn't take care of the aircraft and didn't stress the need of combat, and only wanted to show flying stunts in the air. Comrade Kurishenko made great efforts to fight against this habitual tendency of imperialism to harm the colonial people . . . Kurishenko also slowly said that airplanes are the property of the state. It is not easy for China to transport airplanes from the Soviet Union to China during the war of resistance. If one plane is damaged, there will be one less, and the damaged steel wire will have to be replenished outside Wan Li . . . Soviet volunteer teams are fundamentally different from British and American instructors serving capitalists: for British and American instructors, China has one more plane damaged. In the Soviet Union, however, there were no capitalists. I learned Marxism–Leninism from Comrade Kurishenko's simple words like truth.
> ("kù lǐ shēn kē dà duì zhǎng—zhuī jì kàng rì zhàn zhēng zhōng de sū lián kōng jūn zhì yuàn duì 库里申科大队长—追记抗日战争中的苏联空军志愿队 [Captain Kurishenko—Remembering the Soviet Air Force Volunteer Team in War of Resistance against Japan]", *People's Daily*, October 4, 1949, 6A)

Under the binary opposition created by this text, even if German, British, and American pilots give support to the Chinese Air Force, because China is a "colony", the behavior of Chinese pilots that they don't take good care of their airplanes becomes a behavior that they don't know enough about the hidden dangers of imperialism: damaging Chinese airplanes and buying new ones will contribute to the capital accumulation of "capitalists" in "imperialist" countries. On the contrary, the Soviet Union, which does not implement the capitalist system, and its instructors will be selfless in pursuing actual combat and caring for aircrafts.

Different from the criticism of "camp", the discourse practice of constructing "Japanese imperialism" as "Pernicious-Vestiges" first appeared in *People's Daily* in the early 1950s. This essay entitled "yóu sān fān shì dào tiān jīn 由三藩市到天津 [From San Francisco to Tianjin]", written by Lao She, was published in the column of *People's Garden*, 6A, February 7, 1950, and it was reprinted from the fourth issue of *People's Literature*. This article records Lao She's own experiences when she passed through Tokyo, Japan in October 1949 in a visiting group:

> A visiting group is organized by the U.S. military department, and passengers on board can buy tickets to attend and see Tokyo.
>
> Only four or five hours, I didn't see anything. From Yokohama to Tokyo, all the way was originally an industrial area. Now, it's just a ruined house with no chimney; The factories were bombed out.
>
> On the way, some people are wearing rags without a whole cloth, waiting for the tram. Many women, instead of wearing the gaudy long coat without solid worth, are wearing trousers and short coats.
>
> In Tokyo, people's clothes look slightly neat, but they still can't hide their poverty. Women still wear suits, but their shoes and socks are worn out. Many men are still wearing wartime uniforms and their most hated military hats-the most familiar symbol of violence in China's dramas and pictures during the Anti-Japanese War.
>
> Japanese children, before the war, weren't their faces red and beautiful? Now, they are sallow and emaciated. The hanged war criminal only got one death; Their Pernicious-Vestiges is harmful to future generations!

It can be seen that even though the War of Resistance against Japan's memory has not faded, in the "Pernicious-Vestiges" of imperialism constructed by *People's Daily* in the early days of the founding of the People's Republic of China, calling on Japan's hatred still gave way to emphasizing the confrontation between the two camps in importance, especially after the outbreak of the War to Resist U.S. Aggression and Aid Korea. "Pro-America", "worship of America", and "fear of America" became the most well-documented aspects of the "Pernicious-Vestiges" of imperialism. It also become the "ideological toxin" that *People's Daily* has continuously constructed and emphasized since November 1950, and it marks that the function of *People's Daily* has changed from the exchange of work experience among the CPC members in the early days of its establishment to mass propaganda, which was also verified in the article "bì xū jì xù jìn xíng shí shì zhèng zhì xuān chuán 必须继续进行时事政治宣传 [Political propaganda of current affairs must continue]" published on the 4A of February 4, 1951. It stated that "the imperialists colluded with landlords, comprador and reactionaries to rule China for more than 100 years . . . their ideological and political Pernicious-Vestiges is still deep . . . we must constantly fight with them on the ideological and political front", and its purpose is to "do a good job in the propaganda work to resist U.S. aggression and aid Korea". Subsequently the "Pernicious-Vestiges" of imperialism was equated with the "Pernicious-Vestiges" of American imperialism (for example, *People's Daily*, 4A, February 22, 1951, "hù jī dū tú qiān rén jí huì fā biǎo xuān yán hào zhào quán shì jiè jī dū tú fǎn duì měi dì wǔ zhuāng rì běn 沪基督徒千人集会发表宣言 号召全世界基督徒反对美帝武装日本 [A thousand Christians meeting in Shanghai issued a declaration calling on Christians all over the world to oppose American imperialism to arm Japan]"). This gradually developed into the juxtaposition of "counter-revolution" and "the remnants of Japanese, American and Chiang's cultural thoughts" put forward under the scenario of "the United States arming Japan" (for example, *People's Daily*, 1A, April 5, 1951, "bǎo wèi shì jiè hé píng fǎn měi qīn lüè wěi yuán huì běi jīng fēn huì dìng chū pǔ jí shēn rù kàng měi yuán cháo yùn dòng bàn fǎ yāo qiú quán shì gè qū jí gè dān wèi zuò chū jì huà jìn xíng ài guó xuān chuán jiào yù 保卫世界和平反美侵略委员会北京分会 订出普及深入抗美援朝运动办法 要求全市各区及各单位作出计划进行爱国宣传教育 [Beijing Branch of the Committee for Defending World Peace and Anti-American Aggression formulated the measures for popularizing and deepening the movement to resist U.S. aggression and aid Korea, requiring all districts and units in the city to make plans for patriotic publicity and education]"). By the time the three major movements of land reform, suppression of counter-revolution, and resistance to U.S. aggression and aid Korea were launched in depth, the remnants of imperialism had developed into the idea of "worshiping Britain and the United States, superstitious Germany, exaggerating Japan, doubting the Soviet Union, and not believing in themselves", which was rooted in the influence of imperialist propaganda and was characterized by "the disconnection between teaching and the reality of the motherland" ("cóng wǒ de sī xiǎng tán dào běi jīng dà xué de gōng zuò 从我的思想谈到北京大学的工作 [Talking about Peking University's work from my thoughts]", *People's Daily*, 3A, November 19, 1951, by Ma Dayou, Dean of School of Technology, Peking University). The intention to mobilize and mold the attitude toward war for different groups was increasingly obvious, and the category of "Pernicious-Vestiges" was also expanding.

Around 1954, the original expression of "imperialism, feudalism and bureaucratic capitalism" was rewritten into "feudalism, comprador and fascism", and the ranking of the three "old forces" also indicated that the CCP regime judged the importance of the main social contradictions and their causes at this stage. On August 8, 1954, the 3A of *People's Daily* published the article "wèi péi yǎng shè huì zhǔ yì shè huì quán miàn fā zhǎn de chéng yuán ér nǔ lì 为培养社会主义社会全面发展的成员而努力 [Strive to cultivate members of socialist society with all-round development]" written by Dong Chuncai, then Vice Minister of Education of the Central People's Government, which clearly used this new usage and showed the opposition between socialism and capitalism in "cultural thought" through the discourse construction of "Pernicious-Vestiges". The article points out that "feudal, comprador and fascist ideas" are all reactionary ideological toxins, which need to be eliminated by concentrated efforts. The fundamental reason for the change of rhetoric direction lies in the need to select old textbooks with less ideological toxins in natural science and teach courses necessary for war, so as to learn from the Soviet Union and "pay attention to integrating with practice". Therefore, when educators don't know the specific direction of "learning from the Soviet Union" and can only express their attitude, "dogmatism and formalism" have become the primary obstacles in the process of learning from the Soviet Union. These two doctrines were immediately constructed as "the Pernicious-Vestiges of old education in old China", and they also subtly echoed the priority of "feudal forces" among the three old forces. "Learning from the Soviet Union" was turned into a word game by manipulating words to oppose words themselves.

In June 1957, the anti-rightist struggle began, and the Chinese Communist Party launched an attack on the "bourgeois rightists" who advocated "speaking out loud" in the previous rectification movement. On July 17, *People's Daily* published many speeches at the fourth session of the first National People's Congress. Among them, Pan Dakui, the former leader of China Democratic League, used the words of "bourgeois Pernicious-Vestiges" in his speech of "admitting mistake":

> I have been poisoned by the bourgeois education of American imperialists for a long time . . . My right-wing thoughts are deeply rooted, and my right-leaning friends are many. Since liberation, except for land reform, I haven't participated in various other movements very well. Although my living status is much better than before liberation, no matter from that aspect, my ideology still stays intact on the old foundation. All the Pernicious-Vestiges of old bourgeois democracy still lurks deeply, with little change in outlook on life and slow ideological progress. As a result, once these poisonous bacteria meet the appropriate opportunities, they will unconsciously emerge and endanger the people. In the rectification movement, I did not criticize in good faith from the standpoint of the people. Now I realize this mistake, which makes me feel very ashamed and sad.
> ("我承认错误 潘大逵的发言 [I admit my mistake Pan Dakui's speech]", *People's Daily*, July 17, 1957, 11A)

In this article, Pan Dakui fabricated evidence for his involvement in "bourgeois Pernicious-Vestiges". In addition to "many right-leaning friends" mentioned in the quotation, he was also "born in a landlord family, went to Tsinghua to study since he was 14 years old, and began to be educated by American imperialists, until he returned home when he was twenty-seven". It is these social stratum factors, which are not determined by individuals, rather than their behavior, that make Mr. Pan the antithesis of the "people" and even be charged. As a "rightist", he was excluded from the ranks of the "people" and was not rehabilitated until 1980.

Generally speaking, the "Pernicious-Vestiges" of the bourgeoisie opposed by the anti-rightist struggle is "class nature" based on perception and viewpoint, rather than the capital structure or others in the structural sense, because in this period, the New China was still dominated by the state-owned economy. Therefore, the solution to this "Pernicious-Vestiges" is not asset reorganization but a state-led "movement" with the goal of eliminating or suppressing a specific class, even if this class belongs entirely to the imagination of the initiator of the movement. This was confirmed by Li Jishen, then vice chairman of the Standing Committee of the National People's Congress and vice chairman of the National Committee of the Chinese People's Political Consultative Conference, in his words published in the *People's Daily* in August 1957: "Washing Pernicious-Vestiges is necessary, leaving no trace of it, like breaking the waves and fighting the dragon" ("shuǐ diào gē tóu běi dài hé hǎi yù yǒu gǎn fǎn yòu pài dòu zhēng ér zuò 水调歌头 北戴河 海浴有感反右派斗争而作 [Prelude to Water Melody, Beidaihe Bath in the sea, made by feeling the anti-rightist struggle]", *People's Daily*, August 29, 1957, 2A On the New Year's Day in 1958, the *People's Daily* published a New Year message written by mathematician Duan Xuefu, which revealed the social goal of "Pernicious-Vestiges" in the anti-rightist struggle to build real service:

If the victory of the War to Resist US Aggression and Aid Korea cured the disease of "fear of America", then "Sputnik" cleared away the residual poison of "worshipping America". Rightists' rampant attack on learning the basic policy of the Soviet Union in higher education and scientific research was completely smashed. I believe that in 1958, unswervingly learning from the advanced experience of the Soviet Union and combining our concrete reality will make our higher education and scientific research develop healthily and vigorously along the socialist road.
("wǒ men lái yíng jiē xīn de yī nián 我们来迎接新的一年 [Let's welcome the new year]", *People's Daily*, 7A, January 1st, 1958, by Duan Xuefu)

Here, it seems appropriate for the scientific community to say that the successful launch of the Soviet satellite confirms the correctness of China's Soviet route. Although there is still a big discipline barrier between mathematics and aerospace, it is certain that what really needs to be abandoned as a "Pernicious-Vestiges" is the pro-American and anti-Soviet ideas and the specific individuals or groups who refuse to change this idea, and this is the real meaning of "rightists". On January 18, 1958, the 7A of *People's Daily* published the article "zài gāo děng xué xiào zhí xíng zhī shí fèn zǐ zhèng cè de wèn tí 在高等学校执行知识分子政策的问题 [Problems of implementing intellectuals policy in colleges and universities]" written by Han Ming. This article simply and clearly constructed the "problems of intellectual policy in colleges and universities" as an either-or binary opposition: Adhering to "the party's leadership over intellectuals" is the "proletarian line", otherwise it is "denying the party's leadership over intellectuals and opposing the ideological transformation of intellectuals". This division will make the scope of "enemy" too large, and even lead to a disparity in the number of "enemy" and "friend". Therefore, the author argues that "pro-American anti-Soviet thought" is "the Pernicious-Vestiges of long-term reactionary propaganda of American imperialism and

Kuomintang gangs". By criticizing it, most teachers can know the ugly nature of American imperialism and eliminate their doubts about the Soviet Union.

After the Great Leap Forward movement, the whole country fell into an unprecedented optimism and even fanaticism. On the eve of the National Day in 1959, *People's Daily* systematically reviewed the great achievements of New China in the past 10 years, including this statement:

> It took us only three years to heal the serious trauma caused by the long-term war, completely eliminating the Pernicious-Vestiges of imperialism, feudalism and bureaucratic capitalism, and restoring the national economy on the verge of despair.
> ("huān hū xīn zhōng guó jiàn guó shí zhōu nián！欢呼新中国建国十周年！[Hail the 10th anniversary of the founding of New China!]",
> *People's Daily*, 5A, September 25, 1959, by Li Jishen, chairman of the Revolutionary Committee of the Chinese Nationalist Party)

"Three years" refers to the land reform from the winter of 1950 to the end of 1952. However, if the "three enemies" are "completely eliminated", the phenomenon of "Pernicious-Vestiges" discourse that has increased since 1953 will not be explained. Although the question of when "Pernicious-Vestiges" has been or will be completely "eliminated" has not been answered for the time being, from the report text of *People's Daily*, from 1960–1964, the discourse practice of the juxtaposition of "imperialism, feudalism and bureaucratic capitalism" and the construction of "Pernicious-Vestiges" has fallen into relative silence, which may be a "three-year natural disaster". Perhaps it was a short blank period of "sports governance" before the arrival of the Cultural Revolution, but in any case, it provided more diverse possibilities to spy out what "Pernicious-Vestiges" existed besides class contradictions and ideological camp contradictions.

The short silence of "Pernicious-Vestiges" (1960–1966)

From the beginning of 1960 to May 1964, imperialism, feudalism, and "bureaucratic" capitalism were absent from the discourse construction of "Pernicious-Vestiges" in *People's Daily*. In other words, there was a short period of "discourse interruption" among them. During this period, the "Pernicious-Vestiges" narrative of *People's Daily* only has the general phenomenon of "social disorder" with the "old society" as its source, such as children's education, professional hierarchy, selfish thoughts, commercial window problems, overeating, extravagance and waste, not loving labor, and so on. Until October 1966, this phenomenon of resorting to the marginal areas of personal life was still the only "Pernicious-Vestiges" of the "three mountains", such as "old learning", "yellow music", "serve Qin when in Qin, serve Chu when in Chu", and lack of overall situation. At the same time, this short blank period also cut off the narrative of the "Pernicious-Vestiges" of capitalism into the previous stage of "anti-exploitation" (July 1949–June 1960), which lacked a clear direction, and the Cultural Revolution (October 1966–November 1976), which took class struggle as the key link. The phenomenon may be worthy of the attention of historical researchers—if there is a vacuum stage of ideological discourse and historical paradigm in this historical fragment and is there is the possibility of an alternative discourse generation. Such problems may provide some space for the interpretation of modernity in contemporary China that has not been paid enough attention to.

Since 1960, the discourse practice of "Pernicious-Vestiges" began to slow down in absolute quantity and relative development; especially, the discourse directly used in class struggle was decreasing. On August 1, 1962, Liu Shaoqi's speech "On the Cultivation of Communist party member" at Yan'an Marxist-Leninist College in July 1939 was republished in *Red Flag*, a theoretical journal sponsored by the Central Committee of the Communist Party of China, and *People's Daily* also reprinted it synchronously, so that "every party member must strengthen its own exercise and cultivation in all aspects". Previously, in the rectification movement in the Communist Party of China in 1942, this article was also listed as one of the rectification documents that all party cadres must read. In this article, learning from Marxism–Leninism is divorced from reality, and learning is only regarded as a means to improve one's status and boast about others, and it is constructed as "Pernicious-Vestiges" of the "old society" ("lùn gòng chǎn dǎng yuán de xiū yǎng yī jiǔ sān jiǔ nián qī yuè zài yán ān mǎ liè xué yuàn de jiǎng yǎn 论共产党员的修养 一九三九年七月在延安马列学院的讲演 [On the cultivation of Communist party member: Speech at Yan'an Marxist-Leninist College in July, 1939]", *People's Daily*, 1A, August, 1962, by Liu Shaoqi). Its function is mainly to serve the party's team building rather than the ideological transformation of the masses.

The similar discourse function is also manifested in the literary and artistic creation concept during this period. In June 1964, *People's Daily* published the article "Revolutionizing, Nationalizing and Popularizing—The Urgent Task of the Times for Music Work", which pointed out: "Our society has undergone socialist transformation, and our people have defeated the political attack of the bourgeois Rightists, held high three red flags, and set off the climax of building socialism. In terms of music, it also experienced the criticism of subjective idealism, eliminated the residual poison of bourgeois yellow music, and defeated the conspiracy of right-wingers in the music industry to tamper with revolutionary music tradition and correct music work route. The reason why such a "victory" was achieved was that it strictly followed the historical experience of revolutionary music; "music must obey the requirements of the revolution, reflect the living will of the contemporary people, and serve the revolution and the people" ("gé mìng huà, mín zú huà, qún zhòng huà—yīn yuè gōng zuò pò qiè de shí dài rèn wù 革命化，民族化，群众化—音乐工作迫切的时代任务 [Revolutionizing, nationalizing and popularizing—the urgent task of the times for music work]", *People's Daily*, June 29, 1964, 6A). On August 16, 1964, *People's Daily* published an article on the development of socialist drama written by Ke Qingshi, who was the first secretary of the East China Bureau of the Central Committee of the Communist Party of China and was popular in the "anti-right" movement. The article said, "Some of our drama and literary and art workers came from the old society, or came from exploiting class families, or received bourgeois education, and they were inevitably infected with some Pernicious-Vestiges of capitalism and feudalism". As its title says, such words are constructed to "better serve the socialist economic base" ("dà lì fā zhǎn hé fán róng shè huì zhǔ yì xì jù, gèng hǎo de wèi shè huì zhǔ yì de jīng jì jī chǔ fú wù 大力发展和繁荣社会主义戏剧，更好地为社会主义的经济基础服务 [Vigorously develop and prosper socialist drama to better serve the socialist economic base]", *People's Daily*, 2A, August 16, 1964, by Ke Qingshi).

After 1960, *People's Daily* mainly published two kinds of articles related to "Pernicious-Vestiges", one of which was mainly devoted to shaping and consolidating the concept of public ownership established by the People's Commune movement. For example, in a literary review published by *People's Daily* in 1961, the "Pernicious-Vestiges" discourse constructed by the discussion of the protagonist's image was the People's Commune movement that served the "Great Leap Forward" movement:

> The specific features and close-ups of Wang Jiabin are introduced very clearly. His most outstanding qualities are his loyalty to the party and the socialist cause, and his full enthusiasm. This kind of quality and enthusiasm made him forget himself in his work, and made him break away from the Pernicious-Vestiges of the old times, such as selfishness and narrowness, and become a new type of farmer who measured leniency. The whole process of his purchase of rice seeds in Mei County and his feelings for the property of the agricultural society, such as pigs and mules, fully illustrate this point. These noble qualities of his are combined with his industrious, humble, simple and honest character.
> ("cóng shēng huó sù cái dào yì shù xíng xiàng—tán zhōng de liáng shēng bǎo de xíng xiàng chuàng zào 从生活素材到艺术形象—谈《创业史》中的梁生宝的形象创造 [From life materials to artistic images—on Liang Shengbao's image creation in 'The History of Entrepreneurship']", *People's Daily*, 7A, August 9, 1961, by Li Shiwen)

In this article, by commenting on the characters, the author constructs the opposite of "Pernicious-Vestiges of the old times" and "Pernicious-Vestiges". If the smallholder consciousness that farmers generally had before the public ownership was "Pernicious-Vestiges" of the "old society", then it would be an encouraged quality to take great care of the communal property, whether this "care" refers to rice, seeds, pigs, or mules, as long as they are "public". On the other hand, if "overeating" in the People's Commune movement is equivalent to "households with small population and large labor force take advantage of it", this kind of "flat partnership" that is common in rural areas will become a "bad ethos" and a manifestation of "the residual poison of landlords and gentlemen" ("dà chī dà hē shì huài fēng qì 大吃大喝是坏风气 [Eating and drinking extravagantly is a bad ethos]", *People's Daily*, 2A, November 22, 1964). In 1963, *People's Daily* published an article entitled "An Argument", which emphasized that "I can only look after myself" and "self-cleaning the snow in front of my door" was a kind of "private ownership thought", and the widespread existence of this thought among farmers was another manifestation of the "Pernicious-Vestiges" of the "old society" ("yī chǎng zhēng lùn 一场争论 [An argument]", *People's Daily*, September 19, 1963).

There is another kind of articles, whose main function is not to create or destroy specific classes but to achieve higher industrial and agricultural production goals. For example, on the eve of Children's Day in 1960, a report in *People's Daily* said, "The policy of combining education with productive labor has been generally implemented, the teaching reform in primary and secondary schools is being tested on a large scale, and the Pernicious-Vestiges of bourgeois educational thoughts is being further eliminated" ("quán guó fù lián děng dān wèi lián hé fā chū guān yú qìng zhù 'liù yī' guó jì ér tóng jié tōng zhī cù jìn bǎo yù hé jiào yù gōng zuò dà pǔ jí dà tí gāo 全国妇联等单位联合发出关于庆祝'六一'国际儿童节通知 促进保育和教育工作大普及大提高 [The All-China Women's Federation and other units jointly issued a notice on celebrating the International Children's Day on June 1st to promote the popularization and improvement of conservation and education]", *People's Daily*, 7A, May 19, 1960). In this article, the "Pernicious-Vestiges" of the bourgeoisie has been filled with a new meaning: people and ideas who get something for nothing. In this way, even primary and secondary school students were effectively mobilized to participate in the fiery "socialist construction", and such a policy even became an organic part and advanced model of educational idea innovation at that time.

Similarly, since then, the *People's Daily* article has constructed the idea that "business and service work are inferior" as "the residual poison left by class society" ("zhēn zhèng 'dī rén yī děng' de shì shén me？真正'低人一等'的是什么？ [What is the real 'inferior'?]", *People's Daily*, 6A, June 27, 1963). This view can also be found in the article in August 1964, which promoted the part-time work-study mode in amateur industrial universities. It believed that "the more you learn, the more you despise manual labor and look down on the working people" was a kind of "the most far-reaching Pernicious-Vestiges left by the old society" ("péi yǎng xīn xíng láo dòng zhě de xīn xíng xué xiào 培养新型劳动者的新型学校 [New school for training new laborers]", *People's Daily*, 1A, August 20, 1964), which not only encouraged workers to learn knowledge but also advocated that intellectuals should not be separated from production. On August 30, 1964, *People's Daily* published an article again, with the editorial of "Overcoming the Thought of Ignoring Business" published in *Ta Kung Pao* as the source, encouraging more educated young people to take up "commercial jobs" such as "salespeople and waiters". Its means is to construct the viewpoint of "differentiation between physical labor and mental labor" as "the Pernicious-Vestiges of exploiting class thought", and "the thought of neglecting business is a manifestation of exploiting class thought" ("kè fú qīng shāng sī xiǎng xiàn shēn shāng yè gōng zuò 克服轻商思想 献身商业工作 [Overcoming the disdain for commerce and devoting to commercial work]", *People's Daily*, 2A, August 30, 1964.). In this way, "salespeople, waiters", and other occupations will become reasonable representatives of "commercial jobs", while the educated youth who are unwilling to engage in such occupations will also become the polluters of "the ideological Pernicious-Vestiges of the exploiting class" and thus be excluded from the ranks of "people". Through such language construction, the socialist construction has gained a steady stream of labor force in industry, agriculture, and service industries. However, even in the limited "business" represented by shops at that time, salespeople and waiters were constructed as manual workers and members of the "people", but in October 1964, the commercial department of Beijing still inspected and rectified the shop windows of thousands of shops in the city because "socialist shop windows not only introduce business knowledge but also publicize revolutionary ideas". Therefore, although shop windows are regarded as "silent salespeople", such "salespeople" can't be exempted because of their status as "laborers", among which "some things with feudal Pernicious-Vestiges and advocating bourgeois lifestyle" still need to be cleared ("shāng diàn chú chuāng bù kě xiǎo shì 商店橱窗不可小视 [Shop windows can't be underestimated]", *People's Daily*, 2A, October 27, 1964).

The words of "Pernicious-Vestiges" in 1964 were also shown in *People's Daily* as stimulating people's initiative. Among them, an article entitled "Respecting People and Inspiring People" reads:

> People's little beautiful things and their little contribution to socialism are respected and thanked by their comrades. Here, how tall the image of people is! When a person feels so dignified in everyone's eyes, what good things can't be done! . . . Some people are blinded by the Pernicious-Vestiges of the old society . . . They don't respect themselves . . . Everyone's mind has a heavier code for building socialism, and the speed of building socialism will be even faster.
> ("zūn zhòng rén gǔ wǔ rén 尊重人 鼓舞人 [Respecting people and inspiring people]", *People's Daily*, February 25, 1964, 2A)

Here, being unaware of one's own importance, especially the importance of one's own labor, is contaminated with the "Pernicious-Vestiges" of the "old society", and the opposite of this "Pernicious-Vestiges" is the real purpose of propaganda: to encourage people to accelerate socialist construction through labor. Although there is no sufficient material incentive, labor will be exchanged for the "respect and gratitude" of others. This kind of "words in return" has served as the highest honor that those who respond to the call of the state can get during the limited years of social wealth accumulation.

Similar to these "Pernicious-Vestiges" discourses, which have always been devoted to promoting the enthusiasm of the masses for productive labor, in order to emphasize the great role of "subjective initiative", *People's Daily*'s discourse construction work in this period also targeted the disposable criticism targets at historical resources and historical figures. For example, on July 24, 1964, *People's Daily* reprinted an article published in the fourth issue of *Historical Research* in 1963, trying to encourage people to rebuild their confidence in the "revolutionary cause" that might fail by criticizing Li Xiucheng, an important general of the late Taiping Heavenly Kingdom, who wrote a self-report after he was captured:

> Before he joined the revolution, he was infected by many feudal ideas. The so-called "destiny", "fortunes", "loyal ministers", "enlightened ruler" and "serve Qin when in Qin, serve Chu when in Chu (zài qín wéi qín, zài chǔ wéi chǔ 在秦为秦，在楚为楚)" are all reflections of this ideological Pernicious-Vestiges . . . Because Li Xiucheng has been not only the object of historians' research, but also a figure widely publicized among the masses in various aspects, it is particularly important to correctly estimate his performance . . . Hong Xiuquan, Hong Xiuquan Their sincere revolutionary loyalty, majestic revolutionary spirit, and eternal light in the history of class struggle. They are the beloved revolutionary heroes in our history, and it is this glorious struggle tradition that we should inherit. What about Li Xiucheng? Although he played a great role in the revolutionary history of the Taiping Heavenly Kingdom, he finally lost his revolutionary integrity and betrayed the revolutionary cause of the Taiping Heavenly Kingdom.
>
> ("píng lǐ xiù chéng zì shù—bìng tóng luó ěr gang, liáng hù lú, lǚ jí yì děng xiān shēng shāng què 评李秀成自述——并同罗尔纲，梁岵庐，吕集义等先生商榷 [Comment on Li Xiucheng's self-report—discuss with Luo Ergang, Liang Tonglu, and Lu Jiyi]",
> *People's Daily*, 5A, July 24, 1964, by Qi Benyu)

In this text, Li Xiucheng's self-report of "bowing to the enemy" after being captured is constructed as the product of fatalism and "defection". Although he was a representative figure of peasant uprising in feudal times, Li Xiucheng was described as a completely different figure from Hong Xiuquan and others. The fundamental reason was that the latter did not "defect" when the revolution failed, while the former gave priority to defending his own life. At this point in time, *People's Daily* focused on criticizing the "Pernicious-Vestiges" of feudal thoughts of historical figures in feudal period, not only because Li Xiucheng was a "figure who widely publicized among the masses", but more importantly, in the socialist construction, by criticizing Li Xiucheng and comparing with other leaders of the Taiping Heavenly Kingdom who "persisted in revolution after failure", we created a "model to inspire future generations to fight".

Inheriting the tradition of criticizing the "Pernicious-Vestiges" of the "old society" before the Cultural Revolution, at the beginning of the Cultural Revolution, the words of eliminating the "Pernicious-Vestiges" of the "old society" were first used to establish Mao Zedong's personal authority or even personal worship. In an article published in *People's Daily* in August 1966, "All revolutionary workers" of the Bailongjiang Survey and Design Team of Northwest Survey and Design Institute of Ministry of Water and Electricity wrote, "All revolutionary workers are determined to take the word 'dare' as the head and be fearless in accordance with your great instructions, so as to eliminate all the Pernicious-Vestiges of the old world and create a new world." The real meaning they want to express is another sentence in the article: "We warmly support the CPC Central Committee's decision on the Great Proletarian Cultural Revolution". ("zuì jìng ài de lǐng xiù máo zhǔ xí yǒng yuǎn tóng wǒ men zài yī qǐ 最敬爱的领袖毛主席永远同我们在一起 [The most beloved leader, Chairman Mao, is always with us]", *People's Daily*, August 11, 1966, 2A).

Under such an atmosphere, *People's Daily* published an article "hóng wèi bīng zàn 红卫兵赞 [Praise of Red Guards]" in October, 1966. By using the media and figures in France, Japan, Laos, Congo (Brazzaville), Somalia, Ceylon, and other countries, it expressed its approval of the Red Guards in China through the discourse construction of "eliminating the Pernicious-Vestiges", which was indirectly equivalent to the affirmation of the Cultural Revolution in China. One paragraph reads:

> Under the leadership of contemporary Lenin-Mao Zedong, the young Red Guards in China are cleaning up the muddy water of the past, eliminating all the Pernicious-Vestiges of feudalism, capitalism and imperialism, and opening the way for China's great leap forward; Their experience and victory will all contribute to the international communist movement in Marxism—Leninism.
> ("hóng wèi bīng zàn 红卫兵赞 [Praise of Red Guards]",
> *People's Daily*, 6A, October 22, 1966)

This report was also published in the 5A of *People's Daily*, March 15, 1967 as "wàn suì！zhōng guó de gé mìng chuǎng jiàng hóng wèi bīng—wài guó péng yǒu huān hū zhōng guó wú chǎn jiē jí wén huà dà gé mìng 万岁！中国的革命闯将红卫兵—外国朋友欢呼中国无产阶级文化大革命 [Hooray! China's revolutionary pioneers, the Red Guards—foreign friends cheer the great proletarian cultural revolution in China]". As a result, the discourse construction of "Pernicious-Vestiges" in *People's Daily* seems to have prompted all other countries to accept the historical conceptual framework of "feudalism, capitalism and imperialism" as the source of "Pernicious-Vestiges".

Besides expressing loyalty, determination, and affirmation, the specific direction of the discourse construction of "Pernicious-Vestiges" in the early Cultural Revolution is increasingly empty. In December 1966, *People's Daily* published an article entitled "fān tiān fù dì de biàn huà 翻天覆地的变化 [Earth-shaking changes]". In addition to lamenting that "Pernicious-Vestiges of capitalism, which have not been cleaned up for more than ten years, have been washed away by this huge current today", this article only described the concrete performance of this "huge current" as "under the guidance of the great Mao Zedong Thought, the young Red Guards have made great contributions to the society" ("fān tiān fù dì de biàn huà 翻天覆地的变化 [Earth-shaking changes]", *People's Daily*, 2A, December 2, 1966). By 1967, the situation was even more out of control and the instructions became more and more rude. An article even claimed that,

All revolutionary mass organizations should hold high the great red flag of Mao Zedong Thought, learn from Chairman Mao's works, make great efforts to revolutionize their thinking, practice democratic centralism, break the private sector, and resolutely oppose striving for limelight, mountain-stronghold mentality, cliquish individualism and extreme democratization, I eliminate all the ideological Pernicious-Vestiges left by the private system.

("guì zhōu wú chǎn jiē jí gé mìng zào fǎn zǒng zhǐ huī bù shí xiàng tōng lìng 贵州无产阶级革命造反总指挥部十项通令 [Ten orders of the General Command of the Proletarian Revolution and Rebellion in Guizhou]", *People's Daily*, 1A, February 5, 1967)

But beyond "resolute" and "big-scale", people don't know whether or not this kind of action would succeed, and how the specific implementation path of the action would be. Some articles even put forward the slogan of "eliminating the pernicious influence of economism", but in such articles, the author equates superficial phenomena such as "ostentation and showing off, extravagance and waste of state property" with the connotation of "economism" ("shān xī shí liù gè gé mìng zào fǎn zǔ zhī jiān jué xiǎng yìng máo zhǔ xí de wěi dà hào zhào xiàng quán shěng quán guó fā chū jié yuē nào gé mìng jǐn jí chàng yì 山西十六个革命造反组织坚决响应毛主席的伟大号召 向全省全国发出节约闹革命紧急倡议 [Sixteen revolutionary rebel organizations in Shanxi resolutely responded to Chairman Mao's great call to issue an emergency initiative to save and make revolution throughout the province and the country]", *People's Daily*, 1A, February 9, 1967) or regarded "promoting production and strengthening labor discipline" as a good way to "eliminate the residual poison of economism" ("jiě fàng jūn zhù hā ěr bīn mǒu bù guǎng dà zhǐ zhàn yuán shēn rù gōng chǎng jiāo tōng yùn shū qǐ yè yòng máo zé dōng sī xiǎng wǔ zhuāng wú chǎn jiē jí gé mìng pài duó hǎo quán zhǎng hǎo quán hěn zhuā gé mìng měng cù shēng chǎn 解放军驻哈尔滨某部广大指战员深入工厂交通运输企业 用毛泽东思想武装无产阶级革命派 夺好权掌好权狠抓革命猛促生产 [The vast number of commanders and soldiers of a PLA unit in Harbin went deep into factories and transportation enterprises and armed proletarian revolutionaries in Mao Zedong Thought, seizing and wielding power, paid close attention to revolution and promoted production]", *People's Daily*, 2A, March 23, 1967). In any case, these views have nothing to do with Lenin's criticism of the spontaneity of the workers' movement.

After that, until the beginning of the Cultural Revolution, the articles with "Pernicious-Vestiges" published in *People's Daily* had no obvious trend of increasing or decreasing the number and were also ambiguous in their targeting. Whether it is the remains of the "three enemies" or the discourse construction of the "Pernicious-Vestiges" of the "exploiting class", they are all in a relatively stagnant state. However, such silence is not a permanent tactic between the "Pernicious-Vestiges" discourse and China's propaganda system and historical discourse, but a bigger storm in brewing. We will continue to discuss the discourse origin, the rise and fall process, and the subsequent influence of the "Pernicious-Vestiges" in the Cultural Revolution in Chapter 6 of this book.

References

Assmann, A., & Assmann, J. (2012). Yesterday reappeared: Media and social memory. In Y. Feng & A. Erll (Eds.), *Wen Hua Ji Yi Li Lun Du Ben* 文化记忆理论读本 *Materialbuch Zur Gedächtnisforschung* (pp. 20–42). Beijing: Peking University Press.

Bhatia, A. (2015). *Discursive Illusions in Public Discourse: Theory and Practice*. New York: Routledge.

Dirlik, A. (1996). Reversals, ironies, hegemonies: Notes on the contemporary historiography of modern China. *Modern China*, *22*(3), 243–284.

Olick, J. K., & Robbins, J. (1998). Social memory studies: From "collective memory" to the historical sociology of mnemonic practices. *Annual Review of Sociology*, *24*(1), 105–140.

Songtag, S. (1966/2003). *Against Interpretation and Other Essays* (trans. by C. Wei). Shanghai: Shanghai Translation Publishing House.

Stone, C. B., & Hirst, W. (2014). (Induced) Forgetting to form a collective memory. *Memory Studies*, *7*(3), 314–327.

Zhao, J 赵静蓉. (2013). Ethical dimension of Chinese memory: Rethinking the localization of memory crisis 中国记忆的伦理学向度—对记忆危机的本土化再思考. *Exploration and Free Views* 探索与争鸣, *12*, 77–81.

Zhao, J 赵静蓉. (2015). The virtue of memory and its realistic path to the ethicization of Chinese memory 记忆的德性及其与中国记忆伦理化的现实路径. *Literature and Culture Studies* 文学与文化, *1*, 50–59.

6 Paradigm interruption and re-narration
Historical reversal as a source of "Pernicious-Vestiges"

As far as dominant discourse is concerned, "Pernicious-Vestiges" and its rhetorical object are used to define a kind of individual or collective memory tradition that is blindly inherited without reflection because of its social structure or historical inertia. This memory tradition is often related to the ideology opposed by the current mainstream discourse, which is embodied in a series of thoughts and actions with discourse and body as carriers. So where does the "Pernicious-Vestiges" come from? Does the memory constructed as "Pernicious-Vestiges" really exist? Or is it just the imagination of the discourse subject? What is the purpose of this imagination and what kind of social reality is it to deal with? Counting the rhetorical objects of "Pernicious-Vestiges" in *People's Daily* since 1946, in terms of the construction and imagination of memorized objects, the most striking thing is the frequent appearance of the word "doctrine".

According to Wang (2015), although the upsurge of "ism" once gave the revolutionary youth in China individual meanings and answers, with the change of political power, "ism" has become "an unbreakable dominator in the private sphere". If it's the Three People's Principles or Bolshevism, these "charming words" invariably provide a complete set of political blueprints and roads against a series of old things such as imperialism and warlords, and at the same time, they also provide a cultural script to solve the perplexity of life and become an all-encompassing, exclusive, and self-consistent "justice system" covering life, the country, and the universe. "Doctrine", as a whole in the original sense, was metonymized to the end, and was replaced by a set of fragmented practical methods that could change the realistic predicament and provide an outlet to solve all problems. Similarly, after 1949, so many "isms" appeared in the rhetorical memory objects of "Pernicious-Vestiges" in *People's Daily*, which can be regarded as a re-politicization of the private sphere. Different from the first politicization period, "doctrine" was mostly used to construct public life, collective identity, social mobilization, and action organization. The doctrines rhetorical by "Pernicious-Vestiges" more served the change of regime ideology, which forced the overlapping of China intellectuals' personal pursuit and national destiny into the daily life of the people at the bottom. In addition, carrying forward some specific "isms" and making other "isms" "Pernicious-Vestiges" is also a kind of social mobilization suitable for specific historical and social situations. It realizes the transformation of "isms" from

DOI: 10.4324/9781003409724-6

ideological field to physical imagination by "taking life into the universe of isms", which makes the intervention in private life under the ownership change have the necessary legitimacy and, at the same time, calls back "general personal frustration", which is big enough.

In the process of social construction of memory, "political morality" or memory ethics (Zhao, 2015), embodies the collusion between politics and morality, creates certain social conventions and consciousness for memory, and stipulates its code of conduct and ideological standards. In Chapter 4 and Chapter 5, we introduced all kinds of discourse practices committed to ideological reform that have appeared in the form of "Pernicious-Vestiges" since the founding of *People's Daily* in 1946 and before the Cultural Revolution. However, the real ideological transformation was the most concentrated embodiment during the Cultural Revolution. This violent discourse practice is a link between the past and the future. It not only benefited from the influence of the tradition of constructing the cultural "Pernicious-Vestiges" of intellectuals since the founding of the People's Republic of China, but it was also corrected by the more violent narration of the "Pernicious-Vestiges" of the Cultural Revolution in the subsequent historical rectification, showing two peaks of tit-for-tat discourse construction. Next, in this chapter, we will analyze the root, process, correction process, and subsequent influence of the Cultural Revolution from the aspects of the memory object, memory subject, and its process of narrative construction. We will reveal the rhetorical direction and connotation reflected by the "Pernicious-Vestiges" discourse practice of *People's Daily* and the deeper ethical problems of memory involved.

Cultural "Pernicious-Vestiges" of intellectuals (1949–1971)

Although the "Pernicious-Vestiges" of intellectuals was the most concentrated during the Cultural Revolution, in fact, this language pattern has a long tradition in New China. For a long time after the founding of the People's Republic of China, the ideas of intellectuals that were not welcomed by the ruling goals became "unjust memories" and specific entities that carried such memories. On May 4, 1949, *People's Daily* published an article entitled "Máo zé dōng tóng zhì lùn "wǔ sì" yùn dòng 毛泽东同志论"五四"运动 [Comrade Mao Zedong on the May 4th movement]" in its 4A to commemorate the 30th anniversary of the May 4th movement, which quoted Mao Zedong's view expressed in *On New Democracy*:

> Before the May 4th Movement, the struggle on the cultural front in China was the struggle between the new bourgeois culture and the old feudal culture . . . At that time, the so-called schools, new schools, and western schools were basically bourgeois natural sciences and social sciences (basically, it means that there were many feudal remnants of China in the middle).

Also, in the intellectual world, when "Pernicious-Vestiges" is used as a mobilization discourse to separate from a specific source ideologically, it can also serve the change of ownership and capital structure. In order to further serve the

War to Resist U.S. Aggression and Aid Korea, the focus of "Pernicious-Vestiges of U.S. imperialism" was removed to Yenching University. On February 12, 1951, Yenching University, which had received American subsidies for 32 years, was taken over by the Ministry of Education of the Central People's Government. On the 13th, the 1A of *People's Daily* published the article "Zhōng yāng jiào yù bù jiē shōu yān jīng dà xué, gāi xiào shī shēng jí huì qìng zhù jué xīn sù qīng měi dì wén huà qīn lüè yí dú 中央教育部接收燕京大学 该校师生集会庆祝决心肃清美帝文化侵略遗毒 [The Central Ministry of Education took over Yanjing University where teachers and students gathered to celebrate the determination to eliminate the Pernicious-Vestiges of American imperialism's cultural aggression]". The purpose of winning the War to Resist U.S. Aggression and Aid Korea by strengthening wartime propaganda was interpreted as "thoroughly eliminating the Pernicious-Vestiges of American imperialism's cultural aggression in China". Later, Qián jùn ruì 钱俊瑞, then deputy minister of education, said, "All teachers, students and staff will not only cut off the ties with American imperialism economically, but also eliminate all ideological toxins of American imperialism in the future". Although Yenching University and the American support behind it played an important role in the process of "eliminating the Pernicious-Vestiges of feudalism", once the capital and ownership ran counter to the overall political goal, they completely lost their "cultural" justice.

Since 1952, *People's Daily* has published a series of articles that reflect how Yenching University broke away from the "Pernicious-Vestiges" of American imperialism. These articles more directly show how any clues that are inextricably linked with a particular class can be constructed as "Pernicious-Vestiges" when its existence cannot serve political goals. For example, an article in the 3A of March 10, 1952 wrote:

> In the past three years after liberation, although the American imperialists have been driven out of China, their Pernicious-Vestiges in Yenching university is deeply rooted. Many teachers still seriously retain the decadent ideas of the bourgeoisie, especially the idea of worshipping the United States. Give a few of the most prominent examples. At the first orientation meeting after liberation, the head of the school was still publicly praising the American imperialists, saying that the Americans in yenching university are "good people who can hardly be found in the United States"! When Kē ān xǐ 柯安喜, the former director of the school's western language department, fled back to the United States during the China People's War to Resist US Aggression and Aid Korea, the teachers and students of the western language department had a big farewell party and gave her a pennant with the words "The spring breeze turns the rain, which benefits me a lot". In February, 1951, the school was taken over as a public university, but since a year ago, most of the contents of courses have remained intact. The Department of Politics even bought a large number of reactionary reference books not long ago, including the works of Dulles, Churchill, the warmongers, and Jessup, the executor of the U.S. aggressive policy in the Far East. There are people in the psychology department who continue to

teach lectures that publicly slandered the working people in the past. For example, the wisdom of the 35-year-old working people can only be equivalent to the seven-year-old children of the bourgeoisie. What the Spanish language department tells in class is still ridiculous detective stories, and what it reads after class is still obscene pornographic books. As for teachers' frequent spreading of bourgeois individualism's fame and wealth thoughts and America-worshipping remarks in and out of class, it is a very common phenomenon . . . In order to cooperate with the movement and thoroughly eliminate these ideological filth, Yenching University Economic Inspection Committee held an "exhibition of American imperialist cultural aggression crimes" at the beginning of this month. The exhibition proves with many irrefutable materials that this school founded by the American imperialist church is not only the center of spreading bourgeois ideas, but also the position of American imperialism invading China. The revelation of these facts shattered many people's illusion about Yenching University for more than 30 years.

> ("Sù qīng dì guó zhǔ yì wén huà qīn lüè de yǐng xiǎng—jì yān jīng dà xué 'měi dì guó zhǔ yì wén huà qīn lüè zuì xíng zhǎn lǎn huì' 肃清帝国主义文化侵略的影响——记燕京大学'美帝国主义文化侵略罪行展览会' [Eliminating the influence of imperialist cultural aggression—a record of Yenching University's Exhibition of Crimes of American Imperialist Cultural Aggression]", *People's Daily*, 3A, March 10, 1952, by Xinhua News Agency reporter Shěn róng 沈容)

Four days later, *People's Daily* continued to publish a follow-up report on the educational achievements of this exhibition. Combined with the "anti-corruption, anti-waste, anti-bureaucracy movement" at that time, "the corrosion of bourgeois ideology" and "the Pernicious-Vestiges of American imperialist cultural aggression" were respectively interpreted as the phenomenon of "wasting state property" and "not distinguishing between the enemy and the friend", which also echoed the name of the exhibition sponsor—Economy Inspection Committee. In the report, the final result of this exhibition is,

> Seeing these undeniable facts, the masses have no doubt anymore. Everyone feels that the U.S. imperialists and their agents like "spreading bacteria" bring toxins into our minds. Everyone unanimously demanded that those who wore all kinds of cloaks, but actually echoed with American imperialism and continued to implement the aggressive policy of American imperialism, publicly review.
>
> ("Pī pàn zī chǎn jiē jí sī xiǎng, sù qīng měi dì guó zhǔ yì wén huà qīn lüè yǐng xiǎng, yān jīng dà xué sī xiǎng dòu zhēng jìn rù gāo cháo 批判资产阶级思想，肃清美帝国主义文化侵略影响，燕京大学思想斗争进入高潮 [Criticizing bourgeois ideology and eliminating the influence of American imperialist cultural aggression, Yenching University's ideological struggle reached a climax]", *People's Daily*, 3A, March 14, 1952)

Thus it successfully transformed the goal of supporting the war into a "mass movement". This also shows that, compared with the class, those thoughts carried by intellectuals in social ideological trends will be the easiest to be constructed as "Pernicious-Vestiges" and eliminated, especially through discourse construction such as expressing one's position. Since then, the cultural "Pernicious-Vestiges" of intellectuals has become an extremely prominent aspect in the discourse construction of "Pernicious-Vestiges" in *People's Daily*, and "Pernicious-Vestiges" has also become the core keyword to peek at how the power of contemporary China is turning against intellectuals and how intellectuals are turning against each other.

Since the object of criticism is the intellectuals with various theoretical resources, the criticism of intellectuals' thoughts will be easy to make excuses for because of the abstract nature of the theory itself, so that it is very easy for the logic to be inconsistent. For example, in the article "Guàn chè duì dài zhōng yī de zhèng què zhèng cè 贯彻对待中医的正确政策 [Implementing the correct policy of treating traditional Chinese medicine]" published in the 1A of *People's Daily* on October 20, 1954, the author blamed the failure of leading cadres of health administration to implement the Chinese medicine policy of "unity and cooperation between Chinese and Western medicine" as "they got the Pernicious-Vestiges of bourgeois ideology and looked down on the medical heritage of the motherland" rather than "the Pernicious-Vestiges of imperialism", which is more logically consistent when constructing the binary opposition between China and the West. Combined with other "Pernicious-Vestiges" constructions in this period, it can be found that the intolerance of the intellectuals has become the continuation of the aftermath of criticizing Wǔ xùn zhuàn 武训传. Except for the class criticism consistent with the leader's ideology, other literary and philosophical theoretical orientations that cannot be classified as "proletarian materialism" will be labeled as "bourgeois idealism" and become an integral part of "Pernicious-Vestiges". Even the discourse tradition of directly referring to individuals with "Pernicious-Vestiges" can be traced back to the creation of this kind of cultural "Pernicious-Vestiges" (such as, "Qīng chú hú shì de fǎn dòng zhé xué yí dú—jiān píng yú píng bó yán jiū hóng lóu mèng de cuò wù guān diǎn hé fāng fǎ 清除胡适的反动哲学遗毒——兼评俞平伯研究红楼梦的错误观点和方法 [Clearing the Pernicious-Vestiges of Hu Shih's reactionary philosophy—with a comment on Yu Pingbo's wrong viewpoint and method of studying A Dream of Red Mansions"], *People's Daily*, 3A, November 5, 1954). The author of this article, Wáng ruò shuǐ 王若水, experienced several ups and downs of fate, which became the epitome of the similar fate of contemporary Chinese intellectuals under different life experiences.

Since then, research institutes such as Peking University, Renmin University of China, Beijing Normal University, Henan Normal University, and Tianjin Cultural Academies have successively held "seminars" on "A Dream of Red Mansions", providing intellectuals with the opportunity to express their support for "proletarian materialism". It was true as "a class struggle in the field of academic thought". The correct answer should be like "the existence of bourgeois idealism is the Pernicious-Vestiges of Hu Shih's reactionary philosophy" ("Běi jīng dà xué zhào kāi guān yú 'hóng lóu mèng' yán jiū de zuò tán huì 北京大学召开关于'红楼梦'研究

的座谈会 [Peking University held a symposium on the study of 'A Dream of Red Mansions']", *People's Daily*, 3A, November 9, 1954). Answering that "Yu Pingbo used Hu Shih's reactionary' experimentalism' viewpoint and method to study 'A Dream of Red Mansions' will spread poison" will also help to avoid becoming a part of the "Pernicious-Vestiges", and thus prolong their fragile and uneasy academic life ("Zhōng guó rén mín dà xué děng gāo děng xué xiào shī shēng duì 'hóng lóu mèng' yán jiū zhōng de cuò wù guān diǎn zhǎn kāi pī píng, tiān jīn wén huà xué shù jiè zhào kāi guān yú 'hóng lóu mèng' yán jiū de zuò tán huì 中国人民大学等高等学校师生 对'红楼梦'研究中的错误观点展开批评，天津文化学术界召开关于'红楼梦'研究的座谈会 [Teachers and students of Renmin University of China and other institutions criticize the wrong views in the study of 'A Dream of Red Mansions'; Tianjin cultural academic circles hold a symposium on the study of 'A Dream of Red Mansions']"; *People's Daily*, 3A, November 17, 1954). On December 8th, literary researcher Zhāng xiào hǔ 张啸虎 published a signed article in *People's Daily*, which said:

> Mr. Yu Pingbo's standpoint, viewpoint and method of studying A Dream of Red Mansions were not only directly influenced by the comprador-bourgeois thought represented by Hu Shih, but also inherited and developed the class consciousness of the feudal literati represented by Jin Shengtan, who was called the so-called "great genius" by Hu Shih in all basic aspects. That is to say, the theory and practice of Mr. Yu Pingbo's research on a dream of red mansions is the product of the combination of comprador bourgeois consciousness and feudal scholar-bureaucrat class consciousness . . . It is precisely because Mr. Yu Pingbo's position, viewpoint and method of studying a dream of red mansions are far from the traditional consciousness of Jīn shèng tàn 金圣叹's feudal scholar-bureaucrat class and close to Hu Shih's road of comprador bourgeois idealism; It is precisely because Mr. Yu Pingbo is not the only one who is affected by this kind of influence in the current field of classical literature research, and its poison is extremely deep; Therefore, it is of great practical significance to eliminate the erroneous ideas of the bourgeoisie and the Pernicious-Vestiges of the feudal literati class thoughts.
>
> ("Yú píng bó yán jiū 'hóng lóu mèng' de cuò wù de yòu yī gēn yuán 俞平伯研究'红楼梦'的错误的又一根源 [Another root of Yu Pingbo's mistakes in studying 'A Dream of Red Mansions']", *People's Daily*, 3A, December 8, 1954)

This article adds a new accusation to Yu Pingbo's study of "A Dream of Red Mansions"; he was deeply influenced by Jin Shengtan, who was "the Pernicious-Vestiges of the class thought of feudal literati". Regardless of whether Jin Shengtan, who was active in the late Ming Dynasty and early Qing Dynasty, intended to "attack the working class on the ideological front", the "evidence" that Yu Pingbo was influenced by Jin Shengtan provided by the author is only a personal explanation of "two people's views coincide", and Hu Shih, who is a representative figure of Yu Pingbo's "New Redology", praised Jin Shengtan. In this way, Yu Pingbo not only had the "Pernicious-Vestiges" of the bourgeoisie manifested by reactionary experimental philosophy because of his textual research on "A Dream of Red Mansions" rather than class criticism but also was infected with the "Pernicious-Vestiges" of the feudal scholar-officials because of the "unwarranted" connection. Ironically, the way in which the author of this article constructed and even fabricated "Pernicious-Vestiges" coincides with the feudal dynasty "literary prison", which suffered the most from the literati class in China. Later, in the speech of Guo Moruo, then chairman of the China Federation of Literary and Art Circles, this debate turned into a criticism of "the Pernicious-Vestiges of Hu Shih's reactionary thoughts in literary and art circles and academic circles", and Hu Shih had already moved to the United States and Taiwan. Guo Moruo explained his warning and hope for Yu Pingbo in an article published in *People's Daily* on December 9, 1954:

> It is not surprising that Mr Yu Pingbo used bourgeois idealism to study "Dream of Red Mansions" thirty years ago. Thirty years ago, it was rare for people of our age who studied classical literature to know Marxism. The reason why Mr. Yu Pingbo's research has become a problem is that in the past 30 years, especially since liberation, there has been no change in his thoughts, positions and methods . . . Mr. Yu has admitted his mistakes and is determined to carry out the struggle between the new self and the old self. We hope Mr. Yu's new self can win the struggle.
> ("Sān diǎn jiàn yì 三点建议 [Three suggestions]",
> *People's Daily*, December 9, 1954, 1A)

Guo Moruo concisely expressed the function of constructing the cultural "Pernicious-Vestiges" of intellectuals in his article by comparing with other socialist "Pernicious-Vestiges"; the cultural "Pernicious-Vestiges" with intellectuals as the carrier is not for the purpose of eliminating a specific social class but for launching the "new self's struggle against the old self"—opposing the past self with the present self. The essence of the so-called "new self" is actually to make intellectuals naturalize in the dominant ideology and be loyal to the regime, so as to use their cultural capital to serve the propaganda cause and at the same time reduce the diversity of public opinion, so as to consolidate the public opinion base of the new Republic. At the end of 1954, the criticism of Hu Shih went around again to his teacher John Dewey, and the objectives of anti-imperialism, anti-capitalism, and anti-Chiang finally converged in one place to focus more on criticism ("Chè dǐ sù qīng fǎn dòng zhé xué sī xiǎng shí yòng zhǔ yì de yǐng xiǎng 彻底肃清反动哲学思想实用主义的影响 [Thoroughly eliminating the influence of reactionary philosophical pragmatism]", *People's Daily*, 3A, December 20, 1954). On December 24th, 25th, and 27th, *People's Daily* published three consecutive journals with the title of "Speech at the First Plenary Session of the Second National Committee of China People's Political Consultative Conference", which included articles with the same title from different authors covering the vigilance against "the pernicious influence of landlord and bourgeois ideology" in cultural and educational undertakings (2A, by Shěn yàn bīng 沈雁冰, member of China People's Political

Consultative Conference, also well known by his pen name Mao Dun, a writer); eliminated "the Pernicious-Vestiges of Hu Shih's reactionary thoughts" in the academic and literary circles (2A, by Guo Moruo, member of China People's Political Consultative Conference); and his own "Pernicious-Vestiges of old thoughts" (2A, by Wēng wén hào 翁文灏, member of China People's Political Consultative Conference, a famous geologist who served as the executive dean of the National Government in 1948, lived in Paris in 1949, and returned to Beijing in 1950). At that time, more than a year had passed since the signing of the Korean Armistice Agreement, and the criticism of Yu Pingbo actually served to criticize Hu Shih, and the criticism of Hu Shih and Dewey also served to resist the signing of the mutual defense treaty by the United States. The Chinese intellectuals involved became one of the few possible roles in the local discourse repertoire under international politics. The reason why these plays need to be staged was answered in the article "Zhōng sū yǒu hǎo xié huì wǔ nián lái gōng zuò de bào gào 中苏友好协会五年来工作的报告 [Report on the work of the Sino-Soviet Friendship Association in the past five years]" published in the 2A of *People's Daily* on December 30, 1954.

> Since its establishment, the Sino-Soviet Friendship Association has been carrying out publicity and education among the masses on internationalism of developing and consolidating Sino-Soviet friendship . . . These activities have played an important role in eliminating the residual poison of anti-Soviet propaganda by enemies at home and abroad. In the movement to resist U.S. aggression and aid Korea, the Sino-Soviet Friendship Association widely publicized the comparison of the forces of the two camps in the world, which enhanced the people's confidence in victory and their trust and love for the Soviet Union . . . Sino-Soviet friendship basically reached the level of household names and being deeply rooted in people's hearts.

This protracted debate lasted until the end of 1955. Hu Shih, who "sold the imperial philosophy of American imperialism pragmatism", Zhāng jūn mài 张君劢, who "sold Bergsonism", Liáng shù míng 梁漱溟 and the "others" who "sell New Kantism, New Hegelism and Machism" are all constructed as "scholars of the bourgeoisie and the feudal comprador class" and call on the intelligentsia to "continue to eliminate their legacy" to quiet down temporarily with satisfaction ("Liè níng lùn zhé xué gōng zuò zhě de zhàn dòu gāng lǐng—dú liè níng de 'lùn zhàn dòu wéi wù zhǔ yì dǐ yì yì' 列宁论哲学工作者的战斗纲领—读列宁的'论战斗唯物主义底意义' [Lenin's combat program for philosophers—reading Lenin's 'On the Significance of Combat Materialism']", *People's Daily*, December 27, 1955, 3A).

In 1954, Hú fēng 胡风 wrote a report on the practice of literature and art in recent years to the Central Committee of the Communist Party of China, which triggered nationwide criticism. On January 21, 1955, the 3A of *People's Daily* published the article "Wǒ men bì xū hé hú fēng de wén yì sī xiǎng huà qīng jiè xiàn 我们必须和胡风的文艺思想划清界限 [We must draw a clear line with Hu Feng's literary thought]" by Bào chāng 鲍昌, calling Hu Feng's thought "the Pernicious-Vestiges of Hu Shih School" on the grounds that "Mr. Hu Feng's viewpoint and

Hu Shih School's viewpoint have reached an objective and consistent conclusion". Later, the "abstract concept" used by Hu Feng was called "the residual poison of idealistic sensation theory" ("Pī pàn hú fēng zhé xué sī xiǎng shàng de zhǔ guān wéi xīn lùn 批判胡风哲学思想上的主观唯心论 [Criticizing the subjective idealism of Hu Feng's philosophical thought]", *People's Daily*, 3A, March 3, 1955, by Bao Chang). In May of the same year, Hu Feng was arrested and imprisoned and was designated as the head of Hu Feng's counter-revolutionary group. He was released in 1979, rehabilitated in 1980, and died of illness in 1985.

The movement continued. In February 1956, China People's Political Consultative Conference held the second plenary session of the Second National Committee. The main issue of this meeting is the issue of "intellectuals' transformation". At the meeting, Xú zhèng 徐正, a water conservancy expert, made self-criticism, thinking that he had "always been skeptical about communist party's policies" because of "the Pernicious-Vestiges of deception and propaganda during the Kuomintang rule" ("Zài zhōng guó rén mín zhèng zhì xié shāng huì yì dì èr jiè quán guó wěi yuán huì dì èr cì quán tǐ huì yì shàng de fā yán 在中国人民政治协商会议第二届全国委员会第二次全体会议上的发言 [Speech at the Second Plenary Session of the Second National Committee of China People's Political Consultative Conference]", *People's Daily*, February 13, 1956, 5A).

In addition to press releases, party documents and resolutions, and exchanges of work experience within the party, most literary and artistic works and critical articles published in *People's Daily* are written by well-educated writers and propaganda cadres. Therefore, in the discussion around "Pernicious-Vestiges", there is no lack of self-reflection of intellectuals. For example, in 1956, *People's Daily* published a literary review of Hunan opera, which interpreted and evaluated a story of a pedant failed in the imperial examination repeatedly suddenly died due to excessive excitement after he eventually passed. Finally, the article wrote:

> The era of imperial examinations has long passed, and the image of Shí hào 石灏 can't represent our times, of course. However, it is believed that scholars should be superior to others, and the way for them to 'seek official positions' is to master the writing brush that decides the fate of others and dominate the people's heads. This kind of Pernicious-Vestiges is not left in everyone in modern times.
> ("Tán fěng cì xǐ jù 'jì tóu jīn' de yōu xiù biǎo yǎn 谈讽刺喜剧 '祭头巾'的优秀表演 [On the excellent performance of the satirical comedy 'Sacrificing the headscarf']", *People's Daily*, 7A, July 6, 1956).

This idea may not be unique to "scholars", and it also explains why there have been so many criticisms of intellectuals under various pretexts and even "movements" led by the party and the state since the founding of New China. In the minds of many Chinese people, the ultimate goal of studying is always to achieve class transition and become the one who "lifts his arms and calls out", or it is the only moral way to realize the class transition is not hereditary replacement, nor is it getting rich by doing business; "learning while being excellent makes you an official". This deep-rooted concept hasn't changed quickly in the repeated criticism of "Pernicious-Vestiges". With the help of the shell of criticizing "Pernicious-Vestiges", the tough traditional concept has become the critical thing itself again and again.

In June 1957, the anti-rightist struggle began, and the centralized construction and denunciation of intellectuals' "Pernicious-Vestiges" entered an unprecedented stage. Once again, Mr. Guo Moruo "stepped in" and lost no time in taking the lead on the eve of Army Day by comparing intellectuals with disciplined troops, and he criticized the intellectual groups including himself:

> At present, there are about five million intellectuals in China. If this team can have the same spirit as the People's Liberation Army, how much strength it will exert in cultural and educational construction and production construction! Unfortunately, however, our army of intellectuals is poorly organized. Compared with the working class and the peasant class, we are naturally inferior, and even seem to lag behind the industrial and commercial circles. I don't mean to say this carelessly. Please take a look at Rightists' anti-Party and anti-socialist foolishness this time. Of course, there are Rightists in the industrial and commercial circles, but among the Rightists, intellectuals account for the vast majority, and most of them are dignitaries and core members. This deserves our deep introspection. Under the leadership of the party, our intellectuals have received several years of socialist education, but our experience is not enough. The Pernicious-Vestiges of old-style education is too deep for us, and our spirit is still filled with old-style ideology. It is not easy to get in under the influence of new education. The spirit of many of us is, to be honest, the "Taiwan Province" to be liberated. Such people are demanding unconditional freedom, unlimited personal interests and absolute democracy. Such people, whenever they have the chance, or when they are stirred up, they will engage in foolishness. We can see clearly in this rampant attack by Rightists.
> ("Xiàng zhōng guó rén mín jiě fàng jūn kàn qí—jì niàn zhōng guó rén mín jiě fàng jūn jiàn jūn sān shí zhōu nián 向中国人民解放军看齐—纪念中国人民解放军建军三十周年 [Aligning with China People's Liberation Army—commemorating the 30th Anniversary of China People's Liberation Army]", *People's Daily*, 2A, July 31, 1957)

In this battle message, Mr. Guo seems to criticize himself, but in fact he ran ahead of other intellectuals in pledging allegiance, thus winning the initiative of "turning over a new leaf". At that time, less than 8 years after the establishment of the Chinese Communist Party's political power, there were almost no groups that fully accepted the new democratic education and grew up until they were qualified to become "intellectuals". It can be said that all the intellectual groups at that time were influenced by the "old-style education". However, in the "Pernicious-Vestiges" of "old-style education" constructed in this article, it is still unclear which specific opinions are put forward by people who are "demanding unconditional freedom, unlimited personal interests and absolute democracy" and which actions are "anti-party and anti-socialist folly". However, Guo Moruo still does not hesitate to compare the intellectual group in New China in 1957 to the "Taiwan Province" where the Kuomintang regime is located—both of them are looking forward to the capture and liberation of the Chinese Communist Party again. This kind of intellectual's struggle against himself, which is eager to get rid of himself, can be described as an extremely unbearable scene in the process of "Pernicious-Vestiges" discourse construction.

What's more, in the Great Leap Forward movement in 1958, the discourse of "Pernicious-Vestiges" humiliated this group by juxtaposing intellectuals with "femininity". In this article entitled "Dǎ diào jiāo qì 打掉娇气 [Knocking off the effeminacy]", the author, who self-classified as a "female intellectual" wrote:

> Feminine is the majority. To be more precise, I'm afraid it should be said that femininity is dominated by intellectuals . . . All kinds of femininity can only be formed and established in a society of class exploitation. Without this exploitation as the foundation, the literati can't be elegant, the wit can't be romantic, and the femininity can't take root . . . Since ancient times, women are more effeminate, which has economic foundation and social roots. The sin is not in women themselves, but in the evil old society . . . Now we are the era when working people are masters of their own affairs. Social thoughts and feelings are different, so is the aesthetic outlook . . . Being strong and brave in spirit, not to mention being able to withstand criticism. Even if it is a hurricane, we can stand up, stand firm, not afraid of any difficulties, and always make great strides . . . While setting up a new atmosphere and forming a new style, we must thoroughly eliminate the Pernicious-Vestiges of the old society . . . May all of us intellectuals, especially female intellectuals, including the author herself, become fighters for socialism!
>
> (*People's Daily*, 4A, May 18, 1958, by Yè wén 叶雯)

With the help of the first criticism of China's classical literati's aesthetic standards, the author focuses on the second (self) criticism of the characteristics of intellectuals who can't stand criticism. Through the broad attribution of the "Pernicious-Vestiges of the old society", the author puts the social function of intellectuals, which is more deconstructive than constructive, on the opposite side of the Great Leap Forward movement that pursues the development of productive forces and creates an ideal intellectual image for them who can "stand criticism". Therefore, the initiative provides a sufficient excuse for intellectuals to become the targets of the mass movement launched by the state, and its purpose is exactly the same as the CCP's expectation for intellectuals: to be "strong fighters" who are loyal to political parties and political power and striving to promote the realization of social engineering rather than "cold-eyed bystanders" who are good at criticizing and putting forward different opinions and specialize in theory but are not eager to put them into practice. Sadly, it is also the female intellectuals, rather than others, who played the key role of "opposing themselves" in the national movement to transform intellectuals and femininity at the same time.

A similar situation also appeared in *People's Daily* in late 1959. On December 15th, *People's Daily* reprinted an article from *Anhui Daily* and made a clear criticism of intellectuals' "thinking behind closed doors", arguing that such a move was "divorced from reality, from the masses, from political struggle, and emphasized the role of individuals", and that it was "a Pernicious-Vestiges that has been circulated and has not been thoroughly eliminated yet" ("'Bì mén sī guò' sān cuò '闭门思过'三错 [Three mistakes of thinking behind closed doors]", *People's Daily*, December 15, 1959, 8A). That is to say, even if intellectuals admit their mistakes, they are still considered insufficient. This kind of "rehabilitation" must be "completely convinced" on the basis of fully accepting criticism from the masses and political struggle. In this way, the mode of "the masses" criticizing "intellectuals" has been fixed. This system seems magnanimous without fear of questioning. In fact, it unconditionally expands everyone's right to criticize and even trap intellectuals. For this reason, the tragedy of the Cultural Revolution has laid a foreshadowing that cannot be ignored.

The discussion of "Pernicious-Vestiges" is also widely seen in the debate on how socialist journalism should develop in the articles published in *People's Daily*. In June 1957, Wáng yīng fù 王英富, a student of Beijing University of Political Science and Law, wrote an article in *People's Daily*, refuting the view of Yáng yù qīng 杨玉清, a jurist, that "*People's Daily* has been singing praises for several years, and its editor-in-chief has to step down". He believed that "real literati" could oppose the "status quo" in a society dominated by the exploiting class, but in a society dominated by the working class, "literati" was more concerned with new things, besides, they can only "oppose the Pernicious-Vestiges of the old society" ("'Yáng yù qīng suǒ zhǐ de 'mín' jiū jìng néng bāo kuò duō shǎo rén ? 杨玉清所指的'民'究竟能包括多少人？ [How many people can Yang Yuqing refer to as the 'people'?]", *People's Daily*, June 9, 1957, 2A). This also indirectly tells the basic logic of why *People's Daily* frequently uses the words of "Pernicious-Vestiges" and the heartfelt wishes of the Chinese Communist Party that the propaganda work should be carried out. During the Great Leap Forward movement, more than 260 journalists attended the National Congress of Advanced Workers in Culture and Education. *People's Daily* reprinted an article written by Xinhua News Agency, emphasizing the correctness of the Party's policy of running newspapers and promoting the "two-legged walk" of combining professional journalists with correspondents and the "three combinations" of "leading cadres of the Party, professional journalists and workers directly involved in actual struggles". In this article, the section entitled "Working-class news team is growing" reads:

> In the process of implementing the policy of running a newspaper by the whole party, the working-class news team is growing rapidly. A large number of cadres with practical revolutionary struggle experience and outstanding correspondents from industry and agriculture have joined the ranks of professional journalists . . . After the rectification movement, the former professional journalists have become political leaders, resolutely listened to the party's words, acted in strict accordance with the party's intentions, often

went deep into reality, went deep into the masses, shared the same fate and shared the same breath with them, completed their propaganda tasks, and reformed their own ideological style. In the melting pot of the revolution, he gradually burned the Pernicious-Vestiges of bourgeois news views, accepted the armed forces of Mao Zedong Thought, and became a loyal soldier of the party and a simple servant of the masses.

("Quán dǎng bàn bào de xīn fā zhǎn 全党办报的新发展 [The new development of running newspapers in the whole party]", *People's Daily*, 7A, June 11, 1960, by Xinhua News Agency reporters Yú cháng qīn 于长钦, and Yú huī yīn 余辉音)

Although this passage doesn't state what the "Pernicious-Vestiges of bourgeois news viewpoint" is, it can be seen from the context that the opposite of the respected news viewpoint is "Pernicious-Vestiges"; that is to say, advocating the professionalism of journalists; excluding workers, peasants, and revolutionary struggle cadres from participating in news reports; and questioning or hesitating about the party's orders, intentions, and thoughts will all be the concrete manifestation of holding the "bourgeois news viewpoint" and thus be constructed as the opposite of "the masses". Although this journalistic concept was more vividly reflected through the construction of "Pernicious-Vestiges" in the Great Leap Forward, throughout the history of journalism in New China, it seems that the respect for the concept of de-professional reporting and the emphasis on the role of propaganda are never far away, and this vigilance and contempt for professionalism is exactly the same as the social theme that *People's Daily* has been serving by continuously constructing other "Pernicious-Vestiges" of intellectuals. Thus, in his speech on the work of Xinhua News Agency on June 28, 1956, Liu Shaoqi advocated that "writing journalists' names in front of the news will make journalists famous and beneficial". During the Cultural Revolution, it was framed as "the idea of publish first" and became the "Pernicious-Vestiges of the revisionist news line" that news reporting teams should eliminate ("Jiā qiáng xīn wén bào dào duì wǔ de sī xiǎng jiàn shè 加强新闻报道队伍的思想建设 [Strengthening the ideological construction of news reporting teams]", *People's Daily*, February 27, 1971, 1A). When Chairman Mao's "对《晋绥日报》编辑人员的谈话 [*A talk to the editorial staff of the Shansi-Suiyuan Daily*]" published in 1948 was re-mentioned during the Cultural Revolution, all the situations that were contrary to Mao's "sharp, acerbic, and distinctive revolutionary style" at that time were classified as "decadent style". As for what this style is, it was vaguely described as "living by rumors and sophistry" ("Fā yáng wú chǎn jiē jí de gé mìng wén fēng—xué xí 《Duì jìn suí rì bào biān jí rén yuán de tán huà》发扬无产阶级的革命文风—学习《对<晋绥日报>编辑人员的谈话》 [Carrying forward the revolutionary style of the proletariat—learning from *A talk to the editorial staff of the Shansi-Suiyuan Daily*]", *People's Daily*, 2A, September 27, 1971, by the Shanxi Provincial Committee of the Communist Party of China) and seems that rumors or sophistry do not exist at all in the respected "writing style". As a result, the writing style of news reports has become a "line struggle". These seemingly strange political phenomena are not surprising; no matter which historical period the news work in New China is in, "the Pernicious-Vestiges" discourse is basically reduced to a political tool to dilute the professionalism of news for various purposes.

After the beginning of the Cultural Revolution, intellectuals not only acted as the main targets of being stigmatized and "criticized" (see the corresponding parts of "Fight selfishness and criticize revisionism" and "The Gang of Four and the Cultural Revolution" of this chapter), but the CPC's policy decisions that had the greatest impact on intellectuals were the Wǔ qī zhǐ shì 五·七指示 May 7th Directive and the Qī èr yī zhǐ shì 七·二一指示 July 21st Directive. The idea put forward by Mao Zedong in the latter was quoted into the practice of "Pernicious-Vestiges" discourse construction in *People's Daily*, which complemented the anti-intellectual atmosphere prevailing in the society at that time:

> Universities still need to be set up. What I'm mainly talking about here is that universities of science and engineering still need to be set up, but the academic system should be shortened, education should be revolutionized, proletarian politics should be in command, and Shanghai Machine Tool Works should take the road of training technicians from workers. Students should be selected from workers and peasants with practical experience, and after a few years of schooling, they will return to production practice.–Mao Zedong

> The overthrown bourgeoisie will never be content with their failure, always making use of their influence in the ideological field, exploiting the weakness of intellectuals' world outlook, spreading toxins, trying to recapture their lost "hereditary territory" and competing with the proletariat for intellectuals . . . Workers, peasants and soldiers students have a high awareness of class struggle and line struggle, sharp critical ability and rich practical experience. Once they come into contact with teaching practice, they can see at a glance the "Pernicious-Vestiges" of feudalism, capitalism, and revisionism. They have a profound comparison between school and society. In comparison and identification, it strongly criticized the crawling thought of foreign slaves who had been entrenched in the position of culture and education for a long time. From this point of view, we vigorously carry out the activities of "teaching soldiers by officers, instructors by soldiers, and soldiers by soldiers", and those who are capable are teachers, teaching and learning from each other. By adopting heuristic and discussion-based lecture methods, the initiative and creativity of workers, peasants and soldiers in learning are fully exerted, and a new teacher-student relationship is established.

> ("Wèi chuàng bàn shè huì zhǔ yì lǐ gōng kē dà xué ér fèn dòu 为创办社会主义理工科大学而奋斗 [Struggle for the establishment of socialist universities of science and engineering]", *People's Daily*, 1A, July 22, 1970, signed by Zhù qīng huá dà xué gōng rén, jiě fàng jūn máo zé dōng sī xiǎng xuān chuán duì 驻清华大学工人，解放军毛泽东思想宣传队 workers in Tsinghua University and Mao Zedong Thought Propaganda Team of the People's Liberation Army)

During the whole Cultural Revolution, this discourse illusion successfully established the social impression that intellectuals belonged to the "weak" bourgeoisie, and the workers, peasants, and soldier's college students belonged to the "powerful" proletariat. Under the double blessing of "proletarian politics in command" and "all-powerful teachers", workers, peasants, and soldiers naturally have the right to act as teachers of intellectuals, which is justified in terms of class and ability. It can be said that this article basically fully tells the reality of the existence of the surviving "universities" during the Cultural Revolution and the low status of intellectuals' professionalism. In the remaining "liberal arts universities", it is impossible to study Mao Zedong Thought only in the part related to their major. This idea is constructed as "a reflection that the Pernicious-Vestiges of the old liberal arts has not been eliminated". Therefore, "liberal arts universities must learn Mao Zedong Thought as a whole" ("Yòng gé mìng dà pī pàn gǎi zào wén kē dà xué—fù dàn dà xué 'wǔ · qī' wén kē shì diǎn bān de diào chá bào gào 用革命大批判改造文科大学—复旦大学'五·七'文科试点班的调查报告 [Transforming liberal arts Universities with revolutionary criticism—investigation report of Fudan University's 'May 7th' liberal arts pilot class]", *People's Daily*, June 29, 1971, 2nd edition, originally published in *Red Flag Magazine*, No. 6, 1971, by Fudan University Committee of the CPC).

With the end of the Cultural Revolution and the continuous advancement of reform and opening up, the status of the intellectual class in society has changed. Intellectuals who entered the mainstream after 1990s are powerful supporters, promoters, and beneficiaries of the reform and opening up policy economically. At the same time, Chinese society has become increasingly diverse and complex since the 1990s, and the government's control over intellectuals has become more sophisticated. In other words, intellectuals have gained a certain degree of freedom (Zhao, 2012, p. 3). Reform and opening up have also opened up the "ideological market" in China to a certain extent, and various social ideological trends such as liberalism, nationalism, conservatism, and new leftism are constantly emerging. The diversity of society and the limited freedom gained by intellectuals have accelerated their understanding and differentiation of the current social situation in China, and it is difficult to reproduce the unified anti-institutional discourse initiated by the intellectual class. Therefore, the intellectual class is no longer the object of overall negation and criticism, and the "Pernicious-Vestiges" of intellectuals also fades out of China's news propaganda discourse. However, the trauma brought by this movement to intellectuals will continue to spread in the elite discourse space of China through other varieties of "Pernicious-Vestiges" discourse.

Fight selfishness and criticize revisionism: Whose revision? Whose "Pernicious-Vestiges"? (1966–1976)

Different from the juxtaposition and criticism of "imperialism, feudalism and bureaucratic capitalism" around 1949, the private ownership represented by capitalism, as a social trend of thought, began to appear much later in the discourse construction of "Pernicious-Vestiges" in *People's Daily* because the reflection on this trend of thought will have a realistic soil only after the real knowledge of capitalism and bourgeoisie. Even so, we can still get a glimpse of what "bourgeois ideology" is in the *People's Daily*'s "self-renewal discourse" in the early days of the People's Republic of China:

> To thoroughly eliminate the Pernicious-Vestiges of the old society, we must carry out ideological transformation, especially the ideological transformation of the bourgeoisie . . . The bourgeois ideology is all about making money. The more money you make, the better. The sooner the better. As long as you make more money, you will do whatever it takes. So fraud, bribery, tax evasion, tax dodging, false accounting, stealing information, speculation and hoarding, disrupting the market, and so on . . . any who wish to make more money quickly can do it. During the rule of the Japanese puppet regime and the Kuomintang reactionaries, hoarding was a common occurrence. Bribery, fraud, false accounting, tax evasion, etc. are regarded as necessary means in business. After liberation, for more than two years, while the industry and commerce were improving and the country was being built, many industrial and commercial owners were stirring up again. They used the old methods to attack the cadres of the people's government, bribing, flattering, bowing and scraping, all sorts of dirty and shameless means to lure the cadres into corruption in order to carry out their illegal activities. This was an unforgivable great sin . . . These heinous traitors, in the final analysis, wanted to make a lot of money, that is, the idea of profiteering. So profiteering is the root of all evil. The idea of bourgeois must first be painstakingly eradicated.
> ("Zī chǎn jiē jí sī xiǎng bì xū gǎi zào 资产阶级思想必须改造 [Bourgeois thought must be reformed]", *People's Daily*, 3A, January 29, 1952, by Yú huán chéng 俞寰澄)

That is to say, in the "anti-corruption, anti-waste, anti-bureaucracy movement" in 1952, some property owners, in order to protect themselves, not only interpreted the "bourgeois ideology" as the commercial logic of "profit-seeking" but also joined in many illegal commercial frauds. The two were confused with each other, and together they constituted the so-called "capitalist ideology", which enabled them to be attacked both morally and legally.

By the Great Leap Forward in 1958, industrial and agricultural production was in full swing, and the social service industry also got limited development. *People's Daily* seized this opportunity and published an article criticizing "a few customers and passengers" for being impolite to service personnel. It not only consistently attributed "the idea of despising commercial staff" to the influence of people's "capitalist business practices such as extortion, speculation and fraud, and self-interest", but it also pointed out that "thousands of years of feudal dynasties and Confucianism advocated attaching importance to agriculture over commerce" ("Zài 'rén rén' zhī zhōng 在'人人'之中 [In the 'Everyone']", *People's Daily*, May 25, 1958, 4A). This is an earlier article in *People's Daily*, which explores the shackles of New China's commercial development and its historical roots.

By the time of the Cultural Revolution, bourgeois "Pernicious-Vestiges" and revisionist "Pernicious-Vestiges" appeared at the same time, and the mutual referential relationship between them was gradually fixed. "The Pernicious-Vestiges of revisionism" first appeared in *People's Daily*. It was an editorial published by *China Youth Daily* and *Beijing Daily* on June 16, 1966. The background of this article is "Beijing Municipal Committee of the Communist Party of China and the Central Committee of the Communist Youth League reorganized Beijing Municipal Committee of the Communist Youth League" because "the former Beijing Municipal Committee of the Communist Youth League resisted and resisted the line of Marxism–Leninism and Mao Zedong Thought in youth work, and tried its best to push the revisionist line. They often resist and resist the work principles and decisions put forward by the Central Committee of the Communist Youth League according to the instructions of the CPC Central Committee and Chairman Mao. They spread a lot of bourgeois ideology toxins among the broad masses of teenagers". This article ends like this:

> We believe that the newly reorganized Beijing Municipal Committee of the Communist Youth League, under the leadership of the Beijing Municipal Committee of the Communist Party of China and the Central Committee of the Communist Youth League, will surely hold high the great red flag of Mao Zedong Thought, thoroughly eliminate the Pernicious-Vestiges of the revisionist line of the former Beijing Municipal Committee of the Communist Party of China in youth work, and lead the majority of members and youth to play an active role in the great socialist cause during the Great Proletarian Cultural Revolution and become the right-hand man of the Party.
> Long live the great invincible Mao Zedong Thought!
> ("Máo zé dōng sī xiǎng yǒng yuǎn shì gòng qīng tuán de zuì gāo zhǐ shì 毛泽东思想永远是共青团的最高指示 [Mao Zedong Thought will always be the supreme instruction of the Communist Youth League]", *People's Daily*, 3A, June 16, 1966)

In this way, "revisionist Pernicious-Vestiges" and "bourgeois toxin" can refer to any idea or action that is or is considered to be contrary to Mao Zedong Thought and even "not expressing one's position" can be criticized. The vigorous Cultural Revolution began.

Revisionism originally refers to the incomplete and faithful reinterpretation of Marxist theory, and then it expanded into a kind of words and deeds that are superficially convinced of the socialist line but actually disagree with it. The reason for the prevalence of revisionist "Pernicious-Vestiges" in China after 1966 was not only influenced by the political experience of the former Soviet Union but also effectively connected with the previous announcement of a series of all-round victories of mass movements in New China—the current social contradictions did not come from the incompleteness of various struggles since the founding of New China but from the local problems of those who had shown their conviction in the route but still wanted to fight back. Therefore, compared with the whole class or structural "Pernicious-Vestiges" shaped by imperialism, feudalism, and bureaucrat-capitalism, the revisionist "Pernicious-Vestiges" needs to point out who the specific "counterattacker" is, for instance, "Zhou Yang's activities in the cultural and artistic circles are the most extensive, and there are many Pernicious-Vestiges, which do great harm" ("Zhōu yáng de 'zì yóu huà' dú huà le zhōng yāng měi shù xué yuan 周扬的'自由化'毒化了中央美术学院 [Zhou Yang's liberalization poisoned the Central Academy of Fine Arts]", *People's Daily*, July 16, 1966, 3A). Publicly publicizing the revisionist' literature and art for all program but failing to implement the "literary direction of workers, peasants and soldiers put forward by Chairman Mao", Zhou Yang, a literary theorist, became the leader of the "black line of literature and art", which needed to be thoroughly "eliminated" ("Bù xǔ zhōu yáng cuàn gǎi gōng nóng bīng wén yì fāng xiàng 不许周扬篡改工农兵文艺方向 [Zhou Yang is not allowed to tamper with the literary direction of workers, peasants and soldiers]", *People's Daily*, 4A, July 13, 1966). Because "Xia Yan 夏衍, like Tian Han 田汉, is a general under Zhou Yang, since the 1930s, they have been best friends, pursued Wang Ming's opportunistic line", and "faithfully carried out Zhou Yang's counter-revolutionary revisionist literary black line", Xia Yan, the pioneer of the left-wing film movement in China, was called a counter-revolutionary revisionist, and their "Pernicious-Vestiges" needed to be thoroughly cleared up ("彻底清算电影界'老头子'夏衍的反党罪行 '离经叛道'论是夏衍反革命的宣言书 [Thoroughly liquidating the anti-party crime of Xia Yan, the 'old fellow' in the film industry]", *People's Daily*, December 10, 1966, 6A). Subsequently, similar charges were gradually concentrated on Liu Shaoqi through a similar fabricating way from alluding to name-calling.

Revisionism can also be interchanged with imperialism in a specific context. For example, on July 23, 1966, at the Beijing Science Symposium, an international scientific conference, Vice Premier 聂荣臻 Nie Rongzhen of the State Council delivered a congratulatory message on behalf of the China government at the opening ceremony, saying,

> The scientific culture of the people on four continents serves the people's anti-imperialist revolutionary cause . . . The development of science is first and foremost a political issue. If imperialism is not overthrown and the Pernicious-Vestiges of imperialism is not removed, the people's scientific cause will not develop.
> ("在北京科学讨论会一九六六年暑期物理讨论会开幕式上的贺词 [Congratulatory message at the Opening Ceremony of the 1966 Summer Physics Symposium of Beijing Science Symposium]", *People's Daily*, 4A, July 24, 1966)

The reason why "Pernicious-Vestiges" of imperialism has become an enemy that the four continents need to face together was answered in the welcome speech of 周培源 Zhou Peiyuan, vice chairman of China Association for Science and Technology and head of the China delegation of scientists.

Today, we scientists from so-called 'underdeveloped' countries discriminated against by modern revisionists gather together to organize such a large-scale single-subject academic seminar, which is a very encouraging thing.

("北京物理讨论会隆重开幕 [Grand opening of Beijing Physics Seminar]", *People's Daily*, July 24, 1966, 1A)

In this sense, the word "revisionism" can reclassify the Soviet Union, which has completed socialist transformation, as an "imperialist" country, thus achieving the purpose of more flexibly dividing the line between the enemy and friend.

At the beginning of 1967, the Cultural Revolution movement intensified. In April, some leading revolutionary cadres in Shanghai held a discussion, pointing out that the concrete manifestation of the reactionary bourgeois line was "not trusting the masses and not relying on them", and that the "Pernicious-Vestiges" of these lines and performances had not been completely eliminated. At the same time, the article also pointed out that:

If there were no proletarian revolutionaries who rose up to revolt, the revisionist time bomb buried in the revolutionary ranks would not be dug out, the proletarian regime would be handed over to the bourgeoisie, and China would change its color. To fail to see this is to deny the revolutionary masses and the Great Proletarian Cultural Revolution.

("充分认识革命群众立下的不朽功勋 充分发挥革命群众组织负责人的作用 [Fully understand the immortal feats made by the revolutionary masses and give full play to the role of the heads of revolutionary mass organizations]", *People's Daily*, 3A, April 3, 1967)

These typical landslide arguments have further consolidated the impregnable and irrefutable equivalent relationship between bourgeois "Pernicious-Vestiges", revisionism, and denial of the masses/Cultural Revolution.

Previously, *Red Flag Magazine* had published an editorial trying to use the familiar words of "Pernicious-Vestiges" to reverse the chaotic situation of criticizing all cadres at that time. According to the article,

It is the opinion of those people who put forward the reactionary bourgeois line to treat cadres indiscriminately, reject them and overthrow them all, and that's what they did. This kind of "Pernicious-Vestiges" has not been eliminated in the minds of some comrades, so they have unconsciously made this mistake to a certain extent.

("论革命的'三结合' [On the 'Three Combinations' of the Revolution]", the 5th editorial of *Red Flag Magazine* in 1967, reprinted by *People's Daily* on March 10, 1967, 1A)

The *People's Daily* reprinted the editorial published by Wen Wei Po in Shanghai on April 12, again "Protecting a handful" itself may be the "Pernicious-Vestiges" of the reactionary bourgeois line. What people need to implement is Chairman Mao's cadre policy of "uniting the majority and cracking down on a handful" ("彻底肃清在干部问题上的资产阶级反动路线的流毒 [Completely eliminating the pernicious influence of the reactionary bourgeois line on cadres]", *People's Daily*, April 14, 1967, 1A). However, under the historical trend mentioned earlier, it seemed too late. When the Red Guard Congress of Capital Middle School shouted the slogan of "thoroughly criticizing the reactionary bourgeois line and eliminating its pernicious influence", it didn't talk about what this line was but only targeted the unknown "a handful of capitalist road establishment in the party" ("首都中等学校红卫兵代表大会宣言 [Declaration of the Red Guard Congress of secondary schools in the capital", *People's Daily*, 2A, March 27, 1967), when "Mao Zedong Thought Red Guards of Dongfanghong Commune of Shandong University of Finance and Economics" won the infighting with "Red Guards of Shandong University of Finance and Economics", and labeled the latter as "the Pernicious-Vestiges of reactionary bourgeois line", declaring the overall victory of "educating and uniting the deceived students" ("矛头指向党内走资本主义道路的当权派——争取团结受蒙蔽同学一道干革命的体会 [Pointing at the capitalist establishment in the party—the experience of striving for and uniting the deceived students to join in the revolution]", *People's Daily*, April 1967, 4A), we can see that people had been in a fanatical movement for a long time, and they no longer cared about what the object of criticism was but only cared about how they could criticize.

Take another example to reflect the fanaticism of movements at that time. In order to continue to "mobilize the masses to fight the masses", in a "statement of repentance" published in *People's Daily*, even not reporting others was constructed as a revisionist "Pernicious-Vestiges":

There is no problem in self-examination, but I have concerns about exposing the problems of members. I also think that only when the Party Committee of the Bureau agrees to expose me can I expose it, so that the principle of "collective leadership" of the Party will not be destroyed . . . The revolutionary masses have seen that the poison of our revisionist organizational principle is deep, and there must be a process to remove this Pernicious-Vestiges. Therefore, they have adopted a gradually deepening method of help. Once, more than a dozen of them held a small meeting and encouraged me to expose it. At that time, although there was a word "fear" in my thought, the meeting had already been convened, and the attendees also promised to "keep a secret", so I reluctantly exposed it.

("打碎束缚我彻底革命的精神枷锁 [Breaking the spiritual shackles that bound my complete revolution]", *People's Daily*, 4A, March 26, 1967, by 武宝儒 Wu Baoru, former deputy director of the Political Department of Guizhou Geological Bureau)

In this article, the revisionist "Pernicious-Vestiges" of the party concerned is reflected in the fact that as a leading cadre, insisting on not reporting other people in the organization is considered to be in conflict with Chairman Mao's statement that "slavishness should never be advocated in Communist party member". With the help of such authoritative moral discourse and de-situational interpretation of discourse, the original moral principles and even the moral bottom line have been completely broken down. Of course, the main weapon to realize this de-moralization process is the fear hidden in people's hearts, which is stimulated by labeling revisionism and being excluded from the category of "people".

Driven by fear, people quickly use the word "Pernicious-Vestiges" to demarcate boundaries to express their loyalty. Naturally, the greater the loyalty, the better, regardless of what the revisionism and the "reactionary bourgeois line" they oppose mean. For example, Tuoli Commune, Fangshan County, Beijing, launched a "great revolutionary criticism", which was characterized by "exposing a large number of the largest minority of the party who took the capitalist road, sweeping away the pernicious influence of counter-revolutionary revisionism, learning from Chairman Mao's works, and establishing Mao Zedong Thought" ("坨里公社结合本地的斗批改肃清修正主义流毒 革命大批判有力地促进了革命和生产 [Tuoli Commune combined with local fights to correct the pernicious influence of revisionism, the criticism has promoted revolution and production]", *People's Daily*, 2A, May 10, 1967). The Revolutionary Committee of Hejin County, Shanxi Province, "followed the instruction of Chairman Mao" and absorbed the poor middle peasants to take part in the Mao Zedong Thought class. The learning results are as follows: "With the help of the poor middle peasants, the cadres realized that the Pernicious-Vestiges of 'black cultivation' had not been eliminated, and they lacked a profound understanding of the mass movement" ("县社办学习班有贫下中农参加好 [The class run by the county society has a good participation of the poor middle peasants]", *People's Daily*, February 12, 1968, 1A). The Revolutionary Committee of Guangdong Province held the 'Three Combinations' Mao Zedong Thought class, and one of its 'remarkable results' was that it recognized that 'factionalism among the cadres' was the Pernicious-Vestiges of the reactionary bourgeois line ("从教育着手帮助干部站出来革命 [Helping the cadres stand up for revolution from education]", *People's Daily*, 2A, March 27, 1968).

It should be pointed out that during the Cultural Revolution, there were some exceptions in the discourse construction of "Pernicious-Vestiges". 张富章 Zhang Fuzhang, deputy director of the Revolutionary Committee of Shanghai Instrument and Telecommunications Industry Bureau, tried to protect revolutionary leading cadres with the help of "Pernicious-Vestiges" words:

> Revolutionary cadres, especially revolutionary leading cadres, are familiar with the historical situation of their own units. After more than a year of Cultural Revolution and mass criticism, they had a deeper understanding of the revisionist line of running enterprises promoted by Khrushchev in China. Together with the revolutionary masses, they criticize revisionist black goods, and they will be more able to hit the key points and expose them thoroughly. This is very beneficial to thoroughly eliminate the residual poison of revisionism and do a good job in fighting, criticizing, and correcting this unit.
>
> ("从'三结合'的实践中看干部 [Seeing cadres from the practice of 'Three Combinations']", *People's Daily*, 4A, December 10, 1967)

However, this kind of discourse construction finally brought the particular individual "Khrushchev of China" into the spotlight of criticism.

As the discourse framework of "Khrushchev's revisionism" was gradually accepted or used as a shield, in May 1968, *People's Daily* reported that the mechanical and electrical plant of Benxi Iron and Steel Company had refined high-quality advanced steel grades by reprinting the cable of Shenyang Branch of Xinhua News Agency, saying that it was because "China Khrushchev's" capitulationism and creeping "line and the residual poison of worshipping foreign goods were not eliminated". It is the result of "implementing the line of counter-revolutionary revisionism to run enterprises" ("革命职工以革命大批判推动科学实验 [Revolutionary Workers promote scientific experiments with great criticism of revolution]", *People's Daily*, 4A, July 5, 1968), and this historical attribution is further confluent with the great emphasis on personal initiative constructed by the "Pernicious-Vestiges" discourse during the Great Leap Forward.

Since October 1968, the discourse framework of "removing the Pernicious-Vestiges" has gradually become propaganda, which only reflects the subtle changes in the export number. The "Pernicious-Vestiges" should be "Chinese Khrushchev's counter-revolutionary revisionist line" at first ("工人阶级登上上层建筑斗批改舞台是二十世纪六十年代的伟大事件 [It was a great event in the 1960s that the working class stepped onto the stage to correct the superstructure]", *People's Daily*, 1A, October 3, 1968). Then, the "Pernicious-Vestiges" became "joining the party and being an official" ("广东博罗县革委会运用一分为二的观点总结蹲点办点经验，抓两头带中间推动斗批改深入发展 [Guangdong Boluo County Revolutionary Committee summed up the situation and made some experience to grasp both sides]", *People's Daily*, October 14, 1968, 3A; 甘当人民的老黄牛—彻底批判中国赫鲁晓夫的"入党做官论" being a workhorse of the people—thoroughly criticizing China's Khrushchev's theory of joining the Party and being an official, *People's Daily*, 5A, October 29th, 1968, by The May 7th Ultra-Cadre School Communication Group in Liuhe, Heilongjiang Province). After that, the "Pernicious-Vestiges" had been constructed as "Chinese Khrushchev and his agent's theory of taming tools" ("要敢于坚持真理 [Dare to uphold the truth]", *People's Daily*, October 22, 1968, 4A, by Li Lianrong, a worker of Beijing Shuguang Electric Machinery Factory). Finally, the "Pernicious-Vestiges" was described as "Chinese Khrushchev's theory of the masses lagging behind" ("群众是历史的主人 [The masses are the masters of history]", *People's Daily*, 6A, October 25, 1968, by 辽阳市佟二卜公社头泡大队赵顺才 Zhao Shuncai, Toupao Brigade, Tong Erbu Commune, Liaoyang City). All kinds of "charges" are dazzling. But with the increase of criticized opinions, these opinions gradually converge to one place, making the specific person waiting for criticism.

On November 14, 1968, the author who signed the "Art Publicity Report Group" finally shouted "Eliminate the pernicious influence of Liu Shaoqi's counter-revolutionary revisionist literary thought" ("工人宣传队领导文艺工作者深入展开革命大批判 [Workers' Propaganda Team leads literary and art workers to carry out the Great Revolutionary criticism]", *People's Daily*, November 14, 1968, 3A). Since 1969, the number of articles about "Pernicious-Vestiges" has surged, but it has almost been reduced to loyalty expressed in the form of copying, and its information increment is extremely limited. From January to July 1969 alone, there were 62 articles in the database of *People's Daily* with expressions such as "Pernicious-Vestiges", "residual poison", and "residual harm". Among them, 61 articles all used the phrase "Liu Shaoqi's counter-revolutionary revisionist line" in the same way. The only article with slightly different wording came from an ethnic minority area, which asked for a supplement to the "Outline of Rural Primary and Secondary Education" (draft), hoping to add "eliminating the residual poison of feudalism, capitalism and revisionism" to the syllabus, but did not name Liu Shaoqi personally ("来自少数民族地区的意见 [Opinions from minority areas]", *People's Daily*, 3A, June 21, 1969). But this "line" shows almost everything except the individual (see the "revisionism" line in Table 1.1 for details). The discourse strategy of "Pernicious-Vestiges" even loses the patience of stigmatizing others and instead tries to win with an overwhelming number of propaganda manuscripts. From August to December 1969, the point of "Pernicious-Vestiges" gradually became hidden. In 15 articles, the word "revisionism" was gradually replaced by "bourgeois factionalism" or appeared together with it. In three articles, specific names appeared, criticizing "great traitor" Liu Shaoqi, "counter-revolutionary revisionists" Peng Dehuai, and Luo Ruiqing, respectively. Liu Shaoqi's accusation had become a "philosophy of life" that was contrary to the slogan "You cannot be afraid of hardship or death" ("认真总结经验深入持久地开展革命大批判 [Conscientiously summarizing experience, deeply lasting the Great Criticism of revolution]", *People's Daily*, 2A, August 21, 1969; "把连队建成一不怕苦二不怕死的战斗集体 [Building the company into a fighting collective that is not afraid of hardship or death]", *People's Daily*, 5A, October 13, 1969). On November 12th, 1969, Liu Shaoqi died of illness.

In 1968, "the Pernicious-Vestiges of the revisionist education route in the old school" was once constructed as a shackle for "Red Guards" to mobilize their comrades to "go to the countryside" ("他和群众贴得更紧了 [He sticks closer to the masses]", *People's Daily*, 4A, October 4, 1968), with a relatively clear social orientation. However, in 1970, although the number of articles in *People's Daily* that used the words of "Pernicious-Vestiges" declined, 20 of the 30 articles assigned the role of the carrier of "Pernicious-Vestiges" to specific individuals. First of all, "Liu Shaoqi and Sun Yefang's counter-revolutionary revisionism" had beome the carrier of "Pernicious-Vestiges" ("对孙冶方的批判和经济战线的斗批改 [Criticism of Sun Yefang and correction on the economic front]", *People's Daily*, February 24, 1970, No.2., Signed by Beijing Knitting Factory Workers' Revolutionary Critique Group, Textile Industry Department's Revolutionary Critique Writing Group). Then, "Liu Shaoqi and Kailov's reactionary educational thought of 'intellectual education first'" was also constructed as "Pernicious-Vestiges" ("建设小学以两条路线斗争为纲 结合斗批改实践开展革命大批判 [Jianshe Primary School launches revolutionary critique with the struggle of two routes as the key link and the practice of fight, criticism and correction]", 2A of *People's Daily*, March 6, 1970, Signature: Report Group of Yingkou Revolutionary Committee). Later on, the term "Liu Shaoqi and his agents in Anshan" had been added into the carriers of "Pernicious-Vestiges" ("在毛主席亲自制定的《鞍钢宪法》的灿烂光辉照耀下，鞍钢革命和生产蓬勃发展呈现一派繁荣兴旺的新景象 [A new scene of prosperity and thriving in Angang's revolution and production under the brilliant glory of the Constitution of Angang personally formulated by Chairman Mao]", *People's Daily*, March 23, 1970, 1A). The carriers of "Pernicious-Vestiges" could be counted "from Liu Shaoqi and Gaogang to the No.1 capitalist roader of Northeast China, and their agents Ma Mingfang 马明方, Gu Zhuoxin 顾卓新 and Yu Ping 喻屏" ("伟大的《鞍钢宪法》万岁！—纪念毛主席亲自制定《鞍钢宪法》十周年，《辽宁日报》三月二十二日社论 [Editorial of Liaoning Daily on March 22nd to commemorate the 10th anniversary of Chairman Mao's formulation of Angang Constitution]", *People's Daily*, March 23, 1970). "Liu Shaoqi and his agent, Peng Zhen, the former Beijing Municipal Committee" also become the carriers together ("坚决落实毛主席亲自制定的《鞍钢宪法》, 扎扎实实地深入开展社会主义革命竞赛，首钢革命和生产形势一派大好 [Resolutely implement the Angang Constitution formulated by Chairman Mao himself, carry out the socialist revolutionary competition in a down-to-earth manner, and the revolutionary and production situation in Shougang is excellent]", *People's Daily*, 4A, April 1, 1970). The number of carriers was still expanding, such as "Liu Shaoqi and his agents in Anhui" ("艰苦奋斗，其乐无穷—淮北人民自力更生战天斗地决心彻底改变淮北平原多灾低产面貌 [Hard struggle is endless—Huaibei people are determined to completely change the disastrous and low-yield face of Huaibei Plain through self-reliance]", *People's Daily*, 3A, April 6, 1970), "Four Men, Zhou Yang, Xia Yan, Tian Han and Yang Hansheng, Leaders of the Black Line of Anti-revolutionary Revisionism Literature and Art" ("深入开展革命大批判，认真改造世界观—学习《在延安文艺座谈会上的讲话》 [Carrying out the Great Revolutionary criticism in depth, seriously reforming the world outlook—studying *the speech at Yan'an Literature and Art Symposium*]", 5A, *People's Daily*, May 24, 1970), and so on. The implicated figures include Sun Yefang 孙冶方, a famous economist; Kailov 凯洛夫, a former Soviet educator; Gao Gang 高岗, the vice chairman of the Central People's Government who committed suicide in 1954; Ma Mingfang 马明方, then the third secretary of the Northeast Bureau of the Central Committee of the Communist Party of China; Peng Zhen 彭真, then the third vice chairman of the National People's Congress Standing Committee (NPCSC); and playwrights represented by Zhou Yang 周扬. The discourse construction of "Pernicious-Vestiges" was almost reduced to the exclusive political struggle tool of fabricating accusation in this period. Although from July to August 1970, there was a brief suspension of the construction of the "Pernicious-Vestiges" of a specific individual and the political struggle; instead, the idea of "theory first", which prevented universities from enrolling workers, peasants, and soldiers, was constructed as "Pernicious-Vestiges of bourgeois ideology" ("为创办社会主义理工科大学而奋斗 [Struggle for the establishment of socialist universities of science and engineering]", *People's Daily*, 1A, July 22, 1970). Besides, "take Chairman Mao's works with you" when delivering the much-needed daily necessities and means of production to the poor middle peasants, so as to carry out the performance of "removing the Pernicious-Vestiges of the counter-revolutionary revisionist line and capitalist management ideology and style" ("遵照毛主席关于'发展生产，保障供给'的伟大方针，永泰县商业系统积极支援农业生产 [In accordance with Chairman Mao's great policy of 'developing production and ensuring supply', Yongtai County Commercial System actively supports agricultural production]", *People's Daily*, 2A, August 24, 1970). However, the great inertia of the political struggle made *People's Daily* give up its attempt to solve specific social problems through the discourse construction of "Pernicious-Vestiges" after September of the same year and quickly restored the previously used discourse formula of constructing a specific individual's "Pernicious-Vestiges", and it was increasingly intensified. In October, Yang Xianzhen 杨献珍, then deputy director of the Institute of Philosophy, Department of Philosophy and Social Sciences, China Academy of Sciences, was framed as "Liu Shaoqi's agent in the philosophical circle" because of his unwarranted "philosophical mysticism", and he became a victim under the slogan of "eliminating the Pernicious-Vestiges of Liu Shaoqi and Yang Xianzhen" ("天津工农兵活学活用毛主席哲学著作座谈会纪要 [Summary of Symposium of Tianjin Workers, Peasants and Soldiers' creatively studying and applying Chairman Mao's philosophical works]", *People's Daily*, 1A, October 4, 1970). The unidentified written criticism in the *People's Daily* lasted until the end of 1970.

In 1971, *People's Daily* published a total of 60 articles with the vocabulary of "Pernicious-Vestiges", which was the second highest in the history before the end of the Cultural Revolution after 1969 (77 articles). The carrier of "Pernicious-Vestiges" is still mostly expressed as revisionism, and in a few cases it is juxtaposed with feudalism, old habits, and old traditions. The names of Liu Shaoqi and Wang Ming, the early leader of the Communist Party of China, still appear before "Pernicious-Vestiges" ("发扬无产阶级的革命文风—学习《对<晋绥日报>编辑人员的谈话》 [Carrying forward the revolutionary style of the proletariat— learning from *A talk to the editorial staff of the Shansi-Suiyuan Daily*]", *People's Daily*, 2A, September 27, 1971). Although the "September 13th" incident in which Lin Biao escaped and died in a plane crash was regarded as a watershed of subtle changes in the early and late period of the Cultural Revolution, before and after this date, the discourse construction of "Pernicious-Vestiges" in *People's Daily* did not show obvious differences, which indicated that the word "Pernicious-Vestiges" had great discourse inertia, and the actors who manipulated this set of discourse logic still had the power to publish articles in the official newspapers of the Central Committee of the Communist Party of China.

By 1972, the situation had changed a little. This year, *People's Daily* published 15 articles with the vocabulary meaning of "Pernicious-Vestiges", which had dropped to a quarter of the previous year. In terms of content, although there was still controversy about whether "the iron rice bowl of working people" is "technology" or "socialism", the idea that technology is more important than ideological loyalty is constructed as "the Pernicious-Vestiges of revisionist education route" ("为革命上大学 [Going to university for revolution], *People's Daily*, 4A, January 9, 1972, by Tan Xindi 谭信娣, a radio ceramic device major of Guangdong Institute of Technology). However, some people also started to be alert to the theory that "education is useless", trying to restore the basic right to education of "children of poor middle peasants" ("通过社会调查批判'读书无用论' [Criticizing the useless theory of education through social investigation]", *People's Daily*, 4A, January 7, 1972, by Communication Group of Revolutionary Committee of Luoyang No.2 Middle School of Railway in Henan Province and Communication Group of Luoyang Railway Sub-bureau). The rhetorical phenomenon of "Pernicious-Vestiges" also begins to appear different from slogans, such as criticizing "remembering a few articles" and "reciting epigrams" as "Pernicious-Vestiges of pragmatism" ("在理论联系实践上用苦功夫 [Using hard work in combining theory with practice]", *People's Daily*, 3A, July 5, 1972, by Wang Guangting 王光庭, Party Secretary of Chengguan Commune, Linqu County, Shandong Province). When teenagers write compositions, "Eight-legged essay tune" full of "first country, second schools, and third selves" is called "the Pernicious-Vestiges of Party stereotyped writing", etc. ("选编短小精粹的好文章 [Selected short and pithy articles]", *People's Daily*, 4A, November 2, 1972, by Guo Guanying 郭冠英, Shizuizi School, Chongli, Hebei Province), although these advocates still need to resort to "quotations from Chairman Mao", and there is limited room for criticism. In the changing atmosphere, in 1973, *People's Daily* published only one article praising party member's "thinking for the masses" and criticizing Liu Shaoqi in slogans ("赞一事当前先替群众打算 [Praise for the plan for the masses in advance]", *People's Daily*, 4A, August 4, 1973, by Tang Shengping 唐生平).

In 1974, *People's Daily* published four articles related to "Pernicious-Vestiges". Although the number is small, its content and criticism are rather dangerous. In January, the campaign of criticizing Lin Biao and satirizing Zhou Enlai began to be implemented, and the discourse construction of "Pernicious-Vestiges" quickly followed. An article took the lead in shouting the slogan of eliminating the remnants of the revisionist line of Liu Shaoqi and Lin Biao and equating it with "feudal remnants" such as "underestimating the role of women in marriage, family planning and other issues". The source of these charges is related to Lin Biao's affirmation of the "Way of Confucius and Mencius" before his death ("孔孟之道是束缚和奴役妇女的绳索 [The way of Confucius and Mencius bound and enslaved women]", *People's Daily*, 2A, January 27, 1974, signed by Qing fuwen 青阜文). In solving the internal contradiction of the words of bourgeois "Pernicious-Vestiges" and feudal "Pernicious-Vestiges", an article on March 20th wrote:

> It was in the fierce struggle to crush the two bourgeois headquarters in Liu Shaoqi and Lin Biao that the broad masses of the people broke through the traditional ideas of the reactionary class stubbornly maintained by Liu Shaoqi and Lin Biao, and established the proletarian ideology. The main source of the decadent things stubbornly maintained by Liu Shaoqi and Lin Biao is the reactionary Confucianism and Mencius. The most reactionary part of China's feudal cultural thought is directly inherited from the Tao of Confucius and Mencius. Because the bourgeoisie in China is extremely weak politically and economically, and it has close ties with feudal forces, it has not and cannot completely oppose feudal culture; China's bourgeois cultural thought has always been mixed with many feudal remnants. Liu Shaoqi and Lin Biao,

the bourgeois representatives in the Party, who engage in revisionism, are bound to use the reactionary Confucian and Mencius ways to oppose the proletarian cultural ideology. The reason why Liu Shaoqi and Lin Biao are so eager to grasp ideology, stubbornly advocate reactionary Confucian and Mencius' ways, implement crazy counter-revolutionary dictatorship over the proletariat in all departments under their control, and unleash poisonous weeds is to create public opinion for overthrowing the dictatorship of the proletariat. The purpose of the Great Proletarian Cultural Revolution is to fight against and prevent revisionism, regain the part of the power usurped by the bourgeoisie, implement the all-round dictatorship of the proletariat in the superstructure, including various cultural fields, consolidate and strengthen the socialist economic foundation, prevent the restoration of capitalism, and make our country move forward along the socialist road. In the final analysis, it is to destroy the ideology of the declining exploiting class and transform the world with the proletarian world outlook.

("无产阶级文化大革命对孔孟之道的深刻批判 [Profound criticism of Confucius and Mencius in the Great Proletarian Cultural Revolution]", *People's Daily*, 2A, March 20, 1974, signed by Fang Hai 方海)

In the discourse logic constructed earlier, as both bourgeoisie and feudalism are incompatible with the advanced class of the proletariat, in the sense that they are both reactionary classes, the bourgeoisie and feudalism are naturally equated. As for why they should be "united", the explanation given in the article is that "the bourgeoisie is extremely weak politically and economically" and therefore needs to "contact with feudal forces", but this expression is completely opposite to the judgment that "the bourgeoisie has usurped power" mentioned later. In addition, revisionism and imperialism have converged again, continuing the tradition of criticizing Soviet revisionism in the early stage of the Cultural Revolution. When the domestic ships returned from a long voyage, this technological achievement proved that Chairman Mao's policy of "independence and self-reliance" was great and correct. It also proves that "Liu Shaoqi and Lin Biao worship foreign things and flatter foreigners, and betray their country and surrender" is the residual poison of the revisionist line ("毛主席革命路线指方向 批林批孔运动为动力 国产'风光'轮扬眉吐气远航归来 [Chairman Mao's revolutionary line refers to the direction and the movement of criticizing Lin Biao and Confucius is the driving force, and the domestic 'Fengguang' ship comes back from a long voyage with pride]", *People's Daily*, November 16, 1974, 1A). Therefore, the struggle of criticizing Lin Biao and Confucius needs to read imperialism as capitalism carefully. In this way, "the Pernicious-Vestiges of Liu Shaoqi and Lin Biao's revisionist line" can be eliminated, but these articles don't say a word about why Confucianism is involved with capitalism and imperialism ("反修斗争的强大思想武器——学习《帝国主义是资本主义的最高阶段》 [A powerful ideological weapon of anti-revisionism struggle—learning that imperialism is the highest stage of capitalism]", *People's Daily*, 2A, March 26, 1974, originally published in *Red Flag Magazine*, No.3, 1974). Although there are many internal loopholes in these "Pernicious-Vestiges" discourses, under the threat of long-term anti-intellectual education policies, discourse logic, and dissent intolerance, no one is willing to think about these contradictions or delve into them. People only need to remember that the object of opposition was criticized because they stood on the opposite side of Chairman Mao and the ideology he advocated. If the "Pernicious-Vestiges" carried by the object of opposition can be shown in a variety of completely different or even conflicting faces, it may mean that the ideology advocated by the opponent itself is ambiguous and changeable. On this basis, opposition to "ideology" can only lead to opposition to a specific individual, and opposition to a specific individual can only bring the only certainty: loyalty to the initiator of the opposition.

In 1975, a few words of "the remnants of revisionism has not been eliminated" were found in the excuse of a local county committee for the slow development of local agriculture ("迅速把典型经验推广到面上去——黑龙江省巴彦县委运用典型推动全县农业学大寨运动的经验 [Quickly popularizing typical experiences to the surface—the experience of Bayan County Committee in Heilongjiang Province using typical models to promote the County's Agricultural Learning Dazhai movement]", *People's Daily*, 2A, October 16, 1975), or the suspension of production for the wrong route was dismissed as the remnants of revisionism to provide legitimacy for the resumption of coal mine production ("坚强的战斗堡垒——记淮北煤矿'猛虎掘进队'党支部的先进事迹 [A strong fighting fortress—record the advanced deeds of the party branch of 'Tiger Tunneling Team' in Huaibei Coal Mine]", *People's Daily*, 2A, November 7, 1975). Although the names of people still appear in the carriers of these "residual poisons", the purpose of using discourse strategies is closer to serving the actual needs, rather than stigmatizing specific individuals. Until 1976, articles using the vocabulary of "Pernicious-Vestiges" came late after Mao Zedong's death. Propaganda workers who hadn't found out the wind direction first insisted on "continuing to carry out in-depth struggle against Deng Xiaoping and counter the rightist trend of overturning cases". The editorial staff of *People's Daily*, in collaboration with the workers of the timber factory in the northern suburbs of Beijing, shouted the slogan "Eliminating the Pernicious-Vestiges of Deng Xiaoping's revisionist line" in the "Critique Special Edition" published on October 3, 1976 ("化无限悲痛为巨大战斗力量 [Turning infinite grief into great fighting force]", *People's Daily*, 3A). On October 6th, they continued to call for persisting in "the struggle against Deng Xiaoping and the right-wing reversal of his conviction" and eliminating the "Pernicious-Vestiges" of "the theory of only productivity advocated by Liu Shaoqi and Deng Xiaoping". As this article says, persisting in the struggle is to "turn grief into strength, inherit Chairman Mao's Pernicious-Vestiges, adhere to class struggle as the key link, adhere to the party's basic line and continue the revolution under the dictatorship of the proletariat" ("唯生产力论是个大祸害 [The theory of only productivity is a great scourge]", *People's Daily*, October 6, 1976, 4A). On the evening of October 6th, Hua Guofeng, then the first vice chairman of the CPC Central Committee, and others, on behalf of the Political Bureau of the Central Committee, quarantined Jiang Qing and other related members. These two articles also became the last elegy of the word "revisionist Pernicious-Vestiges" in *People's Daily*. This means that the fabricator of the farce of Cultural Revolution will soon become the vortex of the next wave of discourse construction of "Pernicious-Vestiges": the carrier of a new "Pernicious-Vestiges".

The Gang of Four and the Cultural Revolution: From criticizing to becoming "Pernicious-Vestiges" (1977–2012)

In 1976, *People's Daily* published three articles about "Pernicious-Vestiges". Except for the two articles mentioned in the previous section, which were published in October and still claimed to "inherit the unfulfilled wish of the chairman" and "eliminate the remnants of revisionism", in the third article, the carrier of "Pernicious-Vestiges" and the "enemy of the people" had a huge reversal: The Gang of Four became the target of attack. This article does not directly use the language of "eliminating the lingering poison of the Gang of Four". The word "lingering poison" appears in a local drama "The Gardener's Song" 园丁之歌 attacked by the Gang of Four, and it comes from a drama lyric by the protagonist, "There are struggles everywhere on the journey, and the lingering poison of bourgeois education has not been eliminated" ("扼杀《园丁之歌》也是为了篡党夺权 [Killing the "Gardener's Song" is also to usurp the party and seize power]", *People's Daily*, November 29, 1976, 2A, by the Propaganda Department of the CPC Hunan Provincial Committee), to prove the high ideological awareness of the protagonist, thus demonstrating that the attack of the Gang of Four on this drama is groundless. This reflects two important changes. First, at this time, the discourse function of "Pernicious-Vestiges" changed from stigmatizing the political enemies of the Gang of Four to alienating the Gang of Four itself. Second, although the advocated social goals are completely contrary to each other, the new discourse builders are no longer willing to invent a new set of propaganda methods but hope to "bottle new wine" and make articles on the basis of the "Pernicious-Vestiges" discourse that people are already very familiar with and used to.

The situation changed in 1977. On March 26, 1977, *People's Daily* reprinted an article published in the third journal of *Red Flag Magazine* in 1977, using the expression of "poisonous" of Yao Wenyuan, a member of the Gang of Four. Besides, the Gang of Four's opposition to "eliminating the residual poison of Lin Biao's revisionist line" has also become one of Yao Wenyuan's charges. Ironically, this article accuses Yao Wenyuan of what he did when he controlled *Red Flag Magazine*, and the author of the article signed "The Great Criticism Group of *Red Flag Magazine*". No matter the way of criticism or the style of discourse, it is still highly similar to the Cultural Revolution. This article ends like this:

> The Red Flag initiated by Chairman Mao himself has now returned to the hands of the Party. Under the leadership of the CPC Central Committee headed by President China, we will always hold high the great banner of Chairman Mao, adhere to Chairman Mao's proletarian revolutionary line, rely on the Party and the masses, run the Red Flag well, make efforts to publicize Marxism, Leninism and Mao Zedong Thought, criticize the bourgeoisie and revisionism, and strive for the realization of the great strategic decision

put forward by President China to govern the country by grasping the outline and realizing the great ideal of communism.

("捣乱，失败，灭亡的纪录——揭批姚文元利用《红旗》制造反革命舆论的罪行 [A record of disruption, failure, and destruction—exposing and criticizing Yao Wenyuan's crime of using Red Flag to create counter-revolutionary public opinion]", *People's Daily*, March 25, 1977, 1A, signed by the Great Criticism Group of *Red Flag Magazine*)

Apart from replacing some positions originally belonging to Chairman Mao with the living and incumbent Chairman Hua, the other contents of this passage are the same as those of the critical articles during the Cultural Revolution, even the objects of criticism—the bourgeoisie and revisionism are all the same. If it weren't for "Exposing and criticizing Yao Wenyuan" in the title, it's almost hard to believe that this critical point has continued to history. Observing the words and deeds of the "Great Criticism Group" of *Red Flag Magazine*, the only thing that can be determined is that other people in the magazine were eager to dissociate themselves from those involved. Besides, it is hard to tell whether the 10-year catastrophe had taken away people's imagination of the use of words or completely taken away people's ability and courage to think independently.

The vocabulary of "Eliminating the Residual Poisons of the Gang of Four" officially appeared in *People's Daily* for the first time, and it was completed with the help of the *Korean Labor News*. This article appeared in the 5A on July 12, 1977:

On July 11th, 劳动新闻 Rodong Sinmun published an editorial to celebrate the 16th anniversary of the signing of the DPRK-China Treaty of Friendship, Cooperation and Mutual Assistance . . . The article said: "Today, the brotherly people of China have inherited the Pernicious-Vestiges of their great leader Comrade Mao Zedong and embraced Comrade Hua Guofeng as their wise leader. Under the wise leadership of the Communist Party of China (CPC), headed by Comrade Hua Guofeng, a new upsurge was set off in the socialist revolution and socialist construction. They strengthened the dictatorship of the proletariat, firmly grasped class struggle as the key link, and made great achievements in exposing the crimes of the Gang of Four, thoroughly eliminating their 'Pernicious-Vestiges' and realizing national stability. The people of China are fighting bravely for the grand goal of building their country into a modern socialist power within this century."

("朝鲜《劳动新闻》发表编辑部文章 庆祝朝中友好合作互助条约签订十六周年 [North Korea's Labor News publishes editorial articles to celebrate the 16th anniversary of the signing of the DPRK-China Treaty of Friendship, Cooperation and Mutual Assistance]", *People's Daily*, 5A, July 12, 1977)

On the following August 6th, *People's Daily* published an article, which also adopted the expression of "eliminating the pernicious influence". It not only classified the actions of the Gang of Four as evil deeds rather than good deeds but also further emphasized the most unforgivable of its "evil deeds"—attacking the successor appointed by Chairman Mao:

> On the eve of the fall of the Gang of Four, they attacked Comrade Hua Guofeng, the successor personally selected by Chairman Mao, with the most vicious language, created counter-revolutionary public opinion, engaged in "contingency measures", preparing for sinister undertaking, sharpened their knives, and accelerated the pace of usurping the highest leadership of the party and the state. After the downfall of the Gang of Four, many key members of them tried their best to resist, and some openly made all kinds of counter-revolutionary clamors, pointing the finger at President China and the Party Central Committee; Some secretly step up planning, wait for the opportunity, and prepare to fight back; Some put all their eggs in one basket in an attempt to launch a counter-revolutionary armed riot and make a desperate struggle . . . We must thoroughly criticize the Gang of Four for tampering with the party's purpose, advocating the establishment of the party for private gain, distorting the nature of the party, setting up another party member standard, trampling on the party rules and laws, engaging in gang activities, destroying the party's style, engaging in the evil acts and all kinds of reactionary fallacies of the bourgeois unhealthy tendencies. We must eliminate their pernicious influence, and make them no market within the party and among the people.
> ("彻底粉碎'四人帮'的帮派体系 [Completely crushing the gang system of the Gang of Four]", *People's Daily*, August 6, 1977, 1A, signed by Yu Qing 宇清)

Similar to the position of this passage, at the end of 1977, the writer Zang Kejia 臧克家 published the article "On the Pernicious-Vestiges of Poems 论诗遗典在" in *People's Daily*. In this article, when constructing the indelible harm and "Pernicious-Vestiges" brought by the Gang of Four to the literary style and poetic style of China, the accusation was also that the Gang of Four "rebelled against the teachings of Chairman Mao and opposed the writers' in-depth struggle and life" (4A, December 31). Compared with the Cultural Revolution period charged, these texts are different in that the Gang of Four was constructed as a "Pernicious-Vestiges" instead of being the dominator of the discourse construction of "Pernicious-Vestiges". However, after careful study, the common logic is still chilling; as long as you are loyal to the leader or future leader, it will constitute a positive "revolution"; as long as you attack leaders or future leaders, you must be "counter-revolutionary". No matter in the public political life or in the private life, "revolution" is still the only supreme moral adjective in contemporary China; the only way to become a "revolutionary" person is to be loyal to anyone who may become a leader and, at the same time, have the ability to identify those who can no longer be leaders in time and to be firmly against them. In this sense, living in a "revolutionary" way has become almost impossible for ordinary Chinese people, while it is even more difficult to be a good citizen with independent political judgment and ensure the safety of his or her own life and property in the capricious ideological reform movement, which requires not only wisdom and courage but also a great fortune.

In August 1977, the 11th National Congress of the Communist Party of China was held in Beijing. The congress declared the smashing of the Gang of Four and reaffirmed the fundamental task of building China into a powerful socialist country in this century, which made an end of the Cultural Revolution. In view of the great changes in the national situation, the Fifth National People's Congress was held in February 1978, and Chinese People's Political Consultative Conference, which had not held a congress for 13 years, also held a fifth session—a series of meetings gradually restored the normal order of the country's political and social life disrupted during the Cultural Revolution. However, how to judge the devastating revolution initiated by the ruling party, how to remember, what to remember, and what to forget has become an urgent problem to be solved by the CCP.

By 1978, the discourse construction of social memory had consistently changed into the argument that "the four evils have been eliminated, and the residual poison still exists", and it quickly became slogan. History seemed eager to declare victory and set the tone for the past. Although these articles give different measures on how to eliminate the "Pernicious-Vestiges" of the Gang of Four, and some authors do call for changing the former unhealthy trend of "telling lies" ("文风和认识路线 [Writing style and understanding route]", *People's Daily*, 3A, January 9, 1978, by Shao Huaze 邵华泽), there are still more articles that oppose the Cultural Revolution with the thinking of Cultural Revolution and think that the main problem of the Gang of Four is the "revisionist line". To eliminate the remaining poisons, we only need to:

> Adhere to the direction of serving proletarian politics, workers, peasants and soldiers . . . adhere to the policy of letting a hundred flowers blossom and a hundred schools of thought contend, strictly abide by the six political standards for distinguishing fragrant flowers from poisonous weeds stipulated by Chairman Mao, and eradicate all reactionary prohibitions set by the Gang of Four.
> ("迎接社会主义经济建设高潮和文化建设高潮 在十一大路线指引下多出书出好书 国家出版局在京召开全国出版工作座谈会 [To meet the climax of socialist economic construction and cultural construction, publish more books and produce good books under the guidance of the 11th National Congress Line, and the State Publishing Bureau held a national symposium on publishing work in Beijing]", *People's Daily*, 1A, January 12, 1978)

In other words, it is right to restore the policy line of the late great man and oppose all the orders of the Gang of Four, and the latter idea is undoubtedly extremely dangerous. In the second half of 1978, the number of articles against the Gang of Four in the discourse mode of Cultural Revolution reached its peak. Three quarters of the 44 articles with "Pernicious-Vestiges" vocabulary appeared between July and November. Although the number surged, their contents were highly repetitive and slogans. Except the article "Science and democracy 科学和民主" published on Youth Day, which used "the Pernicious-Vestiges of bureaucratic autocracy left over from China's long feudal society and semi-feudal and semi-colonial society" (*People's Daily*, 2A,

May 4, 1978, by special commentator of the newspaper), the remaining 43 articles focused on exposing and criticizing the "Pernicious-Vestiges" of Lin Biao and the Gang of Four, and many of them acted out the absurdity of using the Cultural Revolution logic to counter the Cultural Revolution practice and advocated the rule of law and democracy with this "Pernicious-Vestiges" construction:

> There are also leading comrades in some units who are still obsessed with catching pigtails. They are always uneasy about the opinions and comments of the masses. What suits their appetite is fine; Those who are not to their liking are regarded as heretics, and they are held in their hands as pigtails, ready to put on some hats and beat you with sticks one day. This can probably be said to be the evil legacy or Pernicious-Vestiges of the Gang of Four! Don't take this Pernicious-Vestiges for granted. Let it go on, not only can it not make people talk, but it will make everyone feel at risk. How can we talk about practicing democracy within the party and among the people? How can we smash spiritual shackles, emancipate our minds, and work hard for socialism?
> ("辫子与民主 [Braids and democracy]", *People's Daily*, 2A, July 6, 1978, by Zhang Leike 张雷克 and Liu Xinru 刘新如)

> To make the law really play a role in safeguarding people's democratic rights, we must carefully eliminate the future troubles and residual poison caused by Lin Biao and the Gang of Four's destruction of the socialist legal system. The unjust, wrong and false cases they have created must be resolutely redressed, rehabilitated and corrected; The use of power to violate the law and discipline must be resolutely stopped; The trend of observing the socialist legal system must be restored and carried forward. Everyone should obey the law. The masses should abide by the law. Cadres should be more law-abiding.
> ("民主和法制 [Democracy and legal system]", *People's Daily*, July 13, 1978, 1A)

Of course, in addition to the text that clearly states what kind of social order we hoped to establish after the remnants of the Gang of Four have been eliminated, some articles set the goal more conservatively before the start of the Cultural Revolution, that is, to restore the order that has been established in the "seventeen years", because the overall picture of this order is more certain and it is more effective to restore it:

> Some comrades have a lingering fear, knowing that there have been many good experiences in management in the past seventeen years, but they lack courage, dare not resume and persist, and adopt the attitude of "one slow, two look, three pass", where they wait and see. Others have "brain poison", and the poison of Lin Biao and the Gang of Four is very deep. They still regard what the Gang of Four advocated as the right thing. As long as "seventeen years" is mentioned, and the good tradition, style and system of the past are

mentioned, they will be out of place. How can you manage the enterprise in such a state of mind? These comrades should be liberated from the spiritual shackles of the Gang of Four as soon as possible, remove the pernicious influence of the Gang of Four from their minds, distinguish right from wrong, stand tall, and focus on enterprise management.

("迅速提高企业管理水平 [Improving enterprise management level rapidly]", *People's Daily*, 2A, July 13, 1978)

Although the order and means advocated for restoration and the fields tried to be reformed are different, the existence of these diverse viewpoints witnessed the internal pluralism briefly presented by *People's Daily* in July 1978, and this pluralism is precisely the concrete embodiment of "emancipating the mind" in practice.

In August 1980, Deng Xiaoping pointed out in his speech "Reform of the Leadership System of the Party and the State" that, on the one hand, we should break the feudal tradition, and, on the other hand, we should oppose bourgeois liberalization. Only by drawing a clear line between socialist democracy and bourgeois democracy and "combining the work of eliminating the residual influence of feudalism with the criticism of bourgeois self-interest, profit-seeking and other corrupt ideas" can we not lose the right direction. Otherwise, it will only plunge our country into anarchy like "Great Democracy" for 10 years, making it more difficult to democratize the country, develop the national economy, and improve people's life ("学习邓小平民主法制思想 发展社会主义民主政治 [Learning Deng Xiaoping's thought of democracy and legal system and developing socialist democratic politics]", *People's Daily*, 10A, September 13, 2004). In the second revolution of reform and opening up, the elimination of the "Pernicious-Vestiges" of the Cultural Revolution has become the basic prerequisite for the reform of the political party and state leadership system.

On the occasion of the 60th anniversary of the National Day in 2009, *People's Daily* published a series of articles reviewing the process of political civilization construction in China in the past 60 years since the founding of the People's Republic of China from the aspects of the national constitution, civic awareness, administrative methods, judicial ideas, changes in the details of the marriage and family system, etc. Among them, the article "The Foundation of the Constitution in China 宪法奠基盛世中国" reviews the formulation and revision of China's constitution in the past 60 years. From the 1954 constitution to the current 1982 constitution, China has successively promulgated four constitutions, and the 1982 constitution has been revised four times (the fifth amendment to the constitution of the People's Republic of China adopted at the first session of the 13th National People's Congress on March 11, 2018). During the Cultural Revolution, state institutions were destroyed, people's congresses stopped working, and people's governments were replaced by "revolutionary committees". During this period, citizens' constitutional rights and freedoms were severely impacted, temporary policies replaced laws, and the "54 Constitution" lost its original legal effect. The "75 Constitution" promulgated in the late period of the Cultural Revolution was also guided by the theory of emphasizing class struggle and the theory of continuing revolution under the dictatorship of the proletariat, which still reflects all the characteristics of the Cultural Revolution. The end of the Cultural Revolution means that the disorder of Chinese society has come to an end, and the law has replaced temporary norms and returned to the center of state and social governance. At the same time, it also means that the Cultural Revolution has completed the historic transformation from criticizing "Pernicious-Vestiges" to officially becoming "Pernicious-Vestiges" at the legal level:

> After the Cultural Revolution, on March 5, 1978, the first session of the Fifth National People's Congress adopted the Constitution of People's Republic of China (PRC), which was called "Constitution 78" in history. Among them, the Pernicious-Vestiges of the Cultural Revolution has been consciously liquidated, and the basic rights of citizens stipulated in the "54 Constitution" have been partially restored. This Constitution not only reflects the achievements of bringing order out of chaos at that time, but also reflects the wrong idea of "two whatevers". Both the guiding ideology and the specific norms are inconsistent with the social objective reality that is undergoing profound changes.
> ("宪法奠基盛世中国 (中国足迹 1949–2009) [The Foundation of the Constitution in China (China Footprint 1949–2009)]",
> *People's Daily*, 6A, September 25, 2009)

In 2011, *People's Daily* published the article "Emancipating the Mind, Breaking Myths and Mistakes: Remembering the End of the Cultural Revolution and the Great Discussion on Truth Standards". The article once again talked about the "Great Discussion on Truth Issues and believed that this ideological debate had formed a torrent of ideological emancipation in the whole country, which had a strong impact on the forbidden area of "two whatevers", thus speeding up the party and the country to get out of the shadow of the Cultural Revolution and realizing a turning point:

> The "Cultural Revolution" was a civil strife that was mistakenly launched by the leaders and used by counter-revolutionary groups, which brought serious disasters to the party, the country and the people of all ethnic groups, and caused the party, the country and the people to suffer the most serious setbacks and losses since the founding of New China.
> ("思想解放破迷误：记'文化大革命'终结和真理标准问题大讨论 [Emancipating the mind, breaking myths and mistakes: remembering the end of the Cultural Revolution 'and the Great Discussion on Truth Standards']",
> *People's Daily*, June 12, 2011, 4A)

On the occasion of the 70th anniversary of the founding of the Party in the Communist Party of China, the organ newspaper of the Communist Party of China once again acknowledged the failure of the Cultural Revolution and the mistakes of the ruling party, as well as the disastrous destruction of Chinese society caused by the Cultural Revolution. It is a reflection on the past and a redefinition of the objects to be remembered and criticized. At the same time, turning mistakes into

"Pernicious-Vestiges" that can be publicly criticized is an effective strategy to publicize and maintain legitimacy; by acknowledging the mistakes and harms of this "Pernicious-Vestiges", the Communist Party of China's "greatness, glory and correctness" of "daring to face up to and correct his own mistakes" can be better reflected ("思想解放破迷误：记'文化大革命'终结和真理标准问题大讨论 [Emancipating the mind, breaking myths and mistakes: remembering the end of the Cultural Revolution 'and the Great Discussion on Truth Standards']").

At the same time, the criticism of the "Pernicious-Vestiges" of the Cultural Revolution has also become a discourse strategy of the CPC in deepening the reform of the economic and political system. In 2012, when the "two sessions" closed, then Premier Wen Jiabao of the State Council met with Chinese and foreign journalists covering the Fifth Session of the Eleventh National People's Congress in the Golden Hall on the third floor of the Great Hall of the People, and he had a routine question-and-answer session. Among them, the reporter of Lianhe Zaobao in Singapore asked two questions about the viewpoint of "political system reform" that Wen repeatedly mentioned and attracted attention at home and abroad: What are the reasons why the Premier repeatedly mentioned the political system reform? What is the difficulty of promoting the political system reform in China? To this, Wen Jiabao had the following reply:

> Wen Jiabao: Yes, I have talked about the reform of the political system many times in recent years. It should be said that it is comprehensive and specific. If you ask me why I am concerned about this matter, I am out of a sense of responsibility. After the downfall of the Gang of Four, although our party made some resolutions on historical issues, it carried out reform and opening up, however, the errors of the Cultural Revolution and the influence of feudalism have not been completely eliminated. With the development of economy, there are some problems such as unfair distribution, lack of honesty, corruption and so on. I am well aware that to solve these problems, we should not only reform the economic system, but also reform the political system, especially the leadership system of the party and the state. Now that the reform has reached a crucial stage, without the success of the political system reform, the economic system reform can't be carried out to the end, the achievements already made may be lost again, and the new problems in society can't be fundamentally solved. Historical tragedies like the Cultural Revolution may happen again. Every responsible party member and leading cadre should have a sense of urgency. Of course, I am well aware of the difficulty of reform, mainly because any reform must have the awakening, support, enthusiasm and creativity of the people. China, a big country with a population of 1.3 billion, must proceed from its national conditions and establish socialist democratic politics step by step. This is not an easy task, but the reform can only advance, not stagnate, not to mention regress, and there is no way out for both stagnation and retrogression.
>
> ("温家宝总理答中外记者问 [Premier Wen Jiabao answers questions from Chinese and foreign journalists]", *People's Daily*, March 15, 2012, 1A)

In Premier Wen Jiabao's reply, the reason for China's political system reform lies in the unfairness, honesty, corruption of power system, etc. that have been constantly appearing in the economic development since the reform and opening up. However, how to deal with the inevitable and concomitant secondary problems in the development of these countries has not completely eliminated the "Pernicious-Vestiges" of the Cultural Revolution and feudalism, which has become the legitimate reason for these problems. Apart from the reconstruction of political civilization, such as the reform of political system and the construction of rule of law, the "Pernicious-Vestiges" of the Cultural Revolution has also been widely used in cultural and social life and has become a new pathogen of "social diseases". For example, in the following text, *People's Daily* attributed the "formalism" style of painting the hills with green paint to meet the requirements of "greening" to the "Pernicious-Vestiges" of the Cultural Revolution:

> Formalism originally refers to the emphasis on form rather than content in art, literature and philosophy, and even emphasizes form to an absolute degree. In our country, formalism was immersed in the social field very early, and reached its peak during the Cultural Revolution. It can be said that this "residual poison" is still deep and still a "social disease". Moreover, everyone knows the existence and harm of this disease in their hearts, and they all feel painful, but they all feel hard to resist and can't help themselves. Today's letters from readers tell all kinds of stories about "responding to the situation", but they just uncover the "tip of the iceberg" of various formalism in today's society.
> ("形式主义：做给别人看的把戏 [Formalism: A trick to show others]",
> *People's Daily*, 19A, March 29, 2011)

Generally speaking, after the end of the Cultural Revolution, history reversed, and social values were re-fixed. The Cultural Revolution itself was shaped as a "Pernicious-Vestiges" and became the object of criticism. In the new revolution of system, economy, and culture since the reform and opening up, the "Pernicious-Vestiges" of the Cultural Revolution has become a new scapegoat, bearing a part of the criticized and generalized "Pernicious-Vestiges" of the "old society".

Reflection on the extreme "left" thought and ambiguous market discourse (1979–present)

In the late stage of discourse construction of "Pernicious-Vestiges" of capitalism, that is, from February 1979–February 1989, "Pernicious-Vestiges" of capitalism was mixed in the narratives against the Gang of Four, the Cultural Revolution, and the extreme "Left" ideological trend, and it was constructed as a series of "obstacles to the construction of spiritual civilization", such as buying and mercenary marriage, breaking the law and discipline, bad work style, old funeral customs, corrupt social atmosphere, uncertain thoughts, etc. In a sense, this new phenomenon of discourse practice has something to do with the rhetoric of "lingering fear of the Gang of Four" and "right phobia" often adopted by *People's Daily* at the same stage. However, as the beginning of China's modernization stage and the watershed of "two decades", why is capitalism still a kind of "Pernicious-Vestiges" in 1979 and the following 10 years?

In the discourse construction of the Gang of Four's "Pernicious-Vestiges", one of the charges is to "smash the unhealthy tendencies of the bourgeoisie" ("彻底粉碎'四人帮'的帮派体系 [Completely smash the gang system of the Gang of Four]", *People's Daily*, August 6, 1977, 1A, signed by Yuqing 宇清); although before that, various political enemies of the Gang of Four had been regarded as carriers of the "Pernicious-Vestiges" for similar reasons. Then, in the process of exposing and criticizing the Gang of Four, should its "Pernicious-Vestiges" be defined as "right" or "left"? This kind of pan-ideology brought about the inconsistency in discourse, which brought a difficult problem to the construction of "Pernicious-Vestiges" discourse after 1978. After a heated debate, the Gang of Four was finally defined as "right in form but left in essence" in the ideological coordinate system and was named "extreme left" to criticize its "remaining poison". Its extreme left performance was constructed as "anarchism" ("围绕批判极'左'思潮的一场激烈斗争 [A fierce struggle around criticizing extreme left thoughts]", *People's Daily*, 2A, March 23, 1977).

Wan Li was one of the first leaders who proposed that China should develop a commodity economy and a market economy. He stressed that democracy and legal system should be well built to ensure the healthy development of commodity economy and market economy. To develop the socialist market economy, if democracy and legal system can't keep up, the achievements of reform and opening up will be destroyed, and socialism will not stand. Problems such as unfair distribution and bribery, which people are generally concerned about, should also be solved through legislation and law enforcement. In June 1977, after Wan Li became the first secretary of Anhui Provincial Committee of the Communist Party of China, he went deep into rural areas to investigate and study, and he risked to approve Shannan Commune in Feixi County and Xiaogang Production Team in Fengyang County to carry out the pilot project of contracting output quotas to households with and without the production team conducting unified accounting, thus opening the road of China's economic reform and opening up from rural areas. At that time, there was a popular saying, "If you want to eat rice, find Wan Li", which shows its influence among the people in China. In this regard, Deng Xiaoping once said that China's reform started from the countryside, and the rural reform started from Anhui. Comrade Wan Li was meritorious. In 1995, the *Selected Works of Wan Li* was published, and *People's Daily* published an article, commenting on Wan Li's contributions to eliminating the influence of "Left" thoughts, eliminating the pernicious influence of feudal thoughts, developing democracy, improving the legal system and reform and opening up, and further criticizing the Cultural Revolution with the core viewpoint of the *Selected Works of Wan Li*:

> The interference of "Left" thoughts "is very severe, which has caused a series of confusion and fallacies in the theory and practice of construction".

Looking back on the road taken since agricultural cooperation, the "Left" tendency has become more and more serious, and the people's commune has become the most powerful form of blind command, administrative intervention, binding and depriving farmers. Once again, the anti-Rightist movement contributed to boasting, divorced from farmers and the actual situation in rural areas. In particular, the Gang of Four criticized the "only productivity theory", which further confused our thinking. For a long time, egalitarianism was mistaken for socialism, and commodity economy was equated with capitalism. Skilled craftsmen in rural areas actively developed commodity production, but they cut it as the "tail of capitalism". At that time, the productivity was still very low, but we were eager to propose to eliminate the difference between urban and rural areas. . . . It seems that when the city is built well, the people in the city will become "revisionists" and our country will become a capitalist society. This trend of thought is extremely absurd, and the damage to economic development is also very serious. History since the founding of the People's Republic of China has proved that the "Left" economy will decline, and the "Left" economy will lead to the wrong country. For decades, the influence of "Left" has been very stubborn. Not daring to take a clear-cut stand against "Left" things is a sign of weakness and inattention.

("坚持改革开放 坚持实事求是 坚持群众路线
[Persisting in reform and opening-up, seeking truth from facts and adhering to the mass line]", *People's Daily*, October 5, 1995, 9A)

This concentrated on Wan Li's criticism of the "Left" line of the Chinese Communist Party during the Cultural Revolution. He believed that this extreme trend of thought was an important reason for interfering with social development and causing social disorder, and not daring to "take a clear-cut stand" against the extreme "Left" trend of thought, was regarded as a sign of weakness and inattention. This was a completely opposite evaluation to that during the Cultural Revolution. It is worth noting that, by comparing the concepts of egalitarianism/socialism and commodity economy/capitalism, *People's Daily* holds that these concepts cannot be simply equated but are in essence a justification for the reform and opening up policy of market economy implemented in socialist countries. While reviewing the extreme "Left" ideological trend, this article mentions the "Pernicious-Vestiges" of feudalism again, and holds that there are "Pernicious-Vestiges" of feudalism in social production command, production and management, commodity circulation, social relations, leadership style, etc. At the same time, the article thinks that another outstanding manifestation of the pernicious feudal ideology is the disregard for democracy and the legal system. In this regard, the *Selected Works of Wan Li* gives the following solutions:

Therefore, for the smooth development of reform, opening up and the four modernizations, while overcoming the influence of "Left" thoughts and eliminating the pernicious influence of feudal thoughts, we must develop socialist democracy and improve the socialist legal system. "Democracy and the legal system must be regarded as one of the fundamental issues in our country's socialist construction. We must make great determination and make great efforts to solve them fundamentally." A high degree of socialist democracy and a sound socialist legal system are the fundamental guarantee for the smooth progress of economic system reform, the long-term stability of our country and the improvement of the socialist system.

("Persisting in Reform and Opening-up, Seeking Truth from Facts and Adhering to the Mass Line")

In *People's Daily*, feudal "Pernicious-Vestiges" and extreme "Left" ideological trend are juxtaposed, and it is considered that these two ideological "Pernicious-Vestiges" points to the poison of the political system, and the important guarantee to eliminate these ideological "Pernicious-Vestiges" is the development and improvement of the political system. By classifying erroneous thoughts as ideological "Pernicious-Vestiges", the official media actually responded to the question about the reform of political system and economic system in the reform and opening up.

Apart from politics and economy, reform and opening up have had a profound impact on the development of China culture. In the 1980s, with the liberation of economy and thought, a "literature craze" arose in China, with the "85" avant-garde literature as the most representative. The literature in the 1980s is a transitional stage, full of various possibilities and choices, and the result of a series of internal and external power struggles, contests, and compromises. Looking back at this period of literary history, the "ideological emancipation" movement did not happen overnight but experienced a tortuous and repeated road from the post-Cultural Revolution period, which was backward-forward-backward-forward again and so was the social development. Nobel Prize winner in literature Mo Yan once commented on the ambiguous relationship between writers and the times (Mo, 2007):

> I think a writer does have a position when writing. It has been repeatedly emphasized by our revolutionary literature theory in the past revolutionary period. Whether a writer's butt sits on the proletarian position or the bourgeois position determines what kind of works you will write. This is a bit absolute, but he does have a certain reason. . . . One of the most basic features of the so-called avant-garde writing in the 1980s is dissatisfaction and confrontation with authority, that is to say, there is a kind of hostility towards the system and politics. This hostility does not mean going to rebel, blow up any building or destroy public facilities. It is a kind of hostility in the cultural sense. A writer puts his position in the same position as the common people. He thinks that he is a member of the common people. He thinks that, like the most ordinary people, he has an innate hostility towards those who are powerful or noble, and a desire to rebel against the officially recognized moral values. He rebelled for the sake of rebellion, and he may not really like it, sometimes even be embarrassed.

As Mo Yan said, the dissatisfaction with absolute authority and the desire to "rebel for the sake of rebellion", represented by writers, are a kind of "hostility" in the cultural sense that is common in Chinese society after the high-handed politics. This rebellious spirit is highly consistent with and highly deviated from the accelerating torrent of market economy. Rock music, avant-garde novels, and the subsequent political turmoil are all born with this huge contradiction. After the "August 9th" political turmoil, the official put forward the policy of "sweeping, squeezing and occupying" for the development of literature and art: "Sweeping away the things that belong to liberalization and 'pornography', squeezing out the negative and unhealthy things, and firmly occupying the ideological and cultural positions with healthy, up-to-date and socialist literature and art works" ("坚持正确导向 推进文艺繁荣 [Adhering to the correct orientation to promote the prosperity of literature and art]", *People's Daily*, 5A, June 27, 1991). At the same time, during this period, the official attitude toward culture was more cautious; limited creative freedom was allowed on the basis of ensuring that the political and ideological direction was consistent with that of the CCP. The objects of literary criticism and memory point to the Cultural Revolution and extreme "Left" thoughts, which continue to assume the role of scapegoats between the political system and social contradictions:

> In view of the fact that the remnants of the "Left" still imprison the thoughts of literary and artistic teams and fetter their literary and artistic creation shortly after the downfall of the Gang of Four, we propose that the literary and artistic teams should further emancipate their minds and "open their hands and feet to engage in creation", and demand that the literary and artistic criticism work should completely abandon some "Left" wrong practices in the past, take fostering literary and artistic flowers as their main task, and jointly create a good public opinion environment.
> ("坚持正确导向 推进文艺繁荣 [Adhere to the correct orientation and promote the prosperity of literature and art]",
> *People's Daily*, 5A, June 27, 1991)

At the same time, in the era of commercialization, "thought" and "economy" began to compete for their own rights and legitimacy. Therefore, apart from reflecting on the extreme "Left" thoughts from all levels, feudal "Pernicious-Vestiges" discourse was once again used to explain the contradiction between political system, market economy, and social thought. For example, *People's Daily*'s literary criticism article said,

> In the eyes of some people, everything in this era is subject to and dependent on the economy, and the need for thought is not so urgent. Indeed, in a period of moderate social conflicts and relatively stable development, literature will lose its novelty and shock in capturing social themes, so it is easy to "give up thinking" and tend to be technical and entertaining.

This article has noticed the problem that the content of literature and art is over-entertaining while the form pursues technicalization and has the following comments on this phenomenon:

When literature is surrounded by brain teaser jokes and mindless art is rampant, it will harm the intellectual health of a nation. Readers are faced with two helpless choices about literature: "abandoning reading" and "being silly". And "foolish people" is the hotbed of feudal Pernicious-Vestiges and tyranny. It is dangerous for a nation to lose the ability and habit of thinking, which will ultimately endanger the development of the whole society.
("思想有深度，文学才有力度 [Thought is deep, literature is powerful]",
People's Daily, June 29, 2010, 24A)

People's Daily has noticed that the salon, film and television, networking, sketch, and vulgarization of contemporary Chinese literature have brought about the problems of excessive entertainment and showmanship, raised the excessive entertainment of literature to the level of endangering the national intellectual health, and linked it with the feudal "Pernicious-Vestiges"; the cultural development situation in which entertainment prevails under the background of market economy is like the "foolish people" behavior of autocratic rule in feudal times and then called on the society to enhance the depth of thought in order to bring powerful literary and artistic works.

At the same time, while reflecting on the past, there are also arguments calling for a new understanding of the past. For example, in one article, by commenting on the details of the traditional etiquette in the movie "Mr. Six" about seniority and inferiority and the cold and warmth of human feelings, they advocate for a new understanding of human relations and etiquette in traditional culture:

Now some people "don't like this", especially some young people think that the "old reason" is empty-headed, full of sour taste, and it also hides some "feudal Pernicious-Vestiges" of the "three cardinal guides and five permanents" style. Some people also think that the social foundation of "old reason" is gone, and "if the skin doesn't exist, how will the hair be attached"? What we should pay attention to now is equality, freedom and so on. Looking in this way may be too linear. In fact, behind the seemingly tedious "etiquette" is "reason", which is the value ethics of being human. From the above, the "living space" of "old reason" has not become smaller, but has been expanded due to the frequent social interaction-the river sometimes waves roll and sometimes waves are as smooth as a mirror, but the riverbed changes so slowly that you can't see. I'm not worried that "old-fashioned" will hinder "modern ethics" such as equality and freedom. In reality, one deals with human relations and the other with legal rights and interests. The two are not in direct conflict, but they can live in peace.
('老理儿'就像温暖的河 ['old reason' is like a warm river]",
People's Daily, 19A, January 19, 2016)

Different from the discourse strategy of "breaking the old and creating the new" in the revolutionary era, the traditional etiquette was removed from the feudal "Pernicious-Vestiges" and the status and social function of the old culture in the new era were reexamined. With regard to the relationship between the old culture and modern ethics such as equality and freedom, the article distinguishes between "human relations" and "legal rights and interests" and looks at the relationship between the old and new cultural systems from the perspectives of human relations and rationality, thus striving for a legitimate living space for the old culture. Generally speaking, with the economic system reform, China's social thoughts and media propaganda discourse strategies have gained limited freedom and pluralism, and the boundary between the subject and object of memory and "Pernicious-Vestiges" has also changed.

If the state needs to control people's memories, then no matter who is in charge of the state, it will never be all the people who have the opportunity to control their memories. Therefore, if the state mechanism tries to forget the experiences that are not in line with its just image, so as to create national identity, it can't avoid another series of questions: Whose experience should be forgotten? Who will benefit from this (Appleby et al., 1995, pp. 128–129)? Who should be the subject of reflective memory? Different from the concept of "functional memory", the normative narration of "Pernicious-Vestiges" discourse opens up a more special functional orientation; the subjects who need to choose individual memories and make them produce individual functions become the selected objects. These individuals who really carry memories often cannot express themselves, and only some of them can enter the space where official discourse is generated and have the opportunity to be reselected and explained. These selected memory materials are not used for personal purposes but serve the official discourse.

Margali (2002, p. 14) pointed out two problems in memory domestication—confusing memory ethics with traditionalism and moralism. Among them, traditionalism often borrows people's loyalty to the past and seeks the legitimacy of realistic rule by controlling collective memory. This discourse pattern has a close relationship between traditionalism and non-democratic rule. Therefore, we can't confuse "memory ethics" with "memory politics", especially to prevent them from being used as "disguised religious forms". The moralism of memory refers to "moral judgment on those who are not suitable for moral judgment" and explains everything in moral terms. In other words, "moralism" takes morality as the key link and regards moral standards as the only standard or the main standard. This practice may make memory blind under the influence of subjective deviation and hinder people from knowing the true and complete history (Zhao, 2015). These problems are particularly common in the narrative of "Pernicious-Vestiges" in *People's Daily*. For example, the "doctrines" as "Pernicious-Vestiges" have been regarded as an integral part of the moral system from the very beginning (Wang, 2015), and the two have gradually merged into one. At least in people's daily life, they will not be strictly distinguished. More specifically, the "Pernicious-Vestiges" initially denied the memory and actions of the perpetrator, and it was a mobilization method that prompted the victim to have resentment against the perpetrator. However, in the process of historical narration, from the point of origin, the reflection memory of "Pernicious-Vestiges" is gradually alienated, and the objects it depicts are repeatedly "stigmatized" (such as "Liu Shaoqi's counter-revolutionary revisionist line"). In this way, the historical dimension of memory is hidden, and the "Pernicious-Vestiges" is no longer related to the perpetrator or victim in history but becomes the historical situation that causes social problems and turns to the criticized object itself.

References

Appleby, J., Hunt, L., & Jacob, M. (1995). *Telling the Truth about History*. New York: W. W. Norton & Company.

Margalit, A. (2002). *The Ethics of Memory*. Cambridge, MA: Harvard University Press.

Mo, Y 莫言., & Yang, Q 杨庆祥. (2007). Avant-garde, folk and bottom 先锋·民间·底层. *Southern Literature 南方文坛*, *2*, 68–73.

Wang, F 王汎森. (2015). "Fánmèn" de běnzhì shì shénme—"Zhǔyì" yǔ zhōngguó jìndài sīrén lǐngyù de zhèngzhìhuà "烦闷" 的本质是什么—"主义" 与中国近代私人领域的政治化. *Forum of Intellectuals 知识分子论丛*, *1*, 263–304.

Zhao, D 赵鼎新. (2012). *Social and Political Movements 社会与政治运动讲义*. Beijing: Tsinghua University Press.

Zhao, J 赵静蓉. (2015). Memory virtues and realistic route of Chinese memory ethicization 记忆的德性及其与中国记忆伦理化的现实路径. *Literature and Culture Studies 文学与文化*, *1*, 50–59.

7 Conclusion

The construction of China's political memory by "Pernicious-Vestiges" media discourse

Summary of the book: The discourse illusion constructed by "Pernicious-Vestiges" and the generation of memory control

In Milan Kundera's novel *Le Livre du rire et de l'oubli*, the author presents readers with an intriguing opening (Kundera, 1978/1993, p. 14):

> It's 1971. Mirek said: The struggle between human beings and power is the struggle between memory and forgetting.

Now, it seems that Milan Kundera's "memory control" opposed by Mirek still has room for further elucidation. This book takes "Pernicious-Vestiges" discourse as the breakthrough point and by studying the discourse practice activities of this discourse resource, it responds to the problem of interruption and reversal of contemporary China's historical paradigm and tries to find the answer to this problem through the relationship between media discourse, memory domestication, and political memory. After the discussion of the discourse pattern of "Pernicious-Vestiges" in the previous parts of this book, we can confirm that a convention needs a parallel "cognitive convention" to be maintained in order to become a legal social system (Douglas, 1986, p. 46). The more fully the system expectations are coded, the more they can control the uncertainty, which further leads to the behavior tending to conform to the system matrix. If this degree of coordination is achieved, disorder and confusion will disappear (pp. 47–48). Schotter (1981) regards institutions as entropy-minimizing devices: from the rule of thumb and norms until all useful information can be stored, and when everything is institutionalized, history or other storage devices are not needed (p. 139). The construction of "Pernicious-Vestiges" discourse is a process of system coding. The official propaganda organization evokes and reconstructs historical events through "Pernicious-Vestiges" discourse narration. In this process, how to cover and domesticate memory is the key coding step. *People's Daily* has adopted a series of dualistic discourse strategies, such as forgetting/remembering, justice/injustice, breaking old/establishing new, and anthropophagic/anthropoemic to construct social memory and political memory selectively and strengthen identity or eliminate and assimilate heterogeneity. Through the construction of "Pernicious-Vestiges" discourse, it has generated

DOI: 10.4324/9781003409724-7

"discourse illusion" to ensure political legitimacy by adopting a series of dualistic discourse strategies, such as "forgetting/remembering", "injustice/justice", "destruction/establishment", and "anthropoemic/anthropophagic", to selectively construct social and political memory, strengthen identity or eliminate/assimilate the heterogeneity.

Let's go back to the word "Pernicious-Vestiges" itself. In Chinese, "yidu/遗毒" is a compound word composed of two words with different meanings. Among them, "yi/遗" means "legacy" and also refers to "the past"; "du/毒" means "poisonous" or "poisonous substance". The combination of these two words means "there is poison left behind". It has rich metaphorical connotations and implies criticism of the "opposite" past. Illusion framework holds that language and symbolic actions represented by metaphorical rhetoric have specific social consequences, and the ultimate purpose of analyzing these metaphors is to reveal the emotions and ideologies created by them, especially the social classification and stereotypes created by ideology. The metaphorical rhetoric behind the "Pernicious-Vestiges" discourse endows abstract political memory and ideology with a more intuitive perception. This rhetorical orientation, which links abstract conceptual fields with specific body organs and diseases, aims to compete for justification and legitimacy for violent revolution and authoritarian politics and highlights the roles of language and symbols in political propaganda.

Looking back over the past 76 years, the historical construction of contemporary China, deeply influenced by Marxist class history view, is full of discourse issues of class opposition. Chapter 4, Chapter 5, and Chapter 6 of this book, through a concrete analysis of the social impact of the "Pernicious-Vestiges" discourse of *People's Daily* through group classification, reveal how the "Pernicious-Vestiges" discourse clearly shows the classification of "us" and "them" and adopts different discourse strategies to establish dissidents as "scapegoats" in the political storm, so as to compete for legitimate discourse resources for the current political power. At the same time, the classification of "Pernicious-Vestiges" is not fixed but changes with the development of contemporary history in China. That is to say, the discourse subject who once opposed the "Pernicious-Vestiges" may also become the opposed "Pernicious-Vestiges" itself. However, the "Pernicious-Vestiges", which has been fiercely criticized, has the opportunity to wash away the guilt of polluting and poisoning the society and return to the mainstream discourse with the change of national politics and culture. The root of the change of subject and object of discourse and memory lies in the formulation and implementation of the ruling party's current decision.

Generally speaking, the "Pernicious-Vestiges" is a rhetorical point that constantly appears in the New China news discourse in the contemporary historical narrative of China, and its function is to reform memory. The narrative practice of "Pernicious-Vestiges" embodies the memory view of power and official discourse construction, and it is also a reflection of contemporary China's historical view. For a long time, the construction of "Pernicious-Vestiges" discourse in China's central news media has been organized and closely relied on realistic politics. They borrowed "enlightenment tools" from the early 20th century to further serve the establishment and unification of a new country. Over the past 76 years, the "Pernicious-Vestiges" narrative continuously constructed by *People's Daily*, the official newspaper of the Central Committee of the Communist Party of China, reflects the views of China's political elites and represents the ruling party's evaluation and reevaluation of social reality and historical events. Its narrative content contains a specific language style and standardization process and uses metaphorical rhetoric to construct "moral persuasion" and "symbol of corruption" in discourse. Through the mutual innuendo of "disease" in the sexual and political fields, the metaphor of "Pernicious-Vestiges" extends its argument field from "body" to personal moral level, thus establishing the rationality of all-round transformation and domestication of private life field and spiritual memory. In terms of form, content, and social consequences, the control mode of "memory domestication" is more concealed than that of "memory masking". Therefore, for specific historical events, the dominant discourse sometimes tends to adopt the strategy of "memory domestication" represented by "Pernicious-Vestiges" discourse, compared with historical masking.

Actually, "Pernicious-Vestiges" is a kind of memory control technique, which not only constructs when ideas, actions, or social entities will be opposed but also makes "opposing the past to open up the future" a deeply rooted and legitimate historical concept. In terms of self-improvement and repair of this concept system, *People's Daily*'s discourse construction of "Pernicious-Vestiges" also has many reflections and responses. First of all, why are there so many "Pernicious-Vestiges drugs"? On December 30, 1951, *People's Daily* published the full text of the report delivered by Huang Yanpei 黄炎培, then deputy prime minister of the State Council and Minister of Light Industry, at the meeting of all the staff of the Central Ministry of Light Industry on December 8, 1951, with the title "我们要彻底地为反贪污反浪费反官僚主义而斗争 [We should thoroughly fight against corruption, waste and bureaucracy]". This article points out some reasons why "Pernicious-Vestiges" words were frequently used at that time, and feudalism, imperialism, and bureaucratic capitalism were regarded as "the three major enemies of the new society" and listed as the source of "Pernicious-Vestiges". According to the data at that time, of the 153 corruption cases discovered in Beijing since the first two years after the founding of New China, only one was due to poverty; "Generally, there are more foreground job than back-office job, and more new cadres than old ones". Therefore, when the trust within the party tries to expand its boundaries but encounters a crisis, it can only be blamed on the temptation of lifestyle brought by higher social classes, but it cannot be admitted that the efforts to "establish new" have not been successful.

So, how long will each "Pernicious-Vestiges" last? In the *People's Daily* published on April 15, 1954, the 1A of the article "Accusations of treating the masses with bureaucratic attitude" explained that "the bureaucratic Pernicious-Vestiges left by the reactionary rule of past dynasties can never be completely eliminated in a short period of time". Wang Zaoshi 王造时, one of the leaders of the May 4th movement and one of the "Seven Gentlemen", in his speech at the third plenary session of the Second National Committee of the Chinese People's Political Consultative Conference, "我们的民主生活一定日趋丰富美满 [Our democratic life must be increasingly rich and happy]" (*People's Daily*, 5A, March 20, 1957), attributed the "Pernicious-Vestiges of bureaucracy" to "the product of feudalism and capitalism", which can be traced back to at least two regimes before New China. In the same year, Wang Zaoshi was wrongly classified as a rightist and rehabilitated in 1960; he was persecuted again during the Cultural Revolution and was rehabilitated again at the end of 1978. At that time, it was more than 7 years since Wang Zaoshi died. This shows that the conceptual system of "opposing the past to open up the future" can't stand scrutiny. As a matter of fact, the extravagant hope of controlling the "future" is tantamount to "gnosticism", while the efforts to stigmatize the past by the words of "Pernicious-Vestiges" actually shut down any possibility for people to restore the truth, distinguish right from wrong, and rebuild justice in history.

"Pernicious-Vestiges" discourse and historical justice: Returning the compressed space of historical criticism

In addition to forgetting and obscuring history, it is also a means that can't be ignored in the process of memory control to domesticate people's understanding of the past with the help of some form of calling and inducing memory. For various reasons, "Pernicious-Vestiges" discourse adopts a memory domestication path that is completely different from "covering" in the traditional sense. Instead, it constructs and opposes a kind of memory through "highlighting" in discourse. Its essence is still to cover up the unfavorable attribution of current social problems, making memory the object of being belittled in history writing; through this kind of belittling, history writing has completed the "negative consensus on the past" that power wants it to establish. Depressing the past is to better affirm the present and achieve another present and future opposite to the past. In a sense, compared with an "ideal" society that only depicts and advocates a lack of reference entities to people, belittling the past reflects the yearning and pursuit of the regime's dominant ideology extremely and even more strongly, and it also has a stronger realistic foundation and social mobilization power.

Admittedly, the control mode of "memory domestication" is more concealed than that of "memory masking" in terms of form, content, and social consequences. Therefore, for specific historical events, the dominant discourse sometimes tends to adopt the strategy of "memory domestication" represented by "Pernicious-Vestiges" discourse, compared with historical masking. This is because, on the one hand, there may be some historical events that are so widespread and influential to cover in any way. On the other hand, and more importantly, re-expressing the past may be useful for the present, while the second explanation is more convincing for the historical events in modern China; the past that should be opposed is not obscured because these histories are still recounted according to the present, thus reconstructing the present significance. Therefore, Kierkegaard's (1843/2013) quote, "it is not worth while remembering that past which can not become a present" (p. 30) may be rewritten as, "it is even worth while remembering that past which should not become a present". From this point of view, as an opposed past, "Pernicious-Vestiges" has undoubtedly become the best "gift" from the past to the present because "the past which should not become a present becomes a present for the present".

Even so, the essence of "knowledge masking" of historical events by "Pernicious-Vestiges" discourse and its metaphorical system cannot be changed (Proctor, 2008). In a sense, the consequences of selective memory or induced memory are no less than another form of selective forgetting and induced forgetting of history (Stone et al., 2017). In Dong Leshan 董乐山's translation of *1984* (Shanghai Translation Publishing House, 2011), "memory hole" is expressed as "forgetting hole":

There is a big oval hole in the wall next to Winston's reach. There are thousands of such holes all over the building, not only in every room, but also in every aisle not far away. This kind of hole is nicknamed the Forgotten Hole. Whenever you think of any document that should be destroyed, you will conveniently lift the lid of the nearby Forgotten Hole, throw the document or waste paper into it, and let a warm air flow blow it into a big boiler somewhere under the building to burn the Times on any day. After all the materials that need to be corrected are collected and checked, the newspaper of that day will be reprinted, and the original newspaper will be destroyed. All documents and books that may have political or ideological significance are applicable. Every day, every hour, every moment, the past is revised to make it conform to the current situation. Any news or opinions that are inconsistent with the current needs are not allowed to be kept on the record. All history is like a parchment that is constantly scraped and rewritten.

As a form of historical work, if we cite the metaphor of "memory holes" created by George Orwell in *1984* as an analogy of "memory masking", then the narrative of "Pernicious-Vestiges" and the "memory domestication" directed by its object are similar to a "memory wall" that openly displays the enemy's "corpse": humiliation of the loser and glory of the winner. At the same time, the safe areas of political life can be defined, and those thoughts that are regarded as dangerous or taboo will all be isolated.

More importantly, historical writing practice bears the right and obligation to lock and unlock memories, and different historical practices can always provide different critical space. As an alternative form of "past practice", "forgetting" actually plays an irreplaceable role in helping people create historical reflection. As Dirlik (1996) pointed out: "This, too, entails questions of power; a past forgotten is a past erased as a possible space from which to view the present critically. While such forgetting has clear utilities in politics, in intellectual activity it makes historical work vulnerable to pressures emanating from its ideological context" (p. 248). According to this view, the words, narratives, and metaphors of "Pernicious-Vestiges" are essentially appeals, which call on people to remember some traditions or heritages marked as "evil" and "harmful" against the natural law of forgetfulness in human society. Dominant discourse blocks the alternative discourse of public reflection on the past, including forgetfulness itself and independent and pluralistic reassessment of historical events based on forgetfulness. It makes the space of historical criticism in the process of generation increasingly cramped and then forms a structural framework of history and politics (Molden, 2016), which is solidified at the bottom of people's consciousness—a memory system or "memory cultures"—and even brings about the return of "cultural unconsciousness".

On this issue, after the policy of "letting a hundred flowers blossom and a hundred schools of thought contend" was introduced in 1956, the *People's Daily* published an article that once reflected on it. The writing purpose of *People's Daily* is mainly to feel that "all things are inferior, only learning is high" as recorded in "Narrative of the "Pernicious-Vestiges" of Kuomintang reactionaries (1946–1958)" in Chapter 5 because a "Pernicious-Vestiges" of the "old society" has bound the reform of the wage system ("十年寒窗苦 [Ten years of cold windows]", *People's Daily*, 2A, July 7, 1956, by 范荣康, for details of the original text, please refer to Chapter 5, "The obscure 'old society' [1949–1966]").

> On July 7th, the *People's Daily* published Comrade Fan Rongkang's "Ten Years of Cold Window", but "criticized" the complaints as grumble . . . The author traced the complaints, it was said that they were not due to grievances, but because they were people who suffered from "suffering through hardships" and "everything is inferior, only studying well". Now, among college graduates, it can't be said that there are absolutely no such people, but I'm afraid they are very few, because their education is not feudal . . . This complaint has a long history, and it didn't "spread" only "in the voice of wage reform". There's nothing to show for it, as evidenced by a limerick: "After ten years of hardship, it's still a hundred and fifty dollars. If you don't use what you've learned, you won't take care of your life. Anyone who raises an opinion will be spanked severely." Of course, the way to spank is not the sticks and boards used by yamen runners in Sanhe County, but the things such as "uneasy work," "individualism", "egalitarianism", "coveting enjoyment", "bargaining with the revolution" and so on. The last one is "you don't understand the revolutionary work" and "you have a problem with your outlook on life" . . . If you don't look at the specific conditions, you will use it as a weapon to criticize the intellectuals . . . This will do no harm to the dead feudal literati, but it is too disrespectful to the living intellectuals, and it doesn't conform to the facts . . . If you don't pay attention to your writing, someone will be aggrieved. Such "criticism" can't help but make people feel wronged.
> ("笔下有冤魂 [There are ghosts under writing]", *People's Daily*, 8A, July 21, 1956, by Gongyang Geng 公羊庚)

This passage, in a speech channel that was once briefly opened but then briefly closed, revealed the absurdity of calling any idea that was inconsistent with the policy various "Pernicious-Vestiges" discourse patterns under various pretexts. It was also during this period that Cai Yi 蔡仪, a famous literary theorist, wrote an article in *People's Daily*, arguing that Huang Yaomian 黄药眠 criticized Zhu Guangqian 朱光潜's aesthetic thought and argued that "the residual poison left by Mr. Zhu's hypocritical theory must not be allowed to spread without being cleaned up" and compared it with Zhu Guangqian's works; he reached a deafening conclusion that "the critic has become another incarnation of the criticized thought" ("评'论食利者的美学' Comments on 'On the Aesthetics of Profit Eaters']", *People's Daily*, 7A, December 1, 1956). Unfortunately, even though some people wake up from this discourse illusion, the word "Pernicious-Vestiges" has been constantly used in the articles of *People's Daily* since then, including when calling for the defense of diverse viewpoints with "Pernicious-Vestiges", which also failed to get rid of the inertia of this discourse mode. According to Tarde's explanation in imitation law, opposition and imitation are two sides because opposition is a unique repetition. In this repetition, things are willing to destroy each other because they are very similar, and fundamental differences cannot confront each other. Only invention can get rid of this imitation law of "opposing itself with itself" and open up new channels for social life and discourse patterns (Tarde, 1903).

Reevaluation of history and its ethical issues have always been one of the spiritual shadows that plague human society. Reviewing the operation of discourse power in "memory domestication" will return the ethical rationality of forgetting itself and reopen the space for reflection on specific historical events and ideologies. On how to mediate the standardization of memory, Adorno's speech on the contention of historical terms in 1959 seems to inspire our current "Pernicious-Vestiges" narrative fanaticism. In this famous speech, Adorno severely criticized Germany's political culture, arguing that trying to bypass the expression of the past by avoiding those difficult memories and "intentionally or unintentionally defending the past crimes" was a sign that both individuals and officials were unwilling to face the past, which would blur the boundaries of democracy and have great potential harm. Adorno further pointed out that although we need to achieve democracy through historical reflection, the reevaluation of history should not be carried out by "conquering the past" but by "working through the past"; historical reflection needs a continuous and self-critical citizen participation (Adorno, 1959/1986). In fact, the official memory itself also has internal competition, and its responsibilities are not constant. Although official memory may influence other forms of memory practice, it cannot completely dominate public memory (Olick, 1998). In any society, the memory discourse finally produced by the historico-political process is the result of wrestling between various forces, including hegemonic dominant discourse, the "silent majority", and resistance to memory challenges (Molden, 2016).

Similar to the whole discourse logic represented by the construction of "Pernicious-Vestiges", since 1960s, the historical reflection expressed by the slogan of "mastering the past" in the German Democratic Federation can only be regarded as a kind of false "self-flagellation" on the level of national will in the eyes of neoconservatives, and its purpose is still to cater to and serve the mainstream ideology of society. In view of this paradox, the solution put forward by Germany in the 1970s and 1980s is "normalizing the past", and its logic also contains the meaning of "confronting the past" (Olick, 1998). In other words, historical reflection should serve memory rather than overstepping its position. There are two main means to regulate history. One view advocates relativization, which holds that the norms of the past should be relative; the history should be divided into two parts, and the merits and demerits should be treated equally. Another view emphasizes ritualization, which is relatively radical and holds that solving domestic economic and development problems has a higher priority, thus shelving the necessity of historical reflection. Specifically, the means used to re-express history also depends on the change of social mainstream groups and their ideology and political environment in a specific period and how events were defined in the past: the path dependence of historical construction (Olick, 1998). Either way, the two normative historical processes will follow different tracks, eventually forming a kind of "hodgepodge" in the post-modern sense (Maier, 1988, p. 171).

Official memory often creates a "present" memory to usurp the memory structure of the "past" (Ben-Amos, 1989, pp. 88–89). Sontag's (1966/2003, pp. 14–17) exposition on the reconstruction of critical space also gives us some enlightenment on how to return the historical reflection space compressed by the "Pernicious-Vestiges" discourse. She advocates that discourse problems should first return to form and thorough description, with clarity as the highest liberating value of criticism and reflection, and descriptive words instead of normative words, so that people's experience of things and themselves can be more real, not more unreal. At the same time, she also stressed that dominant discourse can't equate the explanation of anything with thought or culture, including historical narration and memory practice, but should be devoted to showing how memory and history are like this—even what it is—rather than what it means, so as to dispel the arrogance of explanation.

It should be added that, based on this analysis, we seem to be able to conclude that no matter what kind of "appeal" is made to memory, it will lead to the opposite side of memory: "non-memory" or "anti-memory" including forgetting. However, even if the official discourse does not attempt to manipulate and eliminate individual memory, individual memory needs other preconditions to ensure its credibility. These conditions include the stabilization of the text through the fixation and classicization of the written form and the provision of a space and free space for the social function of memory by the society to ensure the stability of the social use functional context of memory (Assmann & Assmann, 2012).

But in any case, the images of the past are closely related to the current politics and the state of the regime (Rabinbach, 1988). The image of the past is neither dominated by the past nor completely created by the present. Historical images shape and constrain how they will be used to achieve a "successful" present, while the image of the past is actually the product of this continuous dialogue (Olick & Robbins, 1998). Ethics contains knowledge from the past, but it is not the past itself. Although it contains feelings and tendencies such as forgetting, forgiveness, repentance, and gratitude, it is fundamentally based on the present and oriented toward the future (Margalit, 2002, p. 12). The "Pernicious-Vestiges" discourse epitomized by *People's Daily* compresses the reflection space for the retrospective memory that has been "reflected" by the dominant discourse to be criticized again by the alternative discourse, and at the same time, it also shifts people's attention to the fact that the social root of misfortune comes down to the level of power reality, thereby closing the possibility of the generation of prospective memory in the public agenda (Tenenboim-Weinblatt, 2013). In this sense, the protracted existence of the "Pernicious-Vestiges" narrative epitomized by *People's Daily* in the dominant discourse space will not only domesticate our "past" but also domesticate the present and future of China's collective memory.

Historical self-denial dynamic in "Pernicious-Vestiges" discourse

If the construction of political memory is directly related to the orientation and trend of the regime, let's explore why the negative historical "convention" constructed by "Pernicious-Vestiges" was established in the propaganda system of the CPC and served the political system of China for a long time. In the conceptual genealogy of the classification of non-democratic regimes, China is neither a complete post-totalitarianism nor the reappearance of typical authoritarianism; it is a non-democratic regime with the core characteristics of both, showing "various types of authoritarianism". After breaking away from Mao Zedong's rule, China deviated from authoritarianism in three fields: politics, economy, and society. The deviation in politics and society was small, but the deviation in economy was large (Gao, 2014). Since the reform and opening up, the Communist Party of China has mainly formed the basic direction of "economic progress and political stagnation" and "political left and economic right" (Parish & Michelson, 1996). The market transformation under this authoritarian framework is mainly guided and pulled by two forces; one is the infiltration from "development and transformation" and the other is the restriction of "totalitarian heritage". The two struggle endlessly and do not give in to each other (Geng & Chen, 2008). In the process of China's political development, the institutional heritage is an introverted traditional force, while the market force is an extroverted change force (Zhang, 2008). They interact with each other. The regime form, institutional arrangement, institutional environment, and path dependence before and after the institutional change jointly influenced the institutional revision and political change.

Among many theoretical explanations, the theory of development and transformation is a typical modernization theory, which emphasizes the relationship between development and system and holds that economic growth usually changes social structure and promotes democratic politics (Lipset, 1981, pp. 55–70; Deutsch, 1961). In socialist countries, the demand for economic development will inevitably lead to the transformation of members' mentality. The "rational calculation" of economic production predicted by the law of development is often incompatible with the "selfless dedication" required by ideology. Therefore, once the communist countries turn to attach importance to economic development, their utopian political beliefs will be eroded and the political arbitrariness maintained by ideology will be challenged (Lowenthal, 1970). However, the reform and opening up process dominated by the state is full of compromises and concessions for those with vested interests, and the problem of resources and dependence is very obvious. By virtue of the network of relationships and the attachment to the party-state system, the newly rich strata who seize various profit opportunities form "bureaucratic capitalism" (Lu, 2000; Meisner, 1996), coexisting with institutional interests, weakening the power of political transformation, and fully safeguarding the authoritarian system to protect its interests (Yang, 2007).

Different from the theory of development and transformation that the distribution logic of giving priority to efficiency will eventually build a pluralistic social circulation channel and promote the formation of civil society (Nee, 1989), the reinterpretation of ideology by the discourse construction of "Pernicious-Vestiges" examined in this book more strongly supports the explanation of "institutional heritage theory". This kind of viewpoint points out that social change is not only a process of changing from one order to another, but it is a process of "bricolage" by using existing resources (Stark & Bruszt, 2001) to emphasize the path dependence of a system and a specific historical heritage (Arthur, 1994; Thelen, 1999), which is characterized by the phenomenon of "neo-traditionalism" (Jowitt, 1983; Zhao & Zhang, 2005). In the face of the contradiction between the market-oriented reform and the political system, they constantly use the logic of power persistence to bring political influence and its network into the operation of market economy (Bian & Logan, 1996). Institutional dependence is the main obstacle to the path change. On the one hand, this phenomenon comes from the long-term reproduction process of institutions, which has the effect of self-reinforcing, making it difficult for other alternative schemes to be converted or replaced (Arthur, 1994, p. 112–113; Levi, 1997). On the other hand, it comes from the deviation caused by the preference of the political system (status quo bias); the authority hopes to restrict other actors by virtue of political arrangements, especially in a non-democratic environment, and the lack of competition mechanism and a weak learning process increase the difficulty of institutional change (Pierson, 2000), which is characterized by the "bounded rationality" in which actors' interests and structures combine with each other and seek appropriate responses in specific situations. Therefore, the reason why the post-totalitarian system is difficult to transform is the result of the restriction of the "Pernicious-Vestiges" of the communist system. Under this system, all social organizations are subordinate to the party-state system (Geng & Chen, 2008), and the integration of the state and society is carried out through the subordinate organizations of political parties. If there is no social pressure, the post-totalitarian regime will remain unchallenged. The transformation from the revolutionary party of the Communist Party of China to a modern bureaucratic process suitable for ruling has brought difficulties to the reform, resulting in the institutional innovation within the party and the decentralization and autonomy at the grassroots level, which can hardly escape the phenomenon of "involution" (Xu, 2007; Zhao & Zhang, 2005).

Not only that, Zou believes that totalism politics and re-feudalism are also a typical Chinese-style system or revolutionary heritage. Totalism refers to the guiding ideology that the power of political institutions can invade and control every stratum and every field of society at any time without restriction, and omnipotent politics is a political society based on this guiding ideology. It comes from the emergency measure of setting up a strong political party from top to bottom to effectively reorganize the society at the beginning of the 20th century when solving the crisis of national life and death. This kind of social revolution contained the elements of omnipotent politics from the very beginning. Although it sometimes has strong social mobilization ability, once misjudged or out of control, it will have irreparable consequences (1994, pp. 3–5). The correspondence between politics and political-social relations is not inevitable. The consequences of high concentrations of power vary with political-social relations. At the same time, the category of totalism politics is interdependent with the degree of democracy of the system. The basic feature of totalism politics and its system is that there are no areas in the society that cannot be violated by power organs. The freedom and rights of individuals or groups in the society are not guaranteed by morality, public opinion, and constitution, and the size and content of their free activities are determined by political power organs. In addition to the areas directly or indirectly controlled and managed by the state, there are only three exceptional areas in the totalism society, including (1) political institutions making policies according to the needs of social development, and granting independent freedom rights to state units, mass organizations, social groups or individual citizens, (2) political institutions concern strategy or tactics and don't automatically or temporarily control certain social behaviors (for example, giving up the confiscation of landlords' land in Yan'an period), and (3) areas that political institutions don't mind (for example, playing mahjong). In the western democratic regime, these three areas are based on the freedom rights of individuals and groups; are guaranteed by the constitution, laws, public opinion, and morality; and can't be violated by political institutions. They are the foundation of western democratic politics and economic and social life. In fact, the establishment of the New China is guided by the concept of "the masses" rather than "citizens", emphasizing the social and economic rights of a certain social strata but ignoring the freedom rights of individuals (Zou, 1994, pp. 6–8).

Based on the discussion of *People's Daily*'s discourse on "Pernicious-Vestiges" in this book, including the historical view that this discourse practice is shaped by metaphor and social classification, it can be found that different "Pernicious-Vestiges" will be continuously and repeatedly created or temporarily erased according to the specific needs of Chinese society at that time. From the phenomenon point of view, this kind of word practice and the rupture of historical view really support the revolutionary heritage theory rather than the development and transformation theory in the explanation of market-oriented transformation of authoritarian countries. The mass movements in the revolutionary or Mao era were often initiated by the party itself, but in the present China, making a "sound" has become a new "loyal" deception, which also constitutes a unique landscape where the revolutionary authoritarianism heritage is inherited in contemporary times and Chinese society "worships the state" (Su, 1988). The pursuit of stability is often higher than public criticism. In this sense, China never really bid farewell to the revolution (Perry, 2006).

It should be pointed out that the two explanations of revolutionary heritage theory and development and transformation theory seem to conflict, but in fact they may not be contradictory because they may all be based on Schwartz's judgment that the "revolutionary mystery" of China in the first two decades of the 20th century essentially promoted the formation of radicalism (Schwartz, 1972, p. 3). Through the analysis of the long-term existence of the discourse construction of "Pernicious-Vestiges" in this book, we can also presuppose other possibilities of the debate between conservatism and radicalism of China's revolutionary culture; the traditional culture of China is full of egalitarian radicalism tradition, and they further constitute a revolution regarded as radicalism by the West. In fact, the word "revolution" may not be able to summarize the purpose of contemporary China in any historical period, but it has indeed served as a common means of revolution and modernization (Fairbank, 1986, p. 408). A major feature of China's revolution is the strange combination of "radical means" and "conservative goals", which is reflected in the origin of China's traditional culture and the radical tradition of egalitarianism summarized in this book. On the one hand, the radical potential of egalitarianism means that this concept contains a kind of conceptual motivation of "robbing the rich and helping the poor" that constantly weakens the elite to empower the bottom. This "naive justice" is deeply rooted in the Chinese empire that has not been fully baptized by commercial competition, but it doesn't mean that it tends to a static conservative ideology in the western sense, in contrast, it is closer to the "liberal equality" that is infinitely moving, because once the market is introduced as the driving force of modernization, there will surely be more and more "new elites" created in the economic and cultural fields, and these strata will surely become the objects that radical egalitarians who hold power are trying to flatten. On the other hand, the "tradition" of egalitarianism refers to "it has existed since ancient times", and it has been confirmed by the Confucian culture and even the monarchical power by Confucius' saying, "not suffering from scarcity but suffering from inequality". The idea system blessed by monarchical power will be solidified with the hierarchical system of highly recognized authority and become a cultural resource loved by both "emperors" and "subjects".

Echoing the conclusion drawn in this book through the discourse illusion constructed by "Pernicious-Vestiges", ideological hegemony is not only operated through discourse but also closely related to the power balance among groups that hold political and economic power in a specific society. For most people, following the instructions of authority will produce real practical advantages. Therefore, it is meaningful to obey the will of the party with power (Cialdini, 1997). The power, strength, and scale of the majority group with power can effectively dominate and influence the thoughts and actions of the minority groups. This power relationship is reflected in the media discourse, which corresponds to the collective rather than individual discourse illusion. The collective illusion of discourse can create a powerful classification and ultimately shape our experience, as well as people's relationship with others and society (Bhatia, 2015, p. 15). However, the revolution is always unpredictable and uncontrollable (Fairbank, 1986, p. 432), and it is impossible to completely replace the concept system deeply rooted in the Chinese empire for thousands of years with modern political values through several revolutions (Fairbank, 1986, p. 439); so "cultural atavism" is inevitable.

So which end do intellectuals prefer between conservative and radical cultures, and what role do they play between "emperors" and "subjects"? In fact, the presupposition that the belief in thought and cultural change is bound to take precedence over institutional change also comes from the naive derivation of China's traditional ideological resources (Lin, 2022, p. 49). This kind of cultural modernization seems to be "anti-traditional", but it is still fatally born out of the tradition itself with a strong hope or even fantasy of "writing to teach the country" and "literati serving the country". It is the naivety of local intellectuals in China and their lack of vigilance against gnosticism that make them follow the historical track of their own culture's language and thinking and help them understand "revolution" as a simple combination of Marxist class struggle theory and traditional violent revolution. This concept, which has not yet broken away from the context of traditional violent revolution, inevitably brings with it the myth of historical evolution since the 19th century (Chen, 2000, p. 4). As a result, in the polity that has not yet established civic culture, the overall adherence to a radical tradition has become increasingly arrogant. When authoritarianism and the masses who obey authoritarianism select the same enemy, they regard intellectuals who are cultural elites and critics as the sworn enemies of egalitarianism and the idea of a "unified" country. Intellectuals cannot establish their social role as critics institutionally, nor can they shake the political system at all, and they lack the opportunities, strategies, and concrete plans to convince political elites, the masses, and even themselves to accept other ideas beyond the cultural origin. The sad ending of "revolution devouring revolutionaries" will eventually be inevitable (Fairbank, 1986, p. 350).

However, sticking to the radical tradition of egalitarianism in culture does not mean that China's country and society will tend to be steady and stable. On the contrary, the illusion of "Pernicious-Vestiges" discourse constantly produced in contemporary China shows that the changing power of Chinese society is not lacking but rather rampant. No matter whether the Shanghai Women's Congress in October 1949, discussed in "Object and conspiracy of 'class struggle' (1947–1959)" in Chapter 4, constructed the female workers who did not join the trade union and any workers who did not welcome female workers to join the trade union as the carriers of "feudal remnants" or whether the outstanding intellectuals in various periods were first constructed as various "Pernicious-Vestiges" entities under different names, at home or abroad, born from the bottom or elite, with strong imagination and manufacturing power toward the "enemy", it seems that modern China will never lack the object of struggle. As the Constitution of People's Republic of China (Website of People's Republic of China [PRC] Central People's Government, 2018) says:

> In our country, the exploiting class has been eliminated as a class, but class struggle will still exist for a long time in a certain range. The people of China must fight against the hostile forces and elements at home and abroad that are hostile to and destroy our socialist system.

The discourse illusion based on the historical view, metaphor, and otherness relationship order constructed by the "Pernicious-Vestiges" discourse will also be produced intermittently with the "struggles" appearing and disappearing and will be guided and strategically used in all kinds of new "struggles" in China in the future. The motive force of these "struggles" lies not in if the "revolution" itself is full of inertia and unstoppable but in the inherent paradox of "egalitarianism as cultural authority". Once the power balance of social groups changes, the "Pernicious-Vestiges" construction, otherization, and mass struggle against the rising class will inevitably occur. It is this deep-rooted and static cultural blockage that constitutes the real driving force of the continuous social unrest in China, and finally forms a "continuous differentiated universal revolution"—the revolution of everyone to everyone.

Inheriting and reconciling the understanding of the historical self-denial dynamic of modern China from "the theory of development and transformation" and "the theory of institutional heritage", this book holds that "revolution" and "modernization" are not incompatible and mutually substituted conflicts, and the internal parts of these two conceptual processes are not monolithic; the relationship between them is more complicated in present China. If the modernization process of contemporary China is summarized as the fervent desire for economic modernization, the slow iteration of cultural modernization, and the vigorous rejection of political modernization, then at least from the construction and evolution of the "Pernicious-Vestiges" discourse in the propaganda system of the Chinese Communist Party it seems that the revolution and modernization in China are not either/or, but may cooperate. After the obstacles to modernization are removed through revolution, in return, the modern technical tools and bureaucratic rationality turn to serve the next revolution—a "revolution" with technology to make sacrifice more "moral" (Bauman, 1989, p. 159). Therefore, through the words of "Pernicious-Vestiges", new struggle objects are constantly constructed, so that they can serve the overall goal of the country and become the seemingly ups and downs of contemporary China's institutional heritage, the magic weapon of mobilization, and the usual means. This view of history with a strong "patricide complex" may solve the problems left by "parents" in the previous era, but it is more likely to make the historical context return to the same problems that the "grandparents" faced. In this cycle, China's journey of modernization with revolution as the means went back circuitously and staggered away. Judging from its slow-moving silhouette, it may encounter more scenery during the journey, or it may fall into deeper swamps and thorns.

Research limitations and future prospects

Limited by our time, energy, and data availability, there are still some research limitations in this book to be further explored in the future. First of all, from the perspective of methodology, discourse illusion is often used to discuss the tension of social culture, politics, religion, and ideology in the process of generating public discourse consensus in a specific society (Bhatia, 2015, p. 2). However, due to the privilege of the official media in China and the authoritative position of *People's Daily*, we have failed to examine how "Pernicious-Vestiges" is used by intellectuals, social organizations, and individuals and groups of different generations. If Duara's "bifurcated history" is taken as a standard to measure a complete historical representation (Duara, 1996), then it will be far from enough for this book to only examine the embodiment of the official propaganda strategy of the Communist

Party of China in *People's Daily* in the words of "Pernicious-Vestiges". In the face of the suppression of the official narrative, another voice represented by the folk narrative may escape or be absorbed and become a footnote to confirm the existence of the official narrative, or it may be co-opting or resisting. Only by making the "other voice" of individuals or citizens return to the community and completing the transition from darkness to sight in Arendt's sense (Arendt, 1958, p. 71) can it be possible to rebuild public memory and the memory negotiation mechanism between plural groups, so that citizens can truly have autonomy and freedom in moral life (Ren, 2011). The question that should be further considered in the future research is how the alternative history and folk history absorbed or resisted the construction of the "Pernicious-Vestiges" and its corresponding historical view by the official newspaper of the Communist Party of China, thus breaking through the uniformity and bigotry of the linear progressive historical view and realizing the real "bifurcated history" through the reversion of "bifurcated memory" (Duara, 1996).

Second, we also want to remind readers to pay attention to the space-time category of its generalization when using the conclusion of this book. Although the discourse construction of "Pernicious-Vestiges" we investigated was completed by *People's Daily*, this newspaper is the executor of the propaganda work of the CPC, unlike the non-party media. Although around 1951, the readers' criticism column published by *People's Daily* once had great influence in supervising the operation of CCP organizations. For example, during the rectification movement in 1952, Hu Jingyun 胡景澐, deputy governor of the People's Bank of China, published a self-examination of the extravagance and waste of the People's Bank inspection team in *People's Daily*, which was also the result of criticism by *People's Daily*, *Henan Daily*, and their readers. In fact, the influence gained by the Central Committee of the Communist Party of China's official newspaper as an institutional component also benefits from the opportunity structure gained by the CCP as a propaganda machine, but the media itself and later theoretical researchers are oblivious to this (Wang, 2021). Therefore, this kind of institutional influence quickly gave way and served for all kinds of mobilized governance carried out by the CCP. It can be seen that the conclusion of this book on the discourse practice of *People's Daily* can't represent other China newspapers that are not centralized by the central government and not fully publicized, nor can it be extended to other independent media all over the world. Accordingly, future research may explore the similarities and differences between the past and the conclusion of this book when other news media outside *People's Daily* constructed the past as a history that should be opposed and explore the specific reasons for the differences.

Nevertheless, we can't presuppose that *People's Daily*'s "Pernicious-Vestiges" discourse practice has maintained absolute parallelism with political parties in all historical periods examined in this book because the independent judgment of the media may be independent of state regulation and political party control in some specific gaps in history, especially during the market-oriented transformation of other media in China at the end of last century and the digital transformation of propaganda organizations in China in this century. The open impact of market and information communication technology may bring changes to the media ecology in

China, thus urge the *People's Daily* to make corresponding adjustments. In view of this, in the various historical periods mentioned in this book, when *People's Daily* wrote, published, and reprinted different "Pernicious-Vestiges" articles, what the selection criteria were as gatekeepers and what diachronic changes had taken place also need to be further verified by more first-hand experience data.

Finally, the book's investigation on the construction of "Pernicious-Vestiges" in *People's Daily* and its historical context is mainly based on the political, economic, and cultural environment of contemporary China. Although this recontextualization restores are enough to crack the memory domestication process and its social consequences completed by the discourse illusion constructed by "Pernicious-Vestiges" by the Communist Party of China, it seems that it is still insufficient to understand the historical reasons behind the continuous production of this revolutionary discourse. At least, for one of Fairbank's concerns—what is the cause and effect of the co-change relationship between opening up and modernization (Fairbank, 1986, pp. 406–409) —it still needs future research to include a larger time-space coordinate system. Through the dynamic changes of the global political and economic structure in which contemporary China is located, we can understand the intricate interrelation between China's modernization and revolutionary heritage, which may be the purpose, means, and cause and effect of each other.

References

Adorno, T. (1959/1986). What does coming to terms with the past mean? In G. Hartman (Eds.), *Bitburg in Moral and Political Perspective* (pp. 114–129). Bloomington: Indiana University Press.
Arendt, H. (1958). *The Human Condition*. Chicago: University of Chicago Press.
Arthur, W. B. (1994). *Increasing Returns and Path Dependence in the Economy*. Ann Arbor: The University of Michigan Press.
Assmann, A., & Assmann, J. (2012). Yesterday reappeared: Media and social memory. In Y. Feng & A. Erll (Eds.), *Wen Hua Ji Yi Li Lun Du Ben* 文化记忆理论读本 *Materialbuch Zur Gedächtnisforschung* (pp. 20–42). Beijing: Peking University Press.
Bauman, Z. (1989). *Modernity and the Holocaust*. Cambridge: Polity Press.
Ben-Amos, A. (1989). The other world of memory: State funerals of the French third republic as rites of commemoration. *History & Memory, 1*(1), 85–108.
Bhatia, A. (2015). *Discursive Illusions in Public Discourse: Theory and Practice*. New York: Routledge.
Bian, Y., & Logan, J. R. (1996). Market transition and the persistence of power: The changing stratification system in urban China. *American Sociological Review, 61*(5), 739–758.
Chen Jianhua. (2000). *Modernity of Revolution: A Study of China's Revolutionary Discourse*. Shanghai: Shanghai Ancient Books Publishing House.
Cialdini, R. B. (1997). Interpersonal influence. In S. Shavitt & T. C. Brock (Eds.), *Persuasion: Psychological Insights and Perspectives* (pp. 195–217). Boston: Allyn & Bacon.
Deutsch, K. W. (1961). Social mobilization and political development. American *Political Science Review, 55*(3), 493–514.
Dirlik, A. (1996). Reversals, ironies, hegemonies: Notes on the contemporary historiography of modern China. *Modern China, 22*(3), 243–284.
Douglas, M. (1986). *How Institutions Think*. New York: Syracuse University Press.

Duara, P. (1996). *Rescuing History from the Nation: Questioning Narratives of Modern China*. Chicago: University of Chicago Press.
Fairbank, J. K. (1986). *The Great Chinese Revolution, 1800–1985*. New York: Harper Collins.
Gao, J. (2014). Various types of authoritarianism: A probe into the types of regime in China. *Chinese mainland Studies, 57*, 1–38.
Geng, S., & Chen, Y. (2008). Development strategy and constitution of political power: Towards Chinese mainland of "internal division-external connection" system. *Essays on Social Sciences, 2*(2), 191–222.
Jowitt, K. (1983). Soviet Neotraditionalism: The political corruption of a Leninist regime. *Soviet Studies, 35*(3), 275–297.
Kierkegaard, S. (1843/2013). *Kierkegaard's Writings, VI: Fear and Trembling/Repetition*. Princeton: Princeton University Press.
Kundera, M. (1978/1993). *Le Livre du rire et de l'oubli*. Paris: Gallimard.
Levi, M. (1997). A model, a method, and a map: Rational choice in comparative and historical analysis. In M. I. Lichbach & A. S. Zuckerman (Eds.), *Comparative Politics: Rationality, Culture, and Structure* (pp. 19–41). Cambridge: Cambridge University Press.
Lin, Y. (2022). *The Crisis of China's Consciousness: Intense Anti-traditionalism in the May 4th Period*. Taipei: Lianjing Publishing.
Lipset, S. M. (1981). *Political Man: The Social Bases of Politics*. Baltimore and London: Johns Hopkins University Press.
Lowenthal, R. (1970). Development vs. Utopia in communist policy. In C. Johnson (Eds.), *Change in Communist Systems* (pp. 33–116). Stanford: Stanford University Press.
Lu, X. (2000). Booty socialism, bureau-preneurs, and the state in transition: Organizational corruption in China. *Comparative Politics, 32*(3), 273–294.
Maier, C. (1988). *The Unmasterable Past: History, Holocaust, and German National Identity*. Cambridge, MA: Harvard University Press.
Margalit, A. (2002). *The Ethics of Memory*. Cambridge, MA: Harvard University Press.
Meisner, M. J. (1996). *The Deng Xiaoping Era: An Inquiry into the Fate of Chinese Socialism, 1978–1994*. New York: Hill and Wang.
Molden, B. (2016). Resistant pasts versus mnemonic hegemony: On the power relations of collective memory. *Memory Studies, 9*(2), 125–142.
Nee, V. (1989). A theory of market transition: From redistribution to markets in state socialism. *American Sociological Review, 54*(5), 663–681.
Olick, J. K. (1998). What does it mean to normalize the past? Official memory in German politics since 1989. *Social Science History, 22*(4), 547–571.
Olick, J. K., & Robbins, J. (1998). Social memory studies: From "collective memory" to the historical sociology of mnemonic practices. *Annual Review of Sociology, 24*(1), 105–140.
Parish, W. L., & Michelson, E. (1996). Politics and markets: Dual transformations. *American Journal of Sociology, 101*(4), 1042–1059.
Perry, E. J. (2006). Farewell to the revolution and China's political studies. (trans. by L. Ping). *Thoughts and Words, 44*(3), 231–291.
Pierson, P. (2000). Path dependence, increasing returns, and the study of politics. *American Political Science Association, 94*(2), 251–267.
Proctor, R. N. (2008). Agnotology: A missing term to describe the cultural production of ignorance (and its study). In R. N. Proctor & L. Schiebinger (Eds.), *Agnotology: The Making and Unmaking of Ignorance* (pp. 1–35). Palo Alto: Stanford University Press.
Rabinbach, A. (1988). The Jewish question in the German question. *New German Critique, 44*, 159–192.

Ren, J. (2011). Publicity and publicity: An analysis of a concept. *Marxism and Reality*, *6*, 58–65.
Schotter, A. (1981). *The Economic Theory of Social Institutions*. Cambridge: University Press.
Schwartz, B. (1972). Introduction to reflections on the May Fourth Movement: A symposium. In B. Schwartz (Eds.), *Reflections on the May Fourth Movement: A Symposium* (pp. 1–13). Cambridge, MA: Harvard University Press.
Songtag, S. (1966/2003). *Against Interpretation and Other Essays* (trans. by C. Wei). Shanghai: Shanghai Translation Publishing House.
Stark, D., & Bruszt, L. (2001). One way or multiple paths: For a comparative sociology of east European capitalism. *American Journal of Sociology*, *106*(4), 1129–1137.
Stone, C. B., Gkinopoulos, T., & Hirst, W. (2017). Forgetting history: The mnemonic consequences of listening to selective recountings of history. *Memory Studies*, *10*(3), 286–296.
Su, S. (1988). Some problems of the political reform in China. *China Information A Journal on Contemporary China Studies*, *3*(2), 32–37.
Tarde, G. (1903). *The Laws of Imitation*. New York: Henry Holt and Co.
Tenenboim-Weinblatt, K. (2013). Bridging collective memories and public agendas: Toward a theory of mediated prospective memory. *Communication Theory*, *23*(2), 91–111.
Thelen, K. (1999). Historical institutionalism in comparative politics. *Annual Review of Political Science*, *2*(2), 369–404.
Wang, C. (2021). Promoting, responding and supervising: Anti-corruption by public opinion of people's daily in the early years of new China. *Studies on Mao Zedong and Deng Xiaoping Theory*, *10*, 55–68, 107.
Website of People's Republic of China (PRC) Central People's Government (2018). *Constitution of People's Republic of China (PRC)*, March 22. www.gov.cn/guoqing/2018-03/22/content_5276318.htm.
Xu, S. (2007). "Soft discipline restraint": The inner limitation of the political reform of the CPC to strengthen supervision. *Chinese mainland Studies*, *50*(2), 35–60.
Yang, Y. (2007). The model of modernization and the democratic prospect of the communist party of China: The fourth way. *Essays on Political Science*, *33*, 151–192.
Zhang, Z. (2008). The Path of political reform in post-totalitarian authoritarian regime: Taking "inner-party democracy" of the communist party of China as an example. *Essays on Social Sciences*, *2*(2), 63–111.
Zhao, J., & Zhang, Z. (2005). Organizational involution and the adjustment and change of Lenin-style political parties: a case study of the Communist Party of China (CPC). *Journal of Humanities and Social Sciences*, *17*(2), 299–341.
Zou, D. (1994). *Politics in China in the 20th Century: From the Perspective of Macro History and Micro Action*. Hong Kong: Oxford University Press.

Index

absolutism 6, 90; feudal 111; "Pernicious-Vestiges" of 37
Angang Constitution 179
anthropoemic 26, 81, 200–201; strategy 44, 48–50
anthropophagic 26, 81, 200–201; strategy 44, 46–48, 50
anti-corruption, anti-waste, anti-bureaucracy 80, 122, 126, 202; campaign 70; movement 49, 126, 159, 171
Anti-Japanese War 2, 142–143
anti-rightist: movement 71, 77, 148, 194; struggle 29, 82, 138, 145–146, 165

bourgeois liberalization 37, 78, 189
bourgeois rightist 130, 145, 148

categorization 20, 88, 119, 133
Central Committee of the Communist Party of China 3, 9, 34, 36, 104, 110, 114–115, 127, 141, 148, 153, 163, 172, 179, 180, 183–184, 202, 214
Charismatic authority 14, 96; system 15
circle culture 89, 117–118
concession 48, 59–60, 208
Confucius and Mencius 6, 90, 181–182
continuous differentiated universal revolution 213
cultural atavism 211

de-revolutionizing 111
discourse illusion 18–21, 25–26, 53, 56, 78–79, 88, 96, 123, 170, 200–201, 206, 211–215; ideological 17; of progressivism 133
discussion on truth standards 111, 190–191
dock culture 89, 91, 117–118
doctrine 11, 132, 140, 145, 156, 198; piecemeal 92

dogmatism 7, 45, 145
DPRK-China Treaty of Friend- ship, Cooperation and Mutual Assistance 185
Dream of Red Mansions: method of studying 160–161; study of 161; textual research on 80, 162
dross 107–109, 116; backward 110; feudal 112; historical 105

egalitarianism 7–8, 194, 205, 211; as cultural authority 213; radical tradition of 211–212
enlightenment 42–43, 110, 207; ethical 21; movement 33; new 103; tools 38, 201
exploiting class 6–7, 71–72, 76, 85, 90, 98–99, 101, 118–119, 129, 151, 154, 182, 212; families 97, 148; thought 97, 150
extreme left 5, 7, 192; thoughts 90, 105, 193–196; trend 194–195; *see also* ultra-left

factionalism 7, 91, 125, 139–140, 176, 178
fame and fortune 7, 34–35, 139
fanaticism 61, 106, 147, 175
fight selfishness and criticize revisionism 98, 169–170
formalism 6–7, 81, 89, 114, 122, 192; "Pernicious-Vestiges" of 40
four old things 90, 98, 101, 104

The Gardener's Song 184
gnosticism 203, 212

habituation 19, 26
historical aberration 5, 11, 21, 122
historical reversal 2, 5, 9–10, 18, 156
historical work 2, 10, 113, 204
historicity 11, 19, 25; of discourse 26
Homayoun 101

a hundred flowers blossom 28, 187, 205
a hundred schools of thought 28–29, 108, 187, 205
Hu Shih 74–75, 80, 160–164

idealism 7, 28; bourgeois 45, 80, 160–162; reactionary 46; subjective 148
ideological reform 12, 157; movement 2, 126, 186; of teachers 45
imperial examination 13, 59, 164; system 6, 12, 60–61, 90
imperialism, feudalism, and bureaucratic capitalism 82, 90, 138, 141, 147, 202; *see also* three enemies; three mountains
individualism 4, 7, 71–72, 119, 122, 139, 154, 205; bourgeois 159; extreme 116
institutional heritage 208, 213

Jiafeng Style 78–79

Kuomintang reactionaries 5–6, 8, 21, 70, 120–122, 132–137, 141, 171, 205

Learning from the Soviet Union 45, 128, 145–146
legitimation profile 1, 3–4, 6
lingering fear 30–31, 188, 192
literati 129, 166–167; class 162; feudal 105, 161; old 130
living education 41

making the past serve the present 109–110
Mao Zedong Thought 1, 83, 99–101, 110, 153–154, 168–170, 172, 175–176, 184
Marxism–Leninism 28, 81, 148, 172
May 4th movement 13, 42, 107, 157, 202
memory domestication 20, 131, 198, 200–206, 215
metabolism 79–83, 133
Michurin 45–46

New Culture movement 13, 33

officialdom 116–118

party constitution 36–37, 90
past practice 2, 204
Peking Union Medical College (PUMC) 63
People's Commune movement 76–77, 149
People's Volunteer Army 61

Politburo 117
post-colonialism 10
pragmatism 46, 75; American imperialism 163; "Pernicious-Vestiges" of 181; reactionary philosophical 162; technological 46
pro-American anti-Soviet 6, 134, 146

reclassification 89, 119
recontextualization 53
Red Flag Magazine 85, 100, 148, 170, 174, 182, 184–185
Red Guards 85, 100, 153, 175, 178
renaming 56
re-narration 22, 122, 156
resist U.S. aggression and aid Korea 40, 144; movement to 63, 163; war to 70, 84, 143, 158
re-text 26; re-textual 18, 20
revolutionary heritage 11, 209–210, 215

scapegoats 26, 85, 89, 119, 192, 196, 201
self-denial 5; of China's history 9, 16; dynamic 208, 213
sexually transmitted disease 57; *see also* STD
Sino-Soviet Friendship Association 163
speech at Yan'an Literature and Art Symposium 40, 179
Stalin 2, 4, 61
STD 57, 59, 62–64
structured immediacy 25

Ta Kung Pao 33, 150
talk to the editorial staff of the Shansi-Suiyuan Daily 168, 180
three combinations 174, 176
three enemies 82, 147, 154, 202
three mountains 79, 90, 109, 138, 141–142, 147
totalism 14, 209–210

ultra-left 8

victory bond 39–40

workers, peasants and soldiers 169–170, 173, 179–180, 187

yellow songs 46, 99

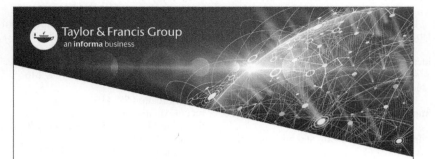